ASSESSMENT, TREATMENT, AND PREVENTION OF SUICIDAL BEHAVIOR

ASSESSMENT, TREATMENT, AND PREVENTION OF SUICIDAL BEHAVIOR

Edited by

ROBERT I. YUFIT and DAVID LESTER

WILEY

John Wiley & Sons, Inc.

Library of Congress Cataloging-in-Publication Data:

Assessment, treatment, and prevention of suicidal behavior   / edited by Robert I. Yufit and David Lester.
    p.   cm.
  Includes bibliographical references and index.
  ISBN 0-471-27264-7 (cloth)
  1. Suicidal behavior—Diagnosis   2. Suicidal behavior—Treatment.   3. Suicide—Prevention.   I. Yufit, Robert I., 1930–   II. Lester, David, 1942–
  RC569.A.776   2004
  616.85′844506—dc22

              2004042224

Printed in the United States of America.

10   9   8   7   6   5   4   3   2   1

Change is a constant in life. By building coping strengths the clinician can help the more vulnerable person cross the therapy bridge and prevent the extreme failure of adaptation: suicide.

We dedicate this book to the mental health clinicians who help suicidal patients build the therapy bridge from hopelessness to wellness, from vulnerability to successful coping with change.

Contents

PART THREE
Special Issues

Foreword

It doesn't seem too long ago that the best answer to the question "How do you know if someone is suicidal?" was (only half-jokingly) "Just ask him/her." Often, it was the only answer in those early years when the first suicide prevention centers and crisis centers were established and the field of suicidology was just beginning. First efforts turned to those most used psychological tests and scales, such as the Rorschach, the TAT, and the MMPI, but these were repeatedly unsuccessful or only minimally helpful. Accordingly, clinicians called on their own resources and made up their own scales using feelings, behaviors, family history, psychosocial factors, medical status, epidemiological and demographic aspects drawn from their own contacts with suicidal individuals along with already existing sociological studies. While these first scales and questionnaires were helpful, they were drawn primarily from clinical experiences with suicidal callers and patients that featured an assessment of immediate short-term risk or the probability of a lethal acting out occurring within the next 24 hours. Kaplan and Lindemann's crisis theory that was developing at about the same period provided a handy theoretical underpinning for the responses that developed.

The difficulty has been that in the intervening years, as studies multiplied and information about the vagaries of suicide increased, its complexity and its multidimensional aspects became more and more apparent. Treatment had to expand to include chronic and long-term suicidal behavior, direct and indirect suicidal behavior, intentional planned and impulsive unplanned behavior, and so on. It became apparent that no one theory and no one therapy could fit all the many manifestations of self-destructive feelings and behaviors. It was increasingly recognized that suicide encompassed a complex, complicated, wide-ranging network of conditions, and that its assessment could only be partial with any one scale or questionnaire. Supplemental procedures and additional sources were necessary to understand more completely the presenting situation. This important fact is repeatedly noted in many chapters in this book, especially in the section on assessment.

This book plays a vital role in helping the reader keep pace with the many changes in assessment that have occurred since those early days. In some instances, it brings the reader up to date with familiar tests by giving their history and indicating its current status, whether useful applicability (Beck scales), or reaffirmations of doubtful help (MMPI, Rorschach in part). But even with unconfirmed scales, there are indications of ways in which they might be useful, as in providing information about specific aspects like impulsivity, handling of guilt feelings, or management of anger and similar conditions that contribute to evaluating suicide status.

A comprehensive view of the major areas of assessment, treatment, and prevention in suicide prevention since its beginnings in the 1950s reveals an uneven development, with studies of treatment of the suicidal individual at first lagging behind the studies of assessment. Within the area of treatment itself, activity was unequal with the majority of the studies focusing on the critical area of crisis response and management as suicide prevention centers appeared throughout the United States and the world. However, as reflected in this book, the focus has shifted and many studies have appeared on individual therapies and long-term treatments, with at least two of the therapies reporting success in working with people at risk of suicide—cognitive behavior therapy and dialectical behavior therapy. For those who still prefer to work with dynamics, there is voice therapy and transactional analysis with their specialized features for providing insights, along with gestalt therapy, interpersonal therapy, insight therapy, and others. Neurobiological aspects and the development of medications specifically targeting the feelings and attitudes most often found in suicide now play an increasingly important role. Guidelines have been formulated specifically for treating the suicidal patient that provide both short-term and long-term procedures and goals, increasing confidence in achieving positive outcomes. Regardless of the kind of therapy practiced, the summaries and conclusions of the chapters in Part Two—the Treatment section of this book—will help every therapist in providing effective and efficient practice with suicidal patients. Like an added special treat in an 18-course intellectual dinner, there is a thoughtful, considered report on the re-emergence of suicide as a weapon of terrorism.

This book provides an invaluable update on the current status of assessment, treatment, and prevention of suicidal behavior.

NORMAN L. FARBEROW, PhD

About the Editors

Robert I. Yufit, PhD, ABPP, is associate professor at the Feinberg School of Medicine at the Northwestern University Medical School and in private practice, focusing primarily on the assessment and treatment of suicidal individuals. He is past-president of the American Association of Suicidology. He is associate editor of the journal, *Suicide and Life-Threatening Behavior,* as well as co-founder of the Illinois Association of Suicidology.

David Lester, PhD, is professor of Psychology at the Richard Stockton College of New Jersey. He has written extensively on both suicide and murder. He was Director of Research and Evaluation at the Suicide Prevention and Crisis Service in Buffalo, New York, and is past-president of the International Association for Suicide Prevention.

Contributors

Robert P. Archer, PhD, ABPP
Eastern Virginia Medical School
Norfolk, Virginia

Elizabeth R. Didie, PhD
Northwestern Memorial Hospital
Chicago, Illinois

Lisa Firestone, PhD
Glendon Association and
Adjunct Faculty
University of California
Santa Barbara, California

Robert R. Fournier, PhD
Private Practice and Department of
    Veterans Affairs
Cape Cod, Massachusetts

Rogina L. Franklin-Scott, PhD
Albert Einstein College of Medicine
Bronx, New York

Alan F. Friedman, PhD
The Feinberg School of Medicine
Northwestern University Medical
    School and Independent Practice
Chicago, Illinois

Ronald J. Ganellen, PhD, ABPP
Department of Psychiatry and
    Behavioral Sciences
The Feinberg School of Medicine
Northwestern University Medical
    School
Chicago, Illinois

Richard W. Handel, PhD
Department of Psychiatry and
    Behavioral Sciences
Eastern Virginia Medical School
Norfolk, Virginia

John Kalafat, PhD
Rutgers University
Piscataway, New Jersey

Antoon A. Leenaars, PhD
Windsor, Canada

David Lester, PhD
The Richard Stockton College of
    New Jersey
Pomona, New Jersey

Ariel Merari
Department of Psychology
Tel Aviv University
Tel Aviv, Israel

Kimberly M. Oney, MA
Department of Counseling
The University of Akron
Akron, Ohio

Lillian M. Range, PhD
University of Southern Mississippi
Hattiesburg, Mississippi

Mark A. Reinecke, PhD
Division of Psychology
The Feinberg School of Medicine
Northwestern University Medical
    School
Chicago, Illinois

Joseph Richman, PhD
Albert Einstein School of Medicine
Bronx, New York

James R. Rogers, PhD
Department of Counseling
University of Akron
Akron, Ohio

Morton M. Silverman, MD
Pritzker School of Medicine
University of Chicago,
Chicago, Illinois

Maureen M. Underwood, ACSW
Private Practice
Morristown, New Jersey

Susanne Wenckstern
The Greater Essex County District
    School Board
Ontario, Canada

Robert I. Yufit, PhD, ABPP
Division of Psychology
The Feinberg School of Medicine
Northwestern University Medical
    School and Independent Practice
Chicago, Illinois

ASSESSMENT, TREATMENT, AND PREVENTION OF SUICIDAL BEHAVIOR

CHAPTER 1

Introduction

Robert I. Yufit and David Lester

The scourge of suicidal behavior touches many lives and knows few boundaries. About 30,000 people are known to take their own lives in the United States each year. In addition, many of those deaths recorded as accidental or undetermined by coroners and medical examiners may have been motivated by suicidal intent. Suicide is the eighth leading cause of death in this country and, among young people 15 to 19 years of age, suicide is exceeded in frequency as a cause of death only by accidental deaths. Suicide occurs in every country in the world and among all racial and ethnic groups. Being destitute and alone increases the risk of suicide, but suicide occurs in all groups of the population, the young and the old, the rich and the poor, the famous and those who remain unnoticed.

For each suicidal death that occurs, there are many more nonfatal suicidal acts ranging in seriousness from mild overdoses and superficially inflicted cuts to potentially lethal acts such as jumping from a high place or ingesting a corrosive poison. It is estimated that there are about a quarter of a million nonfatal suicide attempts each year in the United States. Among people who have made a suicide attempt, about 15 percent will eventually take their own lives; among those who kill themselves, about one-third have previously attempted suicide.

These facts attest to the importance of assessing suicidal risk accurately, providing effective treatment for people who have attempted suicide or who appear to be likely to do so, and implementing preventive strategies that can minimize the emergence of suicidal impulses. Since suicide is unique among causes of death in that it is entirely the result of decisions and actions made by the deceased person, it should be preventable by helping people cope with the chronic predispositions that increase their risk of suicide and the temporary stressors with which they are confronted.

To help clinicians who work with suicidal clients, this book provides a current and comprehensive source of information and guidelines for assessing, treating, and preventing suicidal behavior.

The book consist of three sections: Part One, "Screening and Assessment," examines empirically based assessment techniques that measure important mood states, personality traits, and attitudes that are associated with suicidal behavior. These assessment methods help define the dimensions of vulnerability to becoming self-destructive and also assess the risk of such behavior occurring.

In Chapter 2, James Rogers and Kimberley Oney examine those scales that measure the suicidality of clients. The diversity of these scales means that each clinician and each researcher may use a different scale. As a consequence, their definitions of and judgments about the suicidality of clients may differ considerably. Rogers and Oney discuss the empirical evidence for the reliability and validity of these scales but, more importantly, they discuss how the nature of the relationship between the psychologist and the client can affect this reliability and validity. They propose a model for the clinician to follow that may increase the usefulness of these scales in clinical practice.

One of the most thoughtful and prolific developer of scales to assess the suicidality, mood, and cognitive functioning of clients is Aaron Beck. His scales are based on his theory of psychiatric disorder and the techniques of cognitive therapy that he has proposed. These scales have been used in hundreds, if not thousands, of empirical studies, and so their reliability and validity has been well established. In Chapter 3, Mark Reinecke presents current data on these scales that are of immense value to clinicians working with depressed and suicidal clients.

Several assessment techniques have been used for more than 50 years with suicidal clients. In Chapter 4, Alan Friedman, Robert Archer, and Richard Handel review the use of the old MMPI and the more recent MMPI-2 and MMPI-A with suicidal clients. Not only are these measures still used extensively with potentially suicidal clients, there are also large sets of archival data that have included these measures. Thus, the MMPI in its various forms remains useful for the evaluation of clients, and it also enables archival data sets to be re-examined as new findings on the MMPI become disseminated.

In Chapter 5, Ronald Ganellen reviews research on the use of the Rorschach Ink Blot Test with suicidal clients. Although projective tests such as the Rorschach are not favored by all clinicians, some clinicians still use them and, again, there are large archival data sets from the Rorschach.

Robert Yufit has been involved in research on the assessment of suicidal clients for many years, and he has developed his own approach to assessment based on Karl Menninger's concept of the *Vital Balance,* a balance between the strengths and weaknesses of the client. He presents assessment techniques to evaluate both vulnerability and coping skills in his approach in Chapter 6.

Part Two, "Intervention and Treatment of Suicidality," compares several different approaches for conducting psychotherapy with suicidal clients. The classic systems of psychotherapy have rarely addressed suicidal clients, but in Chapter 7, David Lester brings together the few suggestions that these classic systems (such as psychoanalysis, person-centered therapy, and Gestalt therapy) have made.

Most suicide prevention centers are based on a crisis intervention approach to treating the suicidal client. They do this partly because the suicidal clients they encounter are in crisis, but also because the centers are set up to deal with clients only on a short-term basis and use telephone counseling, both of which limit the techniques that the counselor can use. In Chapter 8, John Kalafat and Maureen Underwood discuss the principles of crisis intervention for suicidal clients.

Having suicidal clients sign contracts that they will not commit suicide has become a common but controversial tactic for psychotherapists. Lillian Range reviews the opinions on this tactic, as well as the research on its usefulness, in Chapter 9.

There are three systems of psychotherapy which have addressed the suicidal client in detail. Mark Reinecke and Elizabeth Didie present cognitive-behavioral therapy in Chapter 10, Lisa Firestone presents voice therapy in Chapter 11, and David Lester presents dialectical behavior therapy approach in Chapter 12.

For many years, Joseph Richman has been the lone therapist advocating the relevance of family therapy for suicidal clients, and he presents his approach in Chapter 13. Suicidal clients have been placed into group therapy since the 1960s when the Los Angeles Suicide Prevention Center first tried this approach. Robert Fournier discusses current practices for group therapy with suicidal clients in Chapter 14.

The final part presents special issues that have relevance today. First, discussions of rational suicide and physician-assisted suicide have become common in recent years, but few psychotherapists have explored how they might become involved in these decisions. In Chapter 15, David Lester discusses the role that counselors and psychotherapists might play in helping the suicidal client come to a decision and in helping the significant others come to terms with the decision.

There is great concern with suicidal behavior in adolescents and students, particularly because many nations have experienced a rise in the suicide rates of young people in recent years and because suicide is one of the leading causes of death for the youth. Antoon Leenaars, David Lester, and Susanne Wenckstern discuss suicide prevention in schools in Chapter 16, while Morton Silverman discusses tactics for helping suicidal college students in Chapter 17.

Finally, we hear much about suicide terrorists who blow themselves up with bombs in their efforts to bring about political change in nations as disparate as Iraq, Chechnya, and Sri Lanka. Ariel Merari concludes this volume by discussing the problems and issues that suicide terrorists present.

This compilation of information concerning the assessment, treatment, and prevention of suicidal behavior is addressed to nurses, psychiatrists, psychologists, social workers, and other mental health professionals, who will find it useful in providing services to patients and clients who have been or may become suicidal or who indulge in self-harm behavior. In addition to its primary audience of mental health professionals, this book will prove valuable to educators, school counselors, and others who are actively engaged with young people and in a position to help them learn improved coping skills. These readers are likely to appreciate the guidance provided for structuring programs to promote coping skills in adolescents that can reduce their potential for suicide. We hope that this book will provide the needed advances in information to help us cross the bridge to a better understanding of how to help suicidal people.

PART ONE

Screening and Assessment

CHAPTER 2

Clinical Use of Suicide Assessment Scales: Enhancing Reliability and Validity through the Therapeutic Relationship

James R. Rogers and Kimberly M. Oney

The search for suicide assessment measures that can reliably and validly inform the clinical assessment of suicide risk or potential has a long history in suicidology (e.g., Farberow, 1981; Jobes, Eyman, & Yufit, 1995; Lester, 1970; Lewinsohn, Garrison, Langhinrichsen, & Marsteller, 1989; Maris, 1992; Range & Knott, 1997; Rothberg & Geer-Williams, 1992; Westefeld et al., 2000). While this search over time has led the field away from its prior focus on the prediction of suicide by means of psychological measures to the more reasonable goal of assessment (Maris, 1992), the ability to inform accurately the clinical assessment of suicide risk or potential using suicide assessment scales remains an elusive goal (Westefeld et al., 2000).

Much of the difficulty in the prediction and assessment of suicidality has been attributed to psychometric weaknesses in suicide assessment scales (e.g., Jobes et al., 1995). Specifically, there has been notable concern about the reliability (i.e., stability and replicability) of scale scores and the validity (i.e., meaningfulness, appropriateness, and usefulness) of the interpretations of those scores vis-à-vis suicidal behavior (Jobes et al., 1995; Maris, 1992; Rothberg & Geer-Williams, 1992).

Conspicuously missing from these discussions, however, has been a consideration of the impact of the relational context of assessment on the psychometric characteristics of reliability and validity at the clinical level. In this chapter, we argue that accurate assessment for clinical work involves not only a consideration of the general psychometric properties of assessment measures based on aggregate data, as has been the primary focus in the past, but also attention to the impact of the context of assessment on the reliability and validity of information collected via those measures at the clinical level. Thus, we posit a two-tiered consideration of reliability and validity, with the first tier consisting of an evaluation of those characteristics at the aggregate level and the second tier focused on issues of reliability and validity at the clinical or phenomenological level.

In keeping with this two-tiered model, we first provide a brief overview of three major reviews of suicide assessment scales published in the past 12 years focusing on reliability and validity based on group or aggregate data. Next, we present an argument supporting the importance of the relational context as a mechanism for enhancing the reliability and validity of data collected via suicide assessment scales in clinical work. Finally, we offer an example of a clinical assessment protocol that incorporates the relational context in the assessment process and, thereby, increases the potential to derive reliable and valid data from suicide assessment scales at the individual level.

TIER ONE: RELIABILITY AND VALIDITY BASED ON AGGREGATE DATA

Three major reviews of suicide assessment scales have appeared in the literature over the past decade. Rothberg and Geer-Williams (1992) reviewed 18 published suicide risk scales and evaluated those scales in terms of their psychometric properties. Similarly, Range and Knott (1997) evaluated 20 suicide assessment instruments, and Westefeld et al. (2000) reviewed 12 suicide assessment scales. Authors of these reviews focused primarily on the psychometric issues of scale reliability and validity derived from aggregate data in their evaluations of the scales and subsequent recommendations. As defined by the Joint Committee on Standards for Educational and Psychological Testing (1999), *validity* is "the degree to which evidence and theory support the interpretations of test scores" (p. 9) while *reliability* refers to the consistency of measurement when "the testing procedure is repeated on a population of individuals or groups" (p. 25) or the extent to which measurement is free from error (Crocker & Algina, 1986). Thus, from a psychometric perspective, the characteristics of validity and reliability are assessed based on the responses of groups of individuals. This information is then used to evaluate the appropriateness of using those instruments at the individual or clinical level.

Rothberg and Geer-Williams

Rothberg and Geer-Williams (1992) reviewed 18 suicide prediction scales in terms of their psychometric properties. These authors categorized the scales into those relying on the direct self-report of the test-taker (six scales) and those relying on a second party, such as documentation from hospital records as the source of information (12 scales). Seventeen of the scales reviewed by Rothberg and Geer-Williams are presented in Table 2.1 along with their original citations. Because it is imbedded in a projective measure of personality and, therefore, not specifically a suicide assessment measure, the Rorschach Suicide Constellation (Exner & Wylie, 1977) is not included in the table.

In summarizing their review, Rothberg and Geer-Williams lamented the general absence in the literature of attention to the psychometric properties of the suicide assessment scales that they included in their work. In an interesting conclusion to their chapter, however, the authors attempted to apply nine of the second-party scales in their review to five case vignettes characterized as ranging from low risk to high risk for suicide (see Berman, 1992, for case summaries). Their application of the scales to the cases resulted in a wide range of risk estimates across four of the five cases. The one case that was rated in a relatively consistent fashion using the nine scales was uniformly identified as a low-risk case. This result suggests that, while the scales may have value in assessing suicide risk as a dichotomous variable (i.e., no risk versus risk), their ability to discriminate across various levels of suicide risk is questionable.

As a result of the dearth of published reliability and validity information on the 18 scales in their review and the lack of agreement among the nine scales used to rate the risk for suicide for four of the five case summaries, the authors refrained from recommending any of the reviewed scales for clinical purposes. Rothberg and Geer-Williams concluded that much more work was needed in developing clinically useful suicide assessment measures but did not make specific recommendations in that regard.

Table 2.1   Suicide Prediction Scales

Title of Measure	Original Citation
Suicide Measures	
Hopelessness Scale[a]	Beck, Weissman, et al., 1974
Brief Reasons for Living Inventory (RFL-B) [b,c]	Ivanoff et al., 1994
Clinical Instrument to Estimate Suicide Risk (CIESR) [a]	Motto et al., 1985
College Student Reasons for Living Inventory (CSRLI) [b,c]	Westefeld et al., 1992, 1996, 1998
Fairy Tales Test (FT) aka Life and Death Attitude Scale or Suicidal Tendencies Test[b,c]	Orbach et al., 1983
Index of Potential Suicide[a]	Zung, 1974
Instrument for the Evaluation of Suicide Potential (IESP) [a]	Cohen et al., 1966
Intent Scale[a]	Pierce, 1977
Lethality of Suicide Attempt Rating Scale (LSARS) [b]	Smith et al., 1984
Life Orientation Inventory (LOI) [b]	Kowalchuk & King, 1988
Los Angeles Suicide Prevention Center Scale (LASPC) [a]	Beck, Resnik, et al., 1974
Modified Scale for Suicide Tendency Scale (MAST) [b]	Miller et al., 1986
Multiattitude Suicide Tendency Scale (MAST) [b,c]	Orbach et al., 1991
Neuropsychiatric Hospital Suicide Prediction Schedule[a]	Farberow & MacKinnon, 1974
Prison Suicidal Behaviors Interview (PSBI) [b]	Ivanoff & Jang, 1991
Reasons for Living Inventory (RFL) [a,b,c]	Linehan et al., 1983
SAD Persons (SP) [a]	Patterson et al., 1983
Scale for Assessing Suicide Risk[a]	Tuckman & Youngman, 1968
Scale for Predicting Suicidal Behavior (SPSB) [a]	Buglas & Horton, 1974
Scale for Suicide Ideation (SSI) [b,c]	Beck et al., 1979
Self-Rated Scale for Suicide Ideation (SSI-SR) [b]	Beck et al., 1988
Short Risk Scale (SRS) [a]	Pallis et al., 1982
Suicidal Death Prediction Scale, Long (SDPS-L) and Short Forms (SDPS-S) [a]	Lettieri, 1974
Suicidal Ideation Questionnaire (SIQ) [b,c]	Reynolds, 1987
Suicidal Ideation Scale (SIS) [b,c]	Rudd, 1989
Suicide Behaviors Questionnaire (SBQ) [b,c]	Linehan, 1981
Suicide Behaviors Questionnaire for Children (SBQ-C) [b]	Cotton & Range, 1993
Suicide Intent Scale aka Suicidal Intent Scale (SNS) [a,b]	Beck, Schuyler, et al., 1974

Table 2.1   *Continued*

Title of Measure	Original Citation
Suicide Intervention Response Inventory (SIRI) [b,c]	Neimeyer & MacInnes, 1981
Suicide Lethality Scale aka Lethality Scale or Suicide Potential Rating Scale (SLS) [b]	Holmes & Howard, 1980
Suicide Opinion Questionnaire (SOQ) [b]	Domino et al., 1982
Suicide Potential Scale (SPS) [a]	Dean et al., 1967
Suicide Probability Scale (SPS) [a,b,c]	Cull & Gill, 1982
Suicide Risk Measure[a]	Plutchik et al., 1989
Suicide Status Form (SSF) [c]	Jobes et al., 1997

Notes: Scales reviewed by: [a]Rothberg and Geer-Williams 1992; [b]Range and Knott, 1997; [c]Westefeld et al., 2000.

Range and Knott

Range and Knott (1997) published a review of 20 suicide assessment instruments, classified as (1) clinician-rated, (2) self-rated, (3) those representing buffers against suicide, (4) assessment measures for adolescents and children, and (5) special purpose scales. The 20 scales reviewed by Range and Knott are also presented in Table 2.1 along with their original citations. Only two of these 20 suicide assessment scales overlapped with those reviewed by Rothberg and Geer-Williams (1992). In fact, Range and Knott purposely excluded many of the second-party informant scales from the earlier review because of their predominant focus on listings of demographic and status variables and the limited reliability and validity information available to support their use.

Range and Knott summarized their review of suicide assessment scales by suggesting that choices among the various instruments be made on the basis of the (1) purpose of assessment (i.e., research, screening, intervention), (2) age of the respondent, (3) time considerations, and (4) psychometric properties of the instrument. In contrast to Rothberg and Geer-Williams, these authors concluded their review by generally recommending three instruments above the rest for the clinical assessment of suicidality. Their recommendations were based on a number of criteria including the existing validity and reliability information, conciseness, and ease of administration. The instruments recommended by Range and Knott included the various forms of the Scale for Suicide Ideation (Beck, Kovacs, & Weissman, 1979), the Reasons for Living Inventory

(Linehan, Goodstein, Nielsen, & Chiles, 1983), and the four-item version of Linehan's (1981) Suicide Behavior Questionnaire (Cole, 1988).

Westefeld and Colleagues

As part of their general overview of suicidology, Westefeld et al. (2000) provided a brief review of 12 suicide-specific measures in terms of their psychometric properties. In addition to examining 11 of the 20 suicide assessment measures reviewed by Range and Knott, these authors also provided a brief review of the Suicide Status Form (Jobes, Jacoby, Cimbolic, & Hustead, 1997), which had not been previously reviewed. These scales are listed in Table 2.1.

While Westefeld et al. took a less critical approach to their review of the various measures in terms of reliability and validity as compared with Rothberg and Geer-Williams and avoided making specific recommendations for choosing any one scale over the others as did Range and Knott, they did suggest that a number of the measures were particularly useful for assessing individuals as to specific suicide-related characteristics and for designing interventions: the Scale for Suicide Ideation (Beck, Kovacs, et al., 1979), the Suicidal Ideation Scale (Rudd, 1989), the Suicide Behavior Questionnaire (Cole, 1988; Linehan, 1981), the Reasons for Living Inventory (Linehan et al., 1983), the Suicide Probability Scale (Cull & Gill, 1982), the Suicidal Ideation Questionnaire (Reynolds, 1987), the Multiattitude Suicide Tendency Scale (Orbach et al., 1991), the Fairy Tales Test (Orbach, Feshback, Carlson, Glaubman, & Gross, 1983), and the Suicide Status Form (Jobes et al., 1997). Thus, Westefeld et al. seemed to have a more positive view of the clinical utility of suicide assessment measures as compared to the views of Rothberg and Geer-Williams (1992) and Range and Knott (1997).

Summary

Over the three reviews, the trend for suicide assessment scales had been to move from measures completed by clinicians based predominantly on demographic and status variables to measures completed by either the potentially suicidal individual or the clinician based on self-reported information obtained through a clinical interview. Additionally, it appears that there has been an appropriate increase in focus on the psychometric issues of reliability and validity in the more current literature. As the first tier, suicide assessment scales that meet acceptable levels of psychometric reliability and validity at the aggregate level can be considered for clinical use. (See Crocker & Algina, 1986, and Joint Committee on Standards for Education and Psychological Testing, 1999, for a thorough discussion of these issues.)

Consistent across the reviews offered by Rothberg and Geer-Williams (1992), Range and Knott (1997), and Westefeld et al. (2000), however, has been a general lack of attention to the context of suicide assessment and the potential impact of that context as to the validity and reliability of self-report responses at the clinical level. Although Rothberg and Geer-Williams attempted to move somewhat beyond the aggregate evaluation of validity and reliability to consider the validity of selected suicide assessment scales at the clinical level, the analogue nature of their analysis and the lack of interrater reliability information about the application of the scales to the case summaries limit the usefulness of their results.

Ultimately, the validity of interpretations of scale scores vis-à-vis suicide risk or suicide potential at the clinical level must be affected by the context of assessment and, more specifically, the quality of the relationship in which assessment occurs. For example, Shea (1998, 1999) has discussed techniques aimed at improving the quality of the information garnered through the clinical interview by reducing client resistance around suicidal communications, and Finn and Tonsager (1992, 1997) have presented their therapeutic assessment model based on the premise that a collaborative approach to assessment can improve the accuracy and subsequent usefulness of the information collected via psychological measures. The conceptualizations of Shea and of Finn and Tonsager are presented later as we see them related to the application of psychometrically sound suicide assessment measures to clinical work with suicidal individuals.

TIER TWO: RELIABILITY AND VALIDITY IN THE CLINICAL CONTEXT

The assessment of risk for suicide most often occurs in the midst of a suicidal crisis: a situation where both the clinician and client are in a heightened state of emotionality. As Bonner (1990) has suggested, suicidal crises represent clinicians' "worst fear, often paralyzing the clinician emotionally and interfering with sound clinical judgment and effective crisis resolution" (p. 232). Training in suicide assessment and intervention is typically based on a crisis intervention model wherein the focus is on a rapid databased assessment of risk for suicide based predominantly on self-report (Clark, 1998; Rogers, 2001; Rogers, Lewis, & Subich, 2002). Risk assessment then leads to a clinical judgment of suicide potential and a subsequent plan for safety and intervention (Kleespies, Deleppo, Mori, & Niles, 1998). In discussing the differences in interview strategies and purposes with a potentially suicidal client as opposed to a nonemergency client, Kleespies et al. suggested:

> In the case of the former, the clinician will be preoccupied with assessing the degree of risk and formulating an appropriate response; in the case of the latter, the clinician may be far more interested in the patient's personal and family history and its relationship to the patient's presenting problem. (p. 42)

Thus, the typical context of suicide risk assessment is replete with strong emotional reactions on the part of both the client and clinician, is time limited and highly structured by the clinician, and is focused on a more narrow range of topics viewed by the clinician as relevant to assessing risk and providing interventions. This is a scenario not particularly conducive to effective and open communication. Just as authors have discussed issues related to the validity of client information solicited in emergency assessment interviews in general (e.g., Kleespies et al., 1998; Shea, 1998), the same concerns exist for information collected via suicide assessment instruments; that is, regardless of appropriate reliability and validity support based on aggregate data, the reliability and validity of self-report information collected in the clinical use of any suicide assessment measure may be compromised as a function of the highly charged, emotional context and the crisis intervention focus on risk assessment and response as secondary to developing a strong therapeutic relationship.

In the following sections, we discuss two general and interconnected approaches to enhancing the reliability and validity of information collected via suicide assessment measures in the clinical setting. The first approach references the work of Shea (1998, 1999) and Michel et al.

(2001) and focuses on overcoming barriers to the open communication of suicide-related content between clinicians and clients within a therapeutic relationship. The development of an effective therapeutic relationship sets the groundwork for scale-based assessment that can be further enhanced by applying practices and principles embedded in Finn and Tonsager's (1992, 1997) therapeutic assessment model and feminist philosophies of assessment (Santos de Barona & Dutton, 1997).

The Therapeutic Context: Setting the Stage for Effective Scale-Based Assessment

Consistent with Kleespies et al's. (1998) observation that clinicians working with suicidal clients are preoccupied with risk assessment and response, Michel et al. (2001) and Shea (1998, 1999) have presented arguments related to the tendency of clinicians working with suicidal clients to minimize attention to the therapeutic relationship. Michel et al. have suggested that a strong therapeutic relationship is a prerequisite for communication about suicidal intent, while Shea has argued that the primary obstacle to collecting reliable and valid information via the clinical interview is low engagement on the part of the client in the interview process. Just as the therapeutic relationship is a precursor to effective communication in the clinical interview, it also provides the context for collecting reliable and valid data via self-report suicide assessment measures; that is, low engagement in the assessment process resulting from a limited therapeutic relationship negatively impacts the reliability and validity of information collected via suicide assessment scales in clinical work. Therefore, the recommendations made by Michel et al. and by Shea to improve the quality of the information garnered through the clinical interview are also relevant to enhancing the reliability and validity of data collected through suicide assessment measures.

Described as sources of resistance, clients' values and beliefs about their own suicidality, Shea suggests, may include viewing suicide as a sign of weakness, seeing suicide as an immoral or sinful act, feeling that suicide is a taboo subject, having concern over being perceived as crazy or fear of being "locked up," and having a true wish to die. Accordingly, these client resistances, which can negatively impact the quality of the information garnered through the clinical interview, must be addressed in order to develop a productive therapeutic relationship. In much the same way, these resistances undoubtedly serve as obstacles to collecting reliable and valid data using suicide assessment scales. This may be especially true when assessment is conducted outside the therapeutic relationship. For example, it is not unusual for clients to complete self-report suicide assessment scales as a result of an initial screening process conducted before meeting with a clinician. Because of the potential complications as a function of clients' resistance-based beliefs and values, any interpretation of the assessment results in this scenario in terms of reliability and validity at the clinical level should be suspect.

In addition to the potential negative impact of client beliefs and values concerning suicidal behavior, unexplored beliefs and values of the clinician concerning suicide can also impede the development of a productive therapeutic relationship between the clinician and client (Shea, 1999). To the extent that clinicians hold and unwittingly communicate beliefs that suicide is a sign of weakness, sinful, unnatural or immoral, or an indication that a person is "crazy," the reliability and validity of information collected in the clinical interview as well as from the use of suicide assessment scales will be negatively affected.

In summary, clients may have a number of personal beliefs and values that affect their willingness and ability to provide reliable and valid self-report responses to suicide assessment scales related to their suicidal thoughts, feelings, and behaviors. In addition, the negative impact of these beliefs and values on the reliability and validity of suicide assessment scales may be exacerbated by the crisis context in which suicide risk assessment is typically conducted in clinical work and the potential negative effects of the personal beliefs and values of the clinician on developing a therapeutic context conducive to open communication about suicide. To enhance the potential to derive reliable responses and valid conclusions from using suicide assessment scales in clinical work, clinicians are encouraged to consider the impact of their own beliefs and values concerning suicide and suicidal behavior, maintain a focus on developing a strong therapeutic relationship despite the crisis context, and explore and overcome potential sources of resistance to open communication that clients may bring with them to the assessment session before using any suicide assessment scale. Shea (1999) and Michel et al. (2001) provide more specific suggestions to clinicians related to improving the therapeutic relationship with suicidal clients, serving to set the stage for the effective use of suicide assessment scales in clinical work.

Collaborative Assessment Using Suicide Assessment Scales

Within the context of a therapeutic relationship focused on overcoming the obstacles to open communication about suicidal content, a collaborative approach to using suicide assessment scales can serve to further enhance their reliability and validity at the clinical level. Finn and Tonsager (1992, 1997) have developed a comprehensive model of psychological assessment, commonly referred to as therapeutic assessment (TA).

According to these authors, TA is unique to the body of literature in assessment in that it is a model grounded in theory, it employs specific techniques, and it represents a collaborative approach between client and therapist. Finn and Tonsager suggest that the primary goal of TA is the creation of a transforming and connecting therapeutic experience for the client in the context of the assessment. Based on the underlying philosophies and the model's impact on the therapeutic relationship, the application of the principles of TA with suicidal clients will result in substantial increases in the reliability of self-report information and the validity of the interpretations of scores derived from suicide assessment measures.

Influential to the development of TA were the humanistic movements of the 1950s and 1960s and the dissonance believed to be associated with the traditional rigid, mechanistic, and impersonal approach to assessment in more recent times (Finn & Tonsager, 1997). These influences on assessment fostered their conceptualization of the assessment process as one that could be therapeutic and beneficial to the client as opposed to being structured solely to provide data for the clinician. Thus, the TA model is viewed by Finn and Tonsager as representing a shift from traditional information-gathering assessment strategies toward more client-centered, collaborative, and therapeutic assessment. Newman and Greenway (1997) described the common processes of the TA model of assessment as beginning with a collaboration between the clinician and the client on the assessment question or questions. Following the assessment, the clinician provides feedback to the client in thematic form, and the client is asked to summarize and validate what he or she has heard from the clinician about the assessment information.

In addition to its humanistic influences, the TA model is consistent with recommendations for change in traditional assessment that have emerged from feminist perspectives. For example, Santos de Barona and Dutton (1997) suggest that assessment grounded in feminist theory would embody a process striving to empower the client and should be collaborative in nature. Thus, assessment from a feminist perspective, much like TA, begins with collaboratively established hypotheses and goals and includes client participation in the collection and interpretation of assessment data, as well as in the recommendations drawn from the assessment. Both TA and feminist assessment philosophies strive to create a therapeutic experience for the client within the assessment process that accentuates collaboration and mutuality.

Although research on therapeutic assessment models is generally sparse, a few empirical studies have focused on Finn and Tonsager's TA model and have found supporting evidence for the efficacy of therapeutic assessment. Finn and Tonsager (1992), for example, examined the effect of the Minnesota Multiphasic Personality Inventory-2 (MMPI-2) test feedback on a group of college students on a counseling center waiting list. Those participants who heard their test results showed a decline in symptomatic distress and an increase in self-esteem and hope concerning their problems, and they experienced a more positive impression of their experience than a group taking the MMPI-2 without feedback. These self-reported benefits continued to be present at a two-week follow-up.

Further evidence of the efficacy of MMPI-2 feedback as an intervention was demonstrated in Newman and Greenway's (1997) replication study of Finn and Tonsager's (1992) earlier work. Newman and Greenway found symptom relief and gains in self-esteem in a group of university students seeking counseling when compared to a control group. Finally, Ackerman, Hilsenroth, Baity, and Blagys (2000) compared a therapeutic assessment model to a basic information-gathering model in an ecologically valid study of counseling dyads at a university counseling center. The authors' findings again suggested the value of therapeutic assessment as evidenced by an increase in adherence to treatment and in the quality of the therapeutic alliance.

Summary

Despite the potential psychometric strengths of any suicide assessment scale in the aggregate, its application at the clinical level may or may not produce reliable data leading to valid interpretations. The primary determining factor is the ability of the client to share his or her suicidal thoughts, feelings, and behaviors with the clinician through item responses. The potential that the client may openly share suicide-related content can be enhanced through a therapeutic relationship focused on minimizing the limiting effects of the crisis situation and addressing sources of client resistances to the communication of that content. In addition, a mutual and collaborative approach to using any suicide assessment scale as embedded in the TA and feminist philosophies should serve to optimize the potential for collecting reliable self-report data and making appropriate interpretations of suicidal risk at the clinical level.

One suicide assessment scale that specifically attempts to address these relationship-based issues as part of its administration protocol is the Suicide Status Form (Jobes, Luoma, Jacoby, & Mann, 2000). Thus, we next provide an overview of this scale and its intended application as an example of how reliability and validity may be enhanced through greater attention to the therapeutic relationship.

A Therapeutically Based Model for Using a
Suicide Assessment Scale

While the TA model has not been specifically applied to suicide risk assessment, Jobes et al. (1997) and Jobes et al. (2000) have presented an assessment model that employs many of the TA and feminist principles. This model, termed the Collaborative Assessment and Management of Suicidality (CAMS) approach, was developed specifically for work with suicidal clients. The assessment instrument used in CAMS is the Suicide Status Form (SSF), a self-report measure of the client's potential for self-harm. According to the authors, the CAMS approach including the SSF has been influenced by many theoretical models, including the work of Beck, Rush, Shaw, and Emery (1979), Shneidman (1993), and Baumeister (1990), and emphasizes the assessment of suicidality within the therapeutic relationship. Similar to the TA and feminist models, the SSF is used in the context of the therapeutic relationship and with the intention of working from a shared perspective between client and clinician. It is, therefore, completed in a collaborative and interactive fashion to provide insight into the underlying variables related to the client's suicidality. Jobes et al. suggest that the unique outcome of the application of the CAMS model is the development of a therapeutic alliance through the process of assessing suicidality, an outcome which is foregone to the mechanistic gathering of data in traditional information-gathering models.

As the cornerstone of the CAMS approach, the SSF is a suicide assessment measure that consists of five theoretically based items self-rated by the client on a five-point rating scale. Three of the items are grounded in Shneidman's (1987) cubic model of suicide (i.e., pain, press, perturbation), one item is a rating of hopelessness based in the work of Beck, Rush, et al. (1979), and one item is a rating of self-hate (Neuringer, 1974). The SSF also includes a self-rating of overall suicide risk to complete its six basic items. Auxiliary items include those related to the client's desire to live, desire to die, and items addressing the relationship between suicidal thoughts and thoughts and feelings related to self and to others. In addition to these rated items, the SSF prompts the suicidal individual to list and rank order in terms of importance up to five reasons for living and five reasons for dying (based on the work of Linehan et al., 1983).

Preliminary psychometric evidence for the six basic items of the SSF has been generally supportive of the use of the measure based on aggregate data (Jobes et al., 1997). For example, two-week test-retest reliability coefficients for the five theoretically based items and the overall rating of risk have ranged from .35 to .69. Although, in a traditional sense, these coefficients are relatively low, given the theoretical conceptualizations of the six basic items as transient and amenable to intervention, this range of coefficients has been interpreted by the authors as reflecting a moderate level of score reliability (Jobes et al., 1997). Construct-related validity evidence for the interpretation of the six SSF items has been supported through convergent procedures. Convergent validity analyses have resulted in validity coefficients ranging from .25 to .74, and claims for the criterion-related validity of the interpretations of the items have been made as a function of the ability of the six items to differentiate statistically between suicidal clients and nonsuicidal college students.

Consistent with the principles of TA and feminist assessment, Jobes et al. have outlined procedures for using the SSF that are intended to promote collaboration between the clinician and the client, augment the therapeutic relationship, and, from our perspective, enhance the reliability of the self-ratings on the SSF and the validity of subsequent interpretations of the scale in relationship to suicide risk. The procedures outlined by Jobes et al. include a thorough discussion of the purposes of the assessment; an open discussion of the client's responses in the context of a warm, accepting, and nonjudgmental relationship; and a collaborative interpretation of the results of the assessment, including the meaning of the results for continued assessment and intervention.

While CAMS provides a generally clear and systematic example of how a suicide assessment scale (i.e., the SSF) can be imbedded into a therapeutic context to enhance the reliability of the responses and the validity of subsequent interpretations, similar processes can be used with any psychometrically sound suicide assessment scale. Thus, rather than administer suicide assessment measures outside the therapeutic relationship where responses may be contaminated by client resistances (based on communication-limiting personal values) and beliefs and by clinician-centered interpretations of the results, exploring possible resistances before assessment and administering suicide assessment scales in a collaborative manner is likely to result in increased reliability of client responses and more meaningful, appropriate, and useful interpretations in relationship to client suicidality.

CONCLUSION

Past reviews of suicide assessment scales have focused almost exclusively on the psychometric characteristics of scale reliability and validity determined from group or aggregate data. Across these reviews, it has been recommended that scales meeting minimal standards of reliability and validity may be considered for use in the clinical assessment of suicidal individuals. Missing from these recommendations, however, has been a consideration of the impact of the assessment setting and various client and clinician values and beliefs about suicide that may negatively impact the reliability and validity of suicide assessment scales at the clinical level, despite the strength of their psychometric properties at the aggregate level.

In this chapter, we have argued that the broad consideration of reliability and validity represents only the first tier in decisions about suicide assessment scales in clinical work and that the second tier should be a consideration of contributions to the reliability and validity of suicide assessment scale responses of the assessment setting, the personal beliefs and values of the suicidal client concerning suicide and suicidal individuals, and the personal beliefs of the clinician about suicide and suicidal individuals. Grounded in the work of Shea (1998, 1999) and

Michel et al. (2001), we have suggested that preassessment attention to these issues through the therapeutic relationship will improve the quality of the response to suicide assessment scales. Additionally, we have argued that the clinical use of a collaborative and mutual therapeutic assessment process as outlined by Finn and Tonsager (1997) and supported by feminist assessment philosophies (Santos de Barona & Dutton, 1997) and extended to suicide assessment by Jobes et al. (2000) will further enhance the reliability of item responses and the validity of interpretations of those responses in the clinical work with suicidal individuals.

While we acknowledge the fact that empirical research in support of these concepts is currently limited, we encourage scientist-practitioners to broaden their approach to investigating the reliability and validity of suicide assessment scales to incorporate a consideration of a clinically based approach to enhancing the usefulness of these scales. To the extent that this occurs, the long-held goal in suicidology to reliably and validly inform the clinical assessment of suicidal individuals via suicide assessment scales may yet be achieved.

REFERENCES

Ackerman, S. J., Hilsenroth, M. J., Baity, M. R., & Blagys, M. D. (2000). Interaction of therapeutic process and alliance during psychological assessment. *Journal of Personality Assessment, 75*(1), 82–109.

Baumeister, R. F. (1990). Suicide as escape from self. *Psychological Review, 97*, 90–113.

Beck, A. T., Kovacs, M., & Weissman, A. (1979). Assessment of suicidal ideation: The scale for suicide ideation. *Journal of Consulting and Clinical Psychology, 47*, 343–352.

Beck, A. T., Resnik, H. L., & Lettieri, D. J. (Eds.). (1974). *The prediction of suicide.* Bowie, MD: Charles Press.

Beck, A. T., Rush, A. J., Shaw, B. F., & Emery, G. (1979). *Cognitive therapy of depression.* New York: Guilford Press.

Beck, A. T., Schuyler, D., & Herman, I. (1974). Development of suicidal intent scales. In A. T. Beck, H. L. P. Resnik, & D. J. Lettieri (Eds.), *The prediction of suicide* (pp. 45–56). Bowie, MD: Charles Press.

Beck, A., Steer, R., & Ranieri, W. (1988). Scale for Suicide Ideation: Psychometric properties of a self-report version. *Journal of Clinical Psychology, 44*, 499–505.

Beck, A. T., Weissman, A., Lester, D., & Trexler, L. (1974). The measurement of pessimism: The Hopelessness Scale. *Journal of Consulting and Clinical Psychology, 42,* 861–865.

Berman, A. L. (1992). Five potential suicide cases. In R. W. Maris, A. L. Berman, J. T. Maltsberger, & R. I. Yufit (Eds.), *Assessment and prediction of suicide* (pp. 235–254). New York: Guilford Press.

Bonner, R. L. (1990). A "M.A.P." to the clinical assessment of suicide risk. *Journal of Mental Health Counseling, 12,* 232–236.

Buglas, D., & Horton, J. (1974). A scale for predicting subsequent suicidal behavior. *British Journal of Psychiatry, 124,* 573–578.

Clark, D. C. (1998). The evaluation and management of the suicidal patient. In P. M. Kleespies (Ed.), *Emergencies in mental health practice: Evaluation and management* (pp. 75–94). New York: Guilford Press.

Cohen, E., Motto, J. A., & Seiden, R. H. (1966). An instrument for evaluating suicide potential: A preliminary study. *American Journal of Psychiatry, 122,* 886–891.

Cole, D. A. (1988). Hopelessness, social desirability, depression and parasuicide in two college student samples. *Journal of Consulting and Clinical Psychology, 56,* 131–136.

Cotton, C. R., & Range, L. M. (1993). Suicidality, hopelessness and attitudes toward life and death in children. *Death Studies, 16,* 79–86.

Crocker, L., & Algina, J. (1986). *Introduction to classical and modern test theory.* Orlando, FL: Holt, Rinehart and Winston.

Cull, J. G., & Gill, W. S. (1982). *Suicide Probability Scale manual.* Los Angeles: Western Psychological Services.

Dean, R. A., Miskimins, W., DeCook, R., Wilson, L. T., & Maley, R. F. (1967). Prediction of suicide in a psychiatric hospital. *Journal of Clinical Psychology, 23,* 296–301.

Domino, G., Moore, D., Westlake, I., & Gibson, L. (1982). Attitudes toward suicide: A factor analytic approach. *Journal of Clinical Psychology, 38,* 257–262.

Exner, J. E., & Wylie, J. (1977). Some Rorschach data concerning suicide. *Journal of Personality Assessment, 41,* 339–348.

Farberow, N. L. (1981). Assessment of suicide. In P. McReynolds (Ed.), *Advances in psychological assessment* (Vol. 5, pp. 124–190). San Francisco: Jossey-Bass.

Farberow, N. L., & MacKinnon, D. R. (1974a). A suicide prediction schedule for neuropsychiatric hospital patients. *Journal of Nervous and Mental Diseases, 158,* 408–419.

Farberow, N. L., & MacKinnon, D. R. (1974b). Prediction of suicide in neu-ropsychiatric hospital patients. In C. Neuringer (Ed.), *Psychological assess-ment of suicidal risk* (pp. 186–224). Springfield, IL: Charles C. Thomas.

Finn, S. E., & Tonsager, M. E. (1992). Therapeutic effects of providing MMPI-2 test feedback to college students awaiting therapy. *Psychological Assessment, 4*(3), 278–287.

Finn, S. E., & Tonsager, M. E. (1997). Information-gathering and therapeutic models of assessment: Complementary paradigms. *Psychological Assess-ment, 9,* 374–385.

Holmes, C. B., & Howard, M. E. (1980). Recognition of suicide lethality fac-tors by physicians, mental health professionals, ministers, and college stu-dents. *Journal of Consulting and Clinical Psychology, 48,* 383–387.

Ivanoff, A., & Jang, S. J. (1991). The role of hopelessness and social desir-ability in predicting suicidal behavior: A study of prison inmates. *Journal of Consulting and Clinical Psychology, 59,* 394–399.

Ivanoff, A., Jang, S. J., Smyth, N. F., & Linehan, M. M. (1994). Fewer reasons for staying alive when you are thinking of killing yourself: The Brief Rea-sons for Living Inventory. *Journal of Psychopathology and Behavioral As-sessment, 16,* 1–13.

Jobes, D. A., Eyman, J. R., & Yufit, R. I. (1995). How clinicians assess sui-cide risk in adolescents & adults. *Crisis Intervention, 2,* 1–12.

Jobes, D. A., Jacoby, A., Cimbolic, P., & Hustead, L. (1997). Assessment and treatment of suicidal clients in a university counseling center. *Journal of Counseling Psychology, 44,* 368–377.

Jobes, D. A., Luoma, J. B., Jacoby, A. M., & Mann, R. E. (2000). *Manual for the collaborative assessment and management of suicidality (CAMS).* Un-published manuscript, Catholic University, Washington, DC.

Joint Committee on Standards for Educational and Psychological Testing. (1999). *The standards for educational and psychological testing.* Washing-ton, DC: American Educational Research Association.

Kleespies, P. M., Deleppo, J. D., Mori, D. L., & Niles, B. L. (1998). The emer-gency interview. In P. M. Kleespies (Ed.), *Emergencies in mental health practice: Evaluation and management* (pp. 75–94). New York: Guilford Press.

Kowalchuk, B., & King, J. D. (1988). *Life Orientation Inventory: A method of assessing suicide risk.* Austin, TX: ProEd.

Lester, D. (1970). Attempts to predict suicidal risk using psychological tests. *Psychological Bulletin, 74,* 1–17.

Lettieri, D. J. (1974). Research issues in developing prediction scales. In C. Neuringer (Ed.), *Psychological assessment of suicidal risk* (pp. 43–73). Springfield, IL: Charles C. Thomas.

Lewinsohn, P. M., Garrison, C. Z., Langhinrichsen, J., & Marsteller, F. (1989). *The assessment of suicidal behavior in adolescents* (Contract Report No. 316774-76, Child and Adolescent Disorders Research Branch). Rockville, MD: National Institute of Mental Health.

Linehan, M. M. (1981). *Suicidal Behaviors Questionnaire.* Unpublished inventory, University of Washington, Seattle.

Linehan, M. M., Goodstein, J., Nielsen, S., & Chiles, J. (1983). Reasons for staying alive when you are thinking of killing yourself: The Reasons for Living Inventory. *Journal of Consulting and Clinical Psychology, 51,* 276–286.

Maris, R. W. (1992). Overview of the study of suicide assessment and prediction. In R. W. Maris, A. L. Berman, J. T. Maltsberger, & R. I. Yufit (Eds.), *Assessment and prediction of suicide* (pp. 3–22). New York: Guilford Press.

Michel, K., Leenaars, A. A., Jobes, D. A., Orbach, I., Valach, L., Young, R. A., et al. (2001). *Meeting the suicidal person: New perspectives for the clinician.* Retrieved November 12, 2002, from http://www.aeschiconference.unibe.ch /index.html.

Miller, I. W., Norman, W. H., Bishop, S. B., & Dow, M. G. (1986). The Modified Scale for Suicide Ideation: Reliability and validity. *Journal of Consulting and Clinical Psychology, 54,* 724–725.

Motto, J. A., Heilbron, D. C., & Juster, R. P. (1985). Development of a clinical instrument to estimate suicide risk. *American Journal of Psychiatry, 142,* 680–686.

Neimeyer, R. A., & MacInnes, W. D. (1981). Assessing paraprofessional competence with the Suicide Intervention Response Inventory. *Journal of Counseling Psychology, 28,* 176–179.

Neuringer, C. (1974). Attitudes toward self in suicidal individuals. *Life-Threatening Behavior, 4,* 96–106.

Newman, M. L., & Greenway, P. (1997). Therapeutic effects of providing feedback to clients at a university counseling service: A collaborative approach. *Psychological Assessment, 9*(2), 122–131.

Orbach, I., Feshback, S., Carlson, G., Glaubman, H., & Gross, Y. (1983). Attraction and repulsion by life and death in suicidal and normal children. *Journal of Consulting and Clinical Psychology, 51,* 661–670.

Orbach, I., Milstein, I., Har-Even, D., Apter, A., Tiano, S., & Elizur, A. (1991). A Multi-Attitude Suicide Tendency Scale for adolescents. *Journal of Consulting and Clinical Psychology, 3,* 398–404.

Pallis, D. J., Barraclough, B. M., Levey, A. B., Jenkins, J. S., & Sainsbury, P. (1982). Estimating suicide risk among attempted suicides: I. The development of new clinical scales. *British Journal of Psychiatry, 141,* 37–44.

Patterson, W. M., Dohn, H. H., Bird, J., & Patterson, G. A. (1983). Evaluation of suicide patients: The SAD Persons Scale. *Psychosomatics, 24,* 343–352.

Pierce, D. W. (1977). Suicidal intent in self-injury. *British Journal of Psychiatry, 130,* 377–385.

Plutchik, R., van Praag, H. M., Conte, H. R., & Picard, S. (1989). Correlates of suicide and violence risk: I. The Suicide Risk Measure. *Comprehensive Psychiatry, 30,* 296–302.

Range, L. M., & Knott, E. C. (1997). Twenty suicide assessment instruments: Evaluation and recommendations. *Death Studies, 21,* 25–58.

Reynolds, W. M. (1987). *Suicide Ideation Questionnaire: Professional manual.* Odessa, FL: Psychological Assessment Resources.

Rogers, J. R. (2001). Suicide risk assessment. In E. R. Welfel & R. E. Ingersoll (Eds.), *The mental health desk reference* (pp. 259–264). New York: Wiley.

Rogers, J. R., Lewis, M. M., & Subich, L. M. (2002). Validity of the Suicide Assessment Checklist in an emergency crisis center. *Journal of Counseling and Development, 80,* 493–502.

Rothberg, J. M., & Geer-Williams, C. (1992). A comparison and review of suicide prediction scales. In R. W. Maris, A. L. Berman, J. T. Maltsberger, & R. I. Yufit (Eds.), *Assessment and prediction of suicide* (pp. 202–217). New York: Guilford Press.

Rudd, M. D. (1989). The prevalence of suicidal ideation among college students. *Suicide and Life-Threatening Behavior, 19,* 173–183.

Santos de Barona, M., & Dutton, M. A. (1997). Feminist perspectives on assessment. In J. Worell & N. G. Johnson (Eds.), *Shaping the future of feminist psychology: Education, research, and practice* (pp. 37–56). Washington, DC: American Psychological Association.

Shea, S. C. (1998). *Psychiatric interviewing: The art of understanding* (2nd ed.). Philadelphia: Saunders.

Shea, S. C. (1999). *The practical art of suicide assessment.* New York: Wiley.

Shneidman, E. S. (1987). A psychological approach to suicide. In G. R. Vandenbos & B. K. Bryant (Eds.), *Cataclysms, crises, and catastrophes* (pp. 151–183). Washington, DC: American Psychological Association.

Shneidman, E. S. (1993). *Suicide as psychache: A clinical approach to self-destructive behavior.* Northvale, NJ: Aronson.

Smith, K., Conroy, R. W., & Ehler, B. D. (1984). Lethality of Suicide Attempt Rating Scale. *Suicide and Life-Threatening Behavior, 14,* 215–242.

Tuckman, J., & Youngman, W. F. (1968). Assessment of suicide risk in attempted suicides. In H. L. Resnik (Ed.), *Suicidal behaviors: Diagnosis and management* (pp. 190–197). Boston: Little, Brown.

Westefeld, J. S., Badura, A., Kiel, J. T., & Scheel, K. (1996a). The College Student Reasons for Living Inventory: Additional psychometric data. *Journal of College Student Development, 37,* 348–351.

Westefeld, J. S., Badura, A., Kiel, J. T., & Scheel, K. (1996b). Development of the College Student Reasons for Living Inventory with African Americans. *Journal of College Student Psychotherapy, 10,* 61–65.

Westefeld, J. S., Cardin, D., & Deaton, W. (1992). Development of the College Student Reasons for Living Inventory. *Suicide and Life-Threatening Behavior, 22,* 442–452.

Westefeld, J. S., Range, L. M., Rogers, J. R., Maples, M. R., Bromley, J. L., & Alcorn, J. (2000). Suicide: An overview. *Counseling Psychologist, 28*(4), 445–510.

Westefeld, J. S., Scheel, K., & Maples, M. R. (1998). Psychometric analysis of the College Student Reasons for Living Inventory utilizing a clinical population. *Measurement and Evaluation in Counseling and Development, 31,* 86–94.

Zung, W. W. K., & Moore, J. (1976). Suicide potential in a normal adult population. *Psychosomatics, 17*(1), 37–41.

CHAPTER 3

Assessment of Suicide: Beck's Scales for Assessing Mood and Suicidality

Mark A. Reinecke and Rogina L. Franklin-Scott

Assessing suicide risk is a complex task that nearly all mental health professionals face in their clinical and research practices. Clinically, suicide should not be thought of as a single entity. Rather, it can be conceptualized along a continuum from ideation to attempt to completed suicide (Pokorny, 1974). Suicide ideators are individuals who have not made recent overt suicide attempts but who currently think about suicide or have plans and wishes to commit suicide. Research suggests that differences may exist among ideators, attempters, and completers (Beck, 1972; Beck, Weissman, Lester, & Trexler, 1976; Pokorny, 1974), and different risk factors may be associated with each group. Thus, suicide ideators, attempters, and completers may be thought of as discrete and relatively independent groups. As such, a thorough assessment of suicide should be idiographic and attempt to assess various points along the continuum from ideation to attempt to completion.

Aaron Beck and his colleagues have been at the forefront of developing measures to assess suicide along this continuum. To date, Beck's scales are among the most widely used in the world for assessing mood and suicidality, and extensive research has been conducted with these scales. The purpose of this chapter is threefold:

1. To briefly review the psychological factors associated with suicide risk
2. To describe Beck's scales for assessing mood and suicidality

3. To provide a brief overview of the research conducted among adult populations using these scales

THE PROBLEM OF BASE RATES AND PREDICTION OF SUICIDE

The goals of clinical assessment include screening, description of symptoms associated with depression and suicide, diagnosis, determination of symptom severity, evaluation of factors contributing to a patient's distress as a means of assisting with case formulation, monitoring of treatment gains, prediction of treatment response, and prediction of suicidal behavior. In pursuit of these goals, the clinician has a number of instruments and approaches to draw from. Different measures are better suited for different purposes; each instrument or approach has practical and psychometric strengths and weaknesses. Prediction of suicidal risk is among the most important and challenging tasks confronting a clinician, and a brief discussion of the problem of base rates is necessary. Pokorny (1983) discussed the difficulties of suicide assessment and suicide research. First, the rare occurrence of completed suicides in clinical and general populations requires research using a prospective study design with a large sample and extremely long-term follow-ups, which is difficult and costly. Furthermore, given the low base rate of suicide, the multivariate statistical models used to predict suicide often yield an unacceptably large number of false positives.

Many researchers have attempted to circumvent the problem of low base rates of completed suicide in the general population suicide by investigating more frequent behaviors (such as suicide ideation, current suicidal intent, and nonfatal attempts), by studying vulnerable or at-risk groups, and by conducting postmortem "psychological autopsies" of completed suicides. It is thought that by understanding predictors of suicide in these groups, it may be possible to develop models for predicting suicidal behavior and completed suicide. Each of these approaches, however, is encumbered by conceptual and methodological limitations. Prediction of suicidal behavior is, in some respects, statistically similar to the prediction of meteorological events, such as tornadoes. We have a general understanding of factors associated with risk of tornadoes (e.g., warm air fronts during the summer in the upper Midwest), so we can make long-term statements about the probability of tornadoes occurring in various regions during different seasons. We also have instruments that allow for detailed, short-term prediction (e.g., Doppler radar), so we can take preventative action minutes before the funnel cloud touches down. Our ability to predict tornadoes in the midterm (i.e., a week or two out), however, is poor. So, too, with the prediction of suicidal behavior. Research has provided us with a general understanding of vulnerability for suicide and with instruments that allow for the prediction of imminent risk. Limits on the reliability of these instruments, in conjunction with the low base rates of completed suicide in both community and at-risk populations, place bounds on our ability to make specific predictions for specific individuals at specific times. Although it is statistically impossible to develop a measure that will accurately predict whether a given individual is going to make a future suicide attempt, research suggests that there are psychological factors associated with an increased risk of suicidal thoughts and behavior. Beck's standardized measures can be used to help identify high-risk individuals.

PSYCHOLOGICAL FACTORS ASSOCIATED WITH IMMINENT RISK

A number of factors appear to be associated with an increasing risk of suicidal ideation, gestures, attempts, and (perhaps) completed suicide. These included depression, hopelessness or pessimism, social problem-solving deficits, cognitive distortions, attributional style, and dysfunctional attitudes or schema. As these factors are associated with vulnerability for suicide, they serve as useful targets for clinical intervention. The ways in which these factors are related to one another and to suicidal behavior, however, are not entirely clear. Although some factors (e.g., hopelessness) appear to be stable and fairly robust predictors of suicidal behavior, others may simply be concomitant of depression and suicidality. As noted, suicide is multiply determined. None of these factors appear to be a necessary or sufficient cause of suicidal behavior. Moreover, these factors appear to be highly correlated with one another, and relationships between them may vary over time. It can be difficult to determine, then, whether each makes an independent, unique, and clinically significant contribution to the prediction of suicide. That said, useful clinical interventions have been developed to address these risk factors. Let us briefly discuss each in turn.

Depression

Empirical research and clinical observation suggest a strong association between mental disorders and suicide. Suicidal ideations and behaviors are more common among psychiatric patients than the general population, and psychiatric illness is more common among persons who have committed suicide than controls. The argument can be made that virtually all completed suicides manifest a diagnosable psychiatric illness at the time of their attempt. Particularly strong associations have been observed between depression and suicide (Davila & Daley, 2000). In their review of follow-up studies, Guze and Robins (1970) suggested that the lifetime prevalence of suicide among clinically depressed persons is 15%. Murphy (1985) found that more than 80% of those who commit suicide are depressed at the time of their attempt. A subsequent study by Klerman (1987) showed that 30% of patients with a major mood disorder die by suicide, which is three to four times higher than that for other psychiatric conditions and more than 20 times higher than the suicide rate in the general population (Pokorny, 1964; Sainsbury, 1986). Level of dysphoria or depression, then, is a robust, albeit nonspecific, predictor of suicidal risk.

Hopelessness

An extensive body of research suggests that hopelessness may be both a concomitant of depression and a predictor of suicidal ideations and behavior (Alloy, Abramson, Metalsky, & Hartlage, 1988; Beck, 1967, 1986; Beck, Steer, Beck, & Newman, 1993; Dyer & Kreitman, 1984; Minkoff, Bergman, Beck, & Beck, 1973). Hopelessness may be conceptualized as a set of negative expectations about the future and may be related to perceptions of personal efficacy or competence for solving problems. These expectations may contain both state and trait components. Hopelessness appears to intensify during periods of emotional distress (e.g., major depressive episodes), and it diminishes as the episode remits (Beck, Brown, Berchick, Stewart, & Steer, 1990). Some individuals experience more chronic, trait-like feelings of pessimism or hopelessness (Young et al., 1996). Research suggests that a patient's trait, or baseline, level of hopelessness predicts future suicide attempts, whereas the incremental increase and total score does not (Young et al., 1996). Hopelessness can be thought of, then, as both a chronic and an acute risk factor for suicide.

Problem-Solving Deficits

Deficits in rational problem solving and problem-solving appraisal also appear to be associated with an increased risk of suicidal thoughts and behavior. Several studies have found that suicidal adults demonstrate deficits in problem solving (D'Zurilla, Chang, Nottingham, & Faccini, 1998; Pollock & Williams, 1998; Priester & Clum, 1993; Rudd, Rajab, & Dahm, 1994). Suicidal adults often experience difficulty generating alternatives, identifying potential solutions to problems, and foreseeing the consequences of given courses of action (Howat & Davidson, 2002; McLeavey, Daly, Murray, O'Riodan, & Taylor, 1987). They lack confidence in their ability to solve problems and have a limited repertoire of active problem-solving strategies (Clum & Febbraro, 1994; Dixon, Heppner, & Anderson, 1991; Eidhin, Sheehy, O'Sullivan, & McLeavey, 2002; Schotte & Clum, 1987). They tend to approach problems in a passive, avoidant, or impulsive manner. Moreover, repeat attempters can be discriminated from nonrepeaters on the basis of problem-solving activity (McAuliffe, Keeley, & Corcoran, 2002). Orbach, Bar-Joseph, and Dror (1990) compared the problem-solving strategies of adult suicide ideators, suicide attempters, and nonsuicidal psychiatric patients. Results indicated that suicidal patients generated solutions that were more negative, more avoidant, less relevant, less resourceful, and less future-oriented than the solutions produced by the nonsuicidal patients. Similar relations between problem solving and suicide have been reported in studies of clinically referred adolescents (Hawton, Kingsbury, Steinhardt, Anthony, & Fagg, 2002; Reinecke, DuBois, & Schultz, 2001).

Although it is not clear whether the problem-solving deficits displayed by suicidal patients are state dependent or more stable (Biggam & Power, 1999; Schotte, Cools, & Payvar, 1990), it is reasonable to hypothesize that suicide may appear to be one of few viable solutions for distressed individuals who have poor problem-solving skills. When individuals view their problems as unendurable and unsolvable, suicide becomes an option. This possibility is consistent with recent research indicating that low self-appraised problem-solving ability and general self-efficacy predicted repeated suicide attempts in a sample of at-risk adults. Moreover, these factors retained their predictive utility even when sex, age, previous suicide attempts, suicide ideation, and medical risk were controlled (Dieserud, Roysamb, Braverman, Dalgard, & Ekeberg, 2003). Although deficits in social problem solving are not explicitly addressed in Beck's model of depression and suicide, they are consistent with it. Evidence suggests that deficits in rational problem solving and problem-solving motivation may mediate relations between stressful life events and hopelessness, a proximal risk factor for suicide. Taken together, findings indicate that rational problem-solving ability and perceived problem-solving efficacy are both concomitants of suicidal ideation and predictors of suicidal behavior.

Cognitive Distortions

Cognitive distortions are another psychological factor associated with suicidal ideation and behavior. Cognitive constriction or *tunnel vision* and polarized or all-or-nothing thinking are cognitive processes that have been most often linked to suicidal ideation. Suicidal individuals have been found to engage in absolutistic or extreme thinking and have been characterized as experiencing difficulty attending to nuances and subtleties (Neuringer, 1961; Neuringer & Lettieri, 1971). They tend to use black-or-white thinking and categorize events and outcomes into polar extremes. Although this approach to understanding events and experiences can be adaptive in that it allows the individual to understand problems in simple terms and thus facilitates rapid responding, it can be maladaptive in that it can lead individuals to view their predicament as more dire than it actually is. Tendencies toward biased information processing can be magnified by state-dependent memory processes (Bower, 1981). An extensive body of research indicates that moods can influence ongoing information processing, including perceptual and memory processes. Depressed individuals tend, for example, to selectively recall past instances of failure and loss and selectively overlook or minimize past successes. Moreover, depressed mood can bias an individual's perceptions of current events (Beck, Rush, Shaw, & Emery, 1979). These cognitive distortions are believed to play a role in the development and maintenance of dysfunctional attitudes and irrational beliefs, which are characteristic of suicidal persons (Beck, Steer, & Brown, 1993; Ranieri et al., 1987). Cognitive distortions, then, are believed to serve as a risk factor for suicidal thoughts and behavior. It is not clear, however, whether cognitive distortions are simply a concomitant of depressed mood or make a unique and independent contribution to the prediction of suicidal behavior.

Attributional Style

Depressed and suicidal individuals are believed, as a group, to make negativistic attributions about the causes of distressing events; that is, they tend to view problems and adverse events as having been caused by personal failures, shortcomings, or flaws. In addition, they tend to view these flaws as global and stable. An extensive body of research suggests that links may exist between attributional style and depression (Sweeney, Anderson, & Bailey, 1986). Moreover, there may be associations between attributional style and both hopelessness (Abramson, Metalsky, & Alloy, 1989) and risk for suicide (Joiner & Rudd, 1995; Priester & Clum, 1992).

The question arises: Is negative attributional style a vulnerability factor for depression and suicide or simply a concomitant of negative mood? Prospective studies with at-risk, albeit asymptomatic, individuals are necessary to answer this question. Longitudinal studies suggest that individuals who manifest a negative attributional style may, in fact, be more likely to experience feelings of depression in response to a stressful life event than are persons who do not (Alloy, Just, & Panzarella, 1997; Reilly-Harrington, Alloy, Fresco, & Whitehouse, 1999). Attributional style, then, may be seen as a risk factor for depression and, perhaps, for suicide.

Schema

Beck (1967) proposed that maladaptive beliefs or schema serve as a distal cause for depression. Schema are tacit beliefs and memory structures that serve to organize the encoding, retrieval, and processing of information. They may be latent much of the time and are believed to be activated by specific life events. Schema are postulated to develop from an early age, to be reinforced and consolidated by life events, and to vary in

their accessibility, strength, and valence. Whereas the schema of nondepressed individuals are believed to be flexible and provide the individual
with a sense of worth, efficacy, and control, the schema of depressed individuals are postulated to be rigid and are characterized by perceptions
of personal inadequacy and loss and the belief that others are unreliable,
unresponsive, or uncaring; that the future is bleak; and that they lack
control over important outcomes in their life. Tacit negativistic beliefs,
such as these, are seen as placing individuals at risk for both depression
and suicide.

Research has been supportive of the descriptive aspects of Beck's
model of depression and partially supportive of developmental and process components of the model (for reviews, see Hammen, 2001; Ingram,
Miranda, & Segal, 1998; Solomon & Haaga, 2003). As Hammen (2001)
cogently notes, however, it is not sufficient to demonstrate that depressogenic schema play a role in the etiology of depression and that they exist
before the onset of the first depressive episode; it is also necessary to
demonstrate that their "contribution is necessary, substantial, and specific to depression" (p. 240), which is a high bar—both conceptually and
empirically. It is possible that cognitive vulnerability factors discussed
previously may act in concert to place individuals at risk for depression
and suicide. Attributional vulnerability and depressogenic schema may,
when activated by stressful life events, contribute to feelings of hopelessness and a loss of perceived problem-solving efficacy. It is these factors that, in conjunction with biological vulnerabilities (as reflected by
variations in the approach-avoidance and impulsivity-restraint systems),
may contribute to the onset of depressive episodes and an increase in
suicidality.

AN INTEGRATED MODEL OF RISK

Cognitive diathesis-stress models have been a dominant paradigm for
understanding vulnerability for depression for more than 30 years
(Abramson et al., 2002; Ingram et al., 1998) and have been used as a
foundation for understanding suicide. These models emphasize the ways
in which perceptual processes guide the interpretation of life events and
the ways in which individuals attempt to cope with them. As these models have evolved, they have challenged us to attend to an ever-wider

range of social, environmental, cognitive, and, most recently, biological and developmental risk and protective factors. A number of authors have proposed integrated cognitive-diathesis-stress models of vulnerability for suicide (Rudd, Joiner, & Rajab, 2001; Schotte & Clum, 1982, 1987). Like the models of depression on which they were based, these integrated models have focused on dysfunctional assumptions or schema, problem-solving deficits, cognitive rigidity, cognitive biases or distortions, problem-solving deficits, and hopelessness. As noted, many of these variables vary in intensity or strength over time, often in reaction to life events. They may be state dependent. Moreover, it is likely that these factors reciprocally influence one another over time. Insofar as individuals function in a dynamic social context, our models must be able to account for the full range of variables associated with risk for suicide, transactional relationships among these variables, and the contexts in which they function. Our models must also serve as a guide for treatment. They must provide us with a parsimonious explanation for the patient's distress that we can share with the patient, and they must direct us toward specific interventions that may be helpful in alleviating the patient's distress. Clinical models of vulnerability for suicide, as such, should be consistent with the empirical literature, relatively comprehensive, parsimonious, and practical.

Rudd, Joiner, and Rajab (2001) have proposed a model for understanding the "suicidal mode" that meets these criteria. Briefly, they propose that predisposing vulnerabilities (e.g., psychiatric diagnoses, prior suicidal behavior, and developmental trauma) interact with triggers (internal or external stressors), a cognitive system (suicidal thoughts, hopelessness, assumptions, and compensatory strategies), a behavioral and motivational system (e.g., death-related preparatory behavior), a physiological system (including autonomic arousal and selective attention), and affect (e.g., negative emotions) in contributing to suicidal thoughts and behavior. Although the model may not, from an experimental perspective, be presented in sufficient detail to allow for empirical test, it is broad and clinically useful. It addresses each of the major variables identified as being associated with vulnerability for suicide and, thus, may be a useful guide for practice. Assessment of suicidality should be based on an understanding of factors found to be associated with risk and should be informed by an integrative model of vulnerability. Assessment of risk for suicide should, when possible, be objective, systematic, and theory-based.

ASSESSMENT OF RISK

Although we cannot, given statistical limitations, predict suicidal behavior for an individual patient with any degree of accuracy, there are clinical features, concomitants, and vulnerability factors that appear to be associated with an increased risk of suicide. It is these factors that should be assessed when evaluating potentially suicidal patients, including:

1. Major and minor life events, social and environmental stressors
2. Perceived social support
3. Psychiatric diagnosis (Axis I & Axis II)
4. Alcohol and substance use
5. Prior suicide attempts (motives, lethality, and intent)
6. Deterrents, reasons for living
7. Hopelessness, pessimism
8. Problem solving (rational problem-solving skills and self-assessed problem-solving efficacy)
9. Depressogenic schema
10. Cognitive rigidity, flexibility
11. Attributional style
12. Cognitive distortions
13. Coping resources

Assessing suicidal risk and treatment planning begins with a clinical interview of patients and, where possible, family members. This interview includes a discussion of patients' motives for considering suicide, whether they viewed their difficulties as intolerable and insurmountable, degree of planning and preparation for their attempt, and their anticipation of rescue, followed by discussions of their impulsivity and distress tolerance, attitudes toward death and suicide, expectations about their future, how have they managed crises in the past, their ability to entertain alternative perspectives or points of view, and their ability to generate and evaluate alternative solutions. Particular attention should be paid to evaluating their current feelings of depression, anxiety, anger, resentment, and pessimism.

Assessing suicidal risk can be complex. Objective self-report and clinician-administered rating scales can be useful for screening, monitoring symptom severity, and treatment planning. In addition to providing a quantitative index of suicidal potential, a review of the items endorsed can provide the therapist with insights into issues that are most problematic for the patient. These scales can serve as a useful stimulus for therapeutic discussion. Although many of these scales have extensive empirical support, many are also face valid and, thus, vulnerable to distortion should a patient wish to magnify or minimize his or her distress. It is important, as such, to seek corroborating evidence from family members and other sources.

BECK DEPRESSION INVENTORY

Perhaps the most widely used and studied measure of depression in the world is the Beck Depression Inventory (BDI; Beck, Ward, Mendelson, Mock, & Erbaugh, 1961). The BDI was based on clinical observations of the attitudes, beliefs, feelings, and symptoms commonly experienced by depressed psychiatric patients. The BDI consists of 21 items assessing attitudes and symptoms of depression: depressed mood, pessimism, failure, anhedonia, guilt, punishment, self-dislike, self-blame, suicidal ideation, crying, irritability, social isolation, difficulty making decisions, body image distortions, work difficulty, insomnia, fatigue, decreased appetite, weight loss, somatic complaints, and impaired libido. Respondents are asked to rate each item on a four-point scale according to how they have felt during the past week. The 21 items are scored from 0 (not at all) to 3 (severe) and are summed to yield a total score ranging from 0 to 63.

The mean BDI score has a skewed distribution in normal populations. Mean scores in unselected, normal populations range from 4 to 6. Suggested BDI cutoff scores are as follows: 0 to 10 (no to minimal depression), 11 to 18 (mild to moderate depression), 19 to 29 (moderate to severe depression), and 30 to 63 (severe depression). The average BDI scores for the minimal, mild, moderate, and severe categories for psychiatric outpatients have been reported as approximately 11, 19, 25, and 30, respectively (Beck, 1967).

Studies indicate that the BDI has adequate psychometric properties. In a review by Beck, Steer, and Garbin (1988), the mean internal consistency estimate (coefficient alpha) was .87, and the test-retest reliabilities were greater than .60. The BDI demonstrates strong relationships with other measures of depression. It differentiates psychiatric patients, medical patients, subtypes of depression, and normal controls. The BDI also discriminates between major depressive and generalized anxiety disorders. Factor analytic studies suggest that the BDI has three highly correlated factors: negative attitudes, performance difficulties, and somatic complaints (Beck, Steer, & Garbin, 1988).

As to content validity, Moran and Lambert (1983) compared the scale's content against the *Diagnostic and Statistical Manual of Mental Disorders,* third edition, revised (*DSM-III-R;* American Psychiatric Association, 1987) criteria and found that the BDI reflects six of nine *DSM-III-R* criteria. Two criteria are only partially represented, and one criterion is not included. Specifically, the BDI assesses decreased appetite and decreased sleep, but it does not inquire about increased appetite or increased sleep; some depressed people experience increased appetite and increased sleep. Finally, psychomotor activity and agitation was included in the *DSM-III-R* criteria, but the BDI does not include an item that directly asks about this criterion.

Although the aforementioned content validity issues have been considered a shortcoming of the BDI (e.g., Moran & Lambert, 1983; Vredenburg, Krames, & Flett, 1985), the omission of items assessing increased appetite, increased sleep, and agitation was intentional. Steer and Beck (1985) reasoned that because increased appetite and increased sleep often occur within normal populations, including these items would yield a higher rate of false positives. Furthermore, they argued that psychomotor activity and agitation is overtly observable and, therefore, somewhat inappropriate for a self-report measure. These issues were addressed with the publication of the BDI-II, a revised version of the scale designed to address the full range of symptoms included in the *Diagnostic and Statistical Manual for Mental Disorders,* fourth edition (*DSM-IV;* American Psychiatric Association, 1994) criteria for major depression.

Studies indicate that BDI scores are highly correlated with suicidal intent. Although the full scale is not consistently predictive of suicidal behavior, the pessimism item of the BDI appears to be strongly associated with suicidal risk (Beck, Steer, Kovacs, & Garrison, 1985). Studies suggest that relations between the BDI and suicidality may be mediated by hopelessness (Beck, Kovacs, & Weissman, 1975), at least in some patient populations.

BECK DEPRESSION INVENTORY-II

Although the BDI is a widely accepted measure of depression, it has not escaped criticism. Concerns about its content validity motivated the development of the scale's second edition, the Beck Depression Inventory-II (BDI-II; Beck, Steer, & Brown, 1996). Twenty-three item changes were made in the BDI-II. Two items were moved to another location, four items (weight loss, body image distortion, work difficulty, and somatic preoccupation) were dropped, and four new items (agitation, worthlessness, concentration difficulty, and loss of energy) were added. The wording was modified for 17 response options. In addition, each BDI-II item contains a header so that the respondent has an idea of the general purpose of the question. Items about sleep and appetite were added, and the time frame in the instructions was changed from one week to two weeks to make the measure consistent with the *DSM-IV* (American Psychiatric Association, 1994) criteria for major depression. Like the BDI, the BDI-II contains 21 items, and each item is rated on a 0- to 3-point scale. Total scores can range from 0 to 63. The recommended cutoff scores on the BDI-II are higher than those on the BDI for categorizing minimal, mild, moderate, and severe depressive symptomatology in clinical samples (Beck, Steer, & Brown, 1996).

The psychometric characteristics of the BDI-II are comparable to those reported for the BDI. The BDI-II has good concurrent validity with respect to clinician-rated depression and anxiety (Beck, Steer, & Brown, 1996) as well as self-reported, SCL-90 ratings of depression and anxiety (Steer, Ball, Ranieri, & Beck, 1997). The average BDI-II score has been found to be 1.54 times higher than the mean BDI score, and the correlation between the two instruments is as high as .93, supporting the convergent validity of the BDI-II. In a psychometric evaluation of the BDI-II, internal consistency was reported to be .91 among college students (Dozois, Dobson, & Ahnberg, 1998), which is comparable to Beck, Steer, and Brown's (1996) reported internal consistency coefficient alpha of .93 in a sample of 120 college students. When the BDI-II was administered to 140 outpatients diagnosed with psychiatric disorders, coefficient alpha for the scale was .91 (Beck, Steer, & Brown, 1996). Beck, Steer, and Brown also report that, on average, psychiatric outpatients reported at least one more symptom on the BDI-II than they did on the BDI and that the mean BDI-II total score was approximately two points higher than it was for the BDI. Because the BDI-II also includes items about appetite and sleep increases, it follows that mean ratings for these items would be higher on the BDI-II than the BDI.

Some differences between the BDI-II and BDI have been found as to factor structure. Dozois et al. (1998) found that on the BDI, the Cognitive-Affective factor consisted of 18 items and the Somatic-Vegetative factor, 3 items. In contrast, the Cognitive-Affective factor of the BDI-II consisted of 10 items and the Somatic-Vegetative factor, 11 items. The BDI-II has consistently been found to yield two factors, representing noncognitive (somatic and affective) and cognitive aspects of self-reported depression in adult psychiatric outpatients with a variety of *DSM-IV* disorders (Beck, Steer, & Brown, 1996), adult psychiatric outpatients with *DSM-IV* depressive disorders (Steer, Ball, Ranieri, & Beck, 1999), and geriatric inpatients with major depressive disorder or an adjustment disorder with depressed mood (Steer, Rissmiller, & Beck, 2000). In contrast, the factor structure of the BDI appears to vary with the clinical sample being studied (Beck, Steer, & Garbin, 1988). Taken together, these findings suggest that the factor structure of the BDI-II is stronger and more defined than that of the BDI.

Many clinicians and researchers have been hesitant to incorporate the BDI-II into their practices given the extensive body of research supporting the original version of the scale. Research, however, suggests that the two measures display comparable psychometric properties and similar patterns association with a range of variables (Beck, Steer, Ball, & Ranieri, 1996). Differences between the scales do not appear to pose a problem with clinical interpretations. The BDI-II, then, can be used with confidence for both clinical and research purposes.

Little research, however, with suicidal patients has been conducted using the BDI-II. Given that the time frame for rating symptoms increased from one week to two weeks, it is possible that the BDI-II may be somewhat less sensitive to changes in depressive symptoms and suicidality over short periods than the original version of the scale. Research is needed to determine the scale's sensitivity to temporal changes as well as its association with risk factors for suicide.

BECK ANXIETY INVENTORY

The Beck Anxiety Inventory (BAI; Beck, Epstein, Brown, & Steer, 1988) is a 21-item self-report scale that measures the symptoms of anxiety. The development of the BAI was motivated by the need for a measure that would reliably discriminate anxiety from depression. Archival data from the Anxiety Checklist (Beck, Steer, & Brown, 1985), *Physician's Desk Reference* (Medical Economics, 1977), and the Situational Anxiety Checklist (Beck, 1982) were used to create the scale. An initial 86-item pool was subjected to a series of item analysis procedures with a sample of 810 psychiatric outpatients. One hundred sixteen psychiatric outpatients were administered a 37-item scale that was based on the items that had been eliminated from the initial 86 items. Subsequent item analysis procedures yielded the final 21-item BAI. The final measure was administered to a subsample of 160 psychiatric outpatients, and analyses were conducted with this sample to determine the reliability and validity of the final BAI scale (Beck, Epstein, et al., 1988).

Respondents are asked to rate how much they have been bothered by each common symptom of anxiety over the past week. Items include: "numbness or tingling," "unable to relax," "shaky," and "faint." Each symptom is rated on a four-point scale ranging from 0 (Not at all) to 3 (Severely-could barely stand it). Total scores can range from 0 to 63. The following cutoff scores have been suggested: 0 to 7 (minimal anxiety), 8 to 15 (mild anxiety), 16 to 25 (moderate anxiety), and 26 to 63 (severe anxiety; Beck & Steer, 1993).

Adequate psychometric properties have been reported for the BAI (Beck, Epstein, et al., 1988; Beck & Steer, 1993). The scale had an internal consistency of .92 and item-total correlations ranging from .30 to .71. The one-week test-retest BAI score in a subsample of 83 patients was .75. An analysis of variance revealed that BAI scores were higher in an anxious group than in either a depressed or a control group. The correlation between the BAI and the BDI was .48. The BAI's correlation with the Hamilton Anxiety Rating Scale-Revised (Hamilton, 1959) and the Hamilton Rating Scale for Depression (Hamilton, 1960) was .51 and .25, respectively, demonstrating adequate convergent and discriminant validity. As to its factor structure, research has shown that the BAI can be factor analyzed into cognitive and somatic components (Hewitt & Norton, 1993).

Relationships between anxiety and suicide can be complex. Although studies suggest that anxiety may not be an independent risk factor for suicide (Rudd, Dahm, & Rajab, 1993), discrepant findings have been reported (Beck, Steer, Sanderson, & Skeie, 1991; Freidman, Jones, Chernen, & Barlow, 1992). Insofar as substantial associations exist between depression and anxiety, the possibility exists that observed links between anxiety and suicide may stem from anxiety's shared variance with depression. Research has suggested that symptoms of anxiety increase short-term suicide risk in patients with comorbid major affective disorder (Fawcett et al., 1990) and that people suffering from panic disorder may be at an increased risk for attempting suicide (Beck, Steer, et al., 1991).

BECK HOPELESSNESS SCALE

The Beck Hopelessness Scale (BHS; Beck, Weissman, Lester, & Trexler, 1974; Beck & Steer, 1988) is a 20-item self-report questionnaire. The BHS assesses respondents' degree of negativity and pessimism about the future. Nine items of the BHS were revisions of items taken from Heimberg's (1961) inventory. Clinicians identified a sample of psychiatric patients who appeared hopeless, and the 11 remaining items were derived from a list of pessimistic statements made by those patients. A sample of depressed and nondepressed patients were then administered the items and asked to give their impressions on the relevance and comprehensibility of the content of the scale. The patients' feedback was then used to make further modifications to the wording of items.

The final version of the BHS consists of 20 true-false statements. Nine items are keyed false, and 11 are keyed true. Each item response is assigned a score of 0 or 1. Items include: "I look forward to the future with hope and enthusiasm," "I can't imagine what my life would be like in 10 years," and "I have enough time to accomplish the things I most want to do." The total hopelessness score is obtained by summing the scores for each item, yielding a possible range of scores from 0 to 20. Total hopelessness scores between 0 and 3 reflect minimal levels of hopelessness, scores between 4 and 8 reflect low levels of hopelessness, scores between 9 and 14 reflect moderate levels of hopelessness, and scores of 15 and above reflect clinically severe hopelessness.

In the original validation study (Beck, Weissman, et al., 1974), a sample of 294 hospitalized patients who had made a recent suicide attempt served as the validation sample. The reliability coefficient was .93, and the item-total correlation coefficients ranged from .39 to .76. The BHS correlated more highly ($r = .63$, $p < .001$) with the pessimism item of the BDI (Beck, 1967) than with any other item on the BDI. When data from the 294 suicide attempters were subjected to factor analysis, three factors emerged: feelings about the future, loss of motivation, and future expectations.

The association between hopelessness and suicide is well documented in the literature. When a highly depressed group of suicide ideators were studied, the BHS was found to be a strong predictor of suicidal intent (Beck, Weissman, et al., 1974). Kovacs, Beck, and Weissman (1975) also found that, among suicide attempters, hopelessness is a better predictor of current suicide ideation than depression. Beck et al. (1975) reported that hopelessness mediated the relationship between depression and suicidal intent among suicide attempters. Furthermore, hopelessness was found to account for 76% of the association between depression and suicidal intent in a sample of 384 hospitalized suicide attempters. As mentioned previously, hopelessness has been identified as being more closely related to the seriousness of intent than was depression itself (Minkoff et al., 1973). Ellis and Ratliff (1986) found that hopelessness discriminates suicidal from nonsuicidal patients with comparable levels of depression, and hopelessness appears to be a strong predictor of suicide among patients who have made a prior suicide attempt (Beck et al., 1975). In one study of suicide attempters, hopelessness was not predictive of eventual suicide, but this may have been because hopelessness was assessed after the initial attempt (Beck & Steer, 1989). In studies where attempters were asked to rate their hopelessness just before their attempt, hopelessness was found to be highly associated with suicide intent (Dyer & Kreitman, 1984).

Hopelessness has received strong empirical support as a risk factor for suicide in prospective studies of both inpatients and outpatients (Beck et al., 1990; Beck, Brown, & Steer, 1989; Beck, Steer, et al., 1985; Fawcett et al., 1987). Longitudinal, prospective studies by Beck and his associates have provided empirical evidence for the BHS's predictive utility. Beck, Steer, et al. (1985) conducted a prospective study with 165 adults hospitalized because of suicidal ideation. The results showed that of the 11 patients in the sample who committed suicide over a 10-year follow-up period, 90% (10) had hopelessness scores greater than 9. There was only one patient with a total hopelessness score below 10 who eventually committed suicide. Similarly, Beck (1986) found that a cutoff score of 10 correctly identified 9 out of 10 eventual suicides, yielding a false negative rate of 10% among psychiatric outpatients. Our confidence in the clinical utility of these findings is reduced, however, given the fact that 1,137 of the 2,164 patients who did not commit suicide (52.5%) had a BHS total score of 10 or above. The specificity rate for a cutoff score of 9 was unacceptably high (47.5%). Given the low rate of completed suicide in this sample, false positives remain a concern. Beck identified a group of high-risk individuals who had a score of 17 or above and noted that individuals with scores of 17 or above had a rate of eventual suicide that was 15 times higher than the rate for other outpatients. Optimum cutoff scores for predicting suicide have also been derived using signal detection theory, and a cutscore of 9 or above on the BHS has been found to yield an accurate prediction of suicide (Beck et al., 1990). More recently, patients with a BHS score of 9 or above were approximately four times more likely than patients who scored 8 or below to commit suicide within a given year of follow-up (Brown, Beck, Steer, & Grisham, 2000).

DYSFUNCTIONAL ATTITUDE SCALE

The Dysfunctional Attitude Scale (DAS; Weissman & Beck, 1978) is a 100-item self-report scale designed to measure assumptions and beliefs thought to reflect the content of relatively stable schemas. Dysfunctional attitudes or schema are believed to be activated by stressful life events and thus serve as a cognitive substrate for different forms of psychopathology (Beck, 1967, 1976). Dysfunctional attitudes can be thought of as latent vulnerability factors for psychopathology. When a salient stressor arises, these attitudes become activated, contributing to the onset and continuance of psychiatric episodes (Beck, 1967).

The DAS items are worded to reflect inflexible and absolute thinking. Items include: "People will probably think less of me if I make a mistake," "It is shameful for a person to display his weaknesses," "If a person does not love me, it means that I am unlovable," and "I ought to be able to solve my problems quickly and without a great deal of effort." Items are scored on a seven-point Likert scale ranging from 1 (totally agree) to 7 (totally disagree). The scale is scored in such a way that higher scores reflect more distorted, maladaptive thinking. The total score represents the overall degree of negative dysfunctional attitudes.

Beck, Steer, and Brown (1993) report a coefficient alpha of .96 for the DAS in a sample of psychiatric outpatients. Beck, Brown, Steer, and Weissman (1991) examined the factor structure of the DAS, and the results of confirmatory and exploratory factor analyses yielded an 80-item scale with nine factors: vulnerability, need for approval (approval), success-perfectionism (perfectionism), need to please others, imperatives, need to impress others (impress others), avoidance of appearing weak (avoidance), control over emotions (control), and disapproval-dependence (disapproval). Beck, Steer, and Brown (1993) reported the coefficient alphas for these nine subscales as .90, .84, .90, .71, .81, .78, .77, .51, and .67, respectively.

Significant associations have been found among dysfunctional attitudes, depression, and suicide. Studies indicate that scores on the DAS often remain elevated among depressed individuals compared to normal controls during periods of remission and that remitted depressives whose DAS scores remain elevated are at greater risk for relapse compared to depressives with lower levels of dysfunctional attitudes (Eaves & Rush, 1984). Ranieri et al. (1987) found that dysfunctional attitude scores were correlated with suicidal ideation among inpatients even after controlling for depression and hopelessness. The results of a stepwise multiple regression analysis indicated that six items on the DAS accounted for approximately 77% of the variance in scores on the Scale for Suicide Ideation. Three of the DAS items reflected perfectionism, and three represented sensitivity to social criticism. In contrast, Beck, Steer, and Brown (1993) found that the overall severity of dysfunctional attitudes was not a significant correlate of suicidal ideation among psychiatric outpatients. Rather, a history of prior suicide attempts and hopelessness was more important than dysfunctional attitudes. The authors suggest that this discrepancy may be attributable to the higher levels of psychopathology presented by inpatients as opposed to outpatients.

Dysfunctional attitudes or schema play a central role in cognitive-behavioral models of depression and suicide. Self-report measures of schema, such as the DAS, appear to be reliable and valid measures of depressive cognitions. It is not clear, though, that they are specific to depression or that they are reliable indicators of stable, tacit beliefs. The notion that specific dysfunctional attitudes may be associated with vulnerability for depression or suicide is interesting and conceptually important. Research bearing on these issues, however, is both complex and contradictory (Clark & Beck, 1999; Ingram et al., 1998). The DAS, however, can provide useful clinical information about dysfunctional attitudes and beliefs that are associated with current distress and suicidality.

SCALE FOR SUICIDAL IDEATION

The Scale for Suicidal Ideation (SSI; Beck, Kovacs, & Weissman, 1979; Beck & Steer, 1991) was constructed to assess the degree to which an individual is currently suicidal. The scale focuses on the intensity, pervasiveness, and characteristics of the ideation and wish to die. Suicidal ideation also includes suicidal threats that have been expressed in overt behavior or stated to others. The scale's items are based on the nature of suicidal wishes rather than on demographics. The scale is administered through a semistructured interview and yields a numerical estimate of the intensity of the interviewee's suicidal thoughts and urges. The scale contains 19 items rated by a clinician on a three-point scale from 0 (least severe) to 2 (most severe). The first five items screen for respondents' desire to live and die. Only individuals who report a wish to make a passive or active suicide attempt are rated on items 6 to 19. The items are related to the duration and frequency of suicidal thoughts, the extent of the wish to die, feelings of control over suicidal wishes, characteristics of a contemplated suicide attempt, strength of the wish to live and the wish to die, means and opportunity of suicide method, internal and external deterrents, and history of previous attempts. Although the scale contains an item assessing the intent to die associated with a suicide attempt, it does not examine the perceived lethality of the attempt. Separate scores are generated for patients' current episode and worst past episode of suicidality.

A self-report version of the SSI has also been developed (Beck, Steer, & Ranieri, 1988). Like the clinical interview, the self-report's screening items assess a person's thoughts, plans, and intent to commit suicide. A list of 19 preoccupations, concerns, wishes, thinking, and behavior patterns was obtained through observations and interviews of suicidal patients. The 19 items, briefly described, are wish to live, wish to die, reasons for living or dying, actual suicidal desire, passive suicidal desire, duration, frequency, attitude toward ideation, control over action, deterrents to attempt, reason for attempt, specificity of planning, means and opportunity, capability, expectancy, actual preparation, suicide note, final acts, and deception or concealment. Items from the self-report measure include: "I have no wish to die; I have a weak wish to die; I have a moderate to strong wish to die" and "I do not expect to make a suicide attempt; I am unsure that I shall make a suicide attempt; I am sure that I shall make a suicide attempt." The 19 items are rated on a three-point scale (0 to 2), and the total scores can range from 0 to 38. Cutoff scores for the SSI are not recommended because any positive response warrants further investigation.

The psychometric properties of the scale were originally reported by Beck, Kovacs, et al. (1979) and were based on a sample of 90 patients hospitalized for suicidal ideation. Item-total score correlations for the scale ranged from .04 to .72, and the reported reliability coefficient was .89. Interrater reliability was .83. The item-total correlation for the suicide note item could not be computed because all of the subjects scored a 0 on that item. The items that did not meet adequate psychometric standards were related to suicide notes, deception, and final acts in preparation for death. These items have a low occurrence rate but are clinically significant and have important meaning as to severity of suicidal intent. Beck, Kovacs, et al. (1979) reasoned that deleting such items would omit important information for assessing suicidal intention, so those items were retained. A factor analysis revealed three factors:

1. *Active suicidal desire* includes items measuring attitudes toward living and dying and characteristics of suicidal ideation.
2. *Preparation* includes items assessing specific formulation of the contemplated suicide attempt.
3. *Passive suicidal desire* includes items measuring passive avoidance of steps to spare the individual's life, courage to carry out the attempt, and concealment of suicidal ideas and plans.

The SSI has been studied with a number of suicidal populations. Pallis, Gibbons, and Pierce (1984) found that, among ideators, the degree of hopelessness appears to be a more powerful indicator of suicidal risk than suicidal intent at the time of hospitalization. Beck, Steer, et al. (1985) found that an inpatient sample of suicide ideators who eventually committed suicide did not score significantly higher on the SSI than those inpatient suicide ideators who did not commit suicide. Although the SSI was not predictive of completed suicide, it appears that the intensity of suicidal wishes among attempters is indicative of short-term risk for suicide. A more recent study by Brown et al. (2000) found that psychiatric outpatients who scored a 3 or higher on the SSI were approximately seven times more likely to commit suicide than those who scored less than 3. Finally, the SSI is a better predictor of hospitalization for suicidal concerns than the BDI, BAI, and BHS (Cochrane-Brink, Phil, Lofchy, & Sakinofsky, 2000).

The assessment of suicidal ideation at its worst point is of particular interest as research suggests that this may identify a subgroup of patients at high risk for suicide (Beck, Brown, Steer, Dahlsgaard, & Grisham, 1999). A new measure of suicidal ideation, the SSI-Worst, was developed using the same item format as the SSI-Current. The SSI-Worst assesses suicide ideation at the worst point in the individual's life. The SSI-Current and the SSI-Worst were administered to a sample of 3,701 psychiatric outpatients (Beck, Brown, & Steer, 1997). The results revealed that patients who scored 16 or above on the SSI-Worst were approximately 14 times more likely to commit suicide than patients who scored less than 16 on the SSI-Worst. Patients who scored 2 or above on the SSI-Current were approximately six times more likely to commit suicide than those who scored less than 2 on the SSI-Current. In a study comparing the psychometric properties of the SSI-Current and the SSI-Worst, the SSI-Worst was more strongly associated with a history of suicide attempts (.50) than was the SSI-Current and previous suicide attempts (.31). The SSI-Worst has high internal consistency (.89). The SSI-Worst and the SSI-Current are moderately correlated with each other (.51), and comparable factor structure has been reported for the two measures (Beck et al., 1999).

SUICIDAL INTENT SCALE

The Suicidal Intent Scale (SIS; Beck, Schuyler, & Herman, 1974) is a 15-item questionnaire administered in the form of a structured clinical interview to persons who have attempted suicide. Suicidal intent is conceptualized as a balance between the wish to die and the wish to live. An assessment of intent is based on ratings made by patients about the probability that their suicide attempt will be successful. Suicidal intent is conceptually different from the lethality of an attempt. Clinically, suicidal individuals may have a high degree of suicidal intent but may choose an ineffective, nonfatal method. The SIS measures the severity of the person's intent to die at the time of the attempt by examining aspects of the attempter's behavior before, during, and after the suicide attempt. Information obtained from the scale provides an index of the risk for future attempts. The scale's items relate to the extent of isolation and the probability of being found, verbalizations about intent, final acts, purpose of attempt, attitudes toward living and dying, and beliefs about lethality and medical recovery. Other items, not included in the total score, assess whether drugs and alcohol were used during the attempt.

Wetzel, Margulies, Davis, and Karam (1980) found that suicide intent and hopelessness were highly correlated in a sample of 73 inpatients. The correlation between suicide intent and depression was also significant. When severity of depression was controlled, the correlation between hopelessness and suicide intent remained highly significant. However, when the effects of hopelessness were statistically controlled, the association between suicide intent and depression was not significant. The precautions subscale of the SIS has been found to be predictive of eventual suicide among alcohol-abusing suicide attempters (Beck, Steer, & Trexler, 1989). Compared to the BDI and BHS, the SIS was the only scale that predicted suicide within that sample over a 5- to 10-year period. The suicide attempters who eventually killed themselves made more efforts to avoid being found at the time of the assessed attempt than those who did not kill themselves.

SOCIAL PROBLEM-SOLVING INVENTORY—REVISED

Social problem solving plays a central role in several cognitive diathesis-stress models of suicide and may mediate relations between stressful life events and hopelessness. The Social Problem-Solving Inventory-Revised (SPSI-R; D'Zurilla & Maydeu-Olivares, 1995; D'Zurilla & Nezu, 1990) is a 52-item self-report inventory designed to assess cognitive affective and behavioral processes by which individuals attempt to identify and implement adaptive coping responses for problematic situations. The scale yields two major factors—Negative Problem Orientation (NPO) and Positive Problem Orientation (PPO)—as well as measures of Rational Problem-Solving (RPS), Impulsivity-Carelessness Style (ICS), and Avoidant Style (AS). The Rational Problem-Solving scale is composed of four subscales: Problem Definition and Formulation (PDF), Generation of Alternative Solutions (GAS), Decision Making (DM), and Solution Implementation and Verification (SIV). The psychometric properties of the SPSI are promising (D'Zurilla & Nezu, 1990). Relations between scores on measures of social problem-solving and suicidal ideations have been examined among both adults (Clum et al., 1996) and adolescents (Reinecke & DuBois, 2001). As noted, findings indicate that suicide may be more closely linked to deficits in problem-solving motivation than to skills in rational problem solving.

CONCLUSIONS

Suicidality may be conceptualized as varying along a continuum from ideation to attempt to completion. A range of objective rating scales has been developed to assess various aspects of suicide along this continuum and to evaluate factors associated with vulnerability for future attempts.

The scales reviewed in this chapter have been developed to measure several components of mood, cognition, and suicidality. Empirical evidence is generally supportive of the reliability and validity of these scales— they are psychometrically sound and can be useful in assessing suicidal risk and in treatment planning. The scales allow us to assess quantitatively the severity of a patient's dysphoria, anxiety, hopelessness, and suicidality, and can be considered individually and qualitatively to identify specific problem areas. Many of these scales are face valid, making them subject to misrepresentation should patients wish to minimize or exaggerate their distress.

Assessing suicide risk for a given individual is a complex task requiring consideration of multiple factors. Standardized, objective measures can be helpful in evaluating risk for suicide, and Beck's scales for assessing mood and suicidality have been found to have clinical and research value with suicidal patients. However, given the multiply determined nature of suicidality and the psychometric limitations of individual measures, estimations of risk for suicide should not be based on a single score, a single scale, or a combination of objective scales. No single clinical scale or combination of scales can replace the need for a complete, idiographic psychiatric assessment for suicide risk, which includes a diagnostic and developmental interview, informant reports, administration of objective rating scales, assessment of suicide risk indicators, and consideration of other risk and protective factors. Beck's scales can, nonetheless, assist this process by providing clear, concise information about suicidality, making the complex and challenging endeavor of assessing suicide risk somewhat less daunting.

REFERENCES

Abramson, L., Alloy, L., Hankin, B., Haeffel, G., MacCoon, D., & Gibb, B. (2002). Cognitive vulnerability-stress models of depression in a self-regulatory and psychobiological context. In I. Gotlib & C. Hammen (Eds.), *Handbook of depression* (pp. 268–294). New York: Guilford Press.

Abramson, L., Metalsky, G., & Alloy, L. (1989). Hopelessness depression: A theory-based subtype of depression. *Psychological Review, 96,* 358–372.

Alloy, L., Abramson, L., Metalsky, G., & Hartlage, S. (1988). The hopelessness theory of depression: Attributional aspects. *British Journal of Clinical Psychology, 27,* 5–21.

Alloy, L., Just, N., & Panzarella, C. (1997). Attributional style, daily life events, and hopelessness depression: Subtype validation by prospective variability and specificity of symptoms. *Cognitive Therapy and Research, 21,* 321–344.

American Psychiatric Association. (1987). *Diagnostic and statistical manual of mental disorders* (3rd ed., rev.). Washington, DC: Author.

American Psychiatric Association. (1994). *Diagnostic and statistical manual of mental disorders* (4th ed.). Washington, DC: Author.

Beck, A. T. (1967). *Depression: Clinical, experimental, and theoretical aspects.* New York: Harper & Row.

Beck, A. T. (1972). *Depression: Causes and treatment.* Philadelphia: University of Pennsylvania Press.

Beck, A. T. (1976). *Cognitive therapy and the emotional disorders.* New York: International Universities Press.

Beck, A. T. (1982). *Situational anxiety checklist.* Philadelphia: University of Pennsylvania, Center for Cognitive Therapy.

Beck, A. T. (1986). Hopelessness as a predictor of eventual suicide. *Annals of the New York Academy of Science, 487,* 90–96.

Beck, A. T., Brown, G., Berchick, R., Stewart, B., & Steer, R. (1990). Relationship between hopelessness and ultimate suicide: A replication with psychiatric outpatients. *American Journal of Psychiatry, 147,* 190–195.

Beck, A. T., Brown, G., & Steer, R. (1989). Prediction of eventual suicide in psychiatric inpatients by clinical ratings of hopelessness. *Journal of Consulting and Clinical Psychology, 57,* 309–310.

Beck, A. T., Brown, G. K., & Steer, R. A. (1997). Psychometric characteristics of the Scale for Suicide Ideation with psychiatric outpatients. *Behavior Research and Therapy, 11,* 1039–1046.

Beck, A. T., Brown, G., Steer, R., Dahlsgaard, K., & Grisham, J. (1999). Suicide ideation at its worst point: A predictor of eventual suicide in psychiatric outpatients. *Suicide and Life-Threatening Behavior, 29,* 1–9.

Beck, A. T., Brown, G., Steer, R. A., & Weissman, A. N. (1991). Factor analysis of the dysfunctional attitude scale in a clinical population. *Psychological Assessment, 3,* 478–483.

Beck, A. T., Epstein, N., Brown, G., & Steer, R. A. (1988). An inventory for measuring clinical anxiety: Psychometric properties. *Journal of Consulting and Clinical Psychology, 56,* 893–897.

Beck, A. T., Kovacs, M., & Weissman, A. (1975). Hopelessness and suicidal behavior: An overview. *Journal of the American Medical Association, 234,* 1146–1149.

Beck, A. T., Kovacs, M., & Weissman, A. (1979). Assessment of suicidal intention: The scale for suicidal ideation. *Journal of Consulting and Clinical Psychology, 47,* 343–352.

Beck, A. T., Rush, A., Shaw, B., & Emery, G. (1979). *Cognitive therapy of depression,* New York: Guilford Press.

Beck, A. T., Schuyler, D., & Herman, I. (1974). Development of suicidal intent scales. In A. Beck, H. Resnick, & D. Lettieri (Eds.), *The prediction of suicide* (pp. 45–56). Philadelphia: Charles Press.

Beck, A. T., & Steer, R. (1988). *Manual for the Beck Hopelessness Scale.* San Antonio, TX: Psychological Corporation.

Beck, A. T., & Steer, R. (1989). Clinical predictors of eventual suicide: A 5- to 10-year prospective study of suicide attempters. *Journal of Affective Disorders, 17,* 203–209.

Beck, A. T., & Steer, R. (1991). *Manual for the Beck Scale for Suicide Ideation.* San Antonio, TX: Psychological Corporation.

Beck, A. T., & Steer, R. (1993). *Manual for the Beck Anxiety Inventory.* San Antonio, TX: Psychological Corporation.

Beck, A. T., Steer, R. A., Ball, R., & Ranieri, W. F. (1996). Comparison of Beck depression inventories-I and -II in psychiatric outpatients. *Journal of Personality Assessment, 67,* 588–597.

Beck, A. T., Steer, R. A., Beck, J. S., & Newman, C. F. (1993). Hopelessness, depression, suicidal ideation, and clinical diagnosis of depression. *Suicide and Life Threatening Behavior, 23,* 139–145.

Beck, A. T., Steer, R. A., & Brown, G. K. (1985). *Beck anxiety checklist.* Unpublished manuscript, University of Pennsylvania.

Beck, A. T., Steer, R. A., & Brown, G. K. (1993). Dysfunctional attitudes and suicidal ideation in psychiatric outpatients. *Suicide and Life-Threatening Behavior, 23,* 11–20.

Beck, A. T., Steer, R. A., & Brown, G. K. (1996). *Manual for Beck Depression Inventory-II.* San Antonio, TX: Psychological Corporation.

Beck, A. T., Steer, R. A., & Garbin, M. G. (1988). Psychometric properties of the Beck Depression Inventory: Twenty-five years of evaluation. *Clinical Psychology Review, 8,* 77–100.

Beck, A. T., Steer, R., Kovacs, M., & Garrison, B. (1985). Hopelessness and eventual suicide: A 10-year prospective study of patients hospitalized with suicidal ideation. *American Journal of Psychiatry, 142,* 559–563.

Beck, A. T., Steer, R. A., & Ranieri, W. F. (1988). Scale for Suicide Ideation: Psychometric properties of a self-report version. *Journal of Clinical Psychology, 44,* 499–505.

Beck, A. T., Steer, R., Sanderson, W., & Skeie, T. (1991). Panic disorder and suicidal ideation and behavior: Discrepant findings in psychiatric outpatients. *American Journal of Psychiatry, 148,* 1195–1199.

Beck, A. T., Steer, R. A., & Trexler, L. D. (1989). Alcohol abuse and eventual suicide: A five to ten year prospective of alcohol abusing suicide attempters. *Journal of Studies on Alcohol, 50,* 202–209.

Beck, A. T., Ward, C., Mendelson, M., Mock, J., & Erbaugh, J. (1961). An inventory for measuring depression. *Archives of General Psychiatry, 4,* 561–571.

Beck, A. T., Weissman, A., Lester, D., & Trexler, L. (1974). The measurement of pessimism: The Hopelessness Scale. *Journal of Consulting and Clinical Psychology, 42,* 861–865.

Beck, A. T., Weissman, A., Lester, D., & Trexler, L. (1976). The classification of suicidal behaviors: 2. Dimensions of suicidal intent. *Archives of General Psychiatry, 33,* 835–837.

Biggam, F., & Power, K. (1999). Suicidality and the state-trait debate on problem-solving deficits: A reexamination with incarcerated young offenders. *Archives of Suicide Research, 5,* 27–42.

Bower, G. (1981). Mood and memory. *American Psychologist, 36,* 129–148.

Brown, G. K., Beck, A. T., Steer, R. A., & Grisham, J. R. (2000). Risk factors for suicide in psychiatric outpatients: A 20-year prospective study. *Journal of Consulting and Clinical Psychology, 68,* 371–377.

Clark, D. A. & Beck, A. T. (1999). *Scientific foundations of cognitive theory and therapy of depression.* New York: Wiley.

Clum, G., & Febbraro, G. (1994). Stress, social support, and problem-solving appraisal/skills: Prediction of suicide severity within a college sample. *Journal of Psychopathology and Behavioral Assessment, 16,* 69–83.

Clum, G., Yang, B., Febbraro, G., Canfield, D., et al. (1996). An investigation of the validity of the SPSI and SPSI-R in differentiating high-suicidal from depressed, low-suicidal college students. *Journal of Psychopathology and Behavioral Assessment, 18,* 119–132.

Cochrane-Brink, K. A., Phil, D., Lofchy, J. S., & Sakinofsky, I. (2000). Clinical rating scales in suicide risk assessment. *General Hospital Psychiatry, 22,* 445–451.

Davila, J., & Daley, S. (2000). Studying interpersonal factors in suicide: Perspectives from depression research. In T. Joiner & M. Rudd (Eds.), *Suicide science: Expanding the boundaries* (pp. 175–200). Boston: Kluwer Academic.

Dieserud, G., Roysamb, E., Braverman, M., Dalgard, O., & Ekeberg, O. (2003). Predicting repetition of suicide attempt: A prospective study of 50 suicide attempters. *Archives of Suicide Research, 7,* 1–15.

Dixon, W., Heppner, P., & Anderson, W. (1991). Problem-solving appraisal, stress, hopelessness and suicide ideation in a college population. *Journal of Counseling Psychology, 38,* 51–56.

Dozois, D. J., Dobson, K. S., & Ahnberg, J. L. (1998). A psychometric evaluation of the Beck Depression Inventory-II. *Psychological Assessment, 10,* 83–89.

Dyer, J., & Kreitman, N. (1984). Hopelessness, depression, and suicidal intent in parasuicide. *British Journal of Psychiatry, 144,* 127–133.

D'Zurilla, T., Chang, E., Nottingham, E., & Faccini, L. (1998). Social problem-solving deficits and hopelessness, depression, and suicide risk in college students and psychiatric inpatients. *Journal of Clinical Psychology, 54,* 1091–1107.

D'Zurilla, T., & Maydeu-Olivares, A. (1995). Conceptual and methodological issues in social problem-solving assessment. *Behavior Therapy, 26,* 409–432.

D'Zurilla, T., & Nezu, A. (1990). Development and preliminary evaluation of the Social Problem-Solving Inventory (SPSI). *Psychological Assessment: A Journal of Consulting and Clinical Psychology, 2,* 156–163.

Eaves, G., & Rush, A. J. (1984). Cognitive patterns in symptomatic and remitted unipolar major depression. *Journal of Abnormal Psychology, 93,* 31–40.

Eidhin, M., Sheehy, N., O'Sullivan, M., & McLeavey, B. (2002). Perceptions of the environment, suicidal ideation and problem-solving deficits in an offender population. *Legal and Criminological Psychology, 7,* 187–201.

Ellis, T., & Ratliff, K. (1986). Cognitive characteristics of suicidal and non-suicidal psychiatric patients. *Cognitive Therapy and Research, 1,* 625–634.

Fawcett, J., Scheftner, W., Clark, D., Hedeker, D., Gibbons, R., & Coryell, W. (1987). Clinical predictors of suicide inpatients with major affective disorders: A controlled prospective study. *American Journal of Psychiatry, 144,* 35–40.

Fawcett, J., Scheftner, W., Fogg, L., Clark, D., Young, M., Hedeker, D., et al. (1990). Time-related predictors of suicide in major affective disorder. *American Journal of Psychiatry, 147,* 1189–1194.

Friedman, S., Jones, J., Chernen, L., & Barlow, D. (1992). Suicidal ideation and suicide attempts among patients with panic disorder: A survey of two outpatient clinics. *American Journal of Psychiatry, 149,* 680–685.

Guze, S., & Robins, E. (1970). Suicide and primary affective disorders. *British Journal of Psychiatry, 117,* 437–438.

Hamilton, M. (1959). The assessment of anxiety states by rating. *British Journal of Medical Psychology, 32,* 50–55.

Hamilton, M. (1960). A rating scale for depression. *Journal of Neurology, Neurosurgery, and Psychiatry, 23,* 56–61.

Hammen, C. (2001). Vulnerability to depression in adulthood. In R. Ingram & J. Price (Eds.), *Vulnerability to psychopathology: Risk across the lifespan* (pp. 226–257). New York: Guilford Press.

Hawton, K., Kingsbury, S., Steinhardt, K., Anthony, J., & Fagg, J. (2002). Repetition of deliberate self-harm by adolescents: The role of psychological factors. *Journal of Adolescence, 22,* 369–378.

Heimberg, L. (1961). *Development and construct validation of an inventory for the measurement of future time perspective.* Unpublished master's thesis, Vanderbilt University, Nashville, TN.

Hewitt, P. L., & Norton, G. R. (1993). The Beck Anxiety Inventory: A psychometric analysis. *Psychological Assessment, 5,* 408–412.

Howat, S., & Davidson, K. (2002). Parasuicidal behaviour and interpersonal problem solving performance in older adults. *British Journal of Clinical Psychology, 41,* 375–386.

Ingram, R., Miranda, J., & Segal, Z. (1998). *Cognitive vulnerability to depression.* New York: Guilford Press.

Joiner, T., & Rudd, M. (1995). Negative attributional style for interpersonal events and the occurrence of severe interpersonal disruptions as predictors of self-reported suicidal ideation. *Suicide and Life-Threatening Behavior, 25,* 297–304.

Klerman, G. (1987). Clinical epidemiology of suicide. *Journal of Clinical Psychiatry, 48,* 33–38.

Kovacs, M., Beck, A. T., & Weissman, A. (1975). Hopelessness: An indicator of suicidal risk. *Suicide, 5,* 98–103.

McAuliffe, C., Keeley, H., & Corcoran, P. (2002). Problem-solving and repetition of parasuicide. *Behavioural and Cognitive Psychotherapy, 30,* 385–397.

McLeavey, B. C., Daly, R. J., Murray, C. M., O'Riodan, J., & Taylor, M. (1987). Interpersonal problem-solving deficits in self-poisoning patients. *Suicide and Life-Threatening Behavior, 17,* 33–49.

Medical Economics. (1977). *Physician's desk reference.* Oradell, NJ: Author.

Minkoff, K., Bergman, E., Beck, A. T., & Beck, R. (1973). Hopelessness, depression, and attempted suicide. *American Journal of Psychiatry, 130,* 455–459.

Moran, P. W., & Lambert, M. J. (1983). A review of current assessment tools for monitoring changes in depression. In M. S. Lambert, E. R. Christenson, & S. DeJulio (Eds.), *The assessment of psychotherapy outcome* (pp. 263–303). New York: Wiley.

Murphy, G. E. (1984). The prediction of suicide: Why is it so difficult? *American Journal of Psychotherapy, 38,* 341–349.

Murphy, G. E. (1985). Suicide and attempted suicide. In R. Michels (Ed), *Psychiatry* (pp. 1–17). Philadelphia: J.R. Lippincott.

Neuringer, C. (1961). Dichotomous evaluations in suicidal individuals. *Journal of Consulting Psychology, 25,* 445–449.

Neuringer, C., & Lettieri, D. (1971). Cognition, attitude, and affect in suicidal individuals. *Suicide and Life-Threatening Behavior, 1,* 106–124.

Orbach, I., Bar-Joseph, H., & Dror, N. (1990). Styles of problem-solving in suicidal individuals. *Suicide and Life-Threatening Behavior, 20,* 56–64.

Pallis, J. J., Gibbons, J. S., & Pierce, D. W. (1984). Estimating suicidal risk among attempted suicides: II. Efficiency of predictive scales after the attempt. *British Journal of Psychiatry, 144,* 139–148.

Pokorny, A. (1964). Suicide rates in various psychiatric disorders. *Journal of Nervous and Mental Diseases, 139,* 499–506.

Pokorny, A. (1974). A scheme for classifying suicidal behaviors. In A. T. Beck, H. L. P. Resnik, & D. J. Lettieri (Eds.), *The prediction of suicide* (pp. 29–44). Bowie, MD: Charles Press.

Pokorny, A. (1983). Prediction of suicide in psychiatric patients: Report of a prospective study. *Archives of General Psychiatry, 40,* 249–257.

Pollock, L., & Williams, J. M. G. (1998). Problem solving and suicidal behavior. *Suicide and Life-Threatening Behavior, 28,* 375–387.

Priester, M., & Clum, G. (1992). Attributional style as a diathesis in predicting depression, hopelessness, and suicide ideation in college students. *Journal of Psychopathology and Behavioral Assessment, 14,* 111–122.

Priester, M., & Clum, G. (1993). Perceived problem-solving ability as a predictor of depression, hopelessness, and suicide ideation in a college population. *Journal of Counseling Psychology, 40,* 79–85.

Ranieri, W. F., Steer, R. A., Lavrence, T. I., Rissmiller, D. J., Piper, G. E., & Beck, A. T. (1987). Relationship of depression, hopelessness, and dysfunctional attitudes to suicide ideation in psychiatric patients. *Psychological Reports, 61,* 967–975.

Reilly-Harrington, N., Alloy, L., Fresco, D., & Whitehouse, W. (1999). Cognitive styles and life events interact to predict bipolar and unipolar symptomatology. *Journal of Abnormal Psychology, 108,* 567–578.

Reinecke, M., & DuBois, D. (2001). Socioenvironmental and cognitive risk and resources: Relations to mood and suicidality among inpatient adolescents. *Journal of Cognitive Psychotherapy, 15,* 195–222.

Reinecke, M., DuBois, D., & Schultz, T. (2001). Social problem-solving, mood, and suicidality among inpatient adolescents. *Cognitive Therapy and Research, 25,* 743–756.

Rudd, M., Dahm, P. F., & Rajab, M. H. (1993). Diagnostic comorbidity in persons with suicidal ideation and behavior. *American Journal of Psychiatry, 150,* 928–934.

Rudd, M., Joiner, T., & Rajab, M. H. (2001). *Treating suicidal behavior: An effective, time-limited approach.* New York: Guilford Press.

Rudd, M., Rajab, M., & Dahm, P. (1994). Problem-solving appraisal in suicide ideators and attempters. *American Journal of Orthopsychiatry, 64,* 136–149.

Sainsbury, P. (1986). The epidemiology of suicide. In A. Roy (Ed.), *Suicide.* Baltimore: Williams & Wilkins.

Schotte, D., & Clum, G. (1982). Suicide ideation in a college population: A test of a model. *Journal of Consulting and Clinical Psychology, 50,* 690–696.

Schotte, D., & Clum, G. (1987). Problem-solving skills in suicidal psychiatric patients. *Journal of Consulting and Clinical Psychology, 55,* 49–54.

Schotte, D., Cools, J., & Payvar, S. (1990). Problem-solving deficits in suicidal patients: Trait vulnerability or state phenomenon? *Journal of Consulting and Clinical Psychology, 58,* 562–564.

Solomon, A., & Haaga, D. (2003). Cognitive theory and therapy of depression. In M. Reinecke & D. Clark (Eds.), *Cognitive therapy across the lifespan: Evidence and practice* (pp. 12–39). Cambridge, England: Cambridge University Press.

Steer, R. A., Ball, R., Ranieri, W. F., & Beck, A. T. (1997). Further evidence for the construct validity of the Beck Depression Inventory-II with psychiatric outpatients. *Psychological Reports, 80,* 443–446.

Steer, R. A., Ball, R., Ranieri, W. F., & Beck, A. T. (1999). Dimensions of the Beck Depression Inventory-II in clinically depressed outpatients. *Journal of Clinical Psychology, 55,* 117–128.

Steer, R. A., & Beck, A. T. (1985). Modifying the Beck Depression Inventory: A reply to Vredenburg, Krames, and Flett. *Psychological Reports, 57,* 625–626.

Steer, R. A., Clark, D. A., Beck, A. T., & Ranieri, W. F. (1995). Common and specific dimensions of self-reported anxiety and depression: A replication. *Journal of Abnormal Psychology, 104,* 542–545.

Steer, R. A., Rissmiller, D. J., & Beck, A. T. (2000). Use of the Beck Depression Inventory-II with depressed geriatric inpatients. *Behaviour Research and Therapy, 38,* 311–318.

Sweeney, P., Anderson, K., & Bailey, S. (1986). Attributional style in depression: A meta-analytic review. *Journal of Personality and Social Psychology, 50,* 974–991.

Vredendurg, K., Krames, L., & Flett, G. L. (1985). Reexamining the Beck Depression Inventory: The long and short of it. *Psychological Reports, 57,* 767–778.

Weissman, A. N., & Beck, A. T. (1978, November). *Development and validation of the Dysfunctional Attitude Scale: A preliminary investigation.* Paper presented at the meeting of the Association for Advancement of Behavior Therapy, Chicago.

Wetzel, R. D., Margulies, T., Davis, R., & Karam, E. (1980). Hopelessness, depression, and suicide intent. *Journal of Clinical Psychiatry, 41,* 159–160.

Young, M. A., Fogg, L. F., Scheftner, W., Fawcett, J., Akiskal, H., & Maser, J. (1996). Stable trait components of hopelessness: Baseline and sensitivity to depression. *Journal of Abnormal Psychology, 105,* 155–165.

CHAPTER 4

Minnesota Multiphasic Personality Inventories (MMPI/MMPI-2, MMPI-A) and Suicide

Alan F. Friedman, Robert P. Archer, and Richard W. Handel

"Of the standard psychological tests, only the Rorschach and the MMPI have potential as predictors of suicidal behavior but, as yet, this potential is unrealized" (Lester, 1970a, p. 1). More than three decades later, this potential continues to be unrealized. The MMPI-2 (Butcher et al., 2001) and its corresponding adolescent version, the MMPI-A (Butcher et al., 1992), are the most widely used objective personality assessment measures in the world (Archer, Maruish, Imhof, & Piotrowski, 1991; Archer & Newsom, 2000; Friedman, Lewak, Nichols, & Webb, 2001). The original form of the MMPI (Hathaway & McKinley, 1942) was subjected to considerable research efforts to identify items, scales, or profile configurations that could reliably differentiate between suicidal and nonsuicidal individuals. However, no reliable markers of suicidal behavior were identified (Eyman & Eyman, 1992). What practical use do the MMPI-2 and MMPI-A have in the assessment of suicidal potential if they are unable to reliably predict eventual suicide? Why is it difficult to identify items or scales that reliably predict suicide? These are two important questions addressed in this chapter. We present an overview of the difficulties inherent in using a personality measure to predict suicide, followed by a review of the extensive MMPI empirical literature that was targeted toward that objective. Next, we provide information on new items that were included on the MMPI-2 and the MMPI-A that are of potential use in the assessment of suicide, followed by a review of the extant literature on suicide assessment with the MMPI-2 and MMPI-A.

We offer some recommendations about the use of the MMPI-2 and MMPI-A in the assessment of suicide and suicide potential. Finally, we close with a case presentation on the MMPI-A.

The primary problem inherent in attempting to predict suicide from personality measures is the base rate issue. Suicide is a low base rate phenomenon (i.e., occurs with a very low frequency in almost all settings and populations), and there are significant difficulties in predicting any phenomena with low base rates of occurrence. The problems related to the prediction of low base rate phenomena have been discussed at length by authors such as Meehl and Rosen (1955) and Wiggins (1973). Stelmachers (1995) noted that attempting to predict suicidal behavior with a psychological test would require sensitivity and specificity close to 99% to reach an acceptable positive predictive power of about 80%. As Nichols (1988) pointed out, in comparison to suicide, the base rates are much less extreme with respect to the frequency of occurrence of suicidal ideation, attempts, and threats, and do not preclude the possibility of useful levels of prediction. For example, in the Marks and Seeman (1963) sample, these behaviors occurred at rates of 23%, 17%, and 5%, respectively. Although no psychological test can currently meet the daunting criteria to accurately predict suicide, objective measures such as the MMPI-2 and MMPI-A may still have a role in the assessment of suicide. Decades of research have shown that the MMPI cannot predict suicide, but several authors have argued that the prediction of suicide potential, rather than the actual prediction of completed suicide, remains an important assessment challenge (e.g., Clopton, 1978; Sepaher, Bongar, & Greene, 1999). Clopton (1979) succinctly stated that the:

> . . . research question of most clinical relevance is whether MMPI data are of assistance in the identification of individuals who will later attempt suicide, not whether MMPI data are sufficient for such identification. (p. 162)

In general, the literature on the prediction of dangerousness, based in great part on psychiatric and forensic subjects, has taught us to move away from trying to predict specific acts of dangerousness or violence in an open-ended time frame. We have come to think in terms of evaluating the probability of an individual perpetrating an act of violence in a briefer and defined window of time, dependent on the knowledge that many factors, which can shift or change rapidly, influence the propensity for violence. The move to a risk assessment model from dangerousness prediction per se can also be applied to MMPI interpretation. Numerous factors influence an individual to think and behave in a suicidal (or homicidal) manner including, but not limited to, changes in personal circumstances such as loss of support from significant others, irreversible business losses, or the worsening of a medical condition with intractable pain. The exacerbation of severe psychiatric symptoms may also increase suicide risk such as command hallucinations, intolerable depressive symptoms, or alcohol and/or drug intoxication. The value of the MMPI lies in being part of a risk assessment mosaic that includes interview data, collateral sources of information, and other psychometric data to help serve the mission of estimating suicide potential rather than the prediction of actual suicide. In this fashion, the test data can help inform and guide a risk management strategy.

The prediction of suicide is too complex a phenomenon to be measured reliably by a single variable or even a combination of indicators on the MMPI or any other psychometric instrument. As mentioned, the base rate problem is one critical factor to consider, but other ingredients come into play, such as individuals' motivation to report accurately their feelings and their own self-awareness of their intentions. In some cases, suicide attempts or gestures are impulsive acts, perhaps unleashed by the disinhibiting effects of a substance such as alcohol, cocaine, or a barbiturate.

The measurement of psychopathology, the major purpose for which the MMPI was developed and is currently used, would naturally lead researchers and clinician users of the test to inquire about the validity of suicide prediction with the instrument. After all, the prevention of suicide or suicide attempts, commonly associated with mental illness, falls well within the province of the responsibilities of mental health practitioners. Psychologists and psychiatrists are looked on by the public and courts to make difficult decisions about the risk status of individuals, frequently as a core element in involuntary hospitalization decisions. The MMPI has been used and studied since its original publication to assess suicide potential and to differentiate suicidal from nonsuicidal individuals (Friedman et al., 2001). The test is used not only clinically in this regard but also forensically. It is not uncommon for a hospital and the clinicians involved in treatment of a suicidal patient to be sued for malpractice, often resulting from incidents in which a patient, either discharged or given a leave or pass, subsequently committed suicide. The MMPI and other test data are usually obtained and examined following these incidents for signs or markers that could have alerted the clinicians and diagnosticians that the patient was a high or at-risk candidate for attempting or completing suicide. These so-called "psychological autopsies" force clinicians to reexamine their decision-making process, and they often rely on the research literature to justify their judgments. The usefulness and the limitations of the MMPI literature in identifying test features predictive of suicide attempts or actual suicide are reviewed in this chapter.

MINNESOTA MULTIPHASIC PERSONALITY INVENTORY RESEARCH FINDINGS

Empirical investigations into the efficacy of the MMPI in differentiating suicide attempters from nonsuicide attempters, or in predicting suicide threateners from actual completed suicides, have generally failed to provide reliable and valid markers for practical clinical application. The MMPI and its derivative forms (MMPI-2 and MMPI-A) are the focus of this chapter, but comprehensive reviews of other personality assessment procedures, including projective and cognitive instruments as well as psychiatric rating scales, have also failed to identify consistently any single instrument or technique that can be exclusively relied on to render important diagnostic decisions and predictions related to suicide. Lester (1970a), in his conclusions from reviewing attempts to predict suicidal risk using psychological tests, stated:

> [I]t is apparent that the use of standard psychological tests in the prediction and identification of suicidal risk has not been fruitful. Even allowing for the methodological weaknesses in their research, very few studies have resulted in the identification of valid and reliable signs. (p. 15)

Eyman and Eyman (1992) stated in their conclusions from reviewing personality assessment methods in suicide prediction that, while personality evaluation can be of use in assessing suicide risk, the "ability to predict immediate suicidal risk has not consistently been supported by research . . ." (p. 197). Clopton (1979) wrote, "to date, neither standard MMPI scales, MMPI profile analysis, nor specific MMPI items have been found to be reliable in predicting suicide at useful levels" (p. 162). He concluded that MMPI scale scores had been found to be unrelated to the method or the lethality of suicide attempts. In a similar commentary, Nichols (1988) concluded that the many research investigations conducted during the 30 years preceding his review produced few valid correlates of, and nothing of substantive clinical value for predicting, suicide. If researchers are to be more productive in this area, Nichols recommended collaborative efforts to build up adequate-size samples of individuals who had completed suicide within a short time frame (e.g., one week) after having completed the MMPI. He opined that since suicide "may more closely approximate the final common pathway of a concatenation of demographic, situational, and personologic variables than a unitary trait disposition, the constitution of suicidal and appropriate comparison groups may require the institution of more extensive and sophisticated inclusion criteria and controls than those found tolerable in previous studies" (Nichols, 1988, p. 103). Unfortunately, few studies have been able to approach the degree of sophistication recommended by Nichols, and he pessimistically concluded that even if such work was to be done, "the clinical payoff for even valid and reliable MMPI correlates of suicide, assuming that such might eventually be found, is most unlikely to compensate the research efforts necessary to develop them" (p. 104). However, such test correlates, if unable to accurately predict suicide, would still add to our general understanding of suicidal behavior.

Suicide studies with the MMPI vary along a number of dimensions. The major areas of these investigations have examined MMPI data in terms of items, scales, and profile configurations or code patterns, with the subjects of these studies varying from suicide threateners, suicide attempters, and suicidal ideators with and without suicidal gestures to those making fatal suicide attempts. Other important subject factors include the age, gender, and personal characteristics of the person, such as his or her voluntary versus involuntary hospitalization status (Leonard, 1977). As to gender, Clopton (1979) noted that studies (e.g., Clopton, Pallis, & Birtchnell, 1979; Leonard, 1977) have demonstrated important differences in the MMPI profile patterns obtained from male and female patients. Clopton's (1979) review of the MMPI literature on suicide led him to recommend that the data for the two sexes always be analyzed separately and that the length of time between MMPI administration and the suicidal act be carefully considered in research studies. These latter time intervals are obviously important because the MMPI measures not just enduring traits, but also changing psychological states such as an individual's mood or affect. Clopton (1979) also concluded that the research on the MMPI and suicide has largely failed to focus on the patients with suicidal characteristics who complete suicide; instead, it has concentrated on examining patients displaying suicidal threats or attempts in efforts to link test data to suicidal behavior.

In 1992, Eyman and Eyman reviewed the status of the MMPI as an aid in suicide assessment. Beginning with a focus on individual test items, they observed that Simon and Gilberstadt (1958) and Clopton and Jones (1975) attempted unsuccessfully to relate MMPI item responses to suicidal behavior. Efforts were also made to develop a suicide threat scale without finding the necessary validity to support such a scale (Clopton & Jones, 1975; Ravensborg & Foss, 1969; Watson, Klett, Walters, & Vassar, 1984). Of the few studies that reported more positive results for individual items, authors typically either failed to adequately identify the useful test items or to describe their subject groups (DeVries, 1967; Koss, Butcher, & Hoffman, 1976). Despite an inadequately described sample of patients in the depressed-suicidal group, for example, Koss et al.'s (1976) depressed-suicidal ideation critical item list is in wide use as part of the Koss-Butcher critical item set. Despite the popularity of these critical items, a comprehensive evaluation of their usefulness has not been undertaken.

A very early study of item content by Simon and Hales (1949), as reported by Clopton (1979), examined the MMPI responses of male psychiatric patients who ruminated about suicide. Only seven Scale 2 (*D*) items and 10 Scale 7 (*Pt*) items were answered in the keyed direction by a majority of the suicidal patients. Farberow and DeVries (1967) created an MMPI suicide threat scale by conducting an item analysis of the MMPI responses of suicidal and nonsuicidal male psychiatric patients. This 52-item scale has failed to replicate, however, and few of these items differentiated the suicidal groups from the nonsuicidal group in independent item analyses (e.g., DeVries, 1966).

Many more studies were initiated exploring the relationship between individual scale elevations and suicidal behaviors, in contrast to investigations at the item level. However, generally mixed findings made it difficult to identify any one scale, or set of scales, that has been consistently related to the accurate prediction of suicidal behavior. Many individual case investigations have reported a relationship between Scale 2 (*D*) elevations on the MMPI and suicidal acts (e.g., Dahlstrom, Welsh, & Dahlstrom, 1972; Simon, 1950), but these findings lacked strong empirical support in empirical investigations of group data. Eyman and Eyman (1992), for example, pointed out that several studies found that MMPI Scale 2 (*D*) elevations did not differentiate significantly between suicide attempters and nonattempters (e.g., Clopton & Jones, 1975; Tarter, Templer, & Perley, 1975; Watson et al., 1984).

Clopton and Jones (1975) reported that male psychiatric patients who committed suicide did not differ significantly from other nonsuicidal psychiatric patients on the MMPI clinical scales. Clopton (1979) compiled mean values for the standard MMPI validity and clinical scales from nine different investigations of psychiatric patients and categorized scores by suicide threateners, suicide attempters, and completed suicides. Among the clinical scales, Scale 2 (*D*) figures prominently in these code patterns, generally representing either the primary or secondary scale elevation. However, other clinical scales, particularly Scale 8 (*Sc*), were also prominently elevated in these profiles, suggesting that relying on a single scale elevation to predict suicide behaviors would often lead to incorrect predictions. It is not surprising that Scale 2 (*D*) elevations would frequently coincide with other clinically significant scale elevations given the extensive item overlap between Scale 2 (*D*) and the other basic clinical scales. Forty-seven of the 60 Scale 2 (*D*) MMPI items, for example, overlap with items from other scales, including substantial overlap with Scale 7 (*Pt*) and Scale 8 (*Sc;* Friedman, Webb, & Lewak, 1989).

The relationship between the method used to attempt or complete suicide and individual scale elevations has also been examined. One early study (Simon, 1950) found a spike on Scale 2 (*D*) to be associated with male patients who attempted suicide by hanging. Later studies by Lester (1970b) and Simon and Gilberstadt (1958), however, failed to provide support for the relationship between MMPI scale scores and the method selected by male psychiatric patients who committed suicide. Tarter et al. (1975) had male and female suicide attempters complete the MMPI and an independent lethality scale but failed to find any relation between the lethality scores and the MMPI standard scores.

The MMPIs of adolescents have been researched by Marks and Haller (1977), who reported that male suicide attempters scored higher on Scales 1 (*Hs*) and 5 (*Mf*) in contrast to male nonattempters. Further, adolescent girls who attempted suicide scored higher on Scales 2 (*D*) and 3 (*Hy*) when compared with female adolescent nonsuicide attempters. Spirito, Faust, Myers, and Bechtel (1988) failed to find differences between adolescent females hospitalized in a general pediatric unit after a suicide attempt and adolescent females who were being psychiatrically evaluated without prior histories of suicide attempts. No clinical scale differentiated reliably between these two groups.

Studies of various codetypes or profile patterns have been the focus of several researchers because codetype interpretation is the basic foundation on which most clinicians base their personality descriptions. Clopton (1979) reviewed several of these studies, and the following summary is drawn in large part from his review. Marks and Seeman (1963) investigated the profiles of female psychiatric inpatients and found that 45% of the inpatients with a 4-8-2 codetype had attempted suicide, followed by 39% of patients with the 4-6 codetype. Other than with the 4-8-2, 2-4-6, 2-7-8, and 2-8 profiles, it appeared that when Scale 2 (*D*) was a salient elevation in the profile, the incidence of suicidal behaviors (including ideation, threats, gestures, and attempts) might be suppressed or absent. This suppression effect was especially evident for cases in which Scales 1 (*Hs*), 3 (*Hy*), and/or Scale 7 (*Pt*) were elevated. These latter scales have been referred to as inhibitor or suppressor scales, whereas Scales 4 (*Pd*), 8 (*Sc*), and 9 (*Ma*) have been referred to as excitor scales. Excitor scales involve correlates such as impulsivity, lack of frustration tolerance, and an action orientation (Friedman et al., 2001). Clinical lore holds that the likelihood of individuals acting on their suicidal impulses increases if their excitor scales are elevated relative to their inhibitor or suppressor scales. While this makes intuitive clinical sense, there is no support in the research literature for this hypothesis. When Clopton et al. (1979) used a cluster analysis of MMPI profiles to identify subtypes of suicidal and nonsuicidal patients, they found that Scale 2 (*D*) was the third most elevated scale in the suicidal clusters. All of the individual MMPI profiles with Scales 7 (*Pt*) and 8 (*Sc*) as the most elevated scales were examined; 64% of the suicidal patients had Scale 2 (*D*) more elevated than Scale 1 (*Hs*), and Scale 1 (*Hs*) was greater than Scale 2 (*D*) for 60% of the nonsuicidal patients. It appeared that within the 7-8/8-7 codetype, the relative elevation of Scales 1 (*Hs*) and 2 (*D*) was important in predicting whether the patient had attempted suicide. These results indicated a prominence of Scale 2 (*D*) in classifying suicidal behavior, which is consistent with the Marks and Seeman (1963) data that showed Scale 2 (*D*) to be associated with more frequent occurrence of suicidal behaviors in selected code patterns.

One of the few studies examining the ability of practicing psychologists to recognize MMPI profiles of suicidal individuals was conducted by Clopton and Baucom (1979). Six psychologists experienced in MMPI interpretation were presented with MMPI profiles of male psychiatric patients who committed suicide and profiles from male nonsuicidal patients. The psychologists were asked to judge the profiles as likely or unlikely to be the profiles of patients who would commit suicide. They also made ratings across several dimensions believed valuable in a suicide risk assessment including impulse control problems, symptomatic depression, and activity level. All of the judges failed to identify suicidal and nonsuicidal patients beyond chance levels, and the clinicians' ratings of patients on suicide factors did not differ for the suicidal versus the nonsuicidal patients.

Clopton (1979), in reviewing the data from several studies (e.g., De-Vries & Farberow, 1967; Farberow, 1956; Rosen, Hales, & Simon, 1954), commented that patients who threaten suicide are the most easily identified suicidal group and that patients who commit suicide are the group most difficult to differentiate from other clinical groups. Not all studies, however, report profile differences among patients who threaten, attempt, or commit suicide. Ravensborg and Foss (1969), for example, compared the MMPI profiles of psychiatric patients who committed suicide with profiles from patients who died of natural causes and with profiles from other psychiatric patients in the same hospital. The mean MMPI profile of the three groups did not differ significantly. In general, it appears that dependence on a codetype pattern to make suicidal predictions is unlikely to yield accurate predictions.

MINNESOTA MULTIPHASIC PERSONALITY INVENTORY-2 AND MINNESOTA MULTIPHASIC PERSONALITY INVENTORY-ADOLESCENT CRITICAL ITEM RESEARCH

The MMPI-2 includes four items that explicitly ask about past or present suicidal ideation or behavior (items 506, 520, 524, and 530). All but one of these items (530) are now included in the revised depression-suicidal ideation critical item grouping of the Koss-Butcher critical items (Butcher et al., 2001; Koss & Butcher, 1973). Specifically, of the 22 items included in the depression-suicidal ideation item group, four items (303, 506, 520, and 524) indicate a self-report of past or present suicidal ideation or behavior. Lachar and Wrobel (1979) also developed a critical item set for the MMPI that includes a depression and worry content area. The Lachar and Wrobel critical items have been retained on the MMPI-2 with the exception of four items (Greene, 2000). Further, the Lachar and Wrobel depression and worry content area includes two items (150 and 303) out of 16 that directly inquire about current suicidal ideation and behavior. Other critical item groupings have been developed, including the original critical item list by Grayson (1951), who gathered a set of 38 items for use with a Veterans Administration (VA) population. Endorsement of any of these items in the course of a psychodiagnostic evaluation was considered sufficient to warrant more detailed clinical inquiry into the content area of the item, regardless of whether the MMPI profile appeared pathological. In some cases, these items were considered pathognomonic of a condition, such as delusions or suicidal ideation. In others, the item would serve as a red flag or a stop sign, forcing an interruption of the diagnostic process in order to explore the patient's grounds for its endorsement. These items came to be called *stop* or *critical* items. Eventually, the Grayson items were recognized to be highly redundant with the F and Sc scales, and 92% of the items were keyed in the "true" direction, rendering the latter items vulnerable to an acquiescent response style.

Another popular critical item list was developed by Caldwell (1969). Although sharing some of the same limitations as the Grayson items, the Caldwell list covered a wider range of problem areas, including a "suicidal thoughts" set of five items and a distress and depression category encompassing 11 items. The Caldwell and Grayson critical items, with their origins in a rational-intuitive item selection process, have demonstrated few empirical relationships with the symptoms and complaints they enunciated. In contrast, Lachar and Wrobel (1979) and Koss and Butcher (1973) constructed empirically based critical items sets, which appear to be conceptually and statistically more sturdy (e.g., Koss et al., 1976).

It is significant that with the exception of the now rarely used Grayson items, all critical item lists subdivide their items into categories determined by content. This type of grouping deemphasizes Grayson's initial conception of these items as standalone or stop items in favor of a perspective that places critical items in a position intermediate between stop items and formally developed and normed scales. See Friedman et al. (2001) for an in-depth discussion of further psychometric theory and methods related to test item content. Friedman et al. noted that critical item lists are not as reliable as scales, primarily because it is possible that a respondent could mark a single item as a result of confusion, misunderstanding, or similar inadvertence. Friedman and his colleagues, therefore, recommended that the endorsement of critical items should lead the clinician to assess these areas further with the patient, but to do so cautiously. The detailed probing of critical items, even when feasible, does not always identify such mishaps or produce satisfactory information. Some respondents deny valid endorsements by claiming disability or faux pas. Many feel excessively pressed and intruded on by close questioning of item responses. For these reasons, it is recommended that the psychologist begin any probing with the least threatening critical items and only then proceed to the most threatening content.

Critical items can be valuable because they can:

afford the clinician a valuable if not always reliable channel of communication with the patient. Single and small sets of items are the means by which the patient can most directly address his or her concerns to the psychologist within the context of the MMPI-2. Although the various scales and indexes of the test serve to identify those problems areas that are of significance in the patient's life and circumstances, it is only through single-item responses that the patient can call the clinician's attention to his or her specific problems. The clinician's access to some of these responses, in the form of critical items, can help to create a channel of communication that stands to facilitate empathy between therapist and patient and build a bridge between the phases of assessment and treatment. (Friedman et al., 2001, p. 345)

In this fashion, critical individual items can serve a useful alerting function and be a springboard to inquiries in the interview, but it is unlikely that they may be used to identify genuine suicide potential or to assign levels of risk for suicidal behavior (Nichols, 1988).

We identified two empirical MMPI-2 studies relevant to the use of selected items in suicide assessment. Sepaher et al. (1999) investigated endorsement frequencies of two MMPI-2 items directly related to suicidal ideation ("I have recently considered killing myself," and "Lately I have thought a lot about killing myself"). These authors used a sample of almost 24,000 well-defined spike (i.e., single scale) and two-point codetypes for their study. A well-defined codetype is one in which the primary scales in the codetype produce T-scores greater than or equal to 65, and all other scales are at least 5 T-score points lower than those of the scales in the codetype (Graham, 2000). Endorsement frequencies of items 506 and 520 were reported by gender for each of the well-defined MMPI-2 codetypes. Sepaher et al. found six codetypes for which these two items were endorsed by more than 20% of men and women (i.e., 6-8/8-6, 2-8/8-2, 7-8/8-7, 3-8/8-3, 1-8/8-1, and 4-8/8-4), one codetype for which they were endorsed by more than 20% of men (2-7/7-2), and two codetypes for which they were endorsed by more than 20% of women (2-6/6-2 and 2-4/4-2). Sepaher et al. indicated that these base rates may be useful to the clinicians as an adjunct to traditional (e.g., clinical interview) methods of assessment for suicide risk.

Although the MMPI/MMPI-2 is ineffective at predicting actual suicide, Glassmire, Stolberg, Greene, and Bongar (2001) reiterated earlier arguments (e.g., Clopton, 1978; Sepaher et al., 1999) suggesting that the prediction of suicide potential remains an important assessment question. Toward this end, Glassmire et al. (2001) developed a Suicidal Potential Scale (SPS) that consists of the six MMPI-2 items (items 150, 303, 506, 520, 524, and 530) that directly indicate a self-report of past or present suicidal ideation or behavior. These authors used a sample of outpatient psychotherapy patients who were asked two questions that directly addressed the presence of suicidal ideation or behavior during a telephone interview as part of the clinic's intake protocol. Glassmire et al. found that a large percentage of patients who endorsed at least one MMPI-2 suicide item also denied suicidal ideation or behavior during the telephone intake interview. Therefore, they concluded that these

MMPI-2 items may provide important clinical information for the assessment of suicidal potential beyond that which is obtained from a clinical interview. Although these authors grouped the items into a single scale, they noted: "Because every item on the SPS directly inquires about suicidal ideation and behavior, raw scores greater than zero should be interpreted as a pathognomonic sign for the reporting of suicidal ideation and behavior" (p. 288).

In addition to MMPI-2 studies, there are also several MMPI-A studies of items and item sets related to suicide. Forbey and Ben-Porath (1998), for example, developed a critical item set for the MMPI-A using a combination of empirical and rational procedures. Their critical item set includes a six-item grouping termed *Depression/Suicidal ideation.* However, there are fewer items on the MMPI-A than on the MMPI-2 that directly inquire about suicidal ideation. Their six-item set includes two items (items 177 and 283) that explicitly inquire about suicidal ideation (i.e., "I sometimes think about killing myself," and "Most of the time I wish I were dead"). Although subsequent research has yet to be conducted on the Forbey and Ben-Porath critical item groupings, the review of the responses to these two items as a component of a comprehensive suicide potential assessment appears to be clinically useful.

Archer and Slesinger (1999) explored the relationship between MMPI-A basic scale profile patterns and MMPI-A items related to suicidal ideation. In addition to the two items mentioned previously that are included in the Forbey and Ben-Porath critical item set, Archer and Slesinger included item 399 ("The future seems hopeless to me") in their analyses. Archer and Slesinger explored the endorsement frequencies of these three items in relation to MMPI-A mean clinical scale elevations and codetype classifications. Archer and Slesinger identified three codetypes (4-8/8-4, 8-9/9-8, and 6-8/8-6) for which participants produced higher item endorsement frequencies on one or more of the three items investigated in their study. Among adolescents producing elevations on single scales, adolescents with spike 2 or spike 8 codetypes tended to endorse these three items more frequently than other adolescents in the clinical sample.

We identified one other MMPI-A study relevant to the assessment of suicide. Kopper, Osman, Osman, and Hoffman (1998) used an inpatient sample of 143 adolescents who completed the MMPI-A and the 36-item

SPS (Cull & Gill, 1982). These authors used the SPS as a dependent measure in a series of hierarchical multiple regression analyses with selected MMPI-A clinical scales, content scales, and Harris Lingoes subscales as independent variables. They reported incremental validity for a variety of content and Harris Lingoes subscales over selected basic clinical scales in the prediction of SPS scores. However, these findings are probably of minimal clinical importance because the SPS is likely to have limited practical utility in the prediction of actual suicidal behavior. Therefore, it is unlikely that the MMPI-A scales used to predict SPS scores would be useful in the prediction of actual suicide.

The available literature from the MMPI, MMPI-2, and MMPI-A provides little evidence that MMPI items, scales, or profile configuration patterns are of practical use in the critical determination involving an adolescent's or adult's probability of engaging in suicidal behavior. Although substantial research has shown that the various forms of the MMPI are not directly useful in the prediction of suicide, numerous researchers and authors have argued that the instrument is useful in prediction to more common aspects related to suicide phenomena, particularly the occurrence of suicidal ideation. The degree to which the endorsement of suicidal ideation on the MMPI-2 or MMPI-A is related to the occurrence of actual suicidal behaviors is probably mediated by numerous factors, including the individual's history of prior suicidal behaviors, family history, access to lethal methods, and the presence or absence of a variety of personality features and/or psychiatric symptoms including depression, impulsivity, alienation, and the occurrence of anger or rage. Suicidal ideation is relatively common among numerous psychiatric groups and even (as we have discussed) relatively common among adolescents in the MMPI-A normative sample. While the MMPI-2 and MMPI-A may not be able to accurately predict the occurrence of suicidal behavior, these tests have potential usefulness in uncovering the presence of suicidal ideation in adolescents and adults and can be of significant value in performing an overall assessment of suicide risk or potential. The MMPI-2 and MMPI-A should always be combined with multiple sources of other data including clinical interview, comprehensive psychosocial history taking, and results from a variety of other psychometric instruments in any evaluation of suicide issues.

———————————————— Case Example ————————————————

Background Information

Caroline is a 17-year-old adolescent female, the oldest of four children from a lower middle-class socioeconomic background. Caroline's mother and father had decided to obtain a divorce, and her father recently left their home to establish a separate residence. Caroline had no history of emotional problems and was generally described as a good student who was responsible, reliable, and cooperative. For the past several weeks, Caroline had been showing symptoms of depression including despondency, lethargy, apathy, weight loss, sleep disturbance, and decreased appetite. She frequently complained of "feeling bad" and "being tired" and recently acknowledged suicidal ideation, but denied any immediate intent to attempt suicide. Caroline agreed to collaborate with her therapist in sharing any significant increase in suicidal ideation or intent.

At the time of her admission to outpatient psychotherapy, Caroline received a diagnosis of dysthymic disorder (*DSM-IV* 300.40) and was administered a clinical interview and mental status examination, the MMPI-A, the Wechsler Adult Intelligence Scale-III, the Rorschach, and the Thematic Apperception Test (TAT). Her mother completed the Child Behavior Checklist (CBCL). While the MMPI-A should always be interpreted within the context of a clinical interview and mental status examination findings in combination with other test and nontest sources of information, the current interpretation is restricted to the major MMPI-A findings in the interest of highlighting the important MMPI-A information. The MMPI-A test manual (Butcher et al., 1992) and interpretive reference works including Archer (1997), Archer and Krishnamurthy (2002), and Butcher and Williams (2000) provides more complete information on the MMPI-A scale correlates and the interpretive process.

Minnesota Multiphasic Personality Inventory-Adolescent Profile Test Results and Interpretation

Caroline's basic scale profile is shown in Figure 4.1, and her Content and Supplementary Scale Profile is presented in Figure 4.2. The examination of Caroline's MMPI-A profiles begins with an evaluation of validity scale data. Caroline responded to all test items ($? = 0$), and her *T*-score

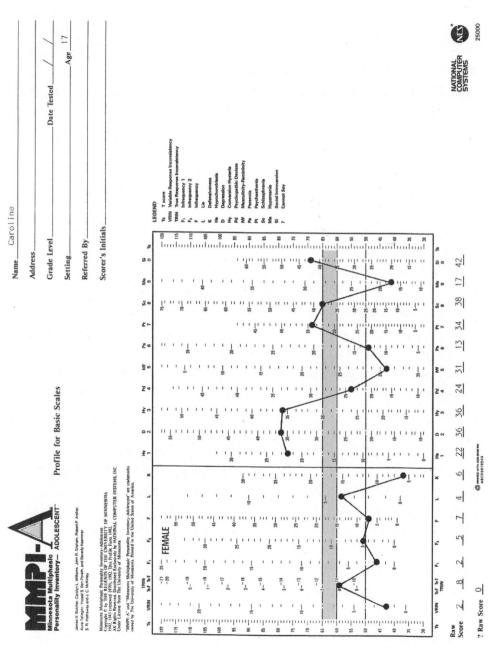

Figure 4.1 Caroline's Basic Scale Profile.

78

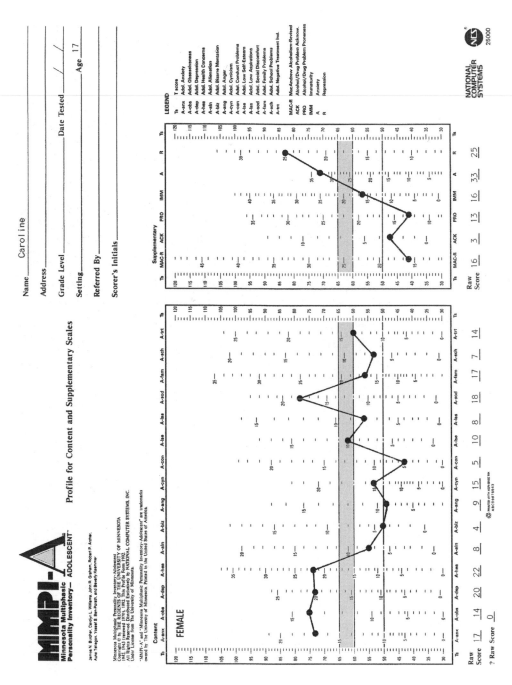

Figure 4.2 Caroline's Supplementary Scale Profile.

79

values of 43 on *VRIN* and 58 on *TRIN* indicate a very consistent item response pattern. This adolescent's normal range *T*-scores on *F* and the *F* subscales show that she responded to items in a conventional and accurate manner. Further, her *T*-scores of 59 on *L* and 37 on *K* suggest that Caroline might be described as a relatively naive girl who is concerned about "doing the right thing," but she is also able to be candid and relatively self-revealing in terms of reporting the occurrence of psychiatric symptomatology. Thus, Caroline's MMPI-A validity scale scores suggest that her self-report on this instrument was consistent and accurate.

Caroline's MMPI-A basic clinical scale profile reveals clinical range elevations on 6 of the 10 basic scales, corresponding to a 2-3-1-0-7-8 codetype. Given the multiplicity of scale elevations, the relative lack of elevation definition for the single scale high point (Scale 2 is identical to Scale 3 in *T*-score value), and the two-point code pattern (Scales 2 and 3 are only two *T*-score points higher than Scale 1), a number of elevation and configural features must be taken into account in interpreting this profile. The primary code patterns involve two-point combinations of Scales 1, 2, and 3 and thus emphasize symptomatology, including overreaction to stress, depression and despondency, and somatic preoccupation including complaints of weakness, fatigability, and tiredness. Major interpersonal themes for Caroline are likely to include unmet needs for attention and approval by others, an interpersonal style that is dependent and ambivalent, and a general fearfulness and hypersensitivity in social interactions. These basic scale characteristics are further supported by clinical range elevations on Content Scales *A-dep* and *A-hea*. For example, adolescent girls who produce elevations on *A-dep* have a higher frequency of despondency, apathy, loneliness, and suicidal ideation, while elevations on *A-hea* for girls have been associated with an increased report of weight problems, limited or no social support, and feelings of tiredness and fatigue.

In addition to her elevations on the neurotic triad (Scales 1, 2, and 3), Caroline also produced clinical range ($T \geq 65$) elevations on Scale 7 (*Pt*) and Scale 8 (*Sc*). Elevations on Scale 7, particularly when combined with elevations on the *A-anx* and *A-obs* content scales and the *A* (*Anxiety*) supplementary scale, are typically obtained by adolescents who are described as anxious, tense, ruminative, indecisive, self-critical, and perfectionistic. While this level of self-dissatisfaction and discomfort is painful for Caroline, it also serves as a powerful motivator to engage in the therapy process. Adolescents who produce elevations on Scale 8 are typically seen as alienated, socially withdrawn, and vulnerable to real or imagined stress and threat. Finally, Caroline's *Si* scale *T*-score of 69 and *A-sod* content scale score of 78 suggest that this teenager might also be described as socially introverted and uncomfortable, with a tendency to be shy, timid, and submissive around others. Among girls, higher scores on *A-sod* have been related to depression, eating disorder problems, social withdrawal and discomfort, fatigue, apathy, and avoidance of conflict and competition with peers.

The elevation on *Si,* particularly in combination with her low *MAC-R* raw score, is also related to a sense of inferiority or lower self-confidence as well as a decreased risk for impulsive or delinquency/conduct-disordered behaviors. Indeed, her relatively low score on the *MAC-R* supplementary scale also supports the view of Caroline as a repressed and sensation-avoidant adolescent. The failure of this latter defense mechanism is shown in Caroline's elevation of the *Repression* (*R*) supplementary scale, which, in combination with her elevation on the *Anxiety* (*A*) scale, indicates her use of repression is ineffective in protecting her from conscious awareness of troubling and distressing thoughts and feelings.

Minnesota Multiphasic Personality Inventory-Adolescent Structural Summary and Critical Item Findings

Figure 4.3 presents the MMPI-A Structural Summary characteristics for Caroline. The MMPI-A Structural Summary form, developed by Archer and Krishnamurthy (1994), initially provides an organization schema for validity scale data relevant to assessment of an adolescent's test-taking attitudes and then organizes data on psychological functioning along eight factor dimensions derived from the 69 scales and subscales of the MMPI-A. The clinician summarizes the adolescent's functioning for each factor through a simple process of placing a check mark next to those scales or subscales that meet the criterion for a critical range score (Krishnamurthy & Archer, 1999). Factor correlates are deemed important in describing the psychological functioning of an adolescent for those factors in which a majority of scales and subscales meet

MMPI-A Structural Summary

Robert P. Archer and Radhika Krishnamurthy

Name: _____Caroline_____   Date: _____

Age: _____17_____   Grade: _____

Gender: _____Female_____   School: _____

Test-Taking Attitudes

1. Omissions (raw score total)

___0___ ? (Cannot Say scale)

2. Consistency (T-score values)

___43___ VRIN

___59___ TRIN

___46___ F_1 vs. ___51___ F_2

3. Accuracy (check if condition present)

Overreport

_____ F scale T score ≥ 90

_____ All clinical scales except 5 and 0 ≥ 60

Underreport

_____ High L ($T \geq 65$)

_____ High K ($T \geq 65$)

_____ All clinical scales except 5 and 0 < 60

Factor Groupings
(enter T-score data)

1. General Maladjustment

- ✓ Welsh's A
- ✓ Scale 7
- ✓ Scale 8
- ✓ Scale 2
- ___ Scale 4
- ✓ D_1 (Subjective Depression)
- ✓ D_4 (Mental Dullness)
- ✓ D_5 (Brooding)
- ✓ Hy_3 (Lassitude-Malaise)
- ___ Sc_1 (Social Alienation)
- ✓ Sc_2 (Emotional Alienation)
- ✓ Sc_3 (Lack of Ego Mastery – Cognitive)
- ___ Sc_4 (Lack of Ego Mastery – Conative)
- ✓ Si_3 (Alienation)
- ___ Pd_4 (Social Alienation)
- ✓ Pd_5 (Self-Alienation)
- ___ Pa_2 (Poignancy)
- ✓ A-dep
- ✓ A-anx
- ✓ A-lse
- ___ A-aln
- ✓ A-obs
- ✓ A-trt

___17___/23 Number of scales with $T \geq 60$

2. Immaturity

- ___ IMM
- ___ Scale F
- ✓ Scale 8
- ___ Scale 6
- ___ ACK
- ___ MAC-R
- ___ Pa_1 (Persecutory Ideas)
- ✓ Sc_2 (Emotional Alienation)
- ___ Sc_6 (Bizarre Sensory Experiences)
- ___ A-sch
- ___ A-biz
- ___ A-aln
- ___ A-con
- ___ A-fam
- ✓ A-trt

___3___/15 Number of scales with $T \geq 60$

Figure 4.3   Caroline's Structural Summary Characteristics.

3. Disinhibition/Excitatory Potential

_____ Scale 9

_____ Ma$_2$ (Psychomotor Acceleration)

_____ Ma$_4$ (Ego Inflation)

_____ Sc$_5$ (Lack of Ego Mastery, Defective Inhibition)

_____ D$_2$ (Psychomotor Retardation) (low score)*

_____ Welsh's R (low score)*

✓ Scale K (low score)*

_____ Scale L (low score)*

_____ A-ang

_____ A-cyn

_____ A-con

_____ MAC-R

_1_ /12 Number of scales with $T \geq 60$ or ≤ 40 for scales with asterisk

4. Social Discomfort

✓ Scale 0

✓ Si$_1$ (Shyness/Self-Consciousness)

_____ Hy$_1$ (Denial of Social Anxiety) (low score)*

_____ Pd$_3$ (Social Imperturbability) (low score)*

✓ Ma$_3$ (Imperturbability) (low scores)*

✓ A-sod

✓ A-lse

✓ Scale 7

_6_ /8 Number of scales with $T \geq 60$ or $T \leq 40$ for scales with asterisk

5. Health Concerns

✓ Scale 1

✓ Scale 3

✓ A-hea

✓ Hy$_4$ (Somatic Complaints)

✓ Hy$_3$ (Lassitude-Malaise)

✓ D$_3$ (Physical Malfunctioning)

_6_ /6 Number of scales with $T \geq 60$

6. Naivete

_____ A-cyn (low score)*

_____ Pa$_3$ (Naivete)

✓ Hy$_2$ (Need for Affection)

_____ Si$_3$ (Alienation–Self and Others) (low score)*

_____ Scale K

_1_ /5 Number of scales with $T \geq 60$ or $T \leq 40$ for scales with asterisk

7. Familial Alienation

_____ Pd$_1$ (Familial Discord)

_____ A-fam

_____ Scale 4

_____ PRO

_0_ /4 Number of scales with $T \geq 60$

8. Psychoticism

_____ Pa$_1$ (Persecutory Ideas)

_____ Scale 6

_____ A-biz

_____ Sc$_6$ (Bizarre Sensory Experiences)

_0_ /4 Number of scales with $T \geq 60$

Note. The presentation of scales under each factor label is generally organized in a descending order from the best to the least effective marker. Within this overall approach, scales are grouped logically in terms of basic clinical scales, Harris-Lingoes and _Si_ subscales, and content scales. The majority of scales included in this summary sheet were correlated $\geq .60$ or $\leq -.60$ with the relevant factor for the MMPI-A normative sample.

PAR Psychological Assessment Resources, Inc.
P.O. Box 998/Odessa, Florida 33556/Toll-Free 1-800-331-TEST

Figure 4.3   (Continued)

the critical criterion. When more than one factor meets this requirement, greater interpretative emphasis is placed on those factors showing
the highest percentage of significant scale or subscale scores.

Caroline produced a pattern of significant *T*-score values on all six of
the scales and subscales associated with the *Health Concerns* dimension.
This indicates that Caroline's concerns about her physical health are a
central aspect of her psychological functioning and that she often views
herself as physically ill, dependent, unhappy, and despondent. She is
likely to fatigue easily and may have weight or sleeping difficulties. Further, Caroline showed significant elevations on six of the eight scales
and subscales associated with the *Social Discomfort* factor. Adolescents
who produce elevations on this factor grouping are likely to feel withdrawn, self-conscious, and uncertain in social situations. They are frequently dominated by their peers and are seen by others as timid, docile,
and socially fearful. These adolescents are also likely to experience significant affective distress and are frequently seen as self-conscious, socially withdrawn, dependent, ruminative, and depressed. They are more
likely than other teenagers to report symptoms of fatigue and tiredness,
and they have a higher frequency of suicidal ideation. In support of this
latter point, a review of the MMPI-A critical item set developed by
Forbey and Ben-Porath (1998) for the content grouping of *Depressed/
Suicidal Ideation* indicates that Caroline endorsed four of the six items
in this category including items 71 (I usually feel that life is worthwhile), 177 (I sometimes think about killing myself), 242 (No one cares
much what happens to me), and 399 (The future seems hopeless to me).

Summary and Implications

The MMPI-A results produced by Caroline reflect a 17-year-old female
who is anxious, tense, despondent, socially uncomfortable, and likely to
express her emotional distress through somatic symptoms including
tiredness, fatigue, and sleep and appetite disturbances. Caroline is likely
to feel dependent and markedly ambivalent about her interpersonal
world, and her feelings of social isolation and alienation are likely to cause
her substantial distress. In response to this distress, undoubtedly increased
by the growing separation of her parents, Caroline acknowledged the occurrence of suicidal ideation in conversations with her mother as well as
in her response to several critical items on the MMPI-A. Caroline's

placement in outpatient psychotherapy appears to be appropriate given her symptomatology, and concerns about her suicide potential are well supported. However, it is also useful to note that suicidal ideation is relatively common, particularly among adolescents, but that suicidal gestures or attempts are relatively rare.

Table 4.1 illustrates the relatively higher endorsement frequency of items related to suicidal ideation among normative adolescents in comparison to normative adults, as reflected in MMPI-A and MMPI-2 normative data reported for the six items on the *Depression/Suicidal Ideation* MMPI-A critical items subgroup developed by Forbey and Ben-Porath (1998). Indeed, while there is no direct counterpart for item 177 in the MMPI-2, 38% of teenager girls in the MMPI-A normative sample endorsed as true the statement, "I sometimes think about killing myself." These data support the observation by Kimmel and Weiner (1995) that 20% to 33% of adolescents may experience suicidal ideation at any given moment, and as many as 65% to 75% of all adolescents experience suicidal ideation at least once during their adolescent development. The authors estimate that approximately 5% of adolescents experiencing suicidal ideation eventually make a suicide attempt or gesture, and they propose four characteristics useful in identifying these adolescents: family instability (including loss of a parent through death,

Table 4.1 Frequency of Endorsement as True for Items in the Forbey and Ben-Porath (1998) Depression/Suicidal Ideation Critical Item Group for Male and Female Adolescents and Adults

MMPI-A

Item Number	Content	MMPI-A Normative Sample (%)		MMPI-2 Normative Sample (%)	
		F	M	F	M
71	I usually feel that life is worthwhile	16	16	5	3
88	I don't seem to care what happens to me	11	12	3	6
177	I sometimes think about killing myself	38	22	—	—
242	No one cares much what happens to you	14	20	9	13
283	Most of the time I wish I were dead	18	13	3	2
399	The future seems hopeless to me	17	17	4	5

Note: MMPI-A item 177 does not have a corresponding item on the MMPI-2. Item endorsement frequencies taken from the MMPI-A (Butcher et al., 1992) and MMPI-2 (Butcher et al., 2001) test manuals.

desertion, or divorce), escalating distress (including mounting feelings of anxiety, hopelessness, and depression), dissolving social relationships (including strong feelings of alienation and lack of social support), and a pattern of unsuccessful problem-solving efforts (typically showing a progression through a series of increasingly desperate attempts to resolve escalating problems). Caroline's test findings and history indicate that she clearly meets several of these high-risk criteria (e.g., parental divorce, high affective distress, strong sense of social isolation/alienation, and failing defenses), underscoring the importance of family and individual therapy in her outpatient treatment program as well as the need for her therapist to carefully monitor her suicide potential. However, the question remains concerning how useful the MMPI-A findings are in accurately predicting the crucial issue of whether Caroline will attempt to take her own life.

The dramatic limitations inherent in accurately predicting suicidal behavior from Caroline's MMPI-A responses are well illustrated by the findings from two provocative studies. Clopton and Baucom (1979), in a study described earlier in this chapter, presented the MMPI profiles of 20 male VA psychiatric inpatients who committed suicide and 20 male inpatients who did not attempt suicide to six clinical psychologists with extensive MMPI expertise. The clinicians were asked to classify each profile into the correct group and to rate these profiles on variables thought to be related to suicide risk, including dimensions such as impulse control, intrapunitiveness versus extrapunitiveness, activity level, depressive symptomatology, and optimism versus pessimism. Clinicians were not able to identify accurately the MMPI profiles of suicidal versus nonsuicidal patients, and their ratings on variables proposed to be relevant to suicide risk were not effective in differentiating patients who did and did not commit suicide.

Directly focused on detection of suicide potential among adolescents, Spirito et al. (1988) compared the profiles of 20 girls hospitalized on a general pediatrics unit following a suicide attempt with a control group of 20 girls without suicide attempt histories who were hospitalized on the same pediatric floor and referred for evaluation to the child psychiatry consultation/liaison service. The latter referrals were based on suspicion of a variety of problems including depression and eating disorders or suspicion that psychological factors played a primary role in these girls' somatic complaints. The mean profile configuration for the adolescent suicide attempters and consultation patients were similar. Additionally, two judges with substantial expertise in using the MMPI with adolescents blindly reviewed the MMPI profiles of both groups, placing each profile into broad diagnostic categories. The MMPI profiles produced by adolescent suicide attempters and by consultation group patients produced two distributions of profiles into normal, invalid, depression, and conduct-disordered groups that were not significantly different. The authors concluded: "No single MMPI profile can help differentiate a female adolescent suicide attempter from a non-attempter. Indeed, primary reliance on the MMPI alone to determine suicide risk seems non-judicious" (p. 210).

In conclusion, the MMPI-A results for Caroline, viewed in isolation, have limited value as a means of predicting her suicide potential. Her MMPI-A test findings, combined with information about her familial and symptom history, however, provide important data for her outpatient therapist in designing treatment interventions and in monitoring her progress on variables associated by Kimmel and Weiner (1995) with adolescent suicide attempts. Carolyn's MMPI-A profile is not within the normal limits range and does suggest psychological maladjustment, which places her in a higher risk category for suicidal gestures and/or attempts. Using her test results as a broad road map for inquiry, a competent clinician would interview her and family members to better understand her risk status as her treatment progresses.

REFERENCES

Archer, R. P. (1997). *MMPI-A: Assessing adolescent psychopathology* (2nd ed.). Mahwah, NJ: Erlbaum.

Archer, R. P., & Krishnamurthy, R. (1994). A structural summary approach for the MMPI-A: Development and empirical correlates. *Journal of Personality Assessment, 63,* 554–573.

Archer, R. P., & Krishnamurthy, R. (2002). *Essentials of MMPI-A assessment.* New York: Wiley.

Archer, R. P., Maruish, M., Imhof, E. A., & Piotrowski, C. (1991). Psychological test usage with adolescent clients: 1990 survey findings. *Professional Psychology: Research and Practice, 22,* 247–252.

Archer, R. P., & Newsom, C. R. (2000). Psychological test usage with adolescent clients: Survey update. *Assessment, 7,* 227–235.

Archer, R. P., & Slesinger, D. (1999). MMPI-A patterns related to the endorsement of suicidal ideation. *Assessment, 6,* 51–59.

Butcher, J. N., Graham, J. R., Ben-Porath, Y. S., Tellegen, A., Dahlstrom, W. G., & Kaemmer, B. (2001). *MMPI-2 manual for administration, scoring, and interpretation.* Minneapolis: University of Minnesota Press.

Butcher, J. N., & Williams, C. L. (2000). *Essentials of MMPI-2 and MMPI-A interpretation* (2nd ed.). Minneapolis: University of Minnesota Press.

Butcher, J. N., Williams, C. L., Graham, J. R., Archer, R. P., Tellegen, A., Ben-Porath, Y. S., et al. (1992). *MMPI-A manual for administration, scoring, and interpretation.* Minneapolis: University of Minnesota Press.

Caldwell, A. B. (1969). *MMPI critical items.* Los Angeles: Author.

Clopton, J. R. (1978). A note on the MMPI as a suicide predictor. *Journal of Consulting and Clinical Psychology, 47,* 135–139.

Clopton, J. R. (1979). The MMPI and suicide. In C. S. Newmark (Ed.), *MMPI: Clinical and research trends* (pp. 149–166). New York: Praeger.

Clopton, J. R., & Baucom, D. H. (1979). MMPI ratings of suicide risk. *Journal of Personality Assessment, 43,* 293–296.

Clopton, J. R., & Jones, W. C. (1975). Use of the MMPI in the prediction of suicide. *Journal of Clinical Psychology, 31*(1), 52–54.

Clopton, J. R., Pallis, D. J., & Birtchnell, J. (1979). MMPI profile patterns of suicide attempters. *Journal of Consulting and Clinical Psychology, 47,* 135–139.

Cull, J. G., & Gill, W. S. (1982). *Suicide Probability Scale.* Los Angeles: Western Psychological Services.

Dahlstrom, W. G., Welsh, G. S., & Dahlstrom, L. E. (1972). *An MMPI handbook: Vol. 1. Clinical interpretation* (Rev. ed.). Minneapolis: University of Minnesota Press.

DeVries, A. G. (1966). Identification of suicidal behavior by means of the MMPI. *Psychological Reports, 19,* 415–419.

DeVries, A. G. (1967). Control variables in the identification of suicidal behavior. *Psychological Reports, 20,* 1131–1135.

DeVries, A. G., & Farberow, N. L. (1967). A multivariate profile analysis of MMPI's of suicidal and non-suicidal neuropsychiatric hospital patients. *Journal of Projective Techniques and Personality Assessment, 31,* 81–84.

Eyman, J. R., & Eyman, S. K. (1992). Personality assessment in suicide prediction. In R. W. Maris, A. L. Berman, J. T. Maltsberger, & R. I. Yufit

(Eds.), *Assessment and prediction of suicide* (pp. 183–201). New York: Guilford Press.

Farberow, N. L. (1956). Personality patterns of suicidal mental hospital patients. In G. S. Welsh & W. G. Dahlstrom (Eds.), *Basic readings on the MMPI in psychology and medicine* (pp. 427–432). Minneapolis: University of Minnesota Press.

Farberow, N. L., & DeVries, A. G. (1967). An item differentiation: Analysis of suicidal neuropsychiatric hospital patients. *Psychological Reports, 20,* 607–617.

Forbey, J. D., & Ben-Porath, Y. S. (1998). *A critical item set for the MMPI-A.* Minneapolis: University of Minnesota Press.

Friedman, A. F., Lewak, R., Nichols, D. S., & Webb, J. T. (2001). *Psychological assessment with the MMPI-2.* Mahwah, NJ: Erlbaum.

Friedman, A. F., Webb, J. T., & Lewak, R. (1989). *Psychological assessment with the MMPI.* Mahwah, NJ: Erlbaum.

Glassmire, D. M., Stolberg, R. A., Greene, R. L., & Bongar, B. (2001). The utility of MMPI-2 suicide items for assessing suicidal potential: Development of a suicidal potential scale. *Assessment, 8,* 281–290.

Graham, J. R. (2000). *MMPI-2: Assessing personality and psychopathyology.* New York: Oxford University Press.

Grayson, H. M. (1951). *A psychological admissions testing program and manual.* Los Angeles: Veterans Administration Center, Neuropsychiatric Hospital.

Greene, R. L. (2000). *The MMPI-2: An interpretive manual* (2nd ed.). Boston: Allyn & Bacon.

Hathaway, S. R., & McKinley, J. C. (1942). *Minnesota Multiphasic Personality Schedule.* Minneapolis: University of Minnesota Press.

Kimmel, D. C., & Weiner, I. B. (1995). *Adolescence: A developmental transition* (2nd ed.). New York: Wiley.

Kopper, B. A., Osman, A., Osman, J. R., & Hoffman, J. (1998). Clinical utility of the MMPI-A content scales and Harris-Lingoes subscales in the assessment of suicidal risk factors in psychiatric adolescents. *Journal of Clinical Psychology, 54,* 191–200.

Koss, M. P., & Butcher, J. N. (1973). A comparison of psychiatric patients self-report with other sources of clinical information. *Journal of Research in Personality, 7,* 225–236.

Koss, M. P., Butcher, J. N., & Hoffman, N. G. (1976). The MMPI critical items: How well do they work? *Journal of Consulting and Clinical Psychology, 44*(6), 921–928.

Krishnamurthy, R., & Archer, R. P. (1999). Empirically based interpretive approaches for the MMPI-A structural summary. *Journal of Personality Assessment, 73,* 245–259.

Lachar, D., & Wrobel, T. A. (1979). Validation of clinicians' hunches: Construction of a new MMPI critical item set. *Journal of Consulting and Clinical Psychology, 47,* 277–284.

Leonard, C. V. (1977). The MMPI as a suicide predictor. *Journal of Consulting and Clinical Psychology, 45,* 367–377.

Lester, D. (1970a). Attempts to predict suicidal risk using psychological tests. *Psychological Bulletin, 74,* 1–17.

Lester, D. (1970b). Personality correlates associated with choice of method of committing suicide. *Personality, 1,* 261–264.

Marks, P. A., & Haller, D. (1977). Now I lay me down for keeps: A study of adolescent suicide attempts. *Journal of Clinical Psychology, 33*(2), 390–400.

Marks, P. A., & Seeman, W. (1963). *The actuarial description of abnormal personality: An atlas for use with the MMPI.* Baltimore: Williams & Wilkins.

Meehl, P. E., & Rosen, A. (1955). Antecedent probability and the efficiency of psychometric signs, patterns, or cutting scores. *Psychological Bulletin, 52,* 194–216.

Nichols, D. S. (1988). Mood disorders. In R. L. Greene (Ed.), *The MMPI: Use with specific populations* (pp. 74–109). Philadelphia: Grune & Stratton.

Ravensborg, M. R., & Foss, A. (1969). Suicide and natural death in a state hospital population: A comparison of admission complaints, MMPI profiles, and social competence factors. *Journal of Consulting and Clinical Psychology, 33*(4), 466–471.

Rosen, A., Hales, W. M., & Simon, W. (1954). Classification of "suicidal" patients. *Journal of Consulting Psychology, 18,* 359–365.

Sepaher, I., Bongar, B., & Greene, R. L. (1999). Codetype base rates for the "I mean business" suicide items on the MMPI-2. *Journal of Clinical Psychology, 55,* 1167–1173.

Simon, W. (1950). Attempted suicide among veterans: A comparative study of fifty cases. *Journal of Nervous and Mental Diseases, 11,* 451–468.

Simon, W., & Gilberstadt, H. (1958). Analysis of the personality structure of 26 actual suicides. *Journal of Nervous and Mental Diseases, 127,* 555–557.

Simon, W., & Hales, W. M. (1949). Note on a suicide key in the MMPI. *American Journal of Psychiatry, 106,* 222–223.

Spirito, A., Faust, D., Myers, B., & Bechtel, D. (1988). Clinical utility of the MMPI in the evaluation of adolescent suicide attempters. *Journal of Personality Assessment, 52,* 204–211.

Stelmachers, Z. T. (1995). Assessing suicidal clients. In J. N. Butcher (Ed.), *Clinical personality assessment: Practical approaches* (pp. 368–378). New York: Oxford University Press.

Tarter, R. E., Templer, D. I., & Perley, R. L. (1975). Social role orientation and pathological factors in suicide attempts of varying lethality. *Journal of Community Psychology, 3,* 295–299.

Watson, C. G., Klett, W. G., Walters, C., & Vassar, P. (1984). Suicide and the MMPI: A cross-validation of predictors. *Journal of Clinical Psychology, 40*(1), 115–119.

Wiggins, J. B. W. (1973). *Personality and prediction: Principles of personality assessment.* Reading, MA: Addison-Wesley.

CHAPTER 5

Rorschach Contributions to Assessment of Suicide Risk

Ronald J. Ganellen

Dear Dr. ——————— :

I am referring Mrs. P to you for a psychological evaluation. Mrs. P is a 54-year-old, married white female with a history of multiple sclerosis. She has been treated for MS for nearly 12 years. Although she has had relatively mild symptoms over the past 1 to 1½ years, she has been more fatigued than usual and has had difficulty keeping up with her responsibilities at home and at work.

When I met with Mrs. P today, she and I agreed she should take a leave of absence from work because she has had considerable difficulty completing work requirements. As we discussed her situation, she became tearful, said she feels worthless, and told me she recently thought about jumping in front of the train she rides to work. At that moment, suicide seemed to Mrs. P to be "an easy solution to my problems" as she thought her children were old enough that they did not need her and she wonders whether her husband needs her. She has never made statements like this before. Naturally, these statements made me very concerned about her.

After I expressed my concern to Mrs. P about her emotional state, I recommended that she meet with you. I told her I have great confidence in you as you have helped a number of my patients in the past. Mrs. P agreed to see you for an evaluation of her psychological state. She and I would appreciate your input concerning appropriate treatment.

Sincerely yours,

Dr. ——————

As mental health clinicians, we shoulder considerable responsibility for our patients. One of the most critical, serious responsibilities we face is assessing an individual's risk for taking his or her own life. As illustrated in the case of Mrs. P, assessing whether an individual who expresses suicidal ideation is speaking figuratively or is dead serious is an extremely grave, weighty, and often worrisome clinical challenge.

From a strictly actuarial perspective, one might argue that clinicians should not attempt to identify whether any single individual who discloses thoughts about suicide will act in a self-destructive manner. Epidemiological studies have estimated that in the United States the rate of suicide for all ages is approximately 12 per 100,000 (Hirschfeld & Russell, 1997; Mosicki, 1997). These figures show that fewer than 1% of the general population commit suicide. Given the extremely low base rate of occurrence of suicide, a clinician would be correct more often than not (99 out of 100 times) if he or she concluded that the odds of a suicide attempt are low in every case in which concerns about suicide are raised without taking into account any clinical information or data derived from psychological tests (Meehl & Rosen, 1955).

As discussed by Bongar (2002), in clinical practice the clinician is not limited simply to determining whether an individual will act on a threat of suicide. Rather than conceptualizing the goal of an evaluation as predicting if a patient will attempt suicide, Bongar stressed that clinicians should assess whether psychosocial characteristics associated with a heightened risk for suicidal behavior are present. This shifts the objective of an evaluation from generating predictions of whether an individual will or will not attempt suicide to identifying, describing, and weighing the clinical features that increase or decrease the risk for self-destructive action. This information can be used in treatment planning to monitor and address characteristics that increase an individual's vulnerability to harm himself or herself.

The extensive literature on suicide indicates that suicidal phenomena are extremely complex and that no single psychological disorder, epidemiological variable, cognitive set, dynamic motivation, or precipitating event universally accounts for self-destructive behavior. This complexity increases the challenge for a clinician evaluating an individual patient for whom concerns about suicide have been raised. While no single method has been accepted to assess suicidal potential, evaluation often includes a clinical interview as well as psychological tests (Bongar, 2002). The Rorschach Comprehensive System (Exner, 2003) is one of the psychological tests frequently used in clinical settings for this purpose. The various ways in which the Rorschach has been used to assess suicide risk and the strengths and weaknesses of these approaches are discussed.

SINGLE SIGN APPROACHES

A number of investigators have attempted to identify Rorschach variables associated with suicide. Early approaches included configurations of multiple Rorschach variables, which were coded as being present or absent (Hertz, 1948; Piotrowski, 1950). In a review of this literature, Goldfried, Stricker, and Weiner (1971) cautioned that these approaches involved complicated, somewhat cumbersome scoring systems that made it difficult to achieve satisfactory levels of interrater reliability. Other approaches involved identifying individual Rorschach variables associated with increased risk of suicidality, such as responses containing color-shading blends (Applebaum & Holtzman, 1962), transparency and cross-section responses (Blatt & Ritzler, 1974), and analysis of symbolic content or language indicating emotional turmoil, morbid preoccupations, or suggestions of decay (Meyer, 1989; Neuringer, 1974; Sapolsky, 1963). For instance, Thomas and Duszynski (1985) reported that persons who later committed suicide used words such as *whirl* or other words suggestive of an agitated, tumultuous emotional state more frequently than nonsuicidal patients.

Color-Shading Blend Responses

The best-known single Rorschach variable claimed to be associated with suicidality is the color-shading blend. Applebaum and Holtzman (1962) reported an association between one or more color-shading blend responses and a history of attempted suicide or what they judged to be a vulnerability to suicidal behavior. They investigated this association by comparing the Rorschach protocols produced by 30 psychiatric patients with mixed diagnoses who committed suicide some time after a hospitalization and the Rorschach protocols of six comparison groups who did not subsequently commit suicide. The comparison groups included a sample of 39 psychiatric inpatients who had previously attempted suicide at least once, 96 psychiatric patients with no known history of suicidal behavior, 53 members of the Kansas Highway Patrol, 50 medical residents in psychiatry, 52 medical patients enrolled in a study of thyroid functioning, and 17 college students. The presence or absence of a color-shading blend response correctly identified 90% of the psychiatric patients who subsequently committed suicide and 82% of the patients with a history of attempted suicide. However, 19% of the nonsuicidal psychiatric patients also produced one or more color-shading blend responses as did 9% of the highway patrol officers, 24% of the psychiatric residents, 17% of the thyroid study medical patients, and 35% of the college students.

Applebaum and Colson (1968) replicated the association between color-shading blend responses and suicidality in a follow-up study. In this study, 42 psychiatric patients with a history of a previous suicide attempt were compared with a group of 35 psychiatric patients with no history of suicide attempts. The suicidal group produced color-shading blends significantly more frequently than the comparison group. However, while 88% of the patients with a history of suicidal behavior produced one or more color-shading blend responses, so did 49% of the comparison group.

Hansell, Lerner, Milden, and Ludolph (1988) examined the relationship between color-shading blends and suicide risk in a sample of 41 inpatients who met diagnostic criteria for an episode of major depression. Suicide risk was assessed using items from the Hamilton Rating Scale for Depression (Hamilton, 1960), which addressed suicidal ideation, intent, and behavior. Patients were identified as having either a moderate to severe risk of suicide or doubtful or no risk of suicide using this scale. Hansell et al. reported that 19% of the total sample produced one or more responses involving color-shading blend responses. No relationship was found between the appearance of a color-shading blend response and a history of a previous suicide attempt. Examination of the association between ratings of suicide risk on the Hamilton Rating Scale for Depression found, contrary to expectations, that 5% of patients with a moderate to severe risk of suicide produced one or more color-shading blend responses while 45% of the low suicide risk gave at least one color-shading blend response.

Silberg and Armstrong (1992) examined the association between color-shading blend responses and suicidality in a sample of adolescent psychiatric inpatients. They compared the Rorschach protocols of 28 adolescent inpatients who had made a serious suicide attempt before being admitted to the hospital with 54 adolescent inpatients identified as having a low risk of suicide. Consistent with predictions, the suicidal group produced significantly more color-shading blend responses than the nonsuicidal group. Silberg and Armstrong concluded that an increased risk of suicide was associated with one or more color-shading blend responses in their sample.

The relationship between color-shading blend responses and suicidality was investigated by Fowler, Hilsenroth, and Piers (2001) in a sample of 122 adult psychiatric inpatients. Fowler, Hilsenroth, et al. examined information contained in patients' hospital records concerning any episodes of self-destructive behavior that occurred within 60 days after administration of the Rorschach. Based on this information, patients were classified as being nonsuicidal if they did not engage in any self-injurious behavior, parasuicidal if self-destructive behavior was minor or involved little risk of serious injury or death, and as engaging in a near-lethal suicide attempt. As predicted, the near-lethal suicide group produced significantly more color-shading blend responses than the other two groups.

Transparency/Cross-Sectional Responses

Blatt and Ritzler (1974) investigated Rorschach variables associated with suicidal behavior. They compared the Rorschach protocols of 12 psychiatric patients who subsequently committed suicide with the protocols of a control group with no history of suicidal behavior. The two groups were matched for age, sex, IQ, and number of Rorschach responses. Blatt and Ritzler reported that the only Rorschach variables differentiating between the two groups were the numbers of transparency and cross-sectional responses. The presence or absence of these variables correctly identified 92% of the patients who committed suicide and 67% of the nonsuicidal comparison group. However, 33% of the controls also gave at least one transparency or cross-sectional response.

Hansell et al. (1988) examined the association between transparency/cross-sectional responses and suicidality in the sample of depressed inpatients described previously. Nineteen percent of their sample produced one or more transparency/cross-sectional responses. While no relationship was found between Hamilton Rating Scale scores for suicide risk and this Rorschach variable, the presence of one or more transparency/cross-sectional responses was significantly related to a history of more than one previous suicide attempt. Hansell et al. noted that they did not assess the lethality of the previous suicide attempts. Therefore, they could not determine whether transparency/cross-sectional responses were associated with a high potential for repeated suicide attempts or for making nonlethal suicidal "gestures."

Silberg and Armstrong (1992) provided additional, although somewhat indirect, support for an association between suicidality and transparency/cross-sectional responses in the adolescent inpatient sample described previously. They reasoned that the Comprehensive System score most similar to the transparency/cross-sectional response is the Vista response. Although different criteria are used to score each type of response, Silberg and Armstrong thought both involve a perception of depth and dimensionality. Consistent with their predictions, they found that the suicidal group produced Vista responses more frequently than the nonsuicidal comparison group.

The relationship among cross-sectional responses, transparency responses, and suicidality was investigated by Fowler, Hilsenroth, et al. (2001) in the sample of 122 adult psychiatric inpatients described previously. Fowler, Hilsenroth, et al. examined information contained in patients' hospital records concerning any episodes of self-destructive behavior that occurred within 60 days after administration of the Rorschach. As predicted, the near-lethal suicide group produced significantly more cross-sectional and transparency responses than the other two groups.

Comment

Studies examining Rorschach signs associated with suicide risk, such as color-shading blend responses and transparency/cross-sectional responses, reported statistically significant differences between groups of suicidal and nonsuicidal individuals. While several studies have replicated an association between suicidality and color-shading blend responses, cross-sectional responses, and transparency responses, a number of methodological issues exist that suggest caution be used when generalizing these findings to an applied clinical setting. These issues include small sample sizes, limited cross-validation in independent samples, differing criteria used to assign individuals to suicidal as opposed to nonsuicidal groups, and variability in time between administration of the Rorschach and the index suicide attempt (Fowler, Piers, Hilsenroth, Holdwick, & Padawer, 2001; Goldfried et al., 1971).

For example, some studies classified individuals as suicidal if they made a suicide attempt whether the attempt was lethal or not, some classified individuals as suicidal only if their suicide attempt was lethal, while others assessed suicide risk based on expression of suicidal ideation during a structured clinical interview. Some studies examined Rorschach protocols of individuals obtained after a suicide attempt, while others examined Rorschach protocols collected before a suicide attempt. It is possible that individuals who have survived a nonlethal suicide attempt may differ from individuals who succeeded in killing themselves or that the psychological state of an individual after a suicide attempt differs from the psychological state of an individual before a suicide attempt. Thus, the criteria used to assign patients to the suicidal as opposed to the nonsuicidal groups may not have adequately distinguished among suicidal ideation, past suicide attempts, and current risk of lethality.

Studies also differed in the temporal relationship between administration of the Rorschach and the episode of suicidal behavior used to identify individuals as suicidal or nonsuicidal. For example, both Applebaum and Holtzman (1962) and Blatt and Ritzler (1974) compared a group of patients who completed a lethal suicide attempt after the Rorschach was administered, whereas Applebaum and Colson (1968) compared a group of patients with a history of a suicide attempt before they took the Rorschach. The length of time between the index suicide attempt and Rorschach administration also varied from study to study. This makes it difficult to determine whether positive findings for the variables investigated in these studies should be viewed as identifying a red flag signaling an imminent risk of suicide as opposed to an enduring psychological characteristic of an individual that contributes to a persistent vulnerability to suicide.

Perhaps even more importantly, although single Rorschach variables effectively identified many suicidal individuals accurately, nonsuicidal individuals also frequently produced these variables. In other words, while single Rorschach signs produced high rates of true positive classification of patients judged to be at risk for suicide, single signs also produced a high false positive rate as individuals who were *not* at risk for suicide were erroneously classified by the Rorschach as being suicidal.

Concerns about the risks of false positive identifications of suicidality are illustrated by examining the frequency with which color-shading blends are produced in the Comprehensive System normative sample. Exner (2003) reported that 252 of the 700 nonpatient adults in the normative sample produced one or more color-shading blend responses. If the presence of at least one color-shading blend response was used to identify a risk of suicidal behavior, 36% of the nonpatient adults would be considered at risk for suicide. This example illustrates the following point made by Fowler, Piers, et al. (2001): Reliance on single-sign approaches to predicting suicide potential (or any other phenomenon for that matter) can be problematic because individual variables nearly always are less reliable and have less statistical power than approaches involving multiple variables. While some support exists for a relationship between suicide and single Rorschach variables (including color-shading blend responses, cross-sectional responses, and transparency responses), the empirical and methodological issues discussed previously indicate that clinicians should not rely exclusively on these signs to assess suicide risk (Eyman & Eyman, 1991).

RORSCHACH SUICIDE CONSTELLATION

A different approach to detecting suicide risk using the Rorschach was taken by Exner and Wylie (1977). Their research differed from previous studies in several other respects. Rather than attempting to identify single Rorschach signs associated with suicide, Exner and Wylie attempted to identify a cluster of Rorschach variables associated with suicidal behavior. Their criterion group of suicidal patients contained only individuals who made a lethal suicide attempt that resulted in their death. Individuals who made a nonlethal suicide attempt were excluded. In addition, they included only the Rorschach protocols of subjects who committed suicide within 60 days *after* the Rorschach had been administered. Rorschach protocols of this criterion group of suicide completers were contrasted with the Rorschach protocols of comparison groups composed of nonpatients as well as psychiatric patients.

Exner and Wylie (1977) empirically identified a cluster of Rorschach variables that correctly identified 75% of the suicide completers. They labeled this cluster the *Rorschach Suicide Constellation* (S-CON). The S-CON was found to have a respectable rate of true positives as well as a low rate of false positives in samples without a history of suicidal behavior within 60 days after the Rorschach was administered. For instance, none of the nonpatient normative sample obtained a positive score on the S-CON. Among a sample of patients diagnosed with schizophrenia hospitalized for the first time, 12% obtained a positive score on the S-CON, while 20% of inpatients who met diagnostic criteria for a mood disorder obtained a positive score on the S-CON.

The design used by Exner and Wylie (1977) improved on earlier studies in several respects. First, they used a prospective design to identify a cluster of multiple Rorschach variables, which, if positive, predicts an immediate, heightened risk for a suicide attempt that has a serious potential for death. Second, the inclusion criteria they used explicitly targeted only subjects who committed suicide within a specified time period after the Rorschach was administered. This eliminates uncertainty as to whether positive findings reflect suicidal ideation, past suicidal behavior, or a present risk of suicidality. Third, they limited findings to a clearly specified time frame, 60 days after administration of the Rorschach. Unlike previous studies, the sample size used to develop the revised S-CON was acceptable.

An effort was made to refine the S-CON using a second, independent sample of 101 individuals who succeeded in killing themselves within 60 days after the Rorschach was administered (Exner, 1993). Inclusion criteria for the criterion group of suicide completers were the same as in the Exner and Wylie (1977) study. The sample of completed suicides was compared with the following groups: 101 patients who met diagnostic criteria for depression, 101 patients who met diagnostic criteria for schizophrenia, and 101 nonpatients. Exner found that including additional variables improved the S-CON's ability to discriminate between the criterion and control groups and reduced the rate of false positives. The revised S-CON correctly identified 83% of the suicide completers while producing a false positive rate of 0% for nonpatients, 6% for inpatient schizophrenics, and 12% for inpatient depressives without a history of subsequent suicide.

Examination of the variables that load on the revised S-CON may help explain the higher false positive rate among depressed patients. Of the 12 variables that make up the revised S-CON, 5 also contribute to the Depression Index (DEPI). Thus, it is possible that a patient who does not experience suicidal ideation and has no history of self-destructive behavior but who meets diagnostic criteria for a current mood disorder and who produces a positive DEPI may get five points on the S-CON simply because of the overlap among variables contained in each index. This is not surprising as many psychological features associated with suicidal behavior overlap with a depressive outlook, rather than the diagnosis of depression per se. These psychological features include a profound sense of intense hopelessness, discouragement, and self-loathing (Beck, Steer, Kovacs, & Garrison, 1985). However, to reach a positive score on the S-CON, depressed individuals must produce positive scores not only for variables related to an outlook colored by pervasive, extreme despair and self-contempt, but also on variables not directly related to their mood and pessimistic mind-set, such as limited self-control over how emotions are expressed or problems perceiving events accurately.

Exner recognized that even though the revised S-CON has a low rate of false positive misidentification of suicidal behavior, a positive S-CON can incorrectly suggest a risk of suicide, particularly among depressed patients who are not suicidal. He recommended that clinicians view a positive S-CON as a serious warning of an increased risk for self-destructive action and take appropriate action to investigate suicidality and ensure the patient's safety. Exner cautioned that a negative S-CON does not necessarily indicate the absence of a risk of suicide, only that the Rorschach provides no indication of current, active suicide potential. He also advised that because the S-CON was developed in a sample of adults and did not contain any subjects under the age of 18, in clinical practice it should not be applied to adolescents or children.

In a thoughtful discussion of the implications of base rates for clinical decision making, Finn and Kamphuis (1995) made several observations that add to Exner's recommendations concerning responsible use of the S-CON. Finn and Kamphuis stressed that psychological test data, such as the S-CON, may have limited clinical utility in making decisions about phenomena with extremely low base rates, such as suicide. They pointed out, however, that the base rate for many clinical events varies in different populations and in different settings. For instance, while suicide, fortunately, is a rare event in the general population, the incidence of suicide is higher for certain populations than for the general population. For instance, some investigators have estimated that the number of patients with manic-depressive illness who kill themselves ranges from 15% to 55% (Goldring & Fieve, 1984). Bongar (2002) pointed out that compared to the general population, the rate of suicide is significantly higher both for patients with medical problems and for patients with a mental illness. Differences between subgroups within these larger groups are also likely to occur. For instance, one might expect the incidence of suicide among patients with depression to differ from the rate of suicide among patients with kleptomania.

The proposals made by Finn and Kamphuis (1995) suggest that the clinician should take into account differences in the rate of suicide in different populations and clinical settings when weighing the significance of a positive score on the S-CON. For example, a positive S-CON produced by a college undergraduate with no history of psychopathology administered the Rorschach to comply with course requirements may have less ominous implications than a positive S-CON produced by a 55-year-old, divorced male battling cancer, who is administered the Rorschach at the request of his psychiatrist to assist with treatment planning for depression and alcohol abuse.

Appraisals of the Rorschach Suicide Constellation

Wood, Nezworski, and Stejskal (1996) raised concerns about the validity and reliability of the S-CON. They pointed out that the reliability of the S-CON has not been reported and that the predictive power of the revised S-CON has not been demonstrated in a cross-validation study. They also questioned the validity of the S-CON based on findings from an unpublished study conducted by Eyman and Eyman (1987), who reported that in a sample of 50 patients who committed suicide, only one produced a positive score on the S-CON.

Wood et al. (1996) pointed out some methodological issues that make interpretation of these results problematic. First, Eyman and Eyman (1987) used the original version of the S-CON, rather than the revised S-CON. Second, although the Rorschach protocols were *scored* according to the guidelines of the Comprehensive System, they were not *administered* using Comprehensive System procedures, but instead were administered using the Rappaport, Gill, and Shafer (1945) system. Third, the length of time between Rorschach administration and suicide ranged from less than 90 days to more than two years. As discussed previously, the S-CON was developed to assess imminent risk of suicide within a specific amount of time (60 days), rather than suicidality over an extended period of time, such as two years. Because Eyman and Eyman did not administer the Rorschach according to the procedures of the Comprehensive System, used the original rather than the revised version of the S-CON, and examined the predictive power of the original S-CON for time frames greater than intended, their results have little bearing on the validity of the revised S-CON. Wood et al. concluded that further research is needed to determine the clinical utility of the revised S-CON.

Fowler, Piers, et al. (2001) responded to several of the issues raised about the S-CON by Wood et al. (1996). They examined the revised S-CON's interrater reliability, predictive validity, discriminant utility, and clinical utility in a sample of 104 adult psychiatric inpatients. Based on their histories, patients were assigned to one of the following three groups: a nonsuicidal group; a parasuicidal group—those who engaged in nonlethal, self-destructive behavior (e.g., superficial self-inflicted wounds or mild drug overdoses) within 60 days after being administered the Rorschach; or a near-lethal suicidal group—those who engaged in serious, self-destructive behavior (e.g., self-inflicted wounds requiring emergency medical attention) within 60 days after the Rorschach was administered.

Fowler, Piers, et al. (2001) reported excellent interrater reliability values for the variables that comprise the revised S-CON (e.g., Kappa greater than .95). As predicted, the near-lethal suicide group scored significantly higher on the S-CON than the nonsuicidal or parasuicidal groups. The discriminant validity of the S-CON was examined by comparing the three groups on other Rorschach indexes, including the DEPI (Depression Index), SCZI (Schizophrenia Index), or CDI (Coping Deficit Index). The groups did not differ on these indexes.

Fowler, Piers, et al. (2001) entered the DEPI, CDI, SCZI, and revised S-CON into a stepwise logistic regression analysis to predict near-lethal suicide attempts. The overall regression analysis was highly significant. The only variable contained in the final regression equation was the S-CON. They also found identification of near-lethal suicidal behavior improved significantly when the S-CON was entered in a regression analysis after demographic and clinical variables and other Rorschach scores. In contrast, elevated scores on the S-CON were not associated with parasuicidal behavior. This indicates that serious suicide attempts were predicted by the S-CON, rather than by demographic variables or Rorschach indicators of depression, deficits in coping, or thought disorder.

In another set of analyses, Fowler, Piers, et al. (2001) computed diagnostic efficiency statistics to examine how effectively the S-CON discriminated between the near-lethal suicide group and the other groups using different cutoff scores for the S-CON. They found that use of the cutoff score recommended by Exner (1993; S-CON ≥ 8) lowered the sensitivity of the S-CON, although there were very few false negatives. A lower cutoff score (S-CON ≥ 7) increased the S-CON's sensitivity (correctly identifying patients who subsequently engaged in serious self-destructive behavior as being at risk) without a substantial increase in the false positive rate (incorrectly identifying patients who did not engage in serious self-destructive behavior as presenting a high risk of suicide). Because Fowler et al.'s sample was composed of psychiatric inpatients, they suggested that a score of 7 or greater on the S-CON may signal an increased risk of suicidality in an inpatient population, although they acknowledged that these findings may not generalize to an outpatient population. Their suggestion that applying different values for the S-CON in different settings and in different patient populations can improve the clinical utility of the S-CON echoes Finn and Kamphuis's (1995) comments discussed previously.

Fowler, Piers, et al. (2001) concluded that their results demonstrated the interrater reliability for the variables that make up the revised S-CON, the discriminant and predictive validity of the S-CON, and the clinical utility of the S-CON. They noted that, in their sample, positive scores on the S-CON were associated with near-lethal suicide attempts while other Rorschach variables (e.g., the DEPI, CDI, and SCZI) were not. Because their study focused only on subjects who made a serious suicide attempt within 60 days after being administered the Rorschach, Fowler et al. emphasized that, consistent with the guidelines that Exner (1993, 2003) proposed for clinical use of the revised S-CON, positive scores on the S-CON should be viewed as signaling an increased risk for imminent self-destructive behavior.

Recent Contributions

As described previously, Fowler, Hilsenroth, et al. (2001) investigated the relationship between self-destructive behavior and four single Rorschach signs of suicidality (color-shading blend responses, cross-sectional responses, transparency responses, and morbid responses). They conducted a stepwise multiple regression analysis in which all four of these variables were used to predict near-lethal suicide attempts. All variables were retained in the final regression equation. Color-shading blends were entered on the first step of the analysis followed by transparencies, morbid responses, and cross-sectional responses.

Based on these findings, Fowler, Hilsenroth, et al. (2001) proposed summing the number of color-shading blend, cross-sectional, transparency, and morbid responses to construct a composite index (called the Riggs Index). Consistent with the preceding discussion concerning the inherent limitations of basing predictions on single variables, they explained that an index combining several variables would be more stable and have greater power in identifying suicide risk than any one variable alone. When Fowler, Hilsenroth, et al. (2001) compared the nonsuicidal, parasuicidal, and near-lethal suicidal groups' scores on the Riggs Index, they found that the near-lethal group produced significantly higher scores than the other groups. Fowler et al. computed diagnostic efficiency statistics for different values of the Riggs Index. Using a cutoff score of 5, they reported respectable levels of correct classification of patients in their sample with a low rate of false positive misidentifications.

Fowler, Hilsenroth, et al. (2001) next examined whether the Riggs Index explained additional variance after the revised S-CON was entered into a regression analysis. The results of a discriminant function analysis showed that the Riggs Index was retained in the regression equation after the S-CON, accounting for additional variance above and beyond that explained by the revised S-CON. Stated differently, these findings support the incremental validity of the Riggs Index. While these results suggest the Riggs Index may be clinically useful, the authors cautioned that additional research and replication of these findings in an independent sample are required to establish the validity and clinical utility of the Riggs Index.

Silberg and Armstrong (1992) attempted to develop an index of Rorschach variables that identifies risk for self-destructive behavior for adolescents. Their effort was prompted by a recognition that Exner (1993) developed the S-CON for use with adults but did not develop a similar index to be used with adolescents. While the need for such an index is obvious, several limitations exist concerning the index developed by Silberg and Armstrong. First, the sample size used to select variables for the adolescent Rorschach suicide index was small with 28 suicidal adolescent patients and 54 nonsuicidal adolescent patients. Second, adolescents were identified as being suicidal if they had made a suicide attempt before their hospital admission and the administration of the Rorschach. Unlike the S-CON, which was developed to predict a lethal suicide attempt that occurred within 60 days *after* administration of the Rorschach, Silberg and Armstrong's adolescent suicide index was based on patients who had engaged in nonlethal self-injurious behavior *before* administration of the Rorschach. Further research is needed to examine the predictive validity of the adolescent Rorschach suicide index before concluding it is a valid, reliable marker that provides useful information concerning suicide potential.

CLINICAL RISK FACTORS FOR SUICIDE AND THE RORSCHACH

Bongar (2002) summarized the extensive literature exploring the association between suicide risk and a wide range of psychological, epidemiological, biological, and cultural variables. For instance, this literature has shown that a history of any type of psychopathology increases the risk for suicide. Research examining the rate of suicide and suicide attempts for specific diagnoses has found that the presence of any type of depressive disorder results in an increased risk for suicidal behavior. Increased risk has also been shown to be associated with a history of alcohol/substance abuse and the presence of a personality disorder, especially borderline personality disorder (BPD) and antisocial personality disorder (APD; Linehan, Rizvi, Welch, & Page, 2000). In addition to psychiatric diagnosis, heightened risk of suicide has been found to be associated with several psychological characteristics. Bongar's (2002) review of this literature identified the following variables as having a relationship with suicidality: a sense of hopelessness or despair, feelings of humiliation or self-hatred, vulnerability to abandonment, feelings of social isolation, and potential for impulsive behavior.

Rorschach data can provide information relevant to some but not all of the psychological variables found to be associated with elevated risk of suicide. Although Rorschach findings are relevant to clinical features of some *DSM-IV* diagnoses (Ganellen, 1996b), the Rorschach is not intended to be used to make specific *DSM-IV* diagnoses (Exner, 2003). It may be more efficient to rely on a structured clinical interview if the goal of an evaluation is specifically to establish a patient's diagnosis. Furthermore, because the Rorschach does not have any indicators of alcohol or substance abuse (Ganellen, 1996a), it is of little use in identifying patients with these conditions.

As discussed later, information provided by the Rorschach variables may be useful in assessing some of the psychological variables established in the literature as being associated with suicidality, including hopelessness, negative self-attitudes, interpersonal dependency, and impulsivity. It must be stressed that, in general practice, positive findings for one or more of these variables should not routinely be considered markers of suicide risk because doing so carries a high risk of false positive misidentifications of suicide for the reasons discussed previously. (See section on single Rorschach signs of suicide risk.) Instead, it is suggested that when conducting an evaluation that focuses on assessment of suicide potential, in addition to clinical information, demographic factors, and other test data, Rorschach variables relevant to the following psychological characteristics associated with suicidality should be reviewed to identify, describe, and weigh factors that may signal a vulnerability for self-destructive behavior or to help the clinician anticipate situations in which self-harm is most likely to occur.

Hopelessness/Despair

Beck and his colleagues have provided strong empirical support that a sense of hopelessness is a strong predictor of suicide (Beck et al., 1985). Other authors have similarly identified hopelessness, helplessness, and feelings of despair as important psychological precursors to suicide (Bongar, 2002; Fawcett, 1988; Maltsberger, 1986; Shneidman, 1989). They suggest that the risk of self-harm is most serious when an individual is unable to manage, modulate, regulate, or cope with intense emotional turmoil. These authors conceptualize one of the central driving forces behind suicide as an effort to escape unrelenting mental pain, which, over time becomes intolerable.

Emotional turmoil, feelings of helplessness, and a pessimistic sense of hopelessness may be reflected on the Rorschach by one of several scores. Individuals who are flooded by intense, disturbing emotions frequently produce low scores on Lambda (scores less than .45), a D Score in the negative range, or a score of zero on one or both sides of the EA. A sense of helplessness, pessimistic concerns that the individual will not be able to control what happens in the future, and hopelessness are measured on the Rorschach by an elevated frequency of inanimate movement and/or shading responses and by numerous morbid responses. These variables, as well as the other Rorschach variables discussed in the following sections, are summarized in Table 5.1.

Guilt/Self-Hatred

Numerous authors have observed that many suicidal patients have extremely negative self-images, often feel guilty, and judge themselves harshly, sometimes to the point of self-hatred or self-loathing (Blumenthal, 1990; Bongar, 2002; Peterson & Bongar, 1989; Shneidman, 1989).

Table 5.1   Suicide Risk and Rorschach Variables

Hopelessness/despair	Lambda < .45
	D Score < 0
	M = 0 or FC+CF+C=0
	m > 2 and/or Y > 2
	MOR > 2
Guilt/self-hatred	V > 0
	FD > 2
	Fr > 0
	Egocentricity Index < .33 or > .44 with Fr = 0
Loss/abandonment	T ≥ 2
	Food > 0
	p > a+1
	Mp > Ma
Loneliness/isolation	Isolation Index > .33
	CDI ≥ 4
	H < (H)+Hd+(Hd)
Impulsivity	D < 0
	FM ≤ 2
	C > 0
	Zd ≤ −.35
	M− or Formless M > 0

These observations suggest that suicide can be provoked by patients' sense of guilt, humiliation, worthlessness, or a conviction that they are a source of shame for their families.

On the Rorschach, negative self-attitudes, guilt, and harshly self-critical attitudes are measured by the presence of Vista responses and an increased number of Form Dimension responses. These features are accentuated in a protocol, which also contains one or more Reflection responses, indicating that narcissism is a core feature of the patient's personality organization. The tendency to react to negative events with shame or humiliation can occur, not only if individuals produce one or more Reflection responses but also (1) if their score on the Egocentricity Index is low, indicating that they struggle with a negative self-concept and doubts about their worth or (2) in the absence of any Reflection responses, if their score on the Egocentricity Index is high, indicating excessive self-preoccupation.

Loss/Abandonment

A number of authors have observed that a disruption or the end of a relationship with an important person can trigger suicidal behavior (Bongar, 2002; Hirschfeld & Davison, 1988; Perlin & Schmidt, 1976), possibly because, for some individuals, interpersonal losses can precipitate emotional turmoil or the onset of an episode of depression. Risk of suicide may be increased for these individuals if they experience a threatened or actual disappointment in an important relationship, such as being rejected, deserted, or betrayed by a spouse or lover.

Individuals who have reacted to a recent loss with a sense of longing, yearning, and frustration that their needs for closeness are not being met often produce an elevated number of Texture responses on the Rorschach. Strong dependency needs, a chronic sense of neediness, and a tendency to rely on, if not cling to, others who contribute to a vulnerability to abandonment may be indicated on the Rorschach by one or more Food responses, two or more Texture responses (especially if there has been no recent history of interpersonal loss), or signs of a passive-dependent orientation in relationships, as indicated by a skewed number of passive movement responses compared to the number of active movement responses.

Loneliness/Isolation

Social isolation is another factor associated with an increased risk of suicidal behavior (Achté, 1988; Bongar, 2002; Fawcett, 1988; Maris, 1989). Feelings of loneliness and isolation can occur as a response to recent losses, changes in the availability of support from the individual's network of family and friends, or long-standing difficulties establishing and maintaining satisfying relationships with others. It is possible that social isolation has both a direct and an indirect relationship with a heightened potential for suicide because positive levels of social involvement can buffer the effects of life stress and prevent the development of depression while low levels of social support constitute a risk factor for depression.

On the Rorschach, a lack of involvement with others is signaled by a positive score on the Isolation Index; chronic difficulties engaging in satisfying, enjoyable social interactions and establishing rewarding relationships are shown by a positive score on the Coping Deficit Index, while disinterest or discomfort with others is manifested by a decreased number of responses involving whole, realistic human figures when compared to the number of imaginary, fantasized, or partial images of people.

Personality Disorders/Impulsivity

Epidemiological studies of risk factors for suicide have consistently found that depression is associated with a significant increase in the risk of self-destructive behavior. This risk is compounded for patients who in addition to depression have a comorbid personality disorder (Bongar, 2002). When specific personality disorders are compared, a diagnosis of a borderline personality disorder (BPD) or antisocial personality disorder (APD) carries a risk of suicidal behavior comparable to that of depression alone (Linehan et al., 2000).

The association among BPD, APD, and heightened risk for suicidality may occur for several reasons. First, one of the central clinical features of both APD and BPD is impulsivity, a psychological factor that increases the risk of suicidality (Joiner, Rudd, & Rajab, 1997). Second, patients with APD or BPD frequently have histories of alcohol and/or substance abuse, another factor that increases the risk for suicide.

Third, patients with BPD or APD may have difficulty obtaining adequate social support given their patterns of dysfunctional interpersonal functioning.

There is no specific configuration of scores on the Rorschach associated with APD (Gacono & Meloy, 1994). While no set of Rorschach scores specifically identifies BPD, some of the most important features of BPD are captured by Rorschach variables. For instance, intense anger, difficulties expressing emotions in a controlled and appropriate manner, and rapidly shifting emotional states may be seen on the Rorschach by an increased number of Space responses, an excessive number of responses involving aggressive movement, a lack of balance in the FC:CF+C ratio, and an elevated number of color-shading blend responses. Problems with thinking in a realistic, logical manner and a tendency to exhibit transient decompensations in functioning, which involve peculiar or strange thinking, can be manifested on the Rorschach by elevated scores on the WSUM6, a large number of responses receiving Special Scores, and problems perceiving stimuli as others do (e.g., low scores on the XA% and WDA% and a high number of M minus responses). The interpersonal neediness, fears of abandonment, and intense responses to interpersonal losses characteristic of BPD may be manifested on the Rorschach by a protocol that has an elevated number of both Texture and Food responses or a protocol that contains one or more Food responses without any Texture responses.

As noted previously, impulsivity is a psychological risk factor for suicide (Joiner et al., 1997), which is also a feature of both APD and BPD. Rorschach signs of a vulnerability to responding to situations in a disorganized, impulsive, poorly thought-through manner include a D Score in the negative range; indications of limited psychological resources to handle both ordinary demands of life as well as unexpected pressures and problems in an effective, controlled manner are shown by lower than expected scores on the EA, while a low number of FM responses indicates a tendency to act before feelings and impulses are consciously recognized and managed in a mature, deliberate fashion. A propensity to respond in an emotionally intense, volatile manner is signaled on the Rorschach when an individual produces more than the expected number of Pure C responses or by an unbalanced FC:CF+C ratio. Another characteristic that can contribute to impulsive action is the tendency to misread situations because of a careless, haphazard cognitive style, which is shown on the Rorschach by a Zd score less than −3.5. In addition, concerns that an individual's capacity to think things through before taking action is significantly impaired are raised if an individual produces one or more M minus or formless M responses.

MRS. P'S RORSCHACH

As recommended by the physician treating her for multiple sclerosis, Mrs. P willingly agreed to meet for a psychological evaluation, which, in addition to a clinical interview and MMPI-2, included the Rorschach. Findings from her Rorschach (see Table 5.2) are reviewed with reference to the guidelines presented previously.

The positive Rorschach S-CON is a worrisome finding. As recommended by Finn and Kamphuis (1995), the significance of a positive S-CON should be determined after considering the base rates of suicide in a specific population. For populations with a low base rate of suicide, a positive S-CON should be viewed as being less alarming than for a population in which suicide is most likely to occur. Among the populations in which the odds of suicidal behavior are increased are patients with a medical disorder as well as patients with a psychiatric disorder (Bongar, 2002). Mrs. P's significant, potentially debilitating medical condition, multiple sclerosis, is one piece of evidence suggesting that the positive S-CON should be taken seriously.

In addition, the positive DEPI and CDI suggest that Mrs. P may present with a mood disorder. In Exner's normative sample, less than 1% of the nonpatient adults earned a score of 6 on the DEPI while 30% of depressed patients had a similar score. While a positive DEPI does not "clinch" a diagnosis of depression, it presents evidence strongly suggestive of depression (Ganellen, 1996a), a possibility that should be explored in more detail during the clinical interview. Mrs. P did report symptoms consistent with a *DSM-IV* diagnosis of major depression when interviewed.

The significance of a positive S-CON for a patient with depression must be evaluated carefully. Since the base rate of suicide is much higher in samples of depressed patients than the general population, a positive S-CON should be taken seriously. On the other hand, one population in which false negative findings for the S-CON are known to occur is

Table 5.2 RIAP™ Structural Summary

Client Information

Client Name: Mrs. P	Gender: Female	Test Date: 08/07/2002
Client ID:	Date of Birth: 11/21/1949	Description: Imported on 01/12/2003 from RIAP3 file 'Hoganson.r3'.

Location Features

Zf	=	11
ZSum	=	28.5
ZEst	=	34.5
W	=	10
(Wv	=	2)
D	=	5
W+D	=	15
Dd	=	2
S	=	3

DQ

			(FQ-)
+	=	5	(2)
o	=	8	(1)
v/+	=	1	(0)
v	=	3	(0)

Form Quality

		FQx	MQual	W+D
+	=	0	0	0
o	=	7	0	7
u	=	5	0	4
-	=	3	0	2
none	=	2	0	2

Determinants

Blends
FC'.FD.FC
FT.FD
FM.FV
FC.FM

Single

M	=	0
FM	=	1
m	=	0
FC	=	0
CF	=	1
C	=	1
Cn	=	1
FC'	=	3
C'F	=	1
C'	=	0
FT	=	0
TF	=	0
T	=	0
FV	=	0
VF	=	0
V	=	0
FY	=	1
YF	=	0
Y	=	0
Fr	=	0
rF	=	0
FD	=	0
F	=	4
(2)	=	1

Contents

H	=	0
(H)	=	1
Hd	=	2
(Hd)	=	3
Hx	=	0
A	=	7
(A)	=	0
Ad	=	0
(Ad)	=	0
An	=	1
Art	=	0
Ay	=	0
Bl	=	1
Bt	=	0
Cg	=	2
Cl	=	0
Ex	=	0
Fd	=	0
Fi	=	0
Ge	=	0
Hh	=	0
Ls	=	2
Na	=	1
Sc	=	0
Sx	=	1
Xy	=	0
Idio	=	1

S-Constellation

☑	FV+VF+V+FD>2
☑	Col-Shd Blends>0
☑	Ego < .31 or > .44
☐	MOR > 3
☑	Zd > ±3.5
☑	es > EA
☑	CF + C > FC
☑	X+% < .70
☐	S > 3
☐	P < 3 or > 8
☑	Pure H < 2
☐	R < 17
8	Total

Special Scores

		Lvl-1		Lvl-2
DV	=	0 x1	0 x2	
INC	=	1 x2	0 x4	
DR	=	4 x3	0 x6	
FAB	=	0 x4	0 x7	
ALOG	=	0 x5		
CON	=	0 x7		

Raw Sum6 = 5
Wgtd Sum6 = 14

AB	= 0		GHR	= 2	
AG	= 0		PHR	= 4	
COP	= 0		MOR	= 0	
CP	= 0		PER	= 0	
			PSV	= 0	

RATIOS, PERCENTAGES, AND DERIVATIONS

R = 17   L = 0.31

EB	=	0 : 3.5	EA	= 3.5	EBPer	=	N/A
eb	=	3 : 8	es	= 11	D	=	-2
			Adj es	= 11	Adj D	=	-2

FM	= 3	SumC'	= 5	SumT	= 1
m	= 0	SumV	= 1	SumY	= 1

AFFECT

FC:CF+C	= 2 : 3
Pure C	= 1
SumC' : WSumC	= 5 : 3.5
Afr	= 0.31
S	= 3
Blends:R	= 4 : 17
CP	= 0

INTERPERSONAL

COP	= 0	AG	= 0
GHR:PHR		= 2 : 4	
a:p		= 2 : 1	
Food		= 0	
SumT		= 1	
Human Content		= 6	
Pure H		= 0	
PER		= 0	
Isolation Index		= 0.24	

IDEATION

a:p	=	2 : 1
Ma:Mp	=	0 : 0
2AB+(Art+Ay)	=	0
MOR	=	0

Sum6	= 5
Lvl-2	= 0
WSum6	= 14
M-	= 0
M none	= 0

MEDIATION

XA%	= 0.71
WDA%	= 0.73
X-%	= 0.18
S-	= 2
P	= 4
X+%	= 0.41
Xu%	= 0.29

PROCESSING

Zf	= 11
W:D:Dd	= 10:5:2
W : M	= 10 : 0
Zd	= -6.0
PSV	= 0
DQ+	= 5
DQv	= 3

SELF-PERCEPTION

3r+(2)/R	= 0.06
Fr+rF	= 0
SumV	= 1
FD	= 2
An+Xy	= 1
MOR	= 0
H:(H)+Hd+(Hd)	= 0 : 6

PTI = 0	☑ DEPI = 6	☑ CDI = 4	☑ S-CON = 8	☐ HVI = No	☐ OBS = No

among depressed patients as some of the Rorschach variables that load on the S-CON are also associated with depression and load on the DEPI (Exner, 1993), which can complicate interpretation of the S-CON for a depressed patient. Because Mrs. P falls into two groups in which the frequency of suicide is increased (medical patients and depressed patients), it seems prudent to view the positive S-CON as signaling an increased risk for self-destructive action.

Other Rorschach variables highlight additional reasons to be concerned about Mrs. P's suicide potential. The risk of suicide is increased when an individual who expresses suicidal ideation feels overwhelmed by an intolerable negative emotional state. The Rorschach describes Mrs. P as being flooded by intense, dysphoric affect, which compromises her capacity to view events in a reasonable, logical manner (Lambda = .31; EA = 0;3.5; D Score = −2).

Another area of concern highlighted by the Rorschach is Mrs. P's extremely negative self-image (3r+2/R = .06; Vista = 1). Suicide attempts are often motivated by harsh self-critical attitudes, which may involve self-hatred, feelings of worthlessness, or guilt. The combination of an extremely low score on the Egocentricity Index and a Vista response shows that Mrs. P is troubled by strong, painful feelings of inadequacy, worthlessness, and inferiority. These scores suggest she sees herself as a failure, as someone who has little to offer others and who worries she is a source of disappointment and embarrassment to her family. Based on these findings, we should anticipate that the risk for self-harm will increase if her feelings of worthlessness intensify or if Mrs. P becomes convinced her family views her as a burden, a source of frustration, and aggravation. While Mrs. P's Rorschach does not suggest that she feels abandoned, unusually needy, or desperate for attention, her responses to the Rorschach raise strong concerns that she could act on impulse without clearly thinking through what she is doing (D Score = −2; M = 0; Zd = −6.0).

Overall, these findings suggest there are substantial reasons to be concerned that Mrs. P could act in a self-destructive manner because she experiences considerable emotional turmoil and is troubled by powerful, negative attitudes toward herself. She is currently disorganized by the intensity of the disturbing reactions, unhappiness, and feelings of worthlessness. The potential for self-harmful behavior should be taken seriously because Ms. P is emotionally overwhelmed, has trouble maintaining perspective on events, and could act on her emotions in an impulsive fashion. Given these concerns, there are pressing reasons for prompt, active intervention to address the factors that contribute to a significant, current risk to harm herself. Clearly, Mrs. P could benefit from treatment for depression. It would be reasonable for treatment to involve both medication and psychotherapy that focuses on increasing her sense of self-worth and examining the reasons she feels useless, unimportant, and not needed by her family. Including her husband and children in the treatment process should be considered to provide a forum for the family to express support for Mrs. P as well as an opportunity for them all to deal with reactions to her illness and changes in the family structure, pattern of interactions, and responsibilities. The therapist should be particularly alert to shifts in Mrs. P's self-image because the potential for self-destructive behavior is likely to be highest if her self-appraisal becomes more negative, if she becomes consumed by a conviction she has nothing to offer and is a worthless failure, or if her feelings of futility and despair deepen.

REFERENCES

Achté, K. (1988). Suicidal tendencies in the elderly. *Suicide and Life-Threatening Behavior, 18,* 55–64.

Applebaum, S. A., & Colson, D. B. (1968). A re-examination of the color shading Rorschach test response. *Journal of Projective Techniques and Personality Assessment, 32,* 160–164.

Applebaum, S. A., & Holtzman, P. S. (1962). The color-shading response and suicide. *Journal of Projective Techniques and Personality Assessment, 26,* 155–161.

Beck, A. T., Steer, R. A., Kovacs, M., & Garrison, B. (1985). Hopelessness and suicide: A 10-year prospective study of hospitalized patients with suicidal ideation. *American Journal of Psychiatry, 142,* 559–563.

Blatt, S. J., & Ritzler, B. A. (1974). Suicide and the representation of transparency and cross-sections on the Rorschach. *Journal of Consulting and Clinical Psychology, 42,* 280–287.

Blumenthal, S. J. (1990). An overview and synopsis of risk factors, assessment, and treatment of suicidal patients over the life cycle. In S. J. Blumenthal & D. J. Kupfer (Eds.), *Suicide over the life cycle: Risk factors, assessment, and treatment of suicidal patients* (pp. 685–733). Washington, DC: American Psychiatric Press.

Bongar, B. (2002). *The suicidal patient: Clinical and legal standards of care* (2nd ed.). Washington, DC: American Psychological Association.

Exner, J. E. (1993). *The Rorschach: A comprehensive system: Vol. I. Basic foundations* (3rd ed.). New York: Wiley.

Exner, J. E. (2003). *The Rorschach: A comprehensive system: Volume I. Basic foundations* (4th ed.). New York: Wiley.

Exner, J. E., & Wylie, J. (1977). Some Rorschach data concerning suicide. *Journal of Personality Assessment, 41,* 339–348.

Eyman, J. R., & Eyman, S. K. (1991). Personality assessment in suicide prediction. *Suicide and Life-Threatening Behavior, 21,* 37–55.

Eyman, S. K., & Eyman, J. R. (1987). *An investigation of Exner's suicide constellation.* Paper presented at the meeting of the American Psychological Association, New York.

Fawcett, J. (1988). Predictors of early suicide: Identification and appropriate intervention. *Journal of Clinical Psychiatry, 49*(Suppl.), 7–8.

Finn, S. E., & Kamphuis, J. H. (1995). What a clinician needs to know about base rates. In J. N. Butcher (Ed.), *Clinical personality assessment: Practical approaches* (pp. 224–235). New York: Oxford University Press.

Fowler, J. C., Hilsenroth, M. J., & Piers, C. (2001). An empirical study of seriously disturbed suicidal patients. *Journal of the American Psychoanalytic Association, 49,* 161–186.

Fowler, J. C., Piers, C., Hilsenroth, M. J., Holdwick, D. J., & Padawer, J. R. (2001). The Rorschach Suicide Constellation (S-CON): Assessing various degrees of lethality. *Journal of Personality Assessment,* 333–351.

Gacono, C. B., & Meloy, J. R. (1994). *The Rorschach assessment of aggressive and psychopathic personalities.* Hillsdale, NJ: Erlbaum.

Ganellen, R. J. (1996a). Comparing the diagnostic efficiency of the MMPI, MCMI-II, and Rorschach: A review. *Journal of Personality Assessment, 67,* 219–243.

Ganellen, R. J. (1996b). *Integrating the Rorschach and MMPI-2 in clinical personality assessment.* Mahwah, NJ: Erlbaum.

Goldfried, M., Stricker, G., & Weiner, I. (1971). *Rorschach handbook of clinical and research applications.* Englewood Cliffs, NJ: Prentice-Hall.

Goldring, N., & Fieve, R. R. (1984). Attempted suicide in manic-depressive disorder. *American Journal of Psychiatry, 38,* 373–383.

Hamilton, M. (1960). A rating scale for depression. *Journal of Neurology, Neurosurgery, and Psychiatry, 23,* 56–62.

Hansell, A. G., Lerner, H. D., Milden, R. S., & Ludolph, P. S. (1988). Single-sign Rorschach indicators: A validity study using a depressed inpatient population. *Journal of Personality Assessment, 52,* 658–669.

Hertz, M. R. (1948). Suicidal configurations in Rorschach records. *Rorschach Research Exchange, 12,* 3–58.

Hirschfeld, R. M. A., & Davison, L. (1988). Risk factors for suicide. In A. J. Frances & R. E. Hales (Eds.), *Review of psychiatry* (Vol. 7, pp. 307–333). Washington, DC: American Psychiatric Press.

Hirschfeld, R. M. A., & Russell, J. M. (1997). Assessment and treatment of suicidal patients. *New England Journal of Medicine, 333,* 910–915.

Joiner, T. E., Rudd, M. D., & Rajab, M. H. (1997). The Modified Scale for Suicidal Ideation: Factors of suicidality and their relation to clinical and diagnostic variables. *Journal of Abnormal Psychology, 106,* 260–265.

Linehan, M. M., Rizvi, S. L., Welch, S. S., & Page, B. (2000). Psychiatric aspects of suicidal behavior. In K. Hawton & K. van Heeringen (Eds.), *International handbook of suicide and attempted suicide* (pp. 147–178). Chichester, Sussex, England: Wiley.

Maltsberger, J. T. (1986). *Suicide risk: The formulation of clinical judgment.* New York: New York University Press.

Maris, R. W. (1989). The social relations of suicide. In D. G. Jacobs & H. N. Brown (Eds.), *Suicide: Understanding and responding* (pp. 87–125). Madison, CT: International Universities Press.

Meehl, P. E., & Rosen, A. (1955). Antecedent probability and the efficiency of psychometric signs, patterns, or cutting scores. *Psychological Bulletin, 52,* 194–216.

Meyer, R. G. (1989). *The clinician's handbook: The psychopathology of adulthood and adolescence* (2nd ed.). Boston: Allyn & Bacon.

Mosicki, E. K. (1997). Identification of suicide risk factors using epidemiologic studies. *Psychiatric Clinics of North America, 20*(3), 499–517.

Neuringer, C. (1974). Rorschach inkblot test assessment of suicidal risk. In C. Neuringer (Ed.), *Psychological assessment of suicide risk* (pp. 74–94). Springfield, IL: Charles C. Thomas.

Perlin, S., & Schmidt, C. W. (1976). Psychiatry. In S. Perlin (Ed.), *A handbook for the study of suicide* (pp. 147–163). New York: Oxford University Press.

Peterson, L. G., & Bongar, B. (1989). The suicidal patient. In A. Lazare (Ed.), *Outpatient psychiatry: Diagnosis and treatment* (2nd ed., pp. 569–584). Baltimore: Williams & Wilkins.

Piotrowski, Z. (1950). A Rorschach compendium, revised and enlarged. *Psychiatric Quarterly, 24,* 543–596.

Rappaport, R., Gill, M., & Shafer, R. (1945). *Diagnostic psychological testing.* Chicago: Yearbook.

Sapolsky, A. (1963). An indicator of suicidal ideation of the Rorschach test. *Journal of Projective Techniques and Personality Assessment, 27,* 332–335.

Shneidman, E. S. (1989). Overview: A multidimensional approach to suicide. In D. G. Jacobs & H. N. Brown (Eds.), *Suicide: Understanding and responding* (pp. 1–30). Madison, CT: International Universities Press.

Silberg, J. L., & Armstrong, J. G. (1992). The Rorschach test for predicting suicide among depressed adolescent inpatients. *Journal of Personality Assessment, 59,* 290–303.

Thomas, C. D., & Duszynski, K. R. (1985). Are words of the Rorschach predictors of disease and death? The case of "whirling." *Psychosomatic Medicine, 47,* 201–211.

Wood, J. M., Nezworski, M. T., & Stejskal, W. J. (1996). The comprehensive system for the Rorschach: A critical examination. *Psychological Science, 7,* 3–10.

CHAPTER 6

Assessing the Vital Balance in Evaluating Suicidal Potential

Robert I. Yufit

There has been little success, thus far, in developing adequate, valid, and reliable assessment techniques for screening or for the assessment of lethality, self-harm, and self-destructive potential.

Some published assessment techniques attempt to evaluate suicide potential, but each has limitations (e.g., too narrow in scope and lacking in sensitivity) and, with a few exceptions, they have not gained wide acceptance mainly because surveys have shown that many clinicians prefer their own assessment or interview techniques (Jobes, Eyman, & Yufit, 1995).

Assessment techniques are needed to detect the presence of self-harm and self-destructive desires in persons who do not express such ideation or behavior. In addition, it would be helpful if assessment techniques could be used to evaluate the *degree of lethality,* to help determine appropriate interventions during a crisis and to plan for subsequent treatment in persons known to have some self-harm or self-destructive intention.

The lack of such acceptable assessment techniques forces the clinician to rely on more subjective methods, such as interviews, which often dilute the specificity of this complex and unique assessment task in which a human life is often in peril. In fact, the most frequent legal action involving psychiatric care is the accusation that the clinician failed to reasonably protect the patient from harming himself or herself (Bongar, 1991).

In many situations, there has been a lack of awareness on the part of the mental health professional in two areas. Either (1) the patient was not considered suicidal, or (2) the degree of self-harm or self-destructive risk was underestimated. Inadequate screening and/or incomplete or erroneous assessment of risk potential has been a major problem in the evaluation of such patients. We address some of these problems in this chapter.

THEORY

The theoretical basis of this chapter is formulated on the assumption that sound mental health can be represented as an equilibrium, or a balance, between one's strengths and weaknesses. This concept can be represented as a *Vital Balance*. The Vital Balance is an indicator of how a person might deal with both everyday and unique stressful situations, including loss, failure, and rejection, which are often major precipitants of anxiety and depression and which, when unresolved, may lead to self-harm feelings or suicidal ideation and result in overt suicidal behavior.

The concept of a Vital Balance is modified from the writings of Karl Menninger, from the publication by that name (Menninger, 1967). Our use of the Vital Balance also incorporates the ideas of Anton Antonovsky (Antonovsky, 1981) and his formulations for coping with stress.

A major assumption in using the concept of a Vital Balance is that a person will be able to cope most effectively if he or she can *adapt to change,* especially to unexpected, major, negative life changes. Presumably, those with an adequate Vital Balance can make adjustments and adapt to change more readily. Then reasonably good coping levels in daily functioning can be expected to resume. Maladaptive reactions to change can include anxiety, frustration, fear, withdrawal, and rigidity, resulting in a sense of hopelessness and eventually depression. Adequate coping is needed to resolve problems of adapting to change and to reduce the stress that has developed.

An equation illustrates this concept:

$$\text{Vital Balance} = \frac{\text{Vulnerability to stress}}{\text{Coping ability}} = \text{Stress reduction}$$

Two characteristics are considered essential for successful coping: resiliency and buoyancy.

Resiliency represents the needed flexibility to maximize adaptation to change and to facilitate coping with stress. *Buoyancy* is an extension of resiliency, the ability not only to be flexible but also to indicate movement, an upward direction in coping—to be able to bounce back and to regain balance and control and, thus, be able to resume coping, rather than sinking into despair, helplessness, and, eventually, hopelessness. These latter characteristics are frequent precursors of suicidal ideation and subsequent overt suicidal behavior, as well as the already cited components of high levels of depression and anxiety, which can also create a vulnerability to suicidal acts. All of these characteristics contribute to rigidity and stagnation, inhibiting the needed resiliency and buoyancy. Loss of a perspective, especially future time perspective, often follows, and such loss usually constricts outlook and adds even more rigidity.

Rigidity, especially *cognitive rigidity,* is a major deficit, limiting an individual's ability to cope adequately. It is also a common correlate of suicidal ideation and behavior. Cognitive rigidity often blocks the development of options to deal with stressful situations and the seeking of alternative solutions to problems. Frequently, the person feels immobilized and trapped, with suicide being considered the *only* way out. The word *only* is frequently used by suicidal persons and is considered an ominous sign, reflecting intense rigidity and constriction in problem-solving attempts. Obsessions may develop, further limiting adaptation to change.

Cognitive rigidity is also a key factor in creating a sense of hopelessness, which is probably the most frequently cited prodromal characteristic in the syndrome of self-harm and suicidal behaviors. Suicide is considered the ultimate failure in not coping with change and usually occurs when the psychological pain (Shneidman's [1996] "psychache") can no longer be endured, and, in the narrow perspective of rigid thinking, suicide then becomes the *only* way out.

Hopefulness and resiliency support each other. Their coexistence allows people to gain a broader time perspective, to widen the horizon of their future, which may then allow space for the development of other solutions to the problem(s), and thereby facilitates adaptation and promotes coping with stressful situations.

Techniques to assess severity of hopefulness, depression, internalized anger, rigidity, and other pertinent variables should be scorable so they can be *quantified* and then used to determine what *degrees* of lethal behavior might be considered by known suicidal individuals, that is, people

Table 6.1   Draft of Suicide Assessment Checklist

Rater _____   Pt. Name _____

Age _____   Sex   M   F   Date _____

SUICIDE ASSESSMENT CHECKLIST

Robert I. Yufit, PhD

Directions: Score each item on basis of interview responses or chart data. Verify doubtful data with family members when possible. If no parenthesis after item, score +1 for each "yes," or use listed weighted score in parenthesis. "No" or "Uncertain" scores = 0. Try to minimize "uncertain" scores. Sum all scores and categorize as indicated. High total score is a danger sign.

	Yes	No	Uncertain
SUICIDE HISTORY: (max section score = 24)			
1. Prior suicide attempt ($\times$ 4); self-harm ($\times$ 2)	_____	_____	_____
2. Two or more highly lethal* attempts in past year ($\times$ 4)	_____	_____	_____
3. Prior suicide threats or ideation	_____	_____	_____
4. Suicide attempts in the family ($\times$ 4)	_____	_____	_____
5. Completed attempts in family ($\times$ 4)	_____	_____	_____
6. Current suicidal preoccupation, threats, attempt ($\times$ 2); detailed, highly lethal plan ($\times$ 2); access to weapon, medication ($\times$ 2); if all three "yes" = 6	_____	_____	_____
7. Ongoing preoccupation with death	_____	_____	_____
PSYCHIATRIC HISTORY: (max score = 20)	Yes	No	Uncertain
8. Drug, alcohol abuse ($\times$ 6)	_____	_____	_____
9. Dx of mental disorder ($\times$ 2); Dx: schiz. or bipolar ($\times$ 4)	_____	_____	_____
10. Poor impulse control; if current ($\times$ 2)	_____	_____	_____
11. Explosive rage episodes (circle: recent or past) ($\times$ 2)	_____	_____	_____
12. Recklessness/accident prone	_____	_____	_____
13. Panic attacks: single ($\times$ 3); recurrent ($\times$ 5)	_____	_____	_____
SCHOOL: (max score = 8) or JOB (max score = 8)	Yes	No	Uncertain
14. Grade failure 14. Demotion ($\times$ 2)	_____	_____	_____
15. Rejection, poor social relations 15. Rejection	_____	_____	_____
16. Probation or school dropout ($\times$ 2) 16. Fired ($\times$ 2)	_____	_____	_____
17. Disciplinary crisis ($\times$ 2) 17. Discip. crisis	_____	_____	_____
18. Unwanted change of schools 18. Unwanted change	_____	_____	_____
19. Anticip. of severe punishment 19. Criminal act	_____	_____	_____
FAMILY: (max score = 30)	Yes	No	Uncertain
20. Recent major negative change (loss: death, divorce $\times$ 4); (serious health problem); (irrevers, loss $\times$ 4); (both = 8)	_____	_____	_____
21. Lack of emotional support, estranged ($\times$ 2)	_____	_____	_____
22. Loss of job (parent, spouse) ($\times$ 4)	_____	_____	_____
23. Major depression in parent, spouse, sibling ($\times$ 2)	_____	_____	_____
24. Alcoholism, other drug use in family member ($\times$ 2)	_____	_____	_____
25. Psychiatric illness in family member ($\times$ 2)	_____	_____	_____
25a. If $23 + 24 + 25 = 6$, add 6 more	_____	_____	_____
26. History of physical or sexual abuse (both = $\times$ 4)	_____	_____	_____
SOCIETAL: (max score = 8)	Yes	No	Uncertain
27. Contagion suicide in community ($\times$ 3)	_____	_____	_____
28. Economic down-shift in community; financial loss	_____	_____	_____
29. Loss of major support system (family; job, career both $\times$ 4)	_____	_____	_____

Table 6.1   *Continued*

PERSONALITY/BEHAVIOR/COGNITIVE STYLE:	Yes	No	Uncertain
(max score = 82)			
30. Hopelessness ($\times$ 6)	_____	_____	_____
31. Depression (intensely depressed $\times$ 2; agitated depress $\times$ 4, both $\times$ 6)	_____	_____	_____
32. Anger, hostility, aggression (all = $\times$ 3); held in (all = $\times$ 6)	_____	_____	_____
32a. If 30 + 31 + 32 = 18, add 10 more	_____	_____	_____
33. Mistrust ($\times$ 2); paranoid level ($\times$ 4)	_____	_____	_____
34. Disgust or despair (both = $\times$ 2)	_____	_____	_____
35. Withdrawn, isolated (loneliness $\times$ 4)	_____	_____	_____
36. Low, or no, future time perspective ($\times$ 6)	_____	_____	_____
37. High or dominant orientation to the past ($\times$ 4)	_____	_____	_____
37a. If 36 + 37 = 10, add 10 more	_____	_____	_____
38. Perfectionism, rigidity, obsessive/compulsive (any = $\times$ 6)	_____	_____	_____
39. Lack of a sense of belonging ($\times$ 5)	_____	_____	_____
40. Indifference, lack of motivation (boredom = $\times$ 2)	_____	_____	_____
41. Worthlessness, no one cares ($\times$ 2)	_____	_____	_____
42. Shame or guilt (both = $\times$ 4) (either one = $\times$ 2)	_____	_____	_____
43. Helplessness	_____	_____	_____
44. Inability to have fun, lacks sense of humor	_____	_____	_____
45. Extreme mood or energy fluctuation (both = $\times$ 2)	_____	_____	_____
46. Giving away valuables	_____	_____	_____
PHYSICAL: (max score = 14)	Yes	No	Uncertain
47. Male ($\times$ 2); Caucasian ($\times$ 2); (both yes = $\times$ 4)	_____	_____	_____
48. Markedly delayed puberty	_____	_____	_____
49. Recent injury leads to impairment, deformity (permanent = $\times$ 3)	_____	_____	_____
50. Loss of appetite, disinterest in food	_____	_____	_____
51. Marked weight loss (more than 10 lbs in past 6 months = $\times$ 2)	_____	_____	_____
52. Sleep disturbed (onset, middle, early awakening) hypersomnia	_____	_____	_____
53. Ongoing physical pain ($\times$ 2)	_____	_____	_____
INTERVIEW BEHAVIOR: (max score = 16)	Yes	No	Uncertain
54. Pt. encapsulated, noncommunicative ($\times$ 2)	_____	_____	_____
55. Negative reaction of pt. to interviewer ($\times$ 3)	_____	_____	———
56. Negative reaction of interviewer to pt.	_____	_____	_____
57. Increasing distance in interaction during interview ($\times$ 4)	_____	_____	_____
58. Increasing hostility, noncooperation by pt. ($\times$ 2)	_____	_____	_____
59. Pt. highly self-critical, self-pitying ($\times$ 2)	_____	_____	_____
60. Discusses death; suicide is only way out ($\times$ 2)	_____	_____	_____
sum of p. 2	_____	_____	_____
sum of p. 1 & p. 2	_____	_____	_____

*Highly lethal: low risk for
    rescue; serious   sum p. 1:   _____ _____ _____

medical injury (comatose); irreversibility

(continued)

Table 6.1   *Continued*

Suicide Risk Potential Guidelines:		Score range	
Very high risk		150–202 (prob. hospitalize)	
High risk		100–149	
Level of ambivalence:	High	Moderate risk	50–99
	Low	Low risk below	49
Current intention:			
seeks attention		Immediate risk (espec. 25a + 32a + 37a = yes)	
escape pain			
punish self/others		Long-term risk:	
harm/injure self			
wants to die		Confidence level: High Low/Manipulating	
		Reasons:	

who have admitted ideation or who have been making verbal threats or overt attempts. What is the probability that such ideation will become overt? What is the *intention* of the person (e.g., to die, to hurt himself or herself, or to seek attention)? Is the intent *clear* or *ambivalent*? If a suicide attempt has been made, what is the lethality level? (Lethality level may be reflected by degree of physical injury.) These are some of the difficult questions that these assessment techniques are attempting to answer.

In this chapter, we describe two clinical assessment instruments that are quantifiable (scorable); and we believe that one, the Suicide Assessment Checklist (SAC), can serve the functions of specific screening and, by the level and content of the total weighted score, provide (1) some estimate of the degree of lethality of a recent attempt and (2) the degree of potential future suicide attempts. (Drafts of the SAC and the Coping Abilities Questionnaire [CAQ] are presented in Tables 6.1 and 6.2.)

The higher the total SAC score, the greater the likelihood that self-harm ideation is present and that overt self-harm behavior may occur. This assumption is based on the *empirical support* of known correlates of suicidal behavior, represented by more highly weighted specific SAC items (such as hopelessness or agitated depression). Such higher weighted items comprise a substantial proportion of the SAC score.

Thus, a *very* high SAC score is considered to indicate not only that self-harm behavior is likely, but also that the *level* of such behavior may be of high lethality and, hence, self-destructive. A high SAC score may also indicate that the risk may be immediate.

Table 6.2   Draft of Coping Abilities Questionnaire

Rater _____   Pt. Name _____

Age _____   Sex M F Date _____

COPING ABILITIES QUESTIONNAIRE

Robert I. Yufit, PhD

Directions: Score each item on basis of interview responses or chart data. Partial weights (maximum weights in parentheses) may be given. "Uncertain" and "no" score on item = 0; try to minimize "uncertain." Sum all scores and categorize as indicated. High total score indicates good coping ability.

		Yes	No	Uncertain
1. Flexible approach in dealing with current adversity	($\times 8$)	_____	_____	_____
2. Firm belief in oneself; feels capable, autonomous	($\times 5$)	_____	_____	_____
3. Sense of trust in self	($\times 8$)	_____	_____	_____
4. Sense of trust in others	($\times 6$)	_____	_____	_____
5. Deals with change adequately	($\times 4$)	_____	_____	_____
6. Has continuity of the self (i.e., has an identity)	($\times 6$)	_____	_____	_____
7. Has/had close relationships; can be intimate	($\times 6$)	_____	_____	_____
8. Maintains adequate perspective in stress situations; not easily overwhelmed; sense of hopefulness	($\times 8$)	_____	_____	_____
9. Has a developed future time perspective	($\times 8$)	_____	_____	_____
10. Enjoys work, achievement oriented; has generativity	($\times 6$)	_____	_____	_____
11. Sense of belonging (to a person, career, etc.)	($\times 8$)	_____	_____	_____
12. Can give, be loving, nurturant, likes to share	($\times 4$)	_____	_____	_____
13. Level of expectations reasonable, reachable	($\times 6$)	_____	_____	_____
14. Well-developed sense of humor, enjoys fun, laughs easily	($\times 3$)	_____	_____	_____
15. Values life in a meaningful manner, enthusiastic	($\times 4$)	_____	_____	_____
16. Has dealt with past adversity with success	($\times 5$)	_____	_____	_____
17. Usually has control over energy level	($\times 3$)	_____	_____	_____
18. Available external support system	($\times 2$)	_____	_____	_____

Scoring Guidelines: Total   _____   _____   _____

　　Excellent coping skills: 90–100   Level of confidence:

　　Good coping skills   70–89   High   Low

　　Fair coping skills   50–69   Reasons:

　　Minimal coping skills   49 and below

SUICIDE ASSESSMENT CHECKLIST (SAC)

The 60-item SAC (see Table 6.1) is scored on the basis of response data from a structured Focused Clinical Interview (FCI). The FCI explores and focuses on those areas to be rated by the SAC. Instructions on the interview procedure and for scoring the SAC are provided to the clinician in a Manual of instructions (Yufit, 1989).

The SAC is also presumed to be a measure of *vulnerability* to stress, and, consequently, a high score reflects the likelihood of a high level of vulnerability. Inability to cope increases the level of vulnerability. A high level of vulnerability is considered to be a common precursor to feelings of helplessness, hopelessness, and despair, which, as mentioned, often lead to subsequent self-harm and self-destructive ideation and, if such feelings intensify, to overt self-destructive behaviors.

COPING ABILITIES QUESTIONNAIRE (CAQ)

The other clinical instrument, the CAQ, is a measure of how well a person may cope with stress (see Table 6.2). The 18-item CAQ is based on specific, positive personality attributes that are thought to facilitate adaptation to change and, thereby, coping. Many CAQ items are derived from Erik Erikson's eight stages framework for human development (Erikson, 1982) and from Henry Murray's need system (Murray, 1938). Coping ability is considered critical for successful adaptation and resolution to stressful ideation and every day life situations (Antonovsky, 1981).

The CAQ is also quantified, and the scoring of each item is based on the Focused Clinical Interview (FCI) response data. Positive attributes of personality are assessed and, based on the theoretical frameworks discussed previously, the higher the CAQ score, the more likely the person has developed reasonably effective coping skills, which should help reduce vulnerability. Capacity for intimacy, a sense of trust in self and others, the degree of flexibility, and a sense of belonging are some of the attributes listed in the CAQ items and can be considered as the basis for good coping skills.

A high total SAC score and a low total CAQ score would be a clinically dangerous combination, indicating a high level of vulnerability and poorly developed coping skills. Such a combination is presumed to indicate a clinically inadequate Vital Balance and suggests a protective environment (such as hospitalization) might be an appropriate intervention. A moderately high SAC score with a higher total CAQ score would be considered indicative of a moderate level of vulnerability and might be managed by outpatient psychotherapy as an appropriate intervention.

The reverse situation, namely, a low score on the SAC (lesser degree of vulnerability) and a high score on the CAQ (effective coping skills), would be indicative of a more desirable Vital Balance, adaptability, and the ability to cope with immediate problems such as major change, especially loss. Continued successful coping would be one step in the development of a sense of confidence and subsequent well-being and may be considered to be an indication of good mental health.

While this conceptualization may seem overly simplistic, the use of such a quantifiable framework gives the clinician a better starting point for organizing and evaluating the existence of the Vital Balance between coping and vulnerability. When coping begins to fail, negative feelings can develop (e.g., hopelessness, depression, despair, and anger) and increase the possible emergence of overt self-harm behaviors if these feelings cannot be controlled or properly channeled.

Such a framework of content may even be related to identifying *intentionality* and *degree of ambivalence* in reference to considering the risk of self-harm behaviors, as both are very important components in evaluating suicide potential. Clarification of the intention usually identifies the degree of ambivalence relating to any plans for suicide. The greater the ambivalence, the more likely therapeutic intervention will be effective.

Specific SAC items are especially important clinical indicators, based on empirical research. These SAC items are more heavily weighted in the scoring scheme, with weights of +2 to +6 when the item is scored as being present from the Focused Interview responses. The degree of weighting is related to the frequency of these clinical items being cited in published empirical research findings plus the consensus of a number of therapists, each with considerable experience assessing and treating suicidal persons. There was good consensus for several variables; therefore, items related to hopelessness, agitated depression, cognitive rigidity, time perspective, and internalized anger all receive higher item-score weighting on the SAC.

In addition, when these weighted items, which are considered to be highly intercorrelated, are scored as positive, the resulting *cluster* of items is given an additional weighting called a *cluster weighted score*. There are three such cluster scores in the SAC, which add significantly (60 points or 30%) to the total score of the SAC when scored as being present. In order of importance, these three clusters are:

1. 32a: Hopelessness/internalized anger/agitated depression (items 30, 31, 32) total = 28 points

2. 37a: Time perspective (minimal future, plus a high past orientation; items 36, 37) total = 20 points

3. 25a: Family psychopathology (alcoholism, depression, and other major psychiatric illness in family member; items 23, 24, 25) total = 12 points

When any (and certainly when all) of these three SAC clusters are scored positive, the index of potential lethality or self-harm is considered to be increased exponentially, as this pattern of significant test-item content is considered to carry the SAC total score above that of a screening function to that of a *sensitivity measure* of *degree of lethality*. The basis for this assumption is that the existence of these known, empirically derived characteristics has an especially strong positive correlation with overt suicidal behavior. When these clusters are in evidence and scored accordingly, they provide the basis for assuming a much higher lethality of any self-harmful behaviors and, therefore, may be properly viewed as an *index of self-destruction* rather than self-harm. They may also be considered to indicate an *immediate* risk of overt self-destructive behavior rather than a long-term risk.

TIME QUESTIONNAIRE

A third suicide assessment technique, the Time Questionnaire (TQ), has been published and in use for more than 25 years as an assessment tool (Yufit & Benzies, 1978). The TQ represents time perspective in a more dimension-specific manner than items in SAC and is considered an important additional measure in evaluating suicide potential.

The lack of a future time perspective is a common (and understandable) finding for most suicidal persons. Such a lack is viewed also as a serious form of cognitive constriction, since the development of an expanded long-term time perspective is reduced. Such constriction often limits also the development of hope, especially in times of stress. When future time perspective is lacking in suicidal persons, as it often is, such a focus further minimizes adaptation to change and curtails resiliency. Focus on the past (especially nostalgia) absorbs emotional energy and further limits any attention to the present or to the future. Cognitive constriction may well be related to a prominent orientation to the past.

Many suicidal persons look to the past with obsessive ruminations ("Why didn't I do this instead of that?") or with nostalgic longings ("Those were the good old days gone forever"). When such time focus is self-absorbing, it can minimize a flexible approach, especially the ability to deal with any sudden change. Such self-absorption can also limit the development of future plans and may minimize the development of hope that current problems can be solved and trust that adaptation to change will eventually take place. Buoyancy becomes restricted. The resulting cognitive constriction may thus tend to limit the development of options in problem solving, creating feelings of being trapped, helpless, and vulnerable. Such a sequence may seriously impair psychological equilibrium of affect and the continuation of a stable Vital Balance.

The Time Questionnaire has a scoring manual and provides measures to quantify past, present, and future time orientations (Yufit & Benzies, 1978). Over the past two decades, the yield of this assessment instrument has consistently revealed that the time profiles of most persons who are suicidal are markedly different from those of persons who are not suicidal. The nonsuicidal person has a more positive and direct involvement in the present and future with minimal involvement in the past, while the suicidal person is usually much more involved in the past, negatively involved in the present, and minimally involved in the future (Yufit, 1991). In the TQ item asking the person to pick a month and year in the future, a high percentage of suicidal persons select the current month and current year, whereas the mean time projection for our control sample is eight years into the future no matter what the age of the person.

ANGER, DEPRESSION, AND HOPELESSNESS

Anger, especially internalized anger, often increases cognitive rigidity and limits resiliency and buoyancy and is considered still another major correlate of self-harm and self-destructive behaviors, especially when the anger is directed inward and focused mainly on oneself (Menninger, 1938).

Depression is also usually viewed as a common correlate of a suicide-prone person but is not always present at a significant level, contrary to popular beliefs. However, when depression is severe, suicidal behavior should be considered a strong possibility.

As mentioned, hopelessness is perhaps the *most consistent* and prominent psychological correlate associated with suicidal behavior, being cited in many studies, and is often mentioned as a very ominous sign by psychotherapists who treat known or latent suicidal persons.

Thus, the presence of hopelessness, internalized anger, depression, cognitive constriction, the lack of a future time perspective, and a preoccupation with the past comprise a clinical syndrome *highly correlated* with increased suicidal potential.

In addition, the existence of illicit drug or alcohol abuse and/or dependency, a history of psychiatric disorders (especially schizophrenia and bipolar affective disorder) in the self and/or in family members, plus a history of prior suicidal attempts comprise additional major clusters of empirically derived suicide correlates. When such clusters are present, they are considered to add substantially to the likelihood of overt suicide attempts, along with higher levels of lethality in any subsequent suicidal behavior. These characteristics relate more to self-destruction than to self-harm. In addition, when an interview reveals a more serious intention, with consequent lower ambivalence, including using a method with higher lethality with less reversibility and less chance to be rescued, self-destruction, rather than self-harm, is indicated. Ongoing pain, physical or psychological, actual or imagined, is also highly correlated with self-destructive ideation and overt suicidal behavior. Such unremitting psychache may foster increasing despair and helplessness and is often present in severe dysphoric states.

As stated, the actual *intention* of the person adds a critical assessment variable of clinical significance to this growing diagnostic profile of significant correlations. Thus, "I really want to die, to end it all," is much different from the desire to shame someone else or to gain attention via a carefully controlled self-harm attempt. Distinguishing intention is a critical task in assessing suicidal potential and the degree of lethality.

Certainly, other factors can be related to assessing suicidal lethality and, for this reason, the total SAC score is to be considered a *guideline* for, a supplement to, and not a replacement of, clinical judgment. A high SAC score, especially when complemented by a low CAQ score, should offer support or confirmation of clinical judgment to hospitalize the person or, when contrary to clinical judgment, should indicate a careful reconsideration and examination of the judgment that has been formed.

False positives in assessing self-harm/suicidal potential have been rare when the pattern of high vulnerability and low coping scores exist. False negatives, based on denial or suppression of feelings or manipulation, can complicate interpretations. Extremely high or low SAC scores should alert the clinicians to such possibilities, and more extensive interviewing plus added psychological projective assessment techniques for the purpose of *serial* assessment may be needed. While malingering is always a thorn in the task of assessment, it may be more difficult to engage in because of the ambiguous nature of many of the stimuli used in projective techniques.

In borderline scoring situations, where the scores are only *moderately* high or low, extended psychological assessment is usually indicated. Middle-range numerical scores may need to be supplemented by additional explorations, such as serial assessments using additional assessment procedures. Such extended assessment can be represented by the concept of a Suicide Assessment Battery (SAB), which consists of a *group* of clinically focused assessment techniques to facilitate clinical judgment in a more comprehensive manner and to increase the sensitivity and specificity of assessing suicide potential.

The SAB is used to assist such borderline, possibly false positive or false negative patterns in these specific assessment situations, and we have been developing additional instruments to comprise such an SAB. The already discussed Focused Clinical Interview, the SAC, the CAQ, and the Time Questionnaire are major assessment techniques that form a core segment of the SAB.

Other projective assessment techniques include a specially devised Sentence Completion Technique, a Word Association Technique, a Draw-a-Person-in-the-Rain Technique, an Experiential Questionnaire, plus specific Thematic Apperception Technique (TAT) cards that have revealed clinical promise in this assessment task, such as TAT cards 1, 3BG, 12BG, and 14.

Unfortunately, the multidimensional components of suicidal behaviors may not be detected with sufficient consistency in response patterns from these latter projective techniques to merit the extensive time involved in administering, scoring, and interpreting these techniques on a more frequent basis. This is partly due to the inadequacy of existing scoring schemes specifically related to self-harm and self-destructiveness.

The traditional projective techniques relate to *general* personality evaluations and usually do not focus on the *specificity* or *sensitivity* of assessing variables empirically related to high suicidal potential. We are trying to develop supplementary scoring schemes for the projective techniques for this purpose, but we may find it more productive to build new assessment techniques to measure the specific correlates, or we may modify existing projective techniques such as the newly developed Word Association, Sentence Completion, and Draw-a-Person-in-the-Rain Techniques, which have all yielded rich clinical data in more than 900 psychological evaluations to date. The Experiential Inventory, which is a listing of positive and negative experiences in the past, present, and future time perspectives, has also proven to be a useful assessment technique, and is modified from concepts of Cottle (1976).

So-called suicide sub-scales, such as those derived from the MMPI, have not been found to be consistently useful, perhaps because major psychological correlates of self-harm are not being tapped. Other published personality questionnaires have not yet achieved widespread acceptance, with the exception of Beck's measures of depression, suicide ideation, and hopelessness (Beck, Kovacs, & Weissman, 1975). Most of these questionnaires lack both focus and comprehensiveness considering the complexity of assessing suicide potential. Furthermore, self-report instruments may not allow significant clinical judgments of observing the demeanor of the patient more directly by asking for specific elaborations to responses via an *inquiry* following the administration.

The nature of projection, in the associations of response patterns on projectives techniques, can also provide data to examine the *intentionality* of the respondent, based on measures of impulsivity, constriction, intensity of focus, and the continuity or pervasiveness of the focus given in the response patterns. The ambiguity of the stimuli of the projective techniques can provide a greater in-depth exploration of intention despite the subjectivity of such interpretations.

PROBLEMS AND LIMITATIONS

As mentioned, sometimes patients have a desire to "look good" or to "look bad." Manipulation and denial are important factors that need to be identified when they are present, as they will often alter the truthfulness and validity of the response.

Asking the same question in a different form or at a later juncture of the interview allows some evaluation of the consistency (or reliability) of a questionable earlier response and is one method of assessing fabrication attempts by the patient. As the saying goes, "The good thing about telling the truth is that you don't have to remember what you said."

A *very* high SAC total score needs to be examined closely, although it would take a psychologically sophisticated patient to know the "right" answers to gain a very high score because most SAC items usually do not have an obvious right or wrong answer. Yet, an extremely high or low score on either the SAC or the CAQ may need further exploration to ascertain possible attempts at fabrication.

Another limitation of these assessment techniques is that they may not always provide valid data with certain special populations, such as the grossly psychotic, the severely intellectually retarded, or organically impaired patients. Such conditions most likely limit the understanding and processing of the questions being asked, and these limitations need to be taken into account in making the assessment. Patients under the age of 14 may have some limitations of life experiences, which might make the CAQ score difficult to interpret for this younger age range.

There is no upper age-range limitation for using the SAC or CAQ, aside from the geriatric patient with severe organicity, who is often characterized by serious cognitive constriction, even without an existing depression. Such constriction could limit understanding and affect response variance. Yet, this very factor of constriction often contributes to suicidal ideation and to subsequent suicide attempts and completed suicides among the elderly.

Life-threatening physical illness, especially with ongoing pain, also constricts outlook and serves as a reality-distorting influence. Such persons often have a desire to consider death as the *only* solution to end their decline in all functions, as well as a way to end physical and/or psychological pain.

The FCI should be conducted by a clinician with adequate experience to gain sufficient rapport so that detailed response data are elicited. The lack of adequate rapport and response data may dilute the accuracy of the scoring of both the SAC and the CAQ and also reduce the sensitivity and the specificity of the measures.

A candid and cooperative patient is especially helpful to facilitate the elicitation of relevant response data to score the CAQ, which is more complex to score, as well as to elicit sufficiently elaborate patient response content. Areas assessed by the CAQ may require more time to explore than the usual interview format allows, so extended time may be needed to complete the administration of the CAQ.

Depressed, withdrawn, and hostile patients usually test the limits of even the skilled clinician who is attempting to collect sufficient pertinent response data for the scoring of any of the assessment procedures, but especially for the CAQ. In-depth interviewing is usually needed to uncover the underlying psychodynamics of such patients, and much more time is needed to gain an adequate response database.

The desire to suppress suicidal intent is a common occurrence that can pose an assessment problem, but the use of the variety of assessment techniques proposed, especially those using indirect questions as projective stimuli, should elicit enough pertinent response data to allow the uncovering of such hidden intentions in a more effective manner than the use of the clinical interview alone. Using an SAB as a multilevel serial assessment strategy is advantageous in more complex screening and diagnostic situations. The factor of added time for administration, scoring, and interpretation, plus integration of the conflicting response date, must be considered, but this may be needed to ensure an adequate database for making a valid and reliable assessment.

APPLICATIONS

The pairing of a high SAC score and low CAQ score is usually an indication for hospitalization, even if psychosis is not present. The Vital Balance is most likely impaired, and vulnerability to stress is probably high.

A high SAC and high CAQ score is an indication that there may be some coping skills for managing the existing vulnerabilities, and intervention with outpatient psychotherapy might be sufficiently adequate treatment, although positive responses to the cited SAC cluster item groupings could still suggest the need for hospitalization regardless of the total SAC score.

A low SAC score and a low CAQ score might suggest the need for some counseling to increase coping abilities, whereas a low SAC score and a high CAQ score would be optimal for a desirable Vital Balance of good mental health and well-being. The response data derived from the SAC and CAQ can be useful in the treatment process. The nature of specific responses or response patterns can often be used as the basis for further explorations in subsequent psychotherapy sessions, and such response data has provided important information for establishing treatment plans and strategies.

Attempts to develop a more defined and meaningful future time perspective have often been found very helpful in the treatment of suicidal persons, especially when there are obsessions with the past that need to be diluted, if not eliminated, so that a person can deal more fully with the present and make plans for the future. Setting reachable goals should be attained more easily and will help develop confidence and self-esteem. By doing so, the reestablishment of the equilibrium between coping and vulnerability needed for the Vital Balance is facilitated.

CURRENT VALUE AND NEEDS

The advent and prominence of managed care have resulted in a dramatic restriction in the utilization of inpatient psychiatric services. In fact, managed care gatekeeping models, utilization review protocols, and the emphasis on short-term outpatient treatment, as well as inpatient treatment, place increasing pressure on clinicians to justify the efficacy of any treatment plan.

Furthermore, the role of managed care in the decision-making process often means that decisions about the level of care can depend on balancing cost containment needs against a clinician's often subjective interpretation of clinical data. Admission for inpatient care, length of stay, and continuation of treatment are often dependent on the clinician's ability to articulate and document medical necessity. *Medical necessity* typically means that a patient's clinical condition represents so severe an illness and impairment that hospitalization and professional treatment are needed. The impairment is usually symptom based. One such impairment is that the person is either a danger to himself or herself or to someone else, so some form of intervention (diagnosis and pertinent treatment) or protection (hospitalization) is necessary immediately. Establishing medical necessity is a major requirement for third-party (insurance) reimbursement.

Instruments such as the SAC and CAQ that can empirically document the degree of vulnerability and of available coping skills should help evaluate the need for hospitalization and degree of suicide risk, and they could be indispensable tools for the clinician who is seeking some empirical and objective support of medical necessity for managed care approval, especially for inpatient care. Determining the immediacy of short-term suicide risk versus long-term risk is also needed.

Many outpatients present ambiguous clinical pictures, requiring the clinician to rely on subjective qualities such as past experience, clinical judgment, and inference in determining the level of risk and the level of care. The SAC and CAQ could offer clarifying, empirically based data, especially when a patient presents with feelings of hopelessness, despair, and/or is significantly depressed. This data in turn would provide documented empirical support for a more accurate diagnosis and could both reduce litigation risks for failing to protect patients from harming themselves and come closer to establishing a higher "standard of care" (Bongar, 1991). Litigation claims of *negligence* are also reduced by the use of extended assessment beyond the use of the clinical interview alone.

As the length of inpatient stays are reduced and as managed care demands more "objective" measures in support of treatment plans, the SAC and CAQ could provide a valuable clinical measure of the patient's current emotional and behavioral stability (or Vital Balance). Frequently, retroactive denials of reimbursement can occur because the patient's chart fails to document medical necessity. If the SAC and CAQ are readministered on a regular basis during inpatient admission and if their scores indicate ongoing suicide risk, this would provide valuable pertinent support for the necessity of continued care. Repeated administration of the SAC can also help evaluate *change* in the patient's level of functioning and can be useful in formulating further treatment plans and ultimate disposition. Repeated evaluation during inpatient stays is also important considering the need for suicide precautions, the privilege of giving passes outside the hospital, as well as for eventual discharge.

The SAC and CAQ are not difficult to administer once qualified clinical psychologists have been trained, and such assessment makes them valuable for emergency psychiatric services, inpatient nursing staff, and office-based mental health professionals, all of whom need an empirically based, quantified database for decision making. The time for completing a SAC and CAQ will vary, dependent on data from the FCI, but should not take more than 30 or 40 minutes if good rapport has been established.

The SAC and CAQ have been informally tested in clinical settings but not yet formally incorporated into a research study. This field testing has resulted in making some revisions in both instruments. More formal research is needed to further evaluate the utility of these instruments, and this will be done.

The experimental design would involve the development of comparison groups. Such groups would be formed by the clinician by use of a general rating of each person to be interviewed by making an estimate of high, low, or moderate suicide potential based on information in the referral questions. Scores of persons in each of these groups would then be compared with this initial rating to determine if the SAC total scores are consistent with these initial rated impressions. Follow-up audits of selected individuals would be carried out to evaluate the degree of validity and reliability of the SAC total scores and how consistent they are with these initial estimates and other related data.

There would also be various intergroup and intragroup comparisons, the latter based on the demographic variables of age, sex, education, and so forth, to determine what distinctive clinical patterns might emerge. Another major goal is to determine whether specific SAC items and/or item clusters are consistent with total SAC scorings to allow briefer versions of the SAC to be developed.

Emergency room (ER) personnel have often requested a briefer version of the SAC, although brevity usually compromises validity and reliability. One brief version (20 items) of the 60-item SAC has been developed and needs to be further field tested in ER settings.

A primary concern is the meaning of intermediate or borderline scores, especially on the SAC, and to what use additional assessment procedures will help clarify this more ambiguous range of scoring. The use of the SAB should play an important role of clarification in such cases by providing a more comprehensive and in-depth assessment in order to increase specificity and sensitivity of the assessment process.

Establishing predictive validity may be a problem, as effective therapeutic treatment over time will likely improve a person's coping abilities. Thus, if such persons with high SAC and low CAQ scores do not make another suicide attempt, the initial high SAC score is not necessarily invalidated because an effective therapeutic intervention may have made a significant impact in reducing vulnerability, improving the person's coping abilities, thereby allowing improved management and adaptation to future stressful situations and significantly decreasing the likelihood of future self-destructive or self-harm behaviors.

It is hoped that a more detailed analysis of the assessment characteristics of the SAC and CAQ might also allow for the assessment of *longer term risk* of self-destructive behavior, and not only *immediate risk,* which is the current aim. The relative strength of coping skills with specific strengths to counter, or not counter, specific vulnerabilities might allow for such an assessment of longer term risk and broaden the sensitivity, specificity, and validity of these new assessment techniques. As mentioned, positive scores on the three cluster-weighted items of the SAC, plus a prior history of suicide attempts, would suggest that immediate suicidal risk exists and that hospitalization may be needed.

Again, being able to identify more clearly the intentionality of the person, along with the degree of *ambivalence* present, will be an important advance in our attempts to improve the *sensitivity* and *specificity* levels of the clinical distinction between self-harm and self-destructive behaviors, as well as providing a more structured framework for the clinician who is attempting to evaluate these very complex behaviors for appropriate intervention and plans for treatment.

The need to use a Focused Clinical Interview to define the variables represented by our assessment instruments should provide much needed structure, thereby assisting the clinician considerably, and is another goal of our efforts to advance assessment technology to a more empirically derived level, ultimately increasing the validity and reliability of evaluating the risk of self-harm and suicidal potential so that appropriate diagnosis, clinical disposition, and recommended treatment plans can be made in a more accurate and clinically meaningful manner. Thus, the patient may be helped to restore a more functional Vital Balance to assist in making adaptations to the stress of daily living, especially important in the insecurity of current geopolitical uncertainty of our present world situation.

REFERENCES

Antonovsky, A. (1981). *Health, stress and coping.* San Francisco: Jossey-Bass.

Beck, A. T., Kovacs, M., & Weissman, A. (1975). Hopelessness and suicidal behavior. *Journal of the American Medical Association, 234,* 1146–1149.

Bongar, B. (1991). *The suicidal patient: Clinical and legal standards of care.* Washington, DC: American Psychological Association.

Cottle, T. J. (1976). *Perceiving time.* New York: Wiley.

Erikson, E. H. (1982). *Life cycle completed.* New York: Norton.

Jobes, D. A., Eyman, J. R., & Yufit, R. I. (1995). How clinicians assess suicide risk. *Crisis Intervention and Time-Limited Treatment, 2,* 1–12.

Menninger, K. (1938). *Man against himself.* New York: Harcourt, Brace & World.

Menninger, K. (1967). *The vital balance.* New York: Viking Press.

Murray, H. A. (1938). *Explorations in personality.* New York: Oxford University Press.

Shneidman, E. S. (1996). *The suicidal mind.* New York: Oxford University Press.

Yufit, R. I. (1989). Developing a suicide screening instrument for adolescents and young adults. In M. L. Rosenberg & K. Baer (Eds.), *Report of the secretary's task force on youth suicide* (Vol. 4, pp. 129–144). Washington, DC: Department of Health and Human Services.

Yufit, R. I. (1991). Suicide assessment in the 1990's. Presidential address, American Association of Suicidology. *Suicide and Life-Threatening Behavior, 21,*152–163.

Yufit, R. I., & Benzies, B. (1978). *Scoring manual for the Time Questionnaire.* Palo Alto, CA: Consulting Psychologist's Press.

PART TWO

Intervention and Treatment of Suicidality

CHAPTER 7

The Classic Systems of Psychotherapy and Suicidal Behavior

David Lester

In many discussions of counseling for suicidal clients, the level of analysis does not proceed much beyond the training given to nonprofessional crisis counselors working at suicide prevention centers, training that focuses on active listening (person-centered therapy), assessment of resources, and formulation of a plan for action. Rudestam (1985–1986) observed that a crisis-oriented approach is rarely useful for chronically suicidal clients, whose level of functioning has been poor throughout most of their life. Such clients need long-term psychotherapy.

The classic systems of psychotherapy are based on well-established theories of human behavior that provide a rationale for therapeutic techniques; yet, academic textbooks on the systems of psychotherapy typically ignore the problem of suicide. Lester (1991) reviewed the scholarly literature on the major systems of psychotherapy, searching for cases in which those systems had been applied to suicidal clients. Whereas some psychotherapists, such as psychoanalysts and cognitive therapists, have occasionally reported applications for their systems to suicidal clients, others, such as Gestalt therapists, have rarely provided such examples.

Psychotherapists who work with suicidal clients need to consider several issues. The first is whether all of the systems of psychotherapy may be used safely with suicidal clients. Some systems, such as person-centered therapy, seem safe enough to use with any client, including suicidal individuals. But what about the more confrontive and emotional therapies, such as Gestalt therapy and primal therapy?

A second and important question is whether the major therapeutic issue is the client's suicidal preoccupation or the problems (such as depression or social isolation) underlying it, a question that relates to whether the suicidal preoccupation is acute or chronic. If the suicidality is chronic, it makes sense for the psychotherapist to focus on the client's underlying psychological problems.

The third issue psychotherapists should consider is whether particular systems of psychotherapy are suitable for particular types of clients. This leads to the problem of devising a taxonomy of suicidal clients that has relevance for psychotherapy (rather than, e.g., research). For example, Fremouw, de Perczel, and Ellis (1990) listed six types of suicidal clients (those who are depressed and hopeless, those with communication and control problems, psychotic clients, alcoholic clients, individuals with organic brain dysfunction, and rational clients), but they kept close to the traditional psychiatric categories and failed to show that classification of suicidal clients into these six types was useful for psychotherapists.

There has been a great deal of research on suicidal behavior in the past 40 years, and some of this research has implications for therapeutic strategies that may be used specifically with suicidal clients. In addition, individual therapists have formulated their own conceptualizations of the genesis of suicidal preoccupation, some of which are empirically based (e.g., Leenaars, 1991) while others are clinically based (e.g., Richman & Eyman, 1990), and they have suggested goals and techniques for psychotherapy based on these conceptualizations.

PSYCHOANALYSIS

Brief mentions of suicidal behavior can be found throughout Freud's writing, and Litman (1967) documented and synthesized these dispersed thoughts. From an analytic perspective, the clinical features of suicidal behavior include guilt over death wishes toward others, identification with a suicidal parent, refusal to accept loss of gratification, suicide as an act of revenge, suicide as an escape from humiliation, suicide as a communication, and the connection between death and sexuality.

The essential feature of suicidal behavior is that the person loses a loved object and energy is withdrawn from this lost loved object, relocated in the ego, and used to re-create the loved one as a permanent feature of the self in an identification of the ego with the lost object. Litman (1967) called this process *ego-splitting*. Even before becoming suicidal, the person has probably already introjected some of the desires of the loved one. Children introject desires of their parents, and adults introject the desires of their lovers. In this way, it is as if part of our mind is symbolic of our loved one. If this person is lost to us, for example, by death or divorce, we still possess those introjected desires; thus the symbolization of the lost loved one remains as part of our mind. This process can lead to suicide if we also harbor hostile wishes toward the lost object, for now we can turn this anger toward the part of our mind that symbolizes the lost object.

More generally, however, one major influence of psychoanalytic theory in the analysis of suicide is the asking of the question, "What is the real reason for this suicide?" Although researchers into suicidal behavior often cite the obvious precipitating event for suicidal preoccupation, such as the breakup of a close relationship, financial problems, or legal problems, the vast majority of people who experience such traumas do not kill themselves. These precipitating events are neither necessary nor sufficient to account for suicide. This had led psychoanalysts to probe for the unconscious motives behind the suicidal act.

For example, the suicide of Sylvia Plath, an American poet, in 1963 was ostensibly precipitated by her husband's adulterous affair. However, Oedipal conflicts appear to have been involved in the suicidal act. In her poem "Daddy" (Plath, 1966), Plath casts her father as a Nazi guard for the concentration camp in which a Jewish Sylvia is interned and as a devil who bites her heart in two. She expresses both affection and anger toward her deceased father, describes her marriage as an attempt to find a father substitute, and casts her suicide as a reunion with Daddy. Gerisch (1998) has provided a detailed analysis of Plath's suicide from a psychoanalytic perspective.

The Goals of Psychoanalysis

There are many goals in psychoanalysis with the suicidal client, but one possible goal is to make conscious to the client what is unconscious. If clients can become conscious of their unconscious desires, they will not necessarily satisfy them directly, but at least they will be able to make more appropriate choices in the future. Psychoanalysis does not attempt to change the client's choice, but rather to make it an informed choice.

Since helping a client to become conscious of unconscious desires may make the client extremely anxious, perhaps to the point of panic, increasing the client's awareness must be done slowly and carefully. Psychoanalysis proceeds cautiously, with three to five meetings a week for three to seven years or longer.

The techniques of psychoanalysis include free association (in which the client permits his or her mind to wander freely from memory to memory and informs the psychoanalyst of the chain of associations), transference (in which the client attributes thoughts and desires to the psychoanalyst that the analyst does not possess), and interpretation (in which the psychoanalyst interprets the client's behavior to the client).

Because many of the client's unconscious desires derive from childhood wishes and many of the client's superego wishes derive from demands that the client's parents made on the client, psychoanalysts place much importance on the client's childhood. In psychoanalysis, much time is spent discussing the early years and the client's parents and siblings. The slow tempo and historical orientation of psychoanalysis make it unsuitable for crisis intervention with acutely suicidal clients.

Discussion

The psychoanalytic position on suicide has generated a good deal of research, much of which is supportive of the theory. For example, in a review of the research on the experience of loss in suicidal people and the relationships between suicide and both anger and depression, Lester (1988) found that the psychoanalytic perspective had been useful in furthering our understanding of suicidal behavior.

Because psychoanalysis is a slow process, it is difficult to document the use of its techniques for dealing with suicidal people. The goal of psychoanalysis is a thorough exploration of the contents of the conscious and unconscious mind, and this has to proceed slowly for both suicidal and nonsuicidal clients. The usefulness of the perspective for suicidal clients can be illustrated in the analysis of particular cases of suicide, such as that of Sylvia Plath, in which a psychoanalytic perspective reveals the deeper motives underlying the superficial precipitating causes for the suicide. However, there are few, if any, cases in which psychoanalytic therapy has been reported as the preferred method for a client whose major presenting problems are suicidal preoccupation and behavior.

Many of the papers by psychoanalysts on suicidal behavior, particularly on the motivations involved and on the problems of countertransference in psychotherapy with suicidal clients, have been collected in one volume by Maltsberger and Goldblatt (1996).

COGNITIVE THERAPY

The cognitive therapies are based on the notion that negative emotions and disturbing behaviors are a consequence of irrational thinking. The symptoms result not from the unpleasant events that we experience, but from our thoughts about those events. It is not the fact that we were fired from our jobs or that our spouse divorced us that makes us anxious or plunges us into despair. Rather, it is what we say to ourselves after these traumatic events that leads us to anxiety and despair.

The first systematic statement of these views was outlined by Ellis (1962, 1973) in his Rational-Emotive Therapy. For example, the client experiences rejection by a lover. This is the activating experience. In the unhealthy sequence, irrational beliefs are activated by this experience: "Isn't it awful that she rejected me? I am worthless. No desirable person will ever accept me. I should have done a better job of getting her to accept me. I deserve to be punished for my ineptness." Intense, unpleasant emotional states result from these irrational beliefs, such as anxiety, depression, worthlessness, or hostility. These emotional states are the consequence. In the healthy sequence, the activating experience is followed by a rational belief: "Isn't it unfortunate (or annoying or a pity) that she rejected me?" The consequence of the rational belief is an emotional state of regret, disappointment, or annoyance.

Cognitive psychotherapy involves teaching clients that their emotional states result not from the activating experiences, but from the irrational, absolutistic, and demanding beliefs they activate. Clients must be taught to dispute their irrational beliefs: "Why is it awful? How am I worthless? Where is the evidence that no one will ever love me? Why should I have done a better job? By what law do I deserve to be punished?" Once clients can substitute rational for irrational beliefs, they will be much happier and make appropriate choices.

Beck's (1976) cognitive-behavioral therapy is a more recent version of cognitive therapy. The goal of cognitive-behavioral therapy is to modify faulty patterns of thinking both directly and indirectly. It focuses on clients' cognitions (thoughts and attitudes) and the assumptions and premises that underlie them.

Clients are taught to recognize their idiosyncratic cognitions. The term *idiosyncratic* is used because the cognitions reflect a faulty appraisal of some aspect of the world. People may have a distorted perception or may misinterpret what they perceive. Despite the fact that the cognitions are faulty, they seem to clients to be plausible, and they occur involuntarily and automatically. Often, they lead to unpleasant emotions.

Clients are taught first to distance themselves from their cognitions. They then learn to examine their cognitions objectively, evaluate them critically, and distinguish between their evaluations and reality. Finally, clients are taught to correct their cognitive distortions. To do this, it helps if clients can specify the particular kind of fallacious thinking they practice. For example, the client who tends to overgeneralize makes unjustified generalizations on the basis of one incident, as when a single failure leads the client to believe that he or she will never succeed at anything.

Therapy provides a safe situation in which to test cognitions. Clients are helped to confront them and examine them. Clients transfer this learning process to real-life situations by directly modifying the thoughts and by rehearsing the reality-oriented thoughts.

Thought Patterns in Suicidal Individuals

Research has identified specific patterns of thought commonly found in suicidal individuals. Awareness of these patterns can help the cognitive therapist who is working with suicidal clients. For example, Neuringer (1988) has shown that suicidal people are prone to dichotomous thinking and tend to have rigid patterns of thought that hinder them in identifying solutions to the problems they face. Hughes and Neimeyer (1990) have elaborated on Neuringer's work, noting that suicidal people have closed themselves off from examining alternative solutions to suicide. In addition, a growing body of research indicates that suicidal people are extremely pessimistic and hopeless about the future (Beck, 1970; Lester, 1992). Even when compared with depressed clients in general, suicidal people have a higher level of hopelessness, which may be caused in part by irrational thinking, as proposed in Ellis's theory (Revere, 1985).

Trexler (1973) has noted that therapists may find it useful to focus cognitive therapy on these distortions. However, the decision to commit suicide is often an impulsive decision. It is important to point out to clients that impulsive decisions are usually bad decisions. It may be helpful to tell suicidal clients that individuals who survive a suicide attempt are almost invariably grateful, as well as to point out that a rash decision made at a time of emotional upheaval would be an error they could not correct. Thus, they should give the decision careful and prolonged consideration.

Several cases of cognitive therapy with suicidal clients have been published. Cautela (1970), Ellis (1989), Burns and Persons (1982), Emery, Hollon, and Bedrosian (1981), and Maultsby, Winkler, and Norton (1975) have reported cases in which they helped suicidal clients using cognitive therapy techniques. In addition, some researchers who are exploring suicidal individuals' cognitive distortions and deficiencies have devised therapeutic strategies to remedy them (Clum & Lerner, 1990; Linehan, Armstrong, Suarez, Allmon, & Heard, 1991).

Therapist Anxiety

Therapists who work with suicidal clients often feel great anxiety over the possibility that the client might commit suicide. If clients do commit suicide, psychotherapists may blame themselves and feel guilt for failing to help the clients. Trexler (1973) pointed out that these feelings are often the result of irrational thinking that needs to be challenged. Although therapists are responsible for their words and actions with clients, clients are ultimately responsible for their decisions and actions. Furthermore, the therapist's input into the client's life is but one small part of the total picture, and the therapist obviously has no control over the other inputs.

Discussion

Cognitive therapy is one of the few therapies for which current research on suicide is providing new insights and guidelines. Researchers are actively exploring the thinking patterns of the suicidal individual, and their discoveries will suggest possible dysfunctional thinking patterns for cognitive therapists to look for in their suicidal clients (Hughes & Neimeyer, 1990; Neuringer, 1988). A more detailed examination of the role of cognitive therapies in helping suicidal clients is presented by Mark Reinecke in Chapter 10 of this book.

TRANSACTIONAL ANALYSIS

Transactional analysis is a simplified, holistic conception of psychoanalysis, and transactional analysts have frequently written about suicidal behavior. They believe, in general, that the genesis of suicidal behavior lies in the early years of life when the child picks up "don't exist" injunctions from the parents and incorporates them into the script of the self (Woollams, Brown, & Huige, 1977). However, with rare exceptions, transactional analysts have not suggested ways in which transactional analysis can work with suicidal clients.

Transactional analysis proposes three ego states: the child ego state, which resembles the state of mind the individual had as a child; the adult ego state, a mature, information-processing state of mind; and the parent ego state, which is a state of mind based on the individual's identification with his or her parents or parent substitutes. Orten (1974) noted that it is the suicidal client's child ego state that is feeling despair and hopelessness and suggested that the counselor attempt to get the client's adult ego state in control at times of suicidal crises. Nurturing responses from the counselor's parent ego state will not accomplish this. Messages that convey, "Somebody loves you," "Promise me you won't kill yourself," or "I won't let you do it," simply reinforce the executive role of the client's child ego stage.

Asking questions designed to elicit information is the most effective method of getting the client's adult ego state to take control. The questions should be nonthreatening, that is, unrelated at first to the problems causing the suicidal preoccupation (e.g., ascertaining the client's current life situation—job, marriage, living arrangements). Prematurely rushing into consideration of the client's problems strengthens the child ego state's position. On being firmly established in the adult ego state, the client may immediately feel relief, because in this ego state he or she sees the world differently and feels more capable of dealing with it.

The counselor can then decide whether it would be useful to begin discussing the problems confronting the client or to postpone such a discussion to the next visit. If the counselor begins an exploration of the personal problems, he or she must be alert for signs that the child ego state is taking control again. If this happens, the counselor should recontact the adult ego state by moving away from the topics that have elicited the child ego state.

BEHAVIOR THERAPY

Behavior therapy focuses on trying to modify the client's behavior with little attention paid to the client's thoughts, desires, or emotions. In some cases, modifying the client's behaviors can result in reduced depression and suicidality. (Training in social skills can be an important technique [Gresham, 1998].) Behavior therapists have described how their techniques can be applied to suicidal clients. Stuart (1967) reported treatment of a suicidal client who was receiving inadequate reinforcement, and Jansson (1984) described a suicidal client with poor social skills. Bostock and Williams (1974) and O'Farrell, Goodenough, and Cutter (1981) have also reported treatment of suicidal clients with behavioral therapy, primarily by reinforcing appropriate behaviors while not reinforcing suicidal behaviors and with the use of behavioral contracts. More controversially, Farrelly and Brandsma (1974) used paradoxical intention with suicidal clients, such as suggesting that suicide would be a solution to clients' problems, softening the approach with humor. (Although paradoxical intention was used by Frankl [1963], who proposed an existential psychotherapy, paradoxical intention is really a simple behavioral therapy technique.)

In recent years, many behavior therapists have begun to include techniques derived from cognitive therapy and dialectical behavioral therapy in their treatment plans (Thorpe & Olson, 1997). For example, Kohlenberg and Tsai (2000) described an approach to working with chronically suicidal women using what they call "functional analytic psychotherapy," which is really a mix of behavior therapy and cognitive therapy. (Indeed, they call their article "Radical Behavioral Help for Katrina.") For example, in addition to teaching the client more empowering ways of thinking (cognitive therapy), they focused on increasing activities that brought pleasure and mastery (behavior therapy).

Rosenthal (1986) outlined steps for treating clients who are suicidal within the context of a learned-helplessness syndrome. First, clients sign a written contract to call the therapist if they feel suicidal. This shows clients that their behavior has had an effect on at least one person, the therapist. There is some debate, however, as to the usefulness of such contracts and the extent to which they should be used with suicidal clients (see Chapter 9 of this book).

Second, it helps if the therapist intervenes in the client's environment. For example, perhaps the therapist can talk to a suicidal teenager's parents. This shows clients that the therapist is on their side and that they do not have to tackle their problems alone. It demonstrates that the situation, although undesirable, is not catastrophic and can be approached rationally.

Third, Rosenthal suggested having clients keep a log of self-defeating thoughts and feelings. Unlike cognitive therapists, Rosenthal did not advocate challenging these thoughts and changing them. He believed that simply tabulating the thoughts lessens their frequency and impact.

Fourth, the therapist can work on anger. Rosenthal believed that anger and suicide are closely related. Shy and timid people need to be taught assertiveness skills and how to express anger in socially acceptable ways. Aggressive clients need to be given homework assignments in which they practice more empathic ways of expressing their feelings.

Finally, Rosenthal suggested that the therapist hold out hope that solutions are possible. For example, a teenager ignored by her parents can be told that the therapist will talk to them, or the teenager can be taught ways of dealing with them. A physically abused wife can be told that tomorrow the therapist will take her to court to get a police protection order and then to a women's shelter.

OTHER SYSTEMS OF PSYCHOTHERAPY

In addition to psychoanalysis, cognitive therapy, transactional analysis, and behavior therapy, other systems of psychotherapy may be useful for suicidal clients. I have discussed the applicability of these systems for the treatment of suicidal clients elsewhere (Lester, 1991), and in this section I briefly outline a few of them.

Primal Therapy

Primal therapy is a derivative of psychoanalysis in which clients are made to experience primal experiences and emotions early in therapy and intensely, and the extreme emotions aroused during primal therapy might be thought to be too stressful for suicidal individuals. However, Janov (1974) has reported using primal therapy with suicidal clients with no adverse effects.

Gestalt Therapy

Gestalt therapy (Perls, Hefferline, & Goodman, 1951), a more confrontive style of therapy than many other systems, might also be thought to be too stressful for suicidal clients. There is also perhaps a danger in having suicidal clients dwell too intensely and too experientially on the "here and now" of their feelings. However, some Gestalt therapists have worked through the current feelings of suicidal clients (e.g., Goulding & Goulding, 1978; Whitaker & Keith, 1981). More recently, Young and Lester (2001) have suggested that some Gestalt therapy techniques may be useful as adjuncts in crisis intervention.

Some psychotherapists may not feel comfortable with encouraging such reencounters. The psychotherapist must be very experienced in using such techniques so that he or she can monitor the client's psychological state carefully during the experiences and calm the client when necessary. In addition, when closing the therapy session with the suicidal client, the therapist should take greater care than usual to ensure that the client has achieved a temporary resolution of the conflicts and feelings just experienced. (Other therapy systems, such as voice therapy [Firestone, 1986; see Chapter 11 of this book], Morita therapy [Reynolds, 1984], psychodrama [Yablonsky, 1976], and movement therapy [Chapman, 1971] have some similarities to aspects of Gestalt therapy and have been used successfully with suicidal clients.)

Alexander and Harman (1988) used Gestalt therapy techniques to help sixth-graders cope with the suicide of a classmate. Their goal was to help the students become aware of their thoughts, feelings, and sensations about the incident and to legitimize their feelings of betrayal and resentment. Many of the students expressed anxiety about losing other friends to suicide and about their own suicidal potential. Among the techniques used was having the students address the chair in which the dead boy sat in the classroom, either verbally, nonverbally or sub-vocally (by looking at the chair and saying goodbye), or in writing. Alexander and Harman also ran short-term and long-term small groups for the students who needed them. Bengesser (1989) has used the empty-chair technique of Gestalt therapy to help the process of catharsis in those who have lost a loved one to suicide. (Bengesser has also used psychodrama to facilitate catharsis and logotherapy to help clients find a meaning in the suicide of their significant other.)

Reality Therapy

Adherents of reality therapy (Wubbolding, 1989), which focuses largely on what the client is doing, making value judgments, and formulating plans, also find that suicidal clients pose no particular problem and can be helped by its standard techniques. Illustrative cases have been de-scribed by Lutter (1980), Wubbolding (1980), and Ingram and Hinkle (1990). Since reality therapists are willing to use any techniques to help clients carry through the plans, their therapy often uses techniques from other systems of psychotherapy. For example, Ingram and Hinkle (1990) helped their suicidal client with behavior therapy techniques—increas-ing interactions with friends and improving her job-hunting activities.

Person-Centered Therapy

Person-centered therapy (Rogers, 1959) has long been the basis for the crisis counseling of suicidal clients (Hamelinck, 1990; Kalafat, 2002). The usefulness of this therapy in suicidal crisis counseling has now been widely acknowledged. Person-centered therapy differs from other therapies in maintaining that simply listening empathically to clients is sufficient for therapy. However, most psychotherapists would not ac-cept this theory. A good example of Carl Rogers's approach to a hypo-thetical case is his analysis of the suicide of Ellen West reported by Ludwig Binswanger (Rogers, 1961).

More recently, Jooste and Cleaver (1992) described the use of metaphorical objects to facilitate person-centered therapy. They pre-sented a piece of charcoal to a woman who had attempted suicide and who felt worthless and unhappy, demonstrating how the charcoal black-ened her fingers and appeared to be strong, but could easily be broken into pieces. The client reflected on the charcoal and saw that it embodied her black mood. She reflected that she looked strong on the outside, but she did not experience herself as strong. She reflected that charcoal could be used to make a fire and that she, too, had a spark of life within her. Jooste and Cleaver observed that the charcoal (used as a metaphor) helped the client to experience aspects of herself of which she had hitherto not been aware.

Existential Therapy

Existential psychotherapy (Yalom, 1980), with its focus on death, isolation, will, and the search for a meaning of life, would seem to have promise for treating suicidal clients. However, existential therapists have not written about suicidal behavior, although occasional case studies of suicidal clients have been published (e.g., Corey, 1991; Frankl, 1963).

Discussion

The usefulness of systematically considering the major forms of psychotherapy for their applicability to the treatment of suicidal clients is that the theorists of each system take a rather narrow and extreme position about the rationale for, purpose of, and techniques of their system of psychotherapy, exploring their perspective to the full, which permits examination of the power of the system acting in isolation. For example, what can psychoanalysis or person-centered therapy achieve if either is used exclusively with a suicidal client? It also reveals where the system of therapy fails, for example, what issues it overlooks, and for which types of suicidal clients it may not be appropriate.

The practicing psychotherapist, in contrast, is able to use whatever theory and techniques best fit the client, both in the long term and in each moment of therapy. Thus, despite their orientation, psychotherapists often need to be eclectic in their approach, drawing on whatever system of psychotherapy seems appropriate in the moment. For example, if the client experiences an acute suicidal crisis, the psychotherapist can use the short-term strategies suggested by transactional analysts and behavior therapists or use a standard crisis-counseling approach. After the suicidal crisis has subsided, the psychotherapist can then switch to more long-term strategies, such as modifying dysfunctional patterns of thinking or undertaking a psychoanalytic exploration of the client's conflicts. Suicidal clients may thus be able to make use of all of the techniques discussed herein to leave the abyss of despair. (A good example is the work of Meech and Wood [2000] with a suicidal 12-year old with a history of severe childhood privation. They described their approach as informed by various models: systemic, solution-focused, narrative, cognitive-behavioral, Ericksonian, provocative, and psychoanalytic. Halgin [1989] worked with a 19-year-old college freshman with suicidal ideation using what Halgin called pragmatic blending, a systematic eclecticism employing psychodynamic, interpersonal, person-centered, and behavioral models.)

REFERENCES

Alexander, J. A. C., & Harman, R. L. (1988). One counselor's intervention in the aftermath of a middle school student's suicide. *Journal of Counseling and Development, 66,* 283–285.

Beck, A. T. (1970). The core problem in depression. *Science and Psychoanalysis, 17,* 47–55.

Beck, A. T. (1976). *Cognitive therapy and emotional disorders.* New York: International Universities Press.

Bengesser, G. (1989). After suicide-postvention. *European Journal of Psychiatry, 3,* 116–119.

Bostock, T., & Williams, C. L. (1974). Attempted suicide as an operant behavior. *Archives of General Psychiatry, 31,* 482–486.

Burns, D., & Persons, J. (1982). Hope and hopelessness. In L. E. Abt & I. R. Stuart (Eds.), *The newer therapies* (pp. 33–57). New York: Van Nostrand Reinhold.

Cautela, J. R. (1970, September). *The modification of behaviors that influence the probability of suicide in elders.* Paper presented at the 78th Annual Convention of the American Psychological Association, Miami.

Chapman, M. (1971). Movement therapy in the treatment of suicidal patients. *Perspectives in Psychiatric Care, 9*(3), 119–122.

Clum, G. A., & Lerner, M. (1990). A problem solving approach to treating individuals at risk for suicide. In D. Lester (Ed.), *Current concepts of suicide* (pp. 194–202). Philadelphia: Charles Press.

Corey, G. (1991). *Case approach to counseling and psychotherapy.* Pacific Grove, CA: Brooks/Cole.

Ellis, A. (1962). *Reason and emotion in psychotherapy.* Secaucus, NJ: Lyle Stuart.

Ellis, A. (1973). *Humanistic psychotherapy.* New York: Julian.

Ellis, A. (1989). Using rational-emotive therapy (RET) as crisis intervention. *Individual Psychology, 45,* 75–81.

Emery, G., Hollon, S. D., & Bedrosian, R. C. (1981). *New directions in cognitive therapy.* New York: Guilford Press.

Farrelly, F., & Brandsma, J. M. (1974). *The beginnings of provocative therapy.* Cupertino, CA: Meta.

Firestone, R. W. (1986). The "inner voice" and suicide. *Psychotherapy, 23,* 439–447.

Frankl, V. E. (1963). *Man's search for meaning.* New York: Pocket Books.

Fremouw, W. J., de Perczel, M., & Ellis, T. E. (1990). *Suicide risk.* New York: Pergamon Press.

Gerisch, B. (1998). This is not death, it is something safer: A psychodynamic approach to Sylvia Plath. *Death Studies, 22,* 735–761.

Goulding, R. C., & Goulding, M. M. (1978). *The power is the patient.* San Francisco: TA Press.

Gresham, F. M. (1998). Social skills training with children. In T. S. Watson & F. M. Gresham (Eds.), *Handbook of child behavior therapy* (pp. 475–497). New York: Plenum Press.

Halgin, R. P. (1989). Pragmatic blending. *Journal of Integrative and Eclectic Psychotherapy, 8,* 320–328.

Hamelinck, L. (1990). Client-centered therapy and psychiatric crisis intervention following suicide attempts. In G. Lietaer, J. Rombauts, & R. van Balen (Eds.), *Client-centered and experiential psychotherapy in the nineties* (pp. 579–597). Leuven, Belgium: Leuven University Press.

Hughes, S. L., & Neimeyer, R. A. (1990). A cognitive model of suicidal behavior. In D. Lester (Ed.), *Current concepts of suicide* (pp. 1–28). Philadelphia: Charles Press.

Ingram, J. K., & Hinkle, J. S. (1990). Reality therapy and the scientist. *Journal of Reality Therapy, 10*(1), 54–58.

Janov, A. (1974). Further implications of "level of consciousness." *Journal of Primal Therapy, 1,* 193–212.

Jansson, L. (1984). Social skills training for unipolar depression. *Scandinavian Journal of Behavior Therapy, 13,* 237–241.

Jooste, E. T., & Cleaver, G. (1992). Metaphors and metaphoric objects. *Journal of Phenomenological Psychology, 23,* 136–148.

Kalafat, J. (2002). Crisis intervention and counseling by telephone. In D. Lester (Ed.), *Crisis intervention and counseling by telephone* (pp. 64–82). Springfield, IL: Charles C. Thomas.

Kohlenberg, R. J., & Tsai, M. (2000). Radical behavioral help for Katrina. *Cognitive and Behavioral Practice, 7,* 500–505.

Leenaars, A. A. (1991). Suicide notes and their implications for intervention. *Crisis, 12,* 1–20.

Lester, D. (1988). *Suicide from a psychological perspective.* Springfield, IL: Charles C. Thomas.

Lester, D. (1991). *Psychotherapy for suicidal clients.* Springfield, IL: Charles C. Thomas.

Lester, D. (1992). *Why people kill themselves.* Springfield, IL: Charles C. Thomas.

Linehan, M. M., Armstrong, H. E., Suarez, A., Allmon, D., & Heard, H. L. (1991). Cognitive-behavioral treatment of chronically parasuicidal borderline patients. *Archives of General Psychiatry, 48,* 1060–1064.

Litman, R. E. (1967). Sigmund Freud on suicide. In E. S. Shneidman (Ed.), *Essay in self-destruction* (pp. 324–344). New York: Science House.

Lutter, A. (1980). Jennifer joins the club. In N. Glasser (Ed.), *What are you doing?* (pp. 1–17). New York: Harper & Row.

Maltsberger, J. T., & Goldblatt, M. J. (1996). *Essential papers on suicide.* New York: New York University Press.

Maultsby, M. C., Winkler, P. J., & Norton, J. C. (1975). Semi-automated psychotherapy with preventive features. *International Academy of Preventive Medicine, 2*(3), 27–37.

Meech, C., & Wood, A. (2000). Reconnecting past, present and future lives. *Australian and New Zealand Journal of Family Therapy, 21*(2), 102–107.

Neuringer, C. (1988). The thinking processes in suicidal women. In D. Lester (Ed.), *Why women kill themselves* (pp. 43–52). Springfield, IL: Charles C. Thomas.

O'Farrell, T. J., Goodenough, D. D., & Cutter, H. S. G. (1981). Behavioral contracting for repeated suicide attempts. *Behavior Modification, 5,* 255–272.

Orten, J. D. (1974). A transactional approach to suicide prevention. *Clinical Social Work Journal, 2,* 57–63.

Perls, F. S., Hefferline, R. F., & Goodman, P. (1951). *Gestalt therapy.* New York: Julian.

Plath, S. (1966). *Ariel.* New York: Harper & Row.

Revere, V. L. (1985). Treatment of suicidal patients. *Independent Practitioner, 5,* 17–18.

Reynolds, D. K. (1984). Morita therapy and suicide prevention. *Crisis, 5,* 37–44.

Richman, J., & Eyman, J. R. (1990). Psychotherapy of suicide. In D. Lester (Ed.), *Current concepts of suicide* (pp. 139–158). Philadelphia: Charles Press.

Rogers, C. R. (1959). A theory of therapy, personality, and interpersonal relationships, as developed in the client-centered framework. In S. Koch (Ed.), *Psychology: A study of a science* (Vol. 3, pp. 184–256). New York: McGraw-Hill.

Rogers, C. R. (1961). The loneliness of contemporary man as seen in "The Case of Ellen West." *Annals of Psychotherapy, 2,* 94–101.

Rosenthal, H. (1986). The learned helplessness syndrome. *Emotional First Aid, 3*(2), 5–8.

Rudestam, K. E. (1985–1986). Suicide and the selfless patient. *Psychotherapy and the Patient, 2,* 83–95.

Stuart, R. B. (1967). Casework treatment of depression viewed as an interpersonal disturbance. *Social Work, 12,* 27–36.

Thorpe, G. L., & Olson, S. L. (1997). *Behavior therapy.* Boston: Allyn & Bacon.

Trexler, L. (1973). The suicidal person and the restoration of hope. *Rational Living, 8*(2), 19–23.

Whitaker, C. A., & Keith, D. V. (1981). Symbolic-experiential therapy. In A. S. Gurman & D. P. Kniskern (Eds.), *Handbook of family therapy* (pp. 187–225). New York: Brunner/Mazel.

Woollams, S., Brown, M., & Huige, K. (1977). What transactional analysts want their clients to know. In G. Barnes (Ed.), *Transactional analysis after Eric Berne* (pp. 487–525). New York: Harper's College Press.

Wubbolding, R. E. (1980). Teenage loneliness. In N. Glasser (Ed.), *What are you doing?* (pp. 120–129). New York: Harper & Row.

Wubbolding, R. E. (1989). Professional issues: Four stages of decision making in suicidal client recovery. *Journal of Reality Therapy, 8*(2), 57–61.

Yablonsky, L. (1976). *Psychodrama.* New York: Basic Books.

Yalom, I. D. (1980). *Existential psychotherapy.* New York: Basic Books.

Young, L., & Lester, D. (2001). Gestalt therapy approaches to crisis intervention with suicidal clients. *Brief Treatment and Crisis Intervention, 1,* 65–74.

CHAPTER 8

Crisis Intervention in the Context of Outpatient Treatment of Suicidal Patients

John Kalafat and Maureen M. Underwood

The goal of this chapter is to provide pragmatic guidelines for the crisis intervention component of outpatient therapy with suicidal patients. We chose this secondary prevention focus for several reasons. First, more mental health professionals are likely to be addressing suicidal crises as part of outpatient treatment in the public or private sector than as staff of specialized crisis services, such as psychiatric emergency services or telephone crisis services. When a client presents with suicidality upon intake, most clinicians recognize the need for some type of risk assessment. When the suicidality arises in the course of established treatment, however, the need to stop, assess, and manage might be overlooked.

Second, the staff of such crisis services are likely to have specialized training in crisis intervention, whereas most graduate training in the core helping professions does not include adequate training in crisis intervention or the treatment and management of suicidal persons (Bongar, 2002). Third, in the current managed care environment, practitioners must be able to work with suicidal patients on an outpatient basis because access to inpatient care is highly restricted. Finally, most community-based suicide prevention programs focus on increasing public awareness of suicide and treatment resources or on the training of gatekeepers, such as school personnel and physicians, to recognize individuals who are at risk for suicide and to refer them to professional treatment. This approach will be effective only if mental health practitioners to whom these individuals are referred are competent to work with suicidal patients.

Crisis intervention is one component in the assessment, management, and treatment of suicidal patients. Additional components of this approach are addressed elsewhere in this volume. This chapter outlines a framework for crisis intervention in suicide management that is guided by a basic conceptualization of suicide that incorporates crisis intervention principles and goals. Additional variables that are critical to clinically sound outpatient management of suicidal patients and issues that tend to be underemphasized by therapists in working with suicidal patients are also addressed.

CONCEPTUALIZING SUICIDE

While a great deal of information about both understanding and assessing suicide risk is available in scholarly volumes (e.g., Jacobs, 1999), the current reality of outpatient treatment in either the public or the private sector tends to be fast-paced, with a press to see as many clients as possible within a given amount of time. Under these circumstances, it may be challenging for all but the most diligent clinician to extrapolate from the available resources a conceptualization of suicide that is both clinically accurate and practical for application in treatment interventions. Certainly, demographic and historical risk factors are relatively easy to ascertain, and checklists exist to facilitate their review in relation to a particular client (Jacobs, 1999). However, while checklists can provide a general guide, risk assessment is best done through an interview by a caregiver who is knowledgeable about the dynamics of suicide. Such knowledge informs the practical and pertinent questions that need to be explored in crisis assessment.

To facilitate the training of mental health professionals in a variety of outpatient settings, we have found that five characteristics of suicide, based in part on three characteristics listed in an early manual of the Los Angeles Suicide Prevention Center (Farbereow, Heilig, & Litman, 1968), provide a framework for specific interview questions about the dynamics of suicide for a particular client. While simple in their approach to what is undeniably a complicated emotional problem, these characteristics recognize the intrapsychic depletion of clients who are contemplating suicide and suggest questions about its personal meaning in a way that encourages meaningful exploration. Their application in a crisis contact begins the process of crisis intervention by focusing on the circumstances that precipitated the current suicidal episode and on the client's feelings about his or her choice of suicide as a problem-solving option. Questions derived from these characteristics of suicide can not only provide an organizing structure to the suicide assessment but also help the client begin to separate and compartmentalize the complex feelings and events that have led him or her to contemplate suicide. These questions acknowledge the client's suicidal crisis in clear, specific detail, thus promoting a climate of open self-disclosure by the client, which is essential to the development of an effective treatment plan that accurately targets the suicidal risks. Just by asking directive questions, the therapist signals his or her willingness to acknowledge and address the client's pain and to support the client in finding a life-affirming solution. Unfortunately, many mental health professionals are intimidated by the suicidal thoughts and feelings of their clients and pursue only cursory examination of either their depths or implications. We cannot overemphasize how important it is that the therapist not simply sit with the client's pain but also confront it in patient, supportive detail. Questions that are derived from the following five characteristics of suicide can provide the structure for these essential interventions:

1. Suicide is viewed as an *alternative,* a solution to a problem or a feeling of intense emotional pain that the client feels is not resolvable by any other means. Asking simply and clearly, "What's going on in your life right now that makes you think that death is the best way out?" focuses the client on the concrete and specific life circumstance that has led to the current suicidal crisis. The response to this question identifies for both the client and the therapist the precipitating problem and joins them in the process of crisis resolution. The therapist immediately becomes part of the solution with this question and is a key element in the crisis intervention strategy, rather than remaining merely an observer of the client's distress.

The client's affective or cognitive confusion, or the complexity of the problem itself, may require that the therapist ask guiding, directive questions to assist the client in articulating what finally pushed him or her over the edge and made suicide seem to be the only remaining problem-solving choice. Because suicidal thoughts and impulses can feel chaotic and overwhelming, clients may need continued directive exploration from the clinician through concrete questions and comments that help clarify the client's state of mind. Though the end product of suicide is death, questions about why a person wants to die can feel ephemeral to clients whose thought processes may be clouded by their current state of psychic depletion. Shneidman (1985) has contended that the main purpose of suicide is cessation of pain; thus, questions about death essentially miss the point. As a 45-year-old female reported:

> When I finally got up the nerve to tell my therapist that I was thinking about suicide, he didn't miss a beat and asked me why I wanted to die. "I just don't want to live," I told him. But then he asked the same question two more times in slightly different ways, and I felt so stupid because I didn't know what answer he wanted, so I told him I didn't really mean it and that was that.

2. A person who is thinking about suicide is in *crisis*. The crisis state is characterized by cognitive constriction or tunnel thinking (Shneidman, 1985). One way to reduce the anxiety that causes such constriction is to acknowledge the client's feelings and encourage the client to express or ventilate feelings. This can provide the cathartic relief that is essential to the resumption of effective personal problem solving.

But it can be challenging, even to a seasoned therapist, to simply listen to the despair of a suicidal client without prematurely pursuing resolution. We all know from personal experience the frustration of trying to express feelings to a listener who is more intent on solving our problem than simply listening to how we are feeling or what we are thinking. Short-circuiting the expression of feelings, especially when they carry the desperation and isolation of suicide, can make the listener feel relieved, while the client feels only half-heard or even misunderstood. Since many suicidal clients report feeling disconnected from both their feelings and the world around them, a therapeutic contact that unintentionally reinforces this sense of disconnection could be devastating. Taking the time to really listen to the nuances and complexities inherent in the client's hopelessness and desperation can not only diminish the intensity of these feelings but also reduce the client's isolation, which is another goal of a crisis contact.

> I no more got the words out of my mouth that I felt like running my car into a tree when the doctor was writing out a prescription for medication. "Here," he said, "take this and you should feel better." He never even let me tell him that my car was in Florida, and I wasn't going there for another couple of months. Or the fact that my dear wife of 46 years had just passed away. I threw the prescription away when I walked out the door.
>
> —Angelo, Age 67

While antidepressant medication can certainly be an effective adjunct to psychotherapy, it should not be recommended prematurely. Even if it is immediately clear that a client could benefit from psychotropic medication, discretion must be used in the timing of the recommendation. Medication should complement, not substitute for, a therapeutic relationship and, at times, it appears that medication recommendations are prompted more by the provider's anxiety than the client's.

3. The thinking of most suicidal clients is characterized by *ambivalence,* and many clients have the awareness that two feelings exist simultaneously: the wish to live versus the wish to die or escape.

> I confused even myself. Within five minutes, I was thinking about what I was going to plant in my garden in the spring, and then I remembered how I wouldn't be here and they could put my ashes in with the lilies if I got them in soon enough. I felt so crazy!
>
> —Tony, age 72

Reminding suicidal people that ambivalent thinking is normal is a critical intervention. Clients who are not used to experiencing dichotomous thinking may be even more confused and frightened by this juxtaposition of thoughts. Therefore, reassuring them that these conflicting thoughts are normal is important. This reassurance must also include the stated therapeutic intention to lend support to the part of the client that wants to live. These two key elements of this intervention must occur in tandem; that is, both the wish to live and the wish to die must be addressed. The client might see ignoring or minimizing the wish to die as being dismissive of his or her most troubling feelings, so it is very important to clearly state the recognition of this side of the ambivalent cognitions. Minimizing the client's negative thoughts can have other unwanted consequences.

> When I talked to my guidance counselor about thinking about wanting to die, she told me that only losers did that. I knew right then I could never tell her that I had taken some pills the other night.
>
> —Nicole, age 14

When clients suspect that the caregiver will apply negative judgments to the behaviors with which they struggle, their honest self-disclosure during the interview may be limited. What is intended by the therapist to be reassuring comments about the client's strengths and personal resiliencies feels punitive and judgmental to the client. These miscommunications may be subtle and insidious, but they point to the critical need for therapists to examine honestly their own feelings and attitudes about suicide and to be conscious and intentional in how they are supportive of their client's distress.

A useful technique for emphasizing and supporting the client's wish to live is to engage the client in a conversation about his or her reasons to live. Linehan's inventory (Linehan, Goodstein, Nielsen, & Chiles, 1983) provides a helpful starting point for this discussion, and the therapist is encouraged to both explore in detail and support the client's reasons to continue living, no matter how trivial or mundane they may seem. Honesty or genuineness is critical at this point because clients in crisis are often keenly perceptive of therapists who offer disingenuous reassurance. It is also important to be alert to potential countertransferential reactions (Maltsberger & Buie, 1974). Initially, clients cannot offer more than one or two reasons to live. As treatment progresses, the number of reasons to live usually increases, even if the reasons to die do not decrease proportionately.

4. There is an *irrational* quality to suicidal thinking. When asked what they think will happen when they die, many suicidal people will relate, with some degree of righteous satisfaction, the details of their funerals or what they expect to happen in their honor after they die. A 12-year-old junior high student wrote in a suicide note to her parents:

> After I die, maybe they'll put up a plaque for me in the front hall of the school. Then all the kids who are mean to me will feel sorry for how they treated me.

These observations can be challenging to refute since details of afterlife are the purview of only the deceased. Rather than engaging in futile discussion about irrational observations that cannot be proved or disproved, a safe therapeutic course is to return to the previous conversation about reasons to live. These very specific, concrete reasons to live, enumerated in the client's own language, can be offered in counterpoint to an amorphous conversation about an afterlife. Also, what the client has offered about his or her perception about life after his or her death can be seen as indicative of the struggles in this life that the client wishes would be resolved, and it may be appropriate to share this observation with the client. These struggles, along with the presenting problem, should direct the course of therapeutic activities in the immediate aftermath of the suicidal crisis. The therapist can help the client to explore ways to attain the recognition or revenge involved in these fantasies that do not involve suicide. For example, as the saying goes, living well is the best revenge.

5. Suicide is an act of *communication*. If we see suicidal behavior as an attempt to *act on* unbearable psychic pain, we can appreciate that the client's ability to *talk about* that pain has vanished. Again, a simple question, "Whom did you want your suicide to send a message to and what is that message?" returns the client to the higher level of verbal functioning where healthier coping options can be explored. There is usually convergence in this answer with the presenting problem and the client's perceived life struggles, and it can be helpful for the therapist to make these connections for the client. We know that crises can compromise communication skills, and clients are often reassured when the therapist can verbally connect the parts of their lives that feel so distressingly disconnected. The therapist needs to find out who else is involved in the suicidal context and ask what their reaction to the client's distress has been and what their anticipated and/or wished for response to the client's suicide would be.

> I felt like there was a sheet of glass separating me from everything and everybody in my life and then, all of a sudden, one of the things I was supposed to do but had forgotten about came crashing into the glass and shattered a piece of me. And when I would try to talk about it, I couldn't find the right words, so I wouldn't say anything at all, which made it even worse. So killing myself was one way I could stop it all. I would shatter the glass so at least I would be prepared for when it was coming. I don't know how my therapist figured this out. I know I never told her because, as I said, I couldn't really tell anyone, but she just got it, and put words to it, and it started to make sense to me.
>
> —Rebecca, age 43

Since every therapeutic encounter is built on communication between the therapist and the client, this final characteristic of suicide is the binding thread that runs through the entire process of crisis intervention. Using both verbal and nonverbal skills, the therapist communicates a safe, predictable, and supportive presence where the client can find the hope and supplemental ego strength that are necessary for resolution of the suicidal crisis.

DEVELOPMENT OF A SUICIDAL CRISIS

In addition to these characteristics, it is helpful to understand the client's experiences that lead to a suicide crisis. The work of Motto (1977) is instructive in outlining a step-by-step progression through a series of cognitive steps, which allow a person to gradually think of suicide as an acceptable means for dealing with pain. For example, a person must:

1. Be faced with a problem that is perceived as unsolvable.
2. View the problem as continuing despite his or her best efforts to solve it.
3. See suicide as the only solution.
4. Conceptualize suicide as ego-syntonic.
5. Disregard all other problem-solving options.
6. Believe death will bring relief.

Other authors have conceptualized the suicidal crisis as a tunnel into which a person at risk descends as he or she struggles with what feels like an unsolvable problem. Healthy problem-solving alternatives gradually give way as the tunnel narrows, and the person feels increasingly alone, discouraged, and helpless in his or her pain. The tunnel finally narrows to its end point, which is suicide. A particularly helpful aspect of this tunnel metaphor is in demonstrating that even one crisis contact can return the suicidal person to the domain of a healthy problem-solving alternative. In sum, these characteristics of suicide can provide a framework for joining with clients, acknowledging and tolerating their morbid feelings, identifying the precipitants of their crises, and exploring alternatives to suicide. At the same time, the therapist must provide a safe, structured holding environment within which helping can take place.

Necessary Components of Outpatient Care of Suicidal Patients

The purpose of hospitalization is to provide a safe holding environment for suicidal patients when they are unable to ensure their own safety. Similarly, the support and structure elements of the crisis approach serve to provide a holding environment on an outpatient basis. Most clinicians understand that a major part of the therapeutic relationship is their ability to "hold" or deal with their patient's anxiety and suicidal feelings—Shneidman's (1985) pain, perturbation, and press (impulse to act). Doing this requires a more active and flexible therapeutic approach than is usually common in most clinical practice, as well as a great deal of self-awareness on the part of the therapist to guard against some of the unfortunate judgments that can compromise effective crisis interventions. While it may be challenging, for example, to remain open-minded with a client who has a history of multiple suicide attempts, Linehan's (1993) work with borderline personality disorders provides lessons about avoiding the pejorative judgment of "manipulative" in work with these types of clients. No matter how experienced the clinician, the *sine qua non* of crisis intervention with suicidal clients is the clinician's willingness to carefully examine his or her biases and prejudices about self-injurious behavior.

Several other critical elements necessary to provide outpatient support and structure to suicidal clients are discussed in the following sections.

Assessment and Diagnosis

Whether the suicidal crisis occurs in the beginning or the middle of therapy, the clinician must conduct an immediate evaluation that includes a suicide risk assessment, mental status exam, and thorough history. With new clients, records of previous treatment and medication must be promptly obtained. The assessment should conclude with a determination of risk status that is based on the clearly delineated variables that were obtained during the interview and a multiaxial diagnosis. Some experts recommend that a brief assessment of suicide risk status be conducted at the start of each session (Jobes & Berman, 1993).

Treatment and Crisis Plans

There must be a written treatment plan derived from this assessment that is agreed to by the patient. In addition, a written crisis plan must be developed with the patient. This crisis plan specifies what the patient and clinician will do if the patient experiences an acute suicidal episode, that is, if his or her suicidal feelings become difficult to control. The crisis plan should record common precipitants to suicidal feelings, alternate ways of coping beside suicidal behavior, and methods of accessing emergency care if the coping plan does not appear to be sufficient for controlling the suicidal urge. The plan should also include an agreement for the patient to contact whatever emergency response resources the clinician and patient have agreed to employ.

Contract

We agree with those who contend that the use of *no-suicide* contracts is ineffective in the management of suicidal clients (e.g., Maltsberger & Buie, 1989). Even the use of the term *contract* implies a legal document, although most clinicians who use this strategy recognize that it would not stand up in court. We believe that an agreement to contact the predetermined emergency response resource is more constructive than a no-suicide contract. No-suicide contracts appear to dismiss the fluctuations in suicidal urges that are often intrinsic to a suicide crisis, whereas an agreement to contact resources acknowledges that suicidal feelings may become acute even after what the client perceives to have been a helpful intervention. Educating the client about the transient nature of suicidal impulses and providing a strategy to respond to them empower the client to take an active role in his or her care. The contract may be to call the clinician, or, if he or she is not available, a local emergency service such as a crisis hotline or psychiatric emergency service. The effectiveness of this intervention may be enhanced by an existing relationship between the therapist and the client, so this strategy is less useful in a psychiatric emergency service.

Radical Availability

Radical availability refers to the ability of the clinician to provide 24-hour emergency response capability. A group practice model in which there is a rotating on-call schedule is one way this availability can be provided in either a public or private outpatient setting. Alternatively, the clinician can instruct the patient to contact a local 24-hour emergency service provider when he or she is not available. If clinicians elect to use a local emergency service, they should obtain a release from the patient, inform the emergency agency of their plan, and provide the agency with basic necessary information about the patient, such as the patient's name, address, phone number, and the crisis response plan agreed on with the patient. Clinicians should provide their own phone number and request that they be contacted if an emergency response such as outreach and/or hospitalization is implemented. This attenuates fragmentation of care and provides the emergency agency with information that is needed when dealing with acute crises.

In some communities, there are crisis hotlines that are not qualified or capable to respond to suicidal callers. Crisis hotlines that are certified by the American Association of Suicidology or Contact USA are so qualified. Essentially, the hotline must have the following *minimum* components:

1. *Screening:* All staff, whether paid or volunteer, should be screened according to standard, written criteria.
2. *Training:* Staff must receive criterion-referenced skills training. That is, they should be trained to an acceptable level of performance through a demonstration-practice-feedback process. Training programs that focus only on content information or consist of a series of guest speakers are insufficient.
3. *Written standard operating procedures:* Procedures for responding to high-risk suicidal callers, contacting backups and other first responders, and tracing or using caller ID must be in place.
4. *Two phone lines at minimum:* This is necessary for contacting backups, tracing calls, and other emergency procedures while maintaining contact with the caller. Many crisis lines also have call-conferencing capacity, which enables helpers to bring other agencies into the call with the caller and ensures smooth referrals.
5. *Twenty-four hour backup* on site or on call by experienced supervisory staff.

6. *Established relationships* with other emergency responders, such as police, medical/psychiatric emergency services, rescue squads, ambulance services, phone companies, and the like.

If any *one* of these is missing, the crisis line cannot be used as a backup.

Another component of radical availability consists of flexibility on the part of the clinician in scheduling sessions. Initially, it may be necessary to see the patient more often than for the standard weekly session (Bongar, Peterson, Harris, & Aissis, 1989). Also, the judicious use of scheduled telephone contacts can help to bridge the gap between sessions and can contribute to the outpatient-holding environment. These contacts can be reduced as the suicidal crisis diminishes in intensity and treatment progresses.

Confidentiality and Informed Consent

At the onset of treatment, clients must be informed of the limits of confidentiality (Simon, 1987). This means that the clinician will break confidentiality and contact emergency responders and/or natural supports if the patient is considered to be at risk for harming himself or herself and/or others. Discussion of both the protections and limits of confidentiality can occur in the context of the provision of informed consent, which refers to efforts to involve the patient in discussions about the risks and benefits of particular courses of action. If the patient disagrees with a recommended course of action, he or she must be informed of his or her right to a second opinion, and the clinician should facilitate such a consultation (Bongar, 2002).

Consultation

The prudent mental health practitioner seeks consultation from trusted and informed colleagues whenever there is a question about a clinically indicated course of action. This consultation is of essential and critical importance when the client is suicidal, and the practitioner is advised to seek consultation on high-risk suicidal patients from a professional colleague who has experience with suicidal patients (Bongar et al., 1989). Basic treatment and crisis plans and major dispositional decisions can be reviewed with this consultant. With a client at risk for suicide, psychiatric consultation is always a sound therapeutic strategy. An evaluation for both psychotropic medication as well as the feasibility of outpatient treatment can be obtained from a psychiatrist who has the ability to admit the client to an inpatient facility if a less restrictive course of treatment appears contraindicated.

Documentation

Careful record keeping is an important part of all clinical work. In the active, crisis-oriented management of suicidal patients, careful and detailed documentation is even more critical. This documentation should include evidence of a suicide risk assessment, the decisions made on the basis of those documented risks, a plan of action that addresses those risks in a timely fashion, and consultation that supports this plan of action. Collateral contacts, either by person or over the telephone, should also be documented, and the wise clinician will also include documentation of even unsuccessful attempts to obtain such ancillary information. In making the point that, if it isn't written down, it did not happen, Gutheil (1980) referred to this process as thinking out loud for the record. For example, Packman and Harris (1998) describe a model risk-benefit progress note as including (1) an assessment of suicide risk, (2) the information that led to the finding of risk, (3) which high and low risk factors were present, (4) what questions were asked and what answers were given by the patient and collateral sources, and (5) how this information led to the actions taken and rejected. Another example involves documenting a consultation. There must be a record of the specific content of the consult, including the questions and/or decisions discussed and the reasons for accepting and/or rejecting the consultant's advice. The thoroughness and even the neatness of the clinical records contribute to the overall judgments as to the adequacy of the treatment and risk management (Bongar, 2002).

Total Environmental Assessment

An environmental assessment recognizes that clients do not exist in isolation and leads to a continuously updated map of the risks (stressors, gaps in support or resources) and benefits (supports, including individuals, organizations, and activities) in the client's environment. Beginning with basic information that includes all relevant phone numbers, the patient's license plate number, and the address and appropriate information about the patient's location (e.g., its remoteness or isolation and whether the client lives alone), the assessment also provides a description of the patient's access to members of his or her social support system. Most critically, it should reflect whether the patient has access to lethal means and, if those means are present, what type of plan has been made to remove them during the period of suicide risk. If the patient or his or her family refuse the therapist's request to remove access to those means, such as guns, this refusal should be clearly indicated in the therapist's clinical notes.

Involvement of Significant Others

In crisis intervention, it is common to contact significant others in the patient's immediate environment to obtain collateral information or enlist their support (Farberow, 1957). When the crisis relates to suicide, an appropriate therapeutic strategy often includes the active involvement of these significant others in shoring up the safety and support that are necessary for the patient's outpatient management. Following the environmental assessment, the clinician must decide, based on the patient's risk status, which resources might play a role in maintaining an ongoing support system for the patient. The clinician can help the patient categorize the members of his or her support system as helpful (willing and able to help and support), neutral (perhaps willing to support but may be uninformed or not know what to do to help), or harmful (avoidant, hostile, blaming, exhausted by the patient's behavior).

For example, for a higher risk patient who requires closer oversight, the clinician may obtain releases from the patient to contact a family member or neighbor to touch base with the patient every day or contact the patient's employer and request to be informed if the patient is absent from work without explanation. Involving the patient in the development of this plan is important because it concretely demonstrates that the patient has the ability to actively participate in constructing strategies for his or her safety. For example, the clinician might say: "I want to ensure your safety and, at least for an initial period of time, I'd like us to identify someone/people who can touch base with you on a regular basis and/or let me know if you depart from your normal routine. I may want to talk to a family member or friend/neighbor, with you present, and review the signs that may signal that you need a little extra help or support. We can routinely review this arrangement to see if we can relax it or need to tighten it up." Again, all releases, contacts, arrangements, and changes in arrangements should be documented.

Activate Benign Cycles

This strategy has received little or no attention in other recommendations for working with suicidal patients, yet it is critically important that clinicians expand their interventions beyond the consulting room to not only assess and mobilize but also enhance the patient's support system or protective factors that may moderate the suicidal impulses. Participation in and contribution to the individual's community is an important protective factor that moderates a variety of risk behaviors (Jessor, Van Den Bos, Vanderryn, Costa, & Turbin, 1995). An assessment of the patient's strengths, avocations, and interests is an important complement to a thorough risk assessment. Once these have been identified, specific opportunities for involvement in the patient's environment should be identified. A plan should be developed with the patient for his or her engagement in an activity or organization that can provide a sense of satisfaction and contribution and would enhance the client's sense of self-efficacy or esteem. Naturally, this intervention must come after the acute crisis has been resolved. In addition, as with any intervention, there is a continuum of clinician involvement that is related to the patient's level of functioning. For example, with lower functioning patients, the clinician assumes primary responsibility to identify and make the initial contact. As the level of client functioning improves, the clinician and patient may plan jointly and, with higher functioning clients, the total responsibility for the initiative may be left to the client. Regardless of level of client functioning, the clinician should be knowledgeable about resources and opportunities in the community or should have access to organizations that provide this information. This may seem beyond the scope of normal clinical practice and may be outside the role of assisting the client through the acute crisis. However, if the goal is to attenuate the likelihood of future suicidal crises, actively enhancing such protective factors is essential. As one patient put it, "I still feel suicidal, but I'm too busy to do it."

Postvention

Postvention refers to the plan for dealing with the aftermath of a suicide. This standard set of interventions was originally developed for school systems (Underwood & Dunne-Maxim, 1997), but it has been expanded to other organizations, such as corporations, health, and mental health agencies. There is also an extensive literature on clinicians' responses to the suicide of a patient (Suicide Information & Education Centre, 1996). Whatever the setting, effective postvention always concludes with a debriefing with the staff that was involved in the crisis. Clinicians who work in health or mental health settings should be knowledgeable about their agency's procedures following a patient suicide completion or attempt. In particular, they should know the extent to which the process is supportive of the clinician or focuses solely on protecting the agency. When agency or organizational liability is the primary concern, clinical staff must seek supportive colleagues with whom they can process their reactions. Practitioners in private settings should also identify knowledgeable colleagues with whom they can debrief after a patient suicide or near lethal attempt.

CONCLUSION

The aim of crisis intervention is to attenuate confusion, anxiety, and agitation or immobilization through the provision of support and structure. Support is derived from an understanding of the dynamics of the suicidal crisis and the subjective experience of the client. Structure is based on the active effort to collaborate with the client in understanding the bases of his or her suicidal crisis, the intervention process, and alternate problem-solving strategies. Interventions must be flexibly tailored to fluctuations in the client's level of functioning. Structure and support are also provided through elements that are necessary for the maintenance of a safe holding environment for the client. This involves going beyond the consulting room to mobilize and enhance protective factors in the client's environment.

REFERENCES

Bongar, B. (2002). *The suicidal patient: Clinical and legal standards of care.* (2nd ed.). Washington, DC: American Psychological Association.

Bongar, B., Peterson, L. G., Harris, E. A., & Aissis, J. (1989). Clinical and legal considerations in the management of suicidal patients: An integrative overview. *Journal of Integrative and Eclectic Psychotherapy, 8,* 53–67.

Farberow, N. L. (1957). The suicidal crisis in psychotherapy. In E. S. Shneidman & N. L. Farberow (Eds.), *Clues to suicide* (pp. 119–130). New York: McGraw-Hill.

Farberow, N. L., Helig, S. M., & Litman, R. E. (1968, December). *Techniques in crisis intervention: A training manual.* Los Angeles: Suicide Prevention Center, Inc.

Gutheil, T. G. (1980). Paranoia and progress notes: A guide to forensically informed psychiatric record-keeping. *Hospital and Community Psychiatry, 31,* 479–482.

Jacobs, D. G. (Ed.). (1999). *The Harvard Medical School guide to suicide assessment and intervention.* San Francisco: Jossey-Bass.

Jessor, R., Van Den Bos, J., Vanderryn, J., Costa, F. M., & Turbin, M. S. (1995). Protective factors in adolescent problem behavior: Moderator effects and developmental change. *Developmental Psychology, 31,* 923–933.

Jobes, D. A., & Berman, A. L. (1993). Suicide and malpractice liability: Assessing and revising policies, procedures, and practice in outpatient settings. *Professional Psychology: Research and Practice, 24,* 91–99.

Linehan, M. M. (1993). *Cognitive behavioral treatment of borderline personality disorder.* New York: Guilford Press.

Linehan, M. M., Goodstein, J. L., Nielsen, S. L., & Chiles, J. A. (1983). Reasons for staying alive when you are thinking about killing yourself: The Reasons for Living Inventory. *Journal of Consulting and Clinical Psychology, 51,* 276–286.

Maltsberger, J. T., & Buie, D. H. (1974). Countertransference hate in the treatment of suicidal patients. *Archives of General Psychiatry, 30,* 625–633.

Maltsberger, J. T., & Buie, D. H. (1989). Common errors in the management of suicidal patients. In D. Jacobs & H. N. Brown (Eds.), *Suicide: Understanding and responding* (pp. 285–294). Madison, CT: International Universities Press.

Motto, J. (1977). Estimation of suicide risk by the use of clinical models. *Suicide and Life-Threatening Behavior, 7,* 236–245.

Packman, W. L., & Harris, E. A. (1998). Legal issues and risk management in suicidal patients. In B. Bongar, A. L. Berman, R. W. Maris, M. M. Silverman, E. A. Harris, & W. L. Harris (Eds.), *Risk management with suicidal patients* (pp. 150–186). New York: Guilford Press.

Shneidman, E. S. (1985). *Definition of suicide.* New York: Wiley.

Simon, R. I. (1987). *Clinical psychiatry and the law.* Washington, DC: American Psychiatric Press.

Suicide Information & Education Centre. (1996, February). *When a patient or client commits suicide* (SIEC Alert #17). Calgary, AB, Canada: Author.

Underwood, M. M., & Dunne-Maxim, K. (1997). *Managing sudden traumatic loss in the schools.* Washington, DC: American Association of Suicidology.

CHAPTER 9

No-Suicide Contracts

Lillian M. Range

A no-suicide contract, also called a no-harm agreement, life-maintenance contract, or safety agreement, is an agreement between client and therapist that the client will refrain from any type of self-harm. No-suicide contracts are a common therapeutic intervention for suicidal or potentially suicidal individuals (Motto, 1999). This chapter describes no-suicide contracts, places them in context, details the existing (albeit sketchy) research on no-suicide contracts, and makes some recommendations about their use.

DESCRIPTION

A no-suicide contract is an agreement between the client and the therapist. As with all types of contracts, no-suicide contracts can vary in the degree of explicitness with which they are negotiated and endorsed by each party (Drew, 2001). The agreement has some standard and some optional components.

One standard component is time parameters, which are typically from a few hours to a few days. Though the amount of time varies from individual to individual, the idea is that the person is making a short-term agreement, which may be easier to keep than a longer agreement. Depressed persons, feeling that they face an eternity of unhappiness, may feel better and more in control if they can hold off on suicidal action for one day, or even one hour (Gutheil, 1999). For example, a therapist and client may agree that the client will not harm herself deliberately or accidentally until her next therapy session, which is the following Monday at 10:00 A.M.

Another standard component is contingencies in case suicidal thoughts and feelings resurface. The contingencies include what the client will do in case the same situation arises that led to the suicidal thoughts and feelings or specific plans for what the client will do if he or she becomes unable to keep the commitment. The contingencies may be people and telephone numbers, an emergency room or crisis center, or a specific action (such as going to see a friend). The no-suicide contract promises too much if it states that the clinician will be reachable at all times (Simon, 1999). Time parameters and contingencies are a part of all no-suicide contracts.

An optional component is whether the no-suicide agreement is oral or written. If it is oral, it may include a handshake. If it is written, it may be an agency form or a statement personalized for the specific client and situation. Written forms sometimes include formal statements of treatment goals and responsibilities for client and therapist. With written forms, the client and the therapist both have a copy. For those who might have comprehension problems, having clients repeat in their own words the terms of the agreement is recommended.

Examples of no-suicide contracts are available. A verbal agreement (see Appendix E for two possibilities) is relatively less formal. Clinicians often use a form of verbal contract, such as by asking, "Can you manage okay until our next appointment?" or "Will you call me if things get to be too much for you?" (Motto, 1999). Questions such as these are commonly used in therapy.

Written no-suicide contracts for adults (see Appendix A) are relatively more formal and include therapy goals and specific times (Bongar, 2002; Fremouw, de Perczel, & Ellis, 1990). Davidson (1996) adapted this adult contract for children, developing an age-appropriate contract for 6- to 8-year-olds (Appendix B), 9- to 11-year-olds (Appendix C), and 12- to 17-year-olds (Appendix D).

In summary, a no-suicide contract can come in many formats. Whether verbal or written, the no-suicide contract should be tailored for the specific individual and his or her specific situation.

NO-SUICIDE CONTRACTS IN CONTEXT

No-suicide contracts arose in an era in which many prominent approaches to therapy used contracts between therapist and client. Two such approaches are behavior therapy and its younger sisters, cognitive-behavior therapy and transactional analysis.

Behavior therapy emerged in the late 1950s as a systematic approach to the assessment and treatment of psychological disorders (Wilson, 2000). Based on modern learning theory, behavior therapy extends classical and operant conditioning to complex forms of human activities. Particularly relevant to no-suicide contracts is operant conditioning, which emphasizes that behavior is a function of its environmental consequences. Behavior therapists stress that people learn best when they are aware of the rules and contingencies governing the consequences of their actions (Wilson). Behavior therapists tailor treatment to specific problems for specific people. No-suicide contracts are consistent with a behavioral approach to treatment.

Behavior therapists and clients mutually contract treatment goals and methods (Prochaska & Norcross, 1999) and frequently use contracts to help the client gain control over contingencies. For example, behavior therapists might contract with a person who wanted to lose weight or stop smoking that the client would deposit $100 and earn the money back through making appropriate responses. Depending on the individual, this type of contract could also be applied to suicidal thoughts and feelings. For example, the client might contract to do pleasant activities, such as going for a walk, taking a dip in the whirlpool, or reading a chapter of an interesting book, to earn back the $100.

A no-suicide contract written from a behavior therapist orientation might involve positive reinforcement (e.g., "If I can refrain from hurting myself for two hours, I can watch my favorite movie") and specific action (e.g., "If thoughts of suicide start to bother me, I will call my best friend to go out for an ice cream"). The contract would be specifically tailored for each suicidal individual.

Behaviorally oriented therapists express concern and give directions and use no-suicide contracts as an expression of this attitude. The therapist might help the client to generate alternative courses of action rather than attempting suicide. The therapist would set highly specific, unambiguous, and short-term goals. For example, the specific, short-term goal might be not cutting oneself for four hours, rather than the global, long-term goal of feeling less suicidal.

Similar to behavior therapy, cognitive-behavior therapy (CBT) is also empirical, present-centered, and problem-oriented. Cognitive-behavior therapy requires explicit identification of problems and the situations in which they occur, as well as the consequences resulting from them. It applies a functional analysis to external experiences as well as to internal experiences, such as thoughts, attitudes, and images. It posits that thoughts, like behaviors, can be modified by active collaboration through behavioral experiments that foster new learning (Beck & Weishaar, 1999). No-suicide contracts are also consistent with a cognitive-behavioral approach to treatment.

Cognitive-behavioral approaches are recommended for suicidal individuals. Short-term CBT that integrates problem solving as a core intervention is effective at reducing suicide ideation, depression, and hopelessness over periods of up to one year, but do not appear to be effective for longer time frames (Rudd, Joiner, Jobes, & King, 1999). Dialectic behavior therapy is recommended for borderline individuals, who are often suicidal (Linehan, Armstrong, Suarez, Allmon, & Heard, 1991).

Another approach to treatment, transactional analysis (TA), can also involve no-suicide contracts. Originated by Eric Berne in the 1950s, TA posits that every individual has three active, dynamic, and observable ego states: parent, adult, and child. Every individual also needs strokes (recognition) and designs a life script (plan) during childhood based on early beliefs about the self and others (Dusay & Dusay, 1989). The simple vocabulary of TA is intentionally designed to enable clients to demystify the esoteric jargon of traditional therapies. Further, TA encourages therapists and clients to use symbols such as circles, arrows, triangles, and bar graphs, all of which increase clarity and understanding.

Contracting is an integral part of a TA approach to treatment (Stummer, 2002). A key question in a TA contract is, "How will both you and I know when you get what you came for?" (Dusay & Dusay, 1989). Throughout the therapy contract, both therapist and client will define their mutual responsibilities in achieving the goal. Further, TA therapists frequently review, update, and even change contracts and may make mini or weekly contracts (Dusay & Dusay). The therapist agrees to provide only those services that he or she can competently deliver, and the client must be competent enough to achieve the goals of the contract. A contract with a 55-year-old person to become the world's champion in the 100-yard dash would not represent competency on the part of the client (Dusay & Dusay).

Transactional analysis defines a no-suicide contract as a statement by the adult ego state of the client to the adult ego state of the therapist. The more the suicidal individual's psychic energy is located in the adult ego state, the more likely the no-suicide contract will be experienced at a primarily cognitive level, and the more likely that such a contract will serve a holding function, keeping the client alive while the therapy takes place. The more the suicidal individual's psychic energy is located in the child ego state, the more likely the no-suicide contract will be experienced at an affective level. In this case, the contract can function as a complete recommitment to life, a full redecision, or as a precursor to such a commitment (Mothersole, 1996). A TA contract with a suicidal person might start with, "Until our appointment at 10:00 A.M. on Monday morning, I will not kill myself accidentally or on purpose."

Transactional analysis theory emphasizes that no-suicide contracts are powerful when they are predicated on a strong therapeutic bond (Mothersole, 1996). When such a bond exists, the client experiences the invitation to make a contract to stay alive as coming from a position of empathic understanding from the therapist. In contrast, when the bond is not present or is weak, there is danger of the client experiencing the contract as prohibiting exploration of self-destructive thoughts and feelings (Mothersole, 1996).

Transactional analysis posits a continuum of ownership of the contract. On the one hand, the client can completely own the commitment to life. Signs of complete ownership would be spontaneously recommitting to life or simply noticing that self-destruction is no longer an option (Mothersole, 1996). On the other hand, the client may disown any commitment to life. Signs of a lack of ownership are nonverbal cues such as lack of eye contact, a tapping foot, or a gallows laugh, and behavioral cues such as voice inflection or great haste in making a no-suicide agreement. Incongruence, within the client or between client and therapist, is characteristic of lack of ownership and is grist for the therapeutic mill (Mothersole). In the case of no-suicide contracts, the therapist must point out and deal with incongruence.

Behavioral contracting is an aspect of treatment for various kinds of behavioral and psychological problems. Written behavioral contracts, usually developed jointly by a health care provider and client, have been effective with a variety of issues, including childhood emotional and behavioral difficulties (Ruth, 1996), alcoholism (Ossip-Klein & Rychtarik,

1993; Silk, Eisner, & Allport, 1994; Vinson & Devera-Sales, 2000), families in which there is a suicidal person (McLean & Taylor, 1994), authorship dilemmas (Hopko, Hopko, & Morris, 1999), incarcerated youth (Hagan & King, 1992), and adherence to an exercise program (Robison, Rogers, & Carlson, 1992). Written contracts are not always helpful, however. For example, contracts were no more helpful than a lecture in promoting safety behavior among mothers (Seal & Swerissen, 1993). With a few exceptions, therefore, the preponderance of evidence indicates that behavioral contracts help people with a wide variety of problems.

Some experts argue, however, that the theory behind therapeutic contracts does not apply to no-suicide contracts. Therapeutic contracts emphasize shared responsibility between clinician and client and define respective contributions, obligations, and roles in the treatment relationship. For therapeutic contracts, two competent, rational individuals make collaborative decisions about treatment aims and plans.

In contrast, some would argue that the threat of suicide makes a true therapeutic contract impossible (Miller, 1999). When the issue is suicide, the central feature of a contract, the element of patient choice, is restricted or removed. When suicide risk is high, the clinician may abandon the collaborative aspect of the relationship and make a plan that the client dislikes. The client no longer chooses, and the clinician acts to protect the client from harm, for instance, by seeking involuntary hospitalization. The clinician does not ignore the client's consent, but rather supplants it with more urgent clinical needs (Miller, 1999).

An alternative is an informed-consent procedure with suicidal individuals (Miller, 1999). In such a procedure, the clinician reviews with the client the variety of treatment options, clarifying the risks and benefits of each. The clinician explains each option to encourage full and voluntary participation in the mutually agreed-on treatment goals. Included in the discussion is a frank acknowledgment of the risk of death from suicide. However, suicide is not the only risk. Overly restrictive plans also carry risks. For example, hospitalization carries risks of regression, dependence and loss of autonomy, family disruptions, and potential job loss. The informed-consent approach creates a realistic framework for appraising treatment options (Miller, 1999).

In the current managed care era, mental health professionals increasingly rely on no-suicide contracts in the treatment of persons at suicide risk (Simon, 1999). Unfortunately, however, the high volume of clients and short lengths of treatment may inhibit development of a therapeutic alliance between therapist and client that forms the basis of suicide prevention intervention.

RESEARCH

Research on no-suicide contracts is scant (Weiss, 2001), especially in comparison to how often they are used (Miller, 1999). Research on no-suicide contracts can take the form of surveys of professionals and nonprofessionals who would be in the position to administer no-suicide contracts. Alternatively, research might involve questioning people who actually use no-suicide contracts.

Surveys of Professionals

The first published report of no-suicide contracts described training clinicians to make no-suicide contracts. After training, 31 trainees reported that they made no-suicide agreements with 609 suicidal persons, 266 of whom were "seriously" suicidal (Drye, Goulding, & Goulding, 1973). This original work was groundbreaking and seemed to indicate that many clinicians used no-suicide contracts after training. However, there were no statistical data, no experimental design, no control group, no check on the self-reports, no mention of the time constraints about when they used these contracts, and no information about whether these clinicians used no-suicide contracts before training. Despite these problems, however, this research opened the door for clinicians and researchers to use and examine no-suicide contracts.

Research on no-suicide contracts has also taken the form of surveys of professionals. These kinds of surveys have asked, "Do you have any experience with no-suicide contracts?" In this kind of survey, the answer is usually yes. By the time of completion of internship or residency, 79% of psychiatrists and 72% of psychologists reported witnessing no-suicide contracts being used. Additionally, most (77% of psychiatrists; 75% of psychologists) stated that their agency recommended no-suicide contracts, and most (86% of psychiatrists; 71% of psychologists) regularly used them (Miller, Jacobs, & Gutheil, 1998). Thus, most clinicians have had some experience with no-suicide contracts early in their careers.

Surveys of professionals have also asked, "Do you actually use no-suicide contracts?" In this kind of survey, the answer is mostly yes. A total of 57% of practicing psychiatrists in Minnesota reported using no-suicide contracts, with those recently out of residency more likely to use them than those out of residency 11 or more years (Kroll, 2000). Among directors of psychiatric hospitals and units, the majority reported using no-suicide contracts, which were typically given by nurses, and typically used with patients who talked, threatened, or attempted suicide. These directors used a variety of types of no-suicide contracts, including hand-written (74%), verbal (72%), and preprinted forms (15%; Drew, 1999). Among head nurses of psychiatric inpatient units, more than 80% said that their units used no-suicide contracts. Further, these head nurses thought no-suicide contracts were useful (Green & Grindel, 1996).

Surveys of professionals have asked, "What do you think about using a no-suicide contract in a specific situation?" When surveyed, licensed psychologists were optimistic about no-suicide contracts with moderately suicidal adults and adolescents, but were neutral to slightly pessimistic about no-suicide contracts with children ages 6 to 11 years and 9 to 12 years. Further, these clinicians viewed no-suicide contracts as helpful with moderately suicidal clients, but only slightly helpful with mildly or severely suicidal clients (Davidson, Wagner, & Range, 1995).

When asked about another specific situation, 368 clinicians who worked with children were mildly to moderately in favor of a written no-suicide agreement regardless of the reading level of the agreement. These practicing professionals saw a no-suicide agreement as more appropriate when a child had no history of academic problems, was relatively older (9 to 11 or 12 to 17) rather than 6 years of age, and relatively free of academic problems (Davidson & Range, 2000). Though clinicians had only moderate faith in the effectiveness of such agreements, they apparently believed that no-suicide contracts would not hurt child clients.

Across a variety of mental health professions, trainees and beginners as well as those with extensive experience are generally in favor of no-suicide contracts.

Surveys of Nonprofessionals

Another research approach is to ask nonprofessionals if no-suicide contracts are a good idea. One group of nonprofessionals is teachers. In one study, 63 practice teachers read a vignette about a suicidal youth and then answered questions about what they would do if confronted with that situation. They reported that they would take direct action, including calling the parents of a suicidal youth, escorting the youth to the school counselor, and staying with the youth until another adult arrived. They were neutral about whether they would use a written or verbal no-suicide agreement, regardless of the age of the student or the level of risk (Davidson & Range, 1997). Thus, although these teachers-in-training expected to act when a student was suicidal, they were neutral about whether this action would be to use a no-suicide contract.

Teachers' less-than-positive attitude may be due to an absence of training in how to deal with suicidal youth during their careers. If so, the good news is that they are responsive to training in this area. After one in-service training module about suicide warning signs and no-suicide contracts, teachers were more certain that they would actively intervene when confronted with a suicidal student. Interventions that they endorsed included physically escorting the suicidal youth to the counselor's office and calling his or her parents. They changed from uncertain/slightly likely to highly likely to use a written or verbal no-suicide agreement (Davidson & Range, 1999). Their opinions became more positive after this single in-service workshop, but there is no indication of how long their positive attitudes lasted.

Another group of nonprofessionals is students. Peers are often the first persons contacted by a suicidal individual. College students have positive attitudes toward no-suicide contracts (Descant & Range, 1997). When given a choice of three different ones that varied in length and specificity, they rated the more detailed contract best (Buelow & Range, 2001). Similarly, high school students thought that therapy that included a no-suicide contract was better than therapy alone (Myers & Range, in press).

Furthermore, students are responsive to training about no-suicide contracts. In a survey of 396 students from 19 health classes at two southwestern high schools, some had been taught to use no-suicide agreements, but few had ever called a crisis hotline or contacted a counseling service. However, about 50% said that they would share suicidal thoughts with a friend. Further, at one- and seven-week follow-ups, those who received training were more likely than others to say that they would obtain a no-suicide contract from a suicidal peer (Hennig, Crabtree, & Baum, 1998).

Professionals are mildly positive about no-suicide contracts. Nonprofessionals may start out only faintly positive, but they seem to be responsive to training that encourages them to use no-suicide contracts.

Surveys of Users

No-suicide contracts are often used in the hospital, and some discharge questionnaires ask people what they think about this aspect of treatment. One survey queried children and adolescents admitted to a psychiatric hospital, most of whom were diagnosed with conduct disorder, major depression, or dysthymia. At one point, the hospital instituted contracts that targeted unauthorized running away from the unit or activities, suicide attempts or suicidal talk, physical aggression, and sexual acting-out. Among 360 children and adolescents treated before the contracts, 16.1% were involved in some sort of incident. Among 570 children and adolescents treated after the contracts, only 1.4% of the children were involved in some sort of incident (Jones, O'Brien, & McMahon, 1993). This study was correlational rather than experimental, so it lacked control groups, random assignment, and systematic controls for other relevant variables, such as staff changes. These flaws often characterize real-world research.

Similarly, in another survey of 39 psychiatrically hospitalized children (mean age = 13.3 years), treatment involved developing a written contingency contract in which children received privileges based on meeting the terms of the behavioral agreement. Children used a variety of contracts, including but not limited to no-suicide contracts. Then, they completed a 32-item questionnaire assessing the efficacy of various treatments they received, including contracting. They rated the contracting "very high" in helping them change their behaviors, but were only moderately interested in continuing to contract after discharge (Jones & O'Brien, 1990). This naturalistic study also lacked random assignment and control groups, but the fact that two samples of hospitalized children reported that no-suicide contracts helped them change their behaviors suggests that children who have used no-suicide contracts found them to be helpful.

In the most extensive research project on users, 135 adult psychiatric inpatients completed a survey at discharge about their written no-suicide contracts. They all had considered or attempted suicide, and their hospital stay averaged five days. Overall, these recent users reported positive attitudes about the therapeutic features of no-suicide contracts, regardless of age, sex, disorder, or ratings of overall treatment helpfulness. However, repeat attempters were not as solid in their attitudes as were the other inpatients. All these inpatients agreed that no-suicide contracts were not coercive and did not lead to detachment (Davis, Williams, & Hays, 2002). This naturalistic study had more participants and more thorough survey instruments than other surveys of users. However, of necessity, it lacked a control group. A prospective, experimental design might entail making a no-suicide agreement part of the check-out procedure for some patients at a psychiatric hospital, then comparing the suicide or suicide attempt rate among those who had this additional step with the rate of those who had a routine procedure (Range et al., 2002). Nevertheless, though the results thus far are correlational rather than causal, the indications are that children as well as adults are in favor of no-suicide agreements.

In a unique approach to studying users of no-suicide contracts, researchers listened unobtrusively to 617 callers at two suicide prevention centers where trained telephone volunteers used no-suicide contracts with callers. The contracts involved refraining from suicide and engaging in follow-up activities to develop a long-term resolution of the suicidal crisis. In the majority of calls (68%), the telephone clinician obtained a no-suicide contract. Researchers classified those who failed to call back in a follow-up as noncompliant. Using this conservative definition, the majority of callers upheld the contracts (54%), some did not make a contract (31%), a minority (14%) failed to keep the contract, and 1% of callers attempted suicide after calling (Mishara & Daigle, 1997). These results, though limited by the high number lost to follow-up, potential biases in retrospective recall, and absence of a control group, suggest that users of a telephone crisis line found no-suicide contracts to be helpful.

There is, therefore, little experimental research on no-suicide contracts, and their use derives more from an oral tradition than from experimental evidence (Miller, 1999). The research that does exist is characterized by the kinds of flaws that occur when research on a low-frequency phenomenon must be conducted in the real world where ethical, treatment, and safety issues must be addressed before experimental design issues can even be considered. Further, no-suicide contracts are typically used in conjunction with a therapeutic situation, and they are never the sole intervention. Taking them out of context to conduct research may be equivalent to assessing a fine Italian dinner with and without pesto sauce. The meal may be better with the sauce, but there are many more aspects of the meal than simply whether it included pesto sauce.

RECOMMENDATIONS

No-suicide contracts, tailored to fit the specific individual and the specific situation, arose against a backdrop of behavioral contracting used in various approaches to psychotherapy. The sketchy research on no-suicide contracts, though limited by serious design flaws, suggests that experts as well as users mildly favor them. Following are guidelines about what to do and what not to do when considering using no-suicide contracts:

- *Do* remember that no-suicide contracts are only one aspect of treatment. They are not the most important part of treatment. The most important aspect of treatment is the relationship between client and helper (Kleespies, Deleppo, & Gallagher, 1999; Rudd et al., 1999). No-suicide contracts that strengthen this relationship are useful; no-suicide contracts that undermine this relationship are harmful. The first step is to form an alliance with the suicidal individual.

- *Don't* get distracted by the paperwork. Paperwork is important to the therapist. Indeed, supervisors, bosses, and agencies demand the paperwork. However, the paperwork is *not* important to the client.

- *Don't* use no-suicide contracts indiscriminately. With some people, it is best to avoid the whole issue of safety contracting. For example, some people with borderline or passive-aggressive characteristics may become embroiled in manipulation around safety-contracting issues. With these clients, reinforce their commitment to the intervention plan, and avoid power struggles that might be brought on by no-suicide contracts (Shea, 1999). Other clients may interpret a no-suicide contract to mean that they may call the clinician only when they are highly dysfunctional, perturbed, and contemplating something lethal (Bongar, 2002). Still other clients who have a compulsive need to be reasonable, rational, grateful, and cooperative may agree to therapeutic arrangements that they cannot fulfill (Bongar, 2002). Weigh carefully the unique dynamics of the therapeutic relationship to see if a no-suicide contract is helpful (Bongar, 2002). Use good judgment.

- *Do* take into account the situation. For first-time meetings, for example, in the emergency room, safety contracting may have little or no impact. However, even in this situation, if the person bonds quickly, safety contracting may have a mild deterrent effect (Shea, 1999). In an inpatient setting, the no-suicide contract has limitations. It may give a false sense of security to client and/or therapist, causing them to overlook other signs and symptoms (Bongar, 2002). Furthermore, repeat suicide attempters may be helped less by written contracts than those who have only considered suicide (Davis et al., 2002).

- *Don't* start a session with a no-suicide contract. Instead, start by encouraging the client/patient to talk. Find out what is troublesome. Encourage communication about suicidal thoughts and impulses (Miller, 1999). Leave some time at the end of the session for the no-suicide contract. One guideline is to introduce the no-suicide contract at about the beginning of the last third of the therapy session.

- *Do* pay attention to how the client makes the agreement. Is the eye contact steady? Is the nonverbal behavior in agreement with the verbal? Some experienced therapists point out that how the client handles the no-suicide contract is its best use (Shea, 1999). Assessment is a continuing process, and no-suicide contracts may help in this aspect of therapy.

- *Do* check to see that the client understands the contract and finds it to be helpful. Rather than using a formal or informal contract, it may be more helpful to focus on an alliance for safety, where client and clinician agree to devote themselves to the task of treatment in a collaborative manner (Gutheil, 1999). The first goal is to protect the client's safety. No-suicide contracts that promote safety are good; no-suicide contracts that do not actively promote safety are a waste of time or worse.

- *Do* reaffirm the no-suicide contract. The no-suicide contract is an alliance to devote time to treatment in a collaborative manner, not just a promise to stay alive for a designated period of time (Bongar, 2002). A potential disadvantage of no-suicide contracts is that they are static—like a photograph. However, therapy is dynamic—like a movie.

- *Do* continue to be vigilant about the possibility of suicide. Unfortunately, the contract against suicide tends to be a specific event, whereas suicide risk assessment is a continuing process (Simon, 1999). A prudent course would be to review at appropriate intervals the person's willingness and ability to call the clinician or to take appropriate actions if suicidal thoughts occur. In addition, it is helpful to review what steps the client and family would take if the same difficulties that led to the suicidal crisis would resurface and to develop alternative methods of coping with these stressors (Brent, 1997).

- *Don't* rely solely on a no-suicide contract. Especially in the case of outpatient treatment, take the time to telephone corroborative sources (Shea, 1999). Such calls take considerable effort, but can be invaluable. The outside source may know of more ominous expressions of suicidal intent than the client disclosed or provide information suggesting other forms of treatment. These sources may also be pivotal in providing help with social support. In the case of inpatient treatment, the person is seriously ill and may not have the capacity to cooperate. In addition, a no-suicide contract may give staff a false sense of security, causing them to overlook other signs and symptoms (Bongar, 2002).

- *Do* have 24-hour clinical backup (Brent, 1997). In the "green card" study, patients who had harmed themselves for the first time were offered rapid, easy access to on-call trainee psychiatrists in the event of further difficulties and were encouraged to seek help at an early stage should such problems arise. After one year, they had fewer subsequent suicide attempts and threats than those who had received standard care (Morgan, Jones, & Owen, 1993). Make sure that the client knows the backup plan.

- *Do* check with a supervisor or colleague. Suicidal individuals are high-stress clients; therapists who work with them may feel anger, frustration, and anxiety (Kleespies et al., 1999). Another perspective on a suicidal client is helpful, especially from someone experienced in dealing with suicidal individuals (Bongar, 2002). Any therapist dealing with suicidal individuals needs a personal backup plan as well as a backup plan for the client.

- *Do* get training. Training in dealing with suicidal individuals should begin early in the training program and continue through internship and postdoctoral experiences (Westefeld et al., 2000).

APPENDIX A _____

NO-SUICIDE CONTRACT—OUTPATIENT

As a part of my therapy program, I, _____ , agree to the following terms:

1. I agree that one of my major therapy goals is to live a long life with more pleasure and less unhappiness than I have now.

2. I understand that becoming suicidal when depressed or upset stands in the way of achieving this goal, and I, therefore, would like to overcome this tendency. I agree to use my therapy to learn better ways to reduce my emotional distress.

3. Since I understand that this will take time, I agree in the meantime to refuse to act on urges to injure or kill myself between this day and _____ (date).

4. If at any time I should feel unable to resist suicidal impulses, I agree to call _____ (name) at _____ (number) or _____ (number). If this person is unavailable, I agree to call _____ (name) at _____ (number) or _____ (number) or go directly to (hospital or agency) at _____ (address).

5. My therapist, _____ , agrees to work with me in scheduled sessions to help me learn constructive alternatives to self-harm and to be available as much as is reasonable during times of crisis.

6. I agree to abide by this agreement either until it expires or until it is openly renegotiated with my therapist. I understand that it is renewable at or near the expiration date of _____ (date). [Includes place for signature, date, countersignature, and date] (Bongar, 2002; Fremouw et al., 1990)

NO-SUICIDE CONTRACT—INPATIENT

I, _____ , commit to not harm or kill myself while I am in the hospital. If I feel I cannot keep this commitment, I will discuss my concerns with a staff member.

APPENDIX B _____

NO-SUICIDE AGREEMENT FOR 6- TO 8-YEAR-OLD CHILD

I, _____ , will do these things:

1. I want to live a long life and be happy.

2. I will come to counseling to learn how to be happy.

3. While I learn how to be happy, I will not hurt or kill myself. I know it will take time to learn how to be happy.

4. If I ever want to hurt or kill myself, I will tell _____ or I will tell _____ .

5. My counselor, _____ , will help me learn how to be happy.

6. I will do all of these things until _____ , when I see my counselor, _____ , again.

_____   _____
Name   Date

Witness:

_____   _____
Name   Date

APPENDIX C _____

NO-SUICIDE AGREEMENT FOR 9- TO
11-YEAR-OLD CHILD

While I am in counseling, I, _____ , will do these things:

1. I want to live a long life and be happy.

2. When I feel bad and I want to hurt myself or kill myself, I cannot be happy. I will come to counseling to learn how to be happy.

3. While I learn how to be happy, I will not hurt or kill myself. I know it will take time to learn how to be happy.

4. If at any time I want to hurt or kill myself, I will tell _____ or I will tell _____ . If I cannot find _____ or _____ , I will call _____ or _____ .

5. My counselor, _____ , agrees to work with me to help me learn how to be happy.

6. I agree to keep this agreement until _____ , when I see my counselor again.

_____   _____
Name   Date

Witness: _____   _____
            Name   Date

APPENDIX D _____

NO-SUICIDE CONTRACT FOR 12- TO 17-YEAR-OLD CHILD/ADOLESCENT

As part of my counseling, I, _____ , will do the following things:

1. I agree that one of my major goals is to live a long life with more happiness than I now have.

2. I understand that wanting to hurt myself or kill myself gets in the way of this goal. I want to learn better things I can do when I feel bad. I want to find answers to my problems.

3. I understand that feeling better will take time, so I will not hurt or kill myself between now and _____ , when I see my counselor again.

4. If at any time I want to hurt or kill myself, I will tell _____ or _____ . If I cannot find _____ or _____ , I will call _____ at _____ or _____ at _____ .

5. My counselor, _____ , will work with me to help me learn better ways to take care of my problems. My counselor, _____ , will be available as much as possible if I feel very upset.

6. I will keep this agreement until it expires or until _____ , when I see my counselor again. My counselor and I can then make another agreement if we need to.

_____   _____
Name   Date

Witness: _____   _____
              Name   Date

APPENDIX E _____

VERBAL AGREEMENT

Version 1

In the event that you begin to develop suicidal feelings, here's what I want you to do: First, use the strategies for self-control that we will discuss, including seeking social support. Then, if suicidal feelings remain, seek me out or whoever is covering for me. If, for whatever reason, you are unable to access help, or if you feel that things just won't wait, call or go to the ER—here is the phone number. (From Joiner, Walker, Rudd, & Jobes, 1999)

Version 2

I will be here (specific place) at (specific future time) no matter what I may think or feel in the meantime. (Adapted from Clarkson, 1992)

REFERENCES

Beck, A. T., & Weishaar, M. E. (1999). Cognitive therapy. In R. J. Corsini & D. Wedding (Eds.), *Current psychotherapies* (6th ed., pp. 241–272). Itasca, IL: Peacock Press.

Bongar, B. (2002). *The suicidal patient: Clinical and legal standards of care* (2nd ed.). Washington, DC: American Psychological Association.

Brent, D. A. (1997). Practitioner review: The aftercare of adolescents with deliberate self-harm. *Journal of Child Psychology and Psychiatry, 38,* 277–286.

Buelow, G., & Range, L. M. (2001). No-suicide contracts among college students. *Death Studies, 25,* 583–592.

Clarkson, P. (1992). The interpersonal field in transactional analysis. *Transactional Analysis Journal, 22,* 89–94.

Davidson, M. (1996). *Age-appropriate "no suicide" contracts: Professionals' ratings of appropriateness and effectiveness.* Doctoral dissertation, University of Southern Mississippi, Hattiesburg.

Davidson, M., & Range, L. (1997). Practice teachers' response to a suicidal student. *Journal of Social Psychology, 137,* 530–532.

Davidson, M., & Range, L. (1999). Are teachers of children and young adolescents responsive to suicide prevention training modules? Yes. *Death Studies, 23,* 61–71.

Davidson, M., & Range, L. (2000). Age appropriate no-suicide agreements: Professionals' ratings of appropriateness and effectiveness. *Education and Treatment of Children, 23,* 143–155.

Davidson, M., Wagner, W., & Range, L. (1995). Clinicians' attitudes toward no-suicide agreements. *Suicide and Life-Threatening Behavior, 25,* 410–414.

Davis, S. E., Williams, I. S., & Hays, L. W. (2002). Psychiatric inpatients' perceptions of written no-suicide agreements: An exploratory study. *Suicide and Life-Threatening Behavior, 32,* 51–66.

Descant, J., & Range, L. M. (1997). No-suicide agreements: College students' perceptions. *Death Studies, 31,* 238–242.

Drew, B. L. (1999). No-suicide contracts to prevent suicidal behavior in inpatient psychiatric settings. *Journal of the American Psychiatric Nurses Association, 5,* 23–28.

Drew, B. L. (2001). Self-harm behavior and no-suicide contracting in psychiatric inpatient settings. *Archives of Psychiatric Nursing, 15,* 99–106.

Drye, R. C., Goulding, R. L., & Goulding, M. E. (1973). No-suicide decisions: Patient monitoring of suicidal risk. *American Journal of Psychiatry, 130,* 171–174.

Dusay, J. M., & Dusay, K. M. (1989). Transactional analysis. In R. J. Corsini & D. Wedding (Eds.), *Current psychotherapies* (6th ed., pp. 405–453). Itasca, IL: Peacock Press.

Fremouw, W. J., de Perczel, M., & Ellis, T. E. (1990). *Suicide risk: Assessment and response guidelines.* New York: Pergamon Press.

Green, J. S., & Grindel, C. G. (1996). Supervision of suicidal patients in adult inpatient psychiatric units in general hospitals. *Psychiatric Services, 47,* 859–863.

Gutheil, T. G. (1999). Liability issues and liability prevention in suicide. In D. G. Jacobs (Ed.), *The Harvard Medical School guide to suicide assessment and intervention* (pp. 561–578). San Francisco: Jossey-Bass.

Hagan, M., & King, R. P. (1992). Recidivism rates of youth completing an intensive treatment program in a juvenile correctional facility. *International Journal of Offender Therapy and Comparative Criminology, 36,* 349–358.

Hennig, C. W., Crabtree, C. R., & Baum, D. (1998). Mental health CPR: Peer contracting as a response to potential suicide in adolescents. *Archives of Suicide Research, 4,* 169–187.

Hopko, D. R., Hopko, S. D., & Morris, T. L. (1999). The application of behavioral contracting to authorship status. *Behavior Therapist, 22,* 93–95, 107.

Jakubczyk, A., Zechowski, C., & Namyslowska, I. (2001). Treatment of adolescent borderline patients in a psychiatric unit. *Archives of Psychiatry and Psychotherapy, 3,* 65–72.

Joiner, T. E., Walker, R. L., Rudd, M. D., & Jobes, D. A. (1999). Scientizing and routinizing the assessment of suicidality in outpatient practice. *Professional Psychology: Research and Practice, 30,* 447–453.

Jones, R. N., & O'Brien, P. (1990). Unique interventions for child inpatient psychiatry. *Journal of Psychosocial Nursing, 28,* 29–31.

Jones, R. N., O'Brien, P., & McMahon, W. M. (1993). Contracting to lower precaution status for child psychiatric inpatients. *Journal of Psychosocial Nursing, 31,* 6–10.

Kleespies, P. M., Deleppo, J. D., & Gallagher, P. L. (1999). Managing suicidal emergencies: Recommendations for the practitioner. *Professional Psychology: Research and Practice, 30,* 454–463.

Kroll, J. (2000). Use of no-suicide contracts by psychiatrists in Minnesota. *American Journal of Psychiatry, 157,* 1684–1686.

Linehan, M. M., Armstrong, H. E., Suarez, A., Allmon, D., & Heard, H. (1991). Cognitive-behavioral treatment of chronically parasuicidal borderline patients. *Archives of General Psychiatry, 48,* 1060–1064.

McLean, P., & Taylor, S. (1994). Family therapy for suicidal people. *Death Studies, 18,* 409–426.

Miller, M. C. (1999). Suicide-prevention contracts: Advantages, disadvantages, and an alternative approach. In D. G. Jacobs (Ed.), *The Harvard Medical School guide to suicide assessment and intervention* (pp. 463–481). San Francisco: Jossey-Bass.

Miller, M. C., Jacobs, D. G., & Gutheil, T. (1998). Talisman or taboo: The controversy of the suicide-prevention contract. *Harvard Review of Psychiatry, 6,* 78–87.

Mishara, B. L., & Daigle, M. S. (1997). Effects of different telephone intervention styles with suicidal callers at two suicide prevention centers: An empirical investigation. *American Journal of Community Psychology, 25,* 861–885.

Morgan, H., Jones, E., & Owen, J. (1993). Secondary prevention of non-fatal deliberate self-harm: The green card study. *British Journal of Psychiatry, 63,* 111–112.

Mothersole, G. (1996). Existential realities and no-suicide contracts. *Transactional Analysis Journal, 26,* 151–159.

Motto, J. A. (1999). Critical points in the assessment and management of suicide risk. In D. G. Jacobs (Ed.), *The Harvard Medical School guide to suicide assessment and intervention* (pp. 224–248). San Francisco: Jossey-Bass.

Myers, S., & Range, L. M. (in press). No-suicide agreements: High school students' perspectives. *Death Studies.*

Ossip-Klein, D. J., & Rychtarik, R. G. (1993). Behavioral contracts between alcoholics and family members: Improving aftercare participation and maintaining sobriety after inpatient alcoholism treatment. In T. J. O'Farrell (Ed.), *Treating alcohol problems: Marital and family interventions* (pp. 281–304). New York: Guilford Press.

Prochaska, J. O., & Norcross, J. C. (1999). *Systems of psychotherapy: A transtheoretical analysis* (4th ed.). Pacific Grove, CA: Brooks/Cole.

Range, L. M., Campbell, C., Kovac, S. H., Marion-Jones, M., Aldridge, H., Kogos, S., et al. (2002). No-suicide agreements: An overview and recommendations. *Death Studies, 26,* 51–74.

Robison, J. I., Rogers, M. A., & Carlson, J. J. (1992). Effects of a 6-month incentive-based exercise program on adherence and work capacity. *Medicine and Science in Sports and Exercise, 24,* 85–93.

Rudd, M. D., Joiner, T. E., Jobes, D. A., & King, C. A. (1999). The outpatient treatment of suicidality: An integration of science and recognition of its limitations. *Professional Psychology: Research and Practice, 30,* 437–446.

Ruth, W. J. (1996). Goal setting and behavior contracting for students with emotional and behavioral difficulties: Analysis of daily, weekly, and total goal attainment. *Psychology in the Schools, 33,* 153–158.

Seal, A. M., & Swerissen, H. (1993). Lectures, prompts and contracts to promote parental safety. *Behaviour Change, 10,* 103–107.

Shea, S. C. (1999). *The practical art of suicide assessment.* New York: Wiley.

Silk, K. R., Eisner, W., & Allport, C. (1994). Focused time-limited inpatient treatment of borderline personality disorder. *Journal of Personality Disorders, 8,* 268–278.

Simon, R. I. (1999). The suicide prevention contract: Clinical, legal, and risk management issues. *Journal of the American Academy of Psychiatry and Law, 27,* 445–450.

Stummer, G. (2002). An update on the use of contracting. *Transactional Analysis Journal, 32,* 121–123.

Vinson, D. C., & Devera-Sales, A. (2000). Computer-generated written behavioral contracts with problem drinkers in primary medical care. *Substance Abuse, 21,* 215–222.

Weiss, A. (2001). The no-suicide contract: Possibilities and pitfalls. *American Journal of Psychotherapy, 55,* 414–419.

Westefeld, J. S., Range, L. M., Rogers, J. R., Maples, M. R., Bromley, J. L., & Alcorn, J. (2000). Suicide: An overview. *Counseling Psychologist, 28,* 445–510.

Wilson, C. T. (2000). Behavior therapy. In R. J. Corsini & D. Wedding (Eds.), *Current psychotherapies* (6th ed., pp. 205–240). Itasca, IL: Peacock Press.

CHAPTER 10

Cognitive-Behavioral Therapy
with Suicidal Patients

Mark A. Reinecke and Elizabeth R. Didie

The treatment of the suicidal patient has undergone a dramatic transformation over the past 75 years. The foundations for cognitive-behavioral therapy for suicidality began with the psychoanalytic formulations of Abraham (1911) and Freud (1927). Early psychodynamic theorists proposed that the suicidal individual suffers from an unconscious loss of a loved object and that feelings of anger and aggression felt toward the lost loved object are redirected inward toward the self. It followed that therapy tended to be insight-oriented and supportive (Mendelson, 1974). Cognitive-behavioral models of depression and suicide were first proposed during the 1960s when limitations in psychodynamic models of depression became apparent (Beck, 1963, 1964, 1967). Trained in psychoanalysis, Aaron Beck attempted to substantiate Freud's theory that depression stemmed from retroflected anger. In a provocative series of studies, Beck observed that depressed adults did not manifest unconscious retroflected anger and aggression. Rather, they demonstrated a negative bias in the processing of information as well as negative views of the self, world, and future (Beck & Weishaar, 1995).

Cognitive-behavioral models of depression and suicide grew out of these seminal works. Research since that time has focused on identifying cognitive, behavioral, and social factors associated with vulnerability for suicide; on articulating models for how these factors interact in placing individuals at risk; and on developing treatments based on these models. Cognitive therapy is based on diathesis-stress models of psychopathology and assumes that depression and suicidality are multiply determined.

Cognitive models assume that the ways in which individuals construe or interpret events influence how they respond, behaviorally and emotionally, to life events. They assume that cognitive processes are knowable and accessible; that is, individuals are able to reflect on and monitor their conscious thoughts. They assume, as well, that cognitive processes and contents can be changed and that behavioral and emotional change can be brought about through cognitive change (Dobson & Dozois, 2001).

In practice, cognitive therapy is active, problem-focused, strategic, and psychoeducational. Cognitive therapists work collaboratively with the patient to identify maladaptive beliefs, attitudes, appraisals, attributions, assumptions, and expectations. These cognitive activities are then subjected to rational analysis and put to empirical test. Through the assignment of cognitive and behavioral tasks, the patient develops social and problem-solving skills, as well as an ability to evaluate and change maladaptive beliefs. Beck (1996) proposed an adaptation of his original cognitive model in an effort to better account for interactions among cognitive, affective, and motivational factors in the development and maintenance of psychopathology, including depression and suicidality. His concept of a "suicidal mode," although interesting, has not yet received empirical scrutiny (Rudd, 2000).

Controlled outcome studies suggest that cognitive-behavioral therapies can be effective for treating clinically depressed adults (D. A. Clark & Beck, 1999; Solomon & Haaga, 2003) and adolescents (Curry, 2001; Reinecke, Ryan, & DuBois, 1998). Cognitive therapy can be effective for treating severe forms of depression (DeRubeis, Gelfand, Tang, & Simons, 1999) and is, in combination with antidepressant medications, more efficacious than either treatment alone for adults with chronic major depression (Keller et al., 2000). Moreover, cognitive-behavioral therapy shows promise as a means of reducing suicidal ideations and behavior (Hawton et al., 1998). Given the strength of these findings, cognitive therapy has attracted a great deal of clinical and research attention over the past quarter-century. The goals of this chapter are, first, to review research on cognitive factors associated with suicidal risk, and second, to discuss evidence for the efficacy of cognitive-behavioral interventions for treating suicidal patients, followed by our conclusions.

FACTORS ASSOCIATED WITH VULNERABILITY FOR SUICIDE

Suicide is multiply determined. Research indicates that a range of social, environmental, biological, psychiatric, and cognitive factors appears to be associated with an increased risk of suicidal ideations, gestures, attempts, and completed suicide. However, we do not have a comprehensive, integrated model for how these variables interact in contributing to the risk for suicide. Although few problems facing clinicians are more urgent or daunting than suicidal behavior, prediction of suicidal risk for individual patients remains a complex and clinically challenging endeavor (Murphy, 1984).

Methodological, statistical, and conceptual factors have complicated attempts to develop and test integrative models of suicide. Suicidal individuals are clinically diverse. Although, by definition, they share a wish or intent to die, they often vary in their motivation for attempting suicide and as to potential deterrents. It appears, as well, that individuals who experience thoughts of suicide may differ in important ways from those who make a gesture or an attempt and that these individuals may differ from individuals who successfully commit suicide. Ideators, attempters, and completers may be distinct, albeit related, groups (Farberow, 1981; Linehan, Chiles, Egan, Devine, & Laffaw, 1986). Moreover, important gender, cultural, ethnic, and age-related differences in suicidal ideations and behavior have been identified. Individuals vary, as well, in how they cope with negative moods and stressful life events. To be clinically useful, our models must be able to account for individual difference factors, such as these, that are associated with vulnerability for suicide.

Statistical factors, however, limit our ability to test multivariate models for predicting suicidal behavior. Limits on the reliability of assessment instruments, in conjunction with low base rates of completed suicide in the general population, make it difficult to test predictive models. Sample sizes necessary to test the multivariate models of suicide with community samples are very large. As a consequence, researchers have tended to focus on developing strategies for predicting and preventing suicide in high-risk groups, such as individuals experiencing suicidal ideations and patients who have been admitted to the hospital after having made a suicide attempt. These efforts have been complicated, however, by the fact that a number of moderator variables appear to exist (as implied by the fact that suicide rates differ among various groups). It is likely that alternative pathways to suicide exist. Clarifying the nature of these pathways is also a complex endeavor. As much of the research has used cross-sectional designs, it is not clear that many of the cognitive, social, and psychiatric factors found to be associated with suicide are, in fact, specific predictors of suicidality. The possibility exists that they are simply concomitants of depressed mood or current psychopathology and that they are neither necessary nor sufficient causes of suicide. It often is not clear whether individual risk factors make independent and unique contributions to the prediction of suicidal thoughts and behavior and how they interact with one another over time.

In sum, our models are not well articulated, our measures are inexact, and we do not yet have a clear understanding of relationships between vulnerability factors and how they lead to suicide. Longitudinal research examining relationships between vulnerability and resilience factors in specific at-risk groups, then, is greatly needed. The possibility exists that identified risk factors (such as level of depression, impulsivity, or hopelessness) may not be applicable for some groups. Moreover, many risk factors have low specificity, leading to an unacceptably high level of false-positive identifications. Vulnerability for suicide is a dynamic state—it tends to fluctuate over time—and may be seen as reflecting a balance between internal and external sources of risk and resilience. It is important, when working with potentially suicidal patients, to bear this in mind. We must attend to environmental, social, and intrapsychic sources of risk, as well as to protective factors, supports, adaptive coping strategies, deterrents, and sources of resilience. Suicidal risk, in short, is not a static entity but a continuously changing state. Suicidal behavior, from this perspective, can be seen as the culmination of a sequence of events, a sequence that can be interrupted in any number of ways. This view is consistent with discussions of a "suicide zone" (Litman, 1990) and a "suicide mode" (Beck, 1996)—constructs proposed to account for the activation and organization of suicidal crises.

A number of factors appear to be associated with an increased risk of suicide. It has long been recognized, for example, that links exist between depression and suicide. Better than 80% of persons who commit suicide are depressed at the time of their attempt (Murphy, 1985), and an early review of follow-up studies by Guze and Robins (1970) suggested that the lifetime incidence of suicide among clinically depressed persons is 15%. A more recent study by Klerman (1987) indicated that fully 30% of patients with a major affective disorder die by suicide. Not surprisingly, treatments found to be effective for treating depressive disorders, such as cognitive therapy, are often used with suicidal patients.

Although depression is strongly associated with suicide, it is neither a necessary nor sufficient cause. Many depressed individuals do not attempt suicide, and many nondepressed individuals make suicide attempts. Additional factors appear to play a role. Cognitive factors associated with an increased risk of suicide include hopelessness, problem-solving deficits, reasons for living, cognitive distortions, maladaptive schemas, and negative attributional style. Feelings of anxiety, social isolation, alcohol or substance abuse, behavioral impulsivity, and deficits in affect regulations also appear to be associated with vulnerability for suicide. Variables such as these are included in descriptive structural models of risk for suicide (Lewinsohn, Rohde, & Seeley, 1996; Schotte & Clum, 1982, 1987; Turner, Korslund, Barnett, & Josiassen, 1998) and serve as the focus of cognitive-behavioral treatments. Given the prominence of cognitive risk factors for our models and treatments, we briefly discuss each in turn.

Hopelessness and Suicide

"When working with suicidal patients, treat hopelessness first" has become something of a truism in the practice of cognitive therapy. Abundant research indicates that feelings of pessimism that accompany depression often contribute to suicidal ideations and motivate suicidal behavior. Suicidality can stem from the individual's belief that his or her problems are so excruciatingly painful that only death can provide relief. Suicidal individuals tend to view their difficulties as both unendurable and unsolvable. Given this predicament, suicide comes to be seen as a viable option.

There is substantial evidence that suicidal individuals tend, as a group, to view their difficulties as insurmountable and feel hopeless in the face of these problems (Beck, Brown, Berchick, Stewart, & Steer,

1990; Beck, Brown, & Steer, 1989). Studies with clinically depressed adults suggest that hopelessness may, in fact, mediate observed relations between depression and suicide. When levels of hopelessness are controlled, associations between severity of depression and suicide typically are reduced to nonsignificance. Hopelessness has been found to be a more powerful predictor of suicidal intent than severity of depression among suicidal ideators (Nekanda-Trepka, Bishop, & Blackburn, 1983). Moreover, the level of pessimism appears to discriminate suicidal from nonsuicidal patients with equivalent levels of depression (Ellis & Ratliff, 1986). Hopelessness has been found to predict completed suicide among individuals diagnosed with major affective disorders (Fawcett et al., 1987), schizophrenia (Drake & Cotton, 1986), and alcohol abuse (Beck, Weissman, & Kovacs, 1976). Finally, longitudinal studies suggest that hopelessness may be a useful long-term predictor of completed suicide (Beck, Brown, & Steer, 1989; Beck, Steer, Kovacs, & Garrison, 1985; Fawcett et al., 1990). In a prospective study of 1,958 outpatients, for example, hopelessness was found to be strongly associated with eventual suicide (Beck et al., 1990). Taken together, findings suggest that hopelessness may be a useful short-term and long-term predictor of suicidal risk among adults and that feelings of pessimism may be an important target for therapy (Freeman & Reinecke, 1993; Reinecke, 2000).

Problem Solving and Suicide

Studies suggest that problem-solving deficits are a risk factor for suicidal behavior (J. Evans, Williams, O'Loughlin, & Howells, 1992; Fremouw, Callahan, & Kashden, 1993; Ivanoff, Smyth, Grochowski, Jang, & Klein, 1992; Priester & Clum, 1993; Rudd, Rajab, & Dahm, 1994; Wilson et al., 1995). It has been hypothesized that, when faced with an external stressor, the suicidal individual is unable to generate solutions and progressively becomes overwhelmed and hopeless. Evidence indicates that suicide attempters demonstrate a range of specific problem-solving deficits. They tend to be more field dependent, show greater cognitive rigidity, have more dichotomous thinking, have greater difficulty generating solutions, and use a passive style of coping with interpersonal problems (Bonner & Rich, 1988; Clum & Febbraro, 1994; Dixon, Heppner, & Anderson, 1991; Linehan, Camper, Chiles, Strosahl,

& Shearin, 1987; Orbach, Bar-Joseph, & Dror, 1990; Pollock & Williams, 1998; Priester & Clum, 1993; Rudd et al., 1994; Schotte & Clum, 1987). As their belief that they are unable to resolve their difficulties and consequent feelings of hopelessness become more severe, depressed individuals become more at risk for suicidal behavior (Dixon, Heppner, & Rudd, 1994). These findings provide a conceptual foundation for interventions that directly address problem-solving deficits. Patients are taught to identify problems and stressful life events that precede suicide attempts, as well as the ability to generate solutions that will impede suicidal gestures (Patsiokas & Clum, 1985; Salkovskis, Atha, & Storer, 1990).

Cognitive Distortions and Suicide

Cognitive models of psychopathology and psychotherapy postulate that individuals assign meanings to events (at both deliberate or conscious and at automatic or implicit levels). These meanings may be adaptive or maladaptive and are influenced by information processing biases or cognitive distortions. Cognitive distortions take several forms and can influence both the assignment of meaning and the perception, encoding, retrieval, and processing of information. Prezant and Neimeyer (1988), in a study of moderately depressed adults, found that selective abstraction (the tendency to selectively attend to information while overlooking more desirable data) and overgeneralization (a tendency to draw broad inferences to a range of unrelated or related situations based on limited information) predicted severity of suicidal ideation. This effect remained even after severity of depression was controlled. Studies suggest that suicidal individuals may also tend to engage in *dichotomous thinking,* that is, categorize events or experiences into opposite extremes, adopting a black-or-white perspective (Neuringer, 1968; Neuringer & Lettieri, 1971; Wetzel, 1976). Although biased information processing is not a specific risk factor for depression, identification, monitoring, and changing cognitive distortions are emphasized in cognitive therapy for depression and suicide.

Schemata and Suicide

The concept of schemata plays a central role in cognitive models of depression. *Schemata* may be defined as organized, tacit bodies of stored knowledge that interact with and guide the processing of information. They are the premises, formulae, and templates that allow individuals to order and integrate their observations so that they can come to meaningful conclusions. Like grammatical structures, they are not taught explicitly. Rather, they are learned through personal experience and vicariously through the observation of others. Schemata influence the full range of cognitive processes, including attention, perception, encoding, and retrieval of information. Schemata are self-perpetuating insofar as they selectively influence both the encoding and availability of information. Cognitive models of depression postulate that depressed persons maintain depressogenic schemata and that these structures contribute to the consolidation of negative views of themselves, the world, and the future (Beck, Rush, Shaw, & Emery, 1979). Studies indicate that, as predicted, depressed individuals tend to selectively recall more negatively valenced adjectives describing themselves, overlook evidence of successful task performance, view others as critical or rejecting, and demonstrate depression-specific attentional bias on dichotic listening tasks (for reviews, see D. A. Clark & Beck, 1999; Ingram, Miranda, & Segal, 1998; Solomon & Haaga, 2003). Stressful events are believed to activate these core beliefs, leading the individual to experience cognitive distortions and negative automatic thoughts.

Studies suggest that a number of dysfunctional attitudes or schemata may be associated with suicidal ideations (Beck, Steer, & Brown, 1993; Bonner & Rich, 1987; Ellis & Ratliff, 1986; Hewitt, Flett, & Turnbull-Donovan, 1992). Schemata of suicidal patients are believed to include:

1. A vulnerability to loss or abandonment in conjunction with a belief that others are rejecting, uncaring, judgmental, and hold unreasonably high expectations for them.
2. Perceptions of personal incompetence and helplessness.
3. Poor distress tolerance.
4. A perception of defectiveness and unlovability.
5. A belief that it is important to impress others (Freeman & Reinecke, 1993; Rudd, Joiner, & Rajab, 2001).

Although dysfunctional attitudes, such as these, are associated with suicidal ideations, it is not clear that they are specific to suicidal patients, that they account for significant variance in predicting suicidality (above and beyond other known predictors, such as hopelessness, problem-solving deficits, and history of prior suicide attempts), or that they predict suicidality among at-risk individuals who are not currently depressed. Nonetheless, tacit beliefs, such as these, can be an important focus of psychotherapy with acutely suicidal patients.

Attributional Style and Suicide

According to the attributional model of depression (Abramson, Metalsky, & Alloy, 1989; Alloy, Abramson, Metalsky, & Hartlage, 1988; Alloy et al., 1999), depressed individuals are more likely to attribute negative life events to internal, stable, and global factors than are nondepressed individuals. A generalized negative attributional style is believed to lead vulnerable individuals to experience depressive symptoms in the presence of negative life events. Furthermore, the combination of negative attributional style and stress is hypothesized to lead to hopelessness (Metalsky & Joiner, 1992), which has, as we have seen, been associated with an increased risk of suicidal thoughts and behavior.

Partial support for an attributional model of suicide was provided by Abramson and colleagues (1998), who observed that cognitively vulnerable older adolescents and young adults were more likely to experience suicidal thoughts during a follow-up period and that these thoughts were mediated by feelings of hopelessness. Along similar lines, Priester and Clum (1992), in a study of college students, observed that a tendency to attribute poor performance on an exam to stable causes was associated with higher levels of depression, hopelessness, and suicidal ideation. Those who attributed positive events to internal causes, however, were less likely to feel depressed, hopeless, or suicidal. More recently, Joiner and Rudd (1995) suggested that negative attributional style may mediate observed associations between interpersonal events and suicidal ideation. They observed that, in situations characterized by high interpersonal stress, a negative attributional style for interpersonal events was associated with increased suicidal ideation. These results are consistent with the observation that experiences of social loss and rejection are a frequent trigger of suicidal thoughts (Berman & Jobes, 1991; Rich, Warsradt, Nemiroff, Fowler, & Young, 1991). Findings have been inconsistent as to relations between attributional style and suicidality among adolescents (Rotheram-Borus, Trautman, Dopkins, & Shrout, 1990;

Spirito, Overholser, & Hart, 1991), raising the possibility of developmental differences in vulnerability for suicide.

Impulsivity, Affect Regulation, and Suicide

Suicidal individuals experience difficulty coping not only with stressful life events but also with negative moods. It is not only the life event or loss that is intolerable; it is the emotional state that accompanies it. Given these difficulties, these individuals respond by engaging in actions that may quickly alleviate their emotional distress (e.g., alcohol or substance use, self-harm, and suicide). Because they lack skills for modulating their rapidly escalating negative moods, these actions are often impulsive. A number of authors have commented on the importance of emotional expression or ventilation (Hawton & Catalan, 1982) and emotion regulation (Koerner & Linehan, 2002) in working with acutely suicidal individuals.

Social, Developmental, and Environmental Risk Factors

Risk factors may be defined as experiences, situations, or proclivities that make a particular outcome, such as suicide, more likely (Reinecke, 2000). Prospective and retrospective studies suggest that stressful life events (such as work or legal problems, humiliating social events, the recent loss of a loved one, and changes in residence) are associated with increased risk for suicide (Hagnell & Rorsman, 1980). Along similar lines, a family history of psychopathology including suicidal behavior has been found to increase the risk for suicide in other family members (Brent, Bridge, Johnson, & Connolly, 1996; Lesage et al., 1994; Roy, Segal, Centerwall, & Robinette, 1991; Wagner, 1997). Other familial variables that appear to be associated with suicidal attempts include early losses, such as divorce, separation, and death (Smith, Mercy, & Conn, 1988; Wagner, 1997). Studies of youth suggest that negative peer relationships, abuse and neglect, family instability, and a chaotic home environment may be associated with both a cognitive vulnerability and later suicidal behavior (Briere & Zaidi, 1989; Wagner, 1997; Yang & Clum, 1996). Finally, a review of factors associated with completed suicide indicated that parental status may be more closely linked with suicide risk than marital status (D. C. Clark & Fawcett, 1992), with those being responsible for young children at lower risk (Fawcett et al., 1987;

Kozak & Gibbs, 1979). Married women without children were more likely to die by suicide than married women with children. Furthermore, married women without children were less likely to die by suicide than unmarried women without children. Among married women, suicide risk declined significantly in proportion to the number of children (Hoyer & Lund, 1993). Women who have been widowed early in their marriage still have the highest suicide rate among any marital status group (Kreitman, 1988).

The question becomes, then, how are we to account for the observed associations between disparate experiences, such as these, and suicide? One possibility is that these experiences are associated with the establishment and consolidation of maladaptive beliefs that, when activated, place the individual at risk for depression and suicide. An alternative possibility is that they may be associated with the establishment of recurrent *interpersonal* processes that serve to corrode social and psychological resources (such as a supportive social network, a positive attributional style, or adaptive problem-solving skills) such that the individual, when confronted by a stressful life event, becomes unable to cope effectively with it. Depressed and suicidal individuals tend, as a group, to receive reduced social support from others. It appears, however, that they may behave in ways that create additional interpersonal stress and elicit rejection from others. They selectively attend to negative feedback and excessively seek reassurance and support from others. Depression and suicide, from this perspective, become recurrent and self-generating. For individuals who experience suicidal ideations that are characterized by a high level of intent, suicidal gestures can come to be seen as an accepted coping strategy or solution. Depressed individuals behave in ways, both subtle and explicit, that exacerbate their distress and place them at risk for recurrent difficulties. In practice, this approach suggests that empirically supported interventions designed to develop social skills and social supports, enhance instrumental and emotional coping skills, and increase effective rates of positive feedback from others may be helpful in reducing both depression and suicidality.

Cognitive-Behavioral Models of Suicide

As noted, cognitive-behavioral models of suicide are based on the assumption that cognitive processes have a direct impact on emotions and subsequent behaviors (Beck et al., 1979). A range of cognitive processes, including perceptual biases, attitudes or schemata, assumptions, automatic thoughts, images, memories, beliefs, goals, attributions, expectations, wishes, plans, inferences, and values influences how an individual responds, behaviorally and emotionally, to life events. Emotional and behavioral problems, including suicidality, are seen as mediated by maladaptive cognitive, behavioral, and interpersonal processes that are learned over the course of development (Reinecke, 2000). A number of cognitive-behavioral models of suicide have been proposed (Bonner & Rich, 1987; Dieserund, Roysamb, & Kraft, 2001; Freeman & Reinecke, 1993; Rudd et al., 2001; Schotte & Clum, 1982). These models are similar in many ways to the cognitive models of depression from which they were derived (Reinecke, 2002). They are based on diathesis-stress paradigms and highlight the ways that cognitive vulnerabilities interact with stressful life events in placing individuals at risk for suicide. Although they differ in emphasis, they are cognitive-mediational and attend to the important role of maladaptive cognitive and perceptual processes in the treatment of suicidal patients.

Strategies and Techniques of Cognitive Therapy

In practice, the cognitive-behavioral therapist and patient work collaboratively to examine the patient's thoughts and beliefs, approaches to problem-solving, social behavior, and emotion regulation skills. Direct attempts are made to develop the patient's ability to monitor changes in his or her mood, identify concomitant thoughts, modify maladaptive social behaviors, and develop adaptive skills. As in cognitive therapy for depression, an emphasis is placed on the use of Socratic questioning. Thoughts are viewed as hypotheses to be tested. It is through systematic questioning and discussion of the adaptiveness (or maladaptiveness) of maintaining a specific perception or a belief (e.g., "I'll never survive this. . . . I might as well be dead") and the rational examination of evidence for and against the belief that assumptions are challenged and more functional, adaptive beliefs are developed. Whereas a primary focus of therapy is on understanding patients' phenomenal world—as reflected in their conscious thoughts, perceptions, memories, and beliefs—the cognitive therapist recognizes the importance of attending to social, environmental, biological, emotional, and behavioral factors that may be contributing to patients' distress. An important goal of therapy is teaching the patient the necessary skills to manage stressful life events independent of the therapist. An explicit goal of cognitive therapy is to facilitate the prevention of relapse and recurrence (Hollon, Haman, & Brown, 2002).

Principles for addressing suicidal ideation and behavior are based on standard cognitive-behavioral approaches for treating depression (Beck et al., 1979). Treatment begins with the establishment of a trusting, collaborative therapeutic relationship. Patients are provided with a venue for expressing their concerns, and relationships among stressful life events, distressing thoughts, and emotional reactions are identified. An explicit goal is to help patients feel understood. A trusting relationship allows for the systematic assessment of cognitive, social, and environmental factors maintaining patients' suicidality. As in cognitive therapy for other disorders, the use of objective rating scales (assessing severity of depression, anxiety, and hopelessness; suicidal ideations and intent; deterrents and reasons for living; social problem solving; dysfunctional attitudes or schema; cognitive distortions; and stressful life events and social supports) is balanced by a sensitive clinical discussion of the patient's subjective views of each of these domains (Maris, Berman, Maltsberger, & Yufit, 1992; Reinecke, 2000; Rudd et al., 2001). As information on each of these areas is collected, the therapist attempts to develop a clear and parsimonious formulation of the patient's concerns. This formulation is shared with the patient and serves as a template for developing a treatment plan. Providing patients with a case formulation helps them come to see that their distress is understandable and that courses of action other than suicide may be possible. The possibility exists, as well, that the development of a therapeutic alliance may, by serving as a reliable social support, itself serve as a barrier against patients acting on suicidal impulses.

Treatment of suicidal patients is systematic, strategic, and problem-focused. An initial emphasis is placed on challenging beliefs that support patients' feelings of hopelessness (Beck et al., 1979). After assessing suicidal risk, patients' motives for considering suicide, and their deterrents, the therapist endeavors to "step into his world and view it through the patient's lens" (p. 212). An idiographic understanding of patients and their perceived difficulties is central to the cognitive model

(Reinecke, 2000). This understanding is achieved through empathizing with patients' despair, understanding their motives for considering suicide, and acknowledging their belief that the future is hopeless. Meanings attached to specific, affect-laden words are carefully explored. What, for example, do patients mean when they describe the loss of their job as "devastating"? Are there situations where they have felt this in the past? How would we define the term *devastation?* Can a country, a city, an individual recover from a "devastating event"? What would be needed to bring this recovery about? The meanings attached to words define, in many ways, how individuals understand themselves and their world. Moreover, our meanings place limits or boundaries on courses of action that are available. To paraphrase Wittgenstein, the limits of our words are the limits of our world.

The acknowledgment of patients' despair does not connote approval of their desire to commit suicide. On the contrary, it directs our attention to a discussion of a wider range of alternative solutions and the identification of a desired end state or solution they would like to bring about. This approach may reduce gains some patients seek through suicidal threats. Patients often are reassured to find that their therapist is comfortable openly discussing their darkest fears and most frightening thoughts and experiences.

As treatment goals are identified, therapy comes to focus on addressing cognitive, social, and environmental mediators of their distress. Direct attempts are made to develop additional deterrents, alleviate stressors, and develop social supports. As noted, impaired rational problem solving, reduced problem-solving motivation, and cognitive distortions often are associated with suicidal thoughts. With this in mind, the therapist actively assists patients to identify a specific *solvable* problem or concern and then to develop their motivation to address it, which may involve reframing or reconceptualizing factors contributing to their distress. If, for example, an individual is suicidal because his wife has filed for a divorce, the goal may or may not center on addressing his marital difficulties and on "making her come back." Rather, treatment may focus on developing an understanding of how the relationship had deteriorated, the meaning of this event for him, and on developing a sense of hope that new relationships and sources of satisfaction may be available in the future. Attempts are made to clarify how he typically copes with problems and to assist him to develop a positive, adaptive, problem-solving orientation. These attempts may involve assisting him to recognize problems as they begin to emerge, to accept that having problems is normal and not to be avoided, to make adaptive attributions about possible causes for problems, to reduce a tendency to magnify or exaggerate the significance of problems, to develop a perception of efficacy or control and an expectation that the problem may be solvable, and to accept that a complete solution may not be possible. The patient's wife may not, when all is said and done, wish to return. This need not mean, however, that suicide is the only viable course of action or the only means of alleviating his distress. As our patient develops a more positive orientation toward problem solving, his tendency to avoid problems, withdraw from challenging situations, or respond in an impulsive manner is reduced.

As patients' problem-solving motivation improves, interventions are introduced to develop rational problem-solving skills. Patients are taught to approach problems in a calm manner. Relaxation training (including controlled breathing and muscle relaxation techniques) can be useful in alleviating feelings of agitation often experienced by suicidal patients. Patients next develop skills in problem identification. They are taught to recognize their most important concern (which may or may not be the event that precipitated the suicidal crisis), as well as the factors that may be maintaining it. An attempt is made to assist the patient to develop reasonable, realistic goals, as well as a clear understanding of the nature of the problem and the steps that may be necessary to resolve it. Patients are encouraged to develop instrumental goals (that is, an understanding of the problem to be addressed) and emotion-focused goals (an understanding of how this problem makes them feel and how it affects their adjustment). This is followed by the development of skills in generating alternative solutions, weighing their pros and cons, evaluating their short- and long-term effectiveness, selecting the most effective solution, implementing it, and evaluating its effectiveness. These skills are typically taught through a combination of psychoeducational exercises, modeling, role plays, and Socratic dialogue.

For patients who view their problems as overwhelming and unsolvable, the therapist assists them in breaking problems into smaller, more manageable units that can be successfully addressed. When potentially harmful coping strategies are being used (such as alcohol and drugs), the therapist works with patients to develop more effective coping skills.

As noted, suicidal crises are often precipitated by interpersonal losses. Suicidal patients frequently feel socially isolated, view others as unsupportive, and behave in ways that elicit ostracism or social rejection. With this in mind, the cognitive therapist attempts to serve as a reliable source of support and works with patients to develop their social skills and their social network. The roles of family members and loved ones in the suicidal crisis are examined and addressed. For many suicidal patients, families are not a source of support, but of stress. Family therapy sessions may be introduced as a means of addressing maladaptive, critical, or coercive interaction patterns.

Given the central role of hopelessness as a proximal risk factor for suicide, a primary goal of therapy is to address patients' sense of pessimism and demoralization. We want patients to perceive that life's problems are solvable (at least in principle) and that they have the ability to bring about this change. This is accomplished through cognitive and behavioral exercises and by modeling effective problem solving and optimism in the face of therapeutic problems (Reinecke, 2000; Rudd et al., 2001).

If patients have a definite plan and appear to be intent on acting on their suicidal wishes, psychiatric hospitalization may be required. For some patients, hospitalization is seen as a relief from dealing with their distress, whereas for others this recommendation may be strongly opposed. It has been suggested that hospitalization be approached in a nonthreatening, collaborative way (Stolberg, Clark, & Bongar, 2002) and that meanings attached to being hospitalized be carefully explored. Hospitalization often carries important meanings for patients. It can affect how they view themselves (e.g., "I'm really sick, just like Dad"), their sense of self-efficacy (e.g., "I couldn't solve this as an outpatient. . . . It's just too big for me"), their families (e.g., "They don't care. . . . They're relieved I'm in here"), their problems (e.g., "There's no solution. . . . It's unstoppable"), and their future (e.g., "I'll never get a job. Who would want to hire someone with a psychiatric history? My life is ruined"). Possible meanings associated with hospitalization should be carefully examined. An emphasis may be placed on envisioning alternative, positive future scenarios and ways of looking at themselves.

In sum, cognitive therapy of suicidal patients is multidimensional and acknowledges the importance of addressing the full range of behavioral, affective, social, and environmental factors associated with vulnerability for suicide. Cognitive interventions include mood and thought monitoring, rational responding, guided imagery, thought stopping, self-instruction, scaling, guided association, reattribution, and examination of idiosyncratic meanings. Behavioral interventions are directed primarily toward developing social and problem-solving skills and include activity scheduling, assertiveness or relaxation training, graded task assignments, mastery and pleasure ratings, behavioral rehearsal, in vivo exposure, and bibliotherapy.

EFFICACY OF COGNITIVE-BEHAVIORAL THERAPY

The utility of cognitive-behavioral therapy for the treatment of depression is well established (for reviews, see Clark & Beck, 1999; Gloaguen, Cottraux, Cucherat, & Blackburn, 1998; Lambert & Davis, 2002; Solomon & Haaga, 2003). Cognitive therapy for depression is among the most widely studied interventions for any psychiatric disorder. Results from controlled clinical trials suggest that cognitive-behavioral therapy is more effective than placebo, treatment-as-usual, or minimal intervention and is as effective as, if not more than, other forms of psychotherapy (Dobson, 1989; Gaffan, Tsaousis, & Kemp-Wheeler, 1995). It is one of the few psychosocial approaches to meet criteria for an empirically supported treatment for depression (DeRubeis & Crits-Christoph, 1998).

There is controversy, however, surrounding the efficacy of cognitive-behavioral therapy for treating severe depression. Findings from the Treatment of Depression Collaborative Research Project (TDCRP) suggest that antidepressant medications may be more efficacious than cognitive therapy for treating severely depressed adult outpatients (Elkin et al., 1989; Thase et al., 1997). Practice guidelines consequently advised that cognitive therapy not be used without concurrent pharmacotherapy for treating severely depressed adults (American Psychiatric Association, 2000). A reanalysis of these and other data indicates, however, that cognitive therapy may be as effective as medication in the treatment of severe depression (Blackburn & Moore, 1997; DeRubeis et al., 1999) and that outcomes for more severely depressed patients may be related to level of therapist experience and competence. Taken together, findings indicate that cognitive therapy can be effective for treating major depression. Outcomes are comparable to those of antidepressant medications, especially when treatment quality or "fidelity" is high (Lambert & Davis, 2002). It is not clear, however, what particular components or facets of cognitive therapy serve as the active ingredients of the treatment, what therapist or patient characteristics are most predictive of treatment response and relapse, or how cognitive therapy exerts its effects. Processes mediating change in cognitive therapy are worthy of careful study (Dimidjian & Dobson, 2003).

Is cognitive psychotherapy effective in reducing suicidal ideations and, more importantly, suicidal behavior? Although few controlled trials are available, preliminary findings suggest that cognitive therapy may be helpful in the acute treatment of some suicidal patients. Patsiokas and Clum (1985) compared brief (three-week) cognitive restructuring, problem-solving therapy, and a nondirective therapy in a study of hospitalized suicide attempters. All three treatments were found to be effective in reducing the severity of suicidal thoughts. Several years later, Salkovskis et al. (1990) examined the effectiveness of a short-term cognitive-behavioral, problem-solving approach among 20 patients at risk for repeated suicide attempts. They found that cognitive-behavioral therapy was effective at reducing severity of suicidal ideations, depression, and hopelessness, and gains were maintained for up to one year. Patients who had received the problem-solving training demonstrated fewer suicide attempts at six months in comparison to controls that received treatment-as-usual. Although patients receiving problem-solving therapy also demonstrated fewer suicidal gestures at 18-month follow-up, these differences were not statistically significant. It appears, then, that more intensive therapy, including follow-up or booster sessions, may be indicated for patients with a history of multiple suicide attempts.

More recently, social problem-solving training was found to be effective in reducing levels of suicidality in a sample of 39 older adolescents and adults who had attempted suicide (McLeavey, Daly, Ludgate, & Murray, 1994). Participants demonstrated reduced levels of hopelessness, as well as improved social problem-solving, self-perceptions, and perceived ability to cope with problems. Although patients receiving problem-solving therapy made fewer suicide attempts during a 12-month follow-up period, these differences were not statistically significant. Problem-solving therapy was also found to be more effective than treatment-as-usual for suicidal young adults (Rudd, Joiner, & Rajab, 1996). Both groups demonstrated a reduction in suicidal thoughts and behavior and an improvement in self-appraised problem-solving ability. Problem-solving therapy was particularly effective with higher risk participants. These gains were maintained at 12-month follow-up. These results are consistent with those of other controlled outcome studies (K. Evans et al., 1999; Lerner & Clum, 1990; Rudd, Rajab, et al., 1996) and are reflected in the positive results of a meta-analytic review of randomized controlled trials of interventions for suicide attempters (van der Sande, Buskens, et al., 1997).

A variant of cognitive-behavioral therapy, dialectical behavior therapy (DBT), also appears to be useful in reducing suicidal behaviors among women diagnosed with borderline personality disorder (Linehan, 1987; Linehan, Armstrong, Suarez, Allmon, & Heard, 1991). The intervention incorporates problem-solving, social skills, and emotion regulation approaches as part of a comprehensive treatment program for chronically parasuicidal patients. Participants were compared with a control group of women who received treatment-as-usual. Women who received DBT demonstrated a significant reduction in the frequency of parasuicidal behaviors, reduced dropout rates, and spent fewer days in the hospital. At six-month follow-up, patients who received DBT displayed less parasuicidal behavior, less anger, and had better self-reported social adjustment (Linehan, Heard, & Armstrong, 1993).

Taken together, these findings suggest that cognitive-behavioral therapy may be more effective than treatment-as-usual in alleviating feelings of depression, reducing suicidal ideations, and preventing suicidal behavior, at least among patients with a history of suicide attempts. However, findings have not been universally positive (Gibbons, Butler, Urwin, & Gibbons, 1978; Hawton et al., 1987; Van der Sande, van Rooijen, et al., 1997).

Research suggests, then, that cognitive-behavioral therapy may be helpful in reducing depression, hopelessness, and suicidal ideations among adults for up to 12 months. Although initial findings have been promising, they have not been uniformly positive. The number of randomized, controlled trials completed to date has been small, and sample sizes generally have been limited. Moreover, it does not appear that gains are maintained for longer time periods, suggesting that follow-up or maintenance interventions may be indicated. More intensive interventions are indicated for chronically suicidal patients and for individuals with comorbid diagnoses (such as alcohol or substance abuse, psychosis, or borderline personality disorder). Although many suicidal patients receive a combination of psychotherapy and psychotropic medications, the efficacy and effectiveness of combined treatments have not been demonstrated. As we have seen, the large majority of outcome studies have emphasized the use of problem-solving interventions. Research is needed on the effectiveness of other cognitive-behavioral strategies, including those targeting maladaptive schema, depressogenic attributional style, social behavior, and cognitive distortions. Comparisons of cognitive-behavioral therapy with other active treatments, including pharmacotherapy, are needed. Further research is necessary to demonstrate the effectiveness of cognitive therapy in community settings.

CONCLUSIONS

Suicide is a tragic and, in many ways, preventable problem. Suicide is multiply determined—a range of biological, social, environmental, developmental, and cognitive factors are associated with an increased risk of suicidal thoughts and behavior. Recognition and appropriate treatment—using empirically supported approaches—may be of value in assisting at-risk individuals and in preventing completed suicide. This chapter has reviewed cognitive-behavioral models and techniques developed for use in treating suicidal patients. Although these approaches are often used in outpatient settings and may be appropriate for patients who have recently been discharged after having made a suicide attempt, they can also be modified for use in day-treatment and inpatient settings. Although research indicates that empirically supported psychotherapies, including cognitive-behavioral therapy, can be effective in reducing suicidal ideations and attempts, they are not widely available or used. The use of psychotherapy for treating depression has declined during recent years, even as potential limitations of psychotropic medications have become apparent. Several recent discussions of evidence-based guidelines and algorithms for treating depressed adults have emphasized new antidepressant medications, augmentation strategies, electroconvulsive therapy, and newer experimental strategies (including vagal nerve stimulation, transcranial magnetic stimulation, and antiglucocorticoid medications) but do not touch on the potential value of psychotherapy (DeBattista & Belanoff, 2002; DeBattista, Trivedi, Kern, & Lembke, 2002). Efforts might be directed toward making mental health professionals better aware of the utility of cognitive-behavioral approaches and making them available to patients in community settings.

Working with suicidal and potentially suicidal patients is challenging. Although patients often readily come to recognize how their beliefs, attitudes, expectations, attributions, approaches to solving problems, and social behavior affect their mood and functioning, it can be difficult for them to change these beliefs. Tacit beliefs are seen as the givens of life and are, to a degree, immutable. All of us tend to understand current experiences in terms of what we already know or believe. Whereas a natural proclivity to assimilate the new to preexisting beliefs can complicate the treatment of depressed or anxious patients, with suicidal patients this tendency can be life threatening. Strongly held beliefs that their pain is unendurable, their problems are insurmountable, others are unavailable, their predicament is futile, and their skills for resolving their problems are inadequate can place individuals at mortal risk. The therapist must work in a focused and incisive manner to demonstrate that these beliefs are not only maladaptive but also incorrect. Moreover, patients must come to see that there may be alternative ways of understanding their experiences and future. We are, in essence, assisting suicidal patients not only to develop problem-solving and social skills but also to construct an alternative understanding of themselves and their life. When individuals can see that an alternative future may exist and that change can be brought about by personal effort, true freedom of action becomes possible. With freedom of action, there is hope.

REFERENCES

Abraham, K. (1911). Notes on the psycho-analytic investigation and treatment of manic-depressive insanity and allied conditions. In *Selected papers on psycho-analysis* (pp. 137–156). London: Hogarth Press.

Abramson, L., Alloy, L., Hogan, M., Whitehouse, W., Cornette, M., Akhavan, S., et al. (1998). Suicidality and cognitive vulnerability to depression among college students: A prospective study. *Journal of Adolescence, 21,* 157–171.

Abramson, L., Metalsky, G., & Alloy, L. (1989). Hopelessness depression: A theory-based subtype of depression. *Psychological Review, 96,* 358–372.

Alloy, L., Abramson, L., Metalsky, G., & Hartlage, S. (1988). The hopelessness theory of depression: Attributional aspects. *British Journal of Clinical Psychology, 27,* 5–21.

Alloy, L., Abramson, L., Whitehouse, W., Hogan, M., Tashman, N., Steinberg, D., et al. (1999). Depressogenic cognitive styles: Predictive validity, information processing and personality characteristics, and developmental origins. *Behaviour Research and Therapy, 37,* 503–531.

American Psychiatric Association (APA). (2000). Practice guideline for the treatment of patients with major depressive disorder (revision). *American Journal of Psychiatry, 157*(Suppl. 4), 1–45.

Beck, A. T. (1963). Thinking and depression: 1. Idiosyncratic content and cognitive distortions. *Archives of General Psychiatry, 10,* 324–333.

Beck, A. T. (1964). Thinking and depression: 2. Theory and therapy. *Archives of General Psychiatry, 10,* 561–567.

Beck, A. T. (1967). *Depression: Clinical, experimental, and theoretical aspects.* New York: Harper & Row.

Beck, A. T. (1996). Beyond belief: A theory of modes, personality, and psychopathology. In P. Salkovkis (Ed.), *Frontiers of cognitive therapy* (pp. 1–25). New York: Guilford Press.

Beck, A. T., Brown, G., Berchick, R., Stewart, B., & Steer, R. (1990). Relationship between hopelessness and ultimate suicide: A replication with psychiatric outpatients. *American Journal of Psychiatry, 147,* 190–195.

Beck, A. T., Brown, G., & Steer, R. (1989). Prediction of eventual suicide in psychiatric inpatients by clinical ratings of hopelessness. *Journal of Consulting and Clinical Psychology, 57,* 309–310.

Beck, A. T., Rush, A., Shaw, B., & Emery, G. (1979). *Cognitive therapy of depression.* New York: Guilford Press.

Beck, A. T., Steer, R., & Brown, G. (1993). Dysfunctional attitudes and suicidal ideation in psychiatric outpatients. *Suicide and Life-Threatening Behavior, 23,* 11–20.

Beck, A. T., Steer, R., Kovacs, M., & Garrison, B. (1985). Hopelessness and eventual suicide: A 10-year prospective study of patients hospitalized with suicidal ideation. *American Journal of Psychiatry, 142,* 559–563.

Beck, A. T., & Weishaar, M. E. (1995). Cognitive therapy. In R. J. Corsini & D. Wedding (Eds.), *Current psychotherapies* (5th ed., pp. 229–261). Itasca, IL: Peacock.

Beck, A. T., Weissman, A., & Kovacs, M. (1976). Alcoholism, hopelessness, and suicidal behavior. *Journal of Studies on Alcohol, 37,* 66–77.

Berman, A., & Jobes, D. (1991). *Adolescent suicide: Assessment and intervention.* Washington, DC: American Psychological Association.

Blackburn, I., & Moore, R. (1997). Controlled acute and follow-up trial of cognitive therapy and pharmacotherapy in outpatients with recurrent depression. *British Journal of Psychiatry, 171,* 328–334.

Bonner, R., & Rich, A. (1987). Toward a predictive model of suicidal ideation and behavior: Some preliminary data in college students. *Suicide and Life-Threatening Behavior, 17,* 50–63.

Bonner, R., & Rich, A. (1988). Negative life stress, social problem-solving, self-appraisal, and hopelessness: Implications for suicide research. *Cognitive Therapy and Research, 12,* 549–556.

Brent, D. A., Bridge, J., Johnson, B. A., & Connolly, J. (1996). Suicidal behavior runs in families. *Archives of General Psychiatry, 53,* 1145–1152.

Briere, J., & Zaidi, L. (1989). Sexual abuse histories and sequelae in female psychiatric emergency room patients. *American Journal of Psychiatry, 146,* 1602–1606.

Clark, D. A., & Beck, A. (1999). *Scientific foundations of cognitive theory and therapy for depression.* New York: Wiley.

Clark, D. C., & Fawcett, J. (1992). Review of empirical risk factors for evaluation of the suicidal patient. In B. Bongar (Ed.), *Suicide: Guidelines for assessment, management, and treatment* (pp. 16–48). New York: Oxford University Press.

Clum, G., & Febbraro, G. (1994). Stress, social support, and problem-solving appraisal/skills: Prediction of suicide severity within a college sample. *Journal of Psychopathology and Behavioral Assessment, 16,* 69–83.

Curry, J. (2001). Specific psychotherapies for childhood and adolescent depression. *Biological Psychiatry, 49,* 1091–1100.

DeBattista, C., & Belanoff, J. (2002). Novel strategies in the treatment of psychotic major depression. *Psychiatric Annals, 32,* 695–698.

DeBattista, C., Trivedi, M., Kern, J., & Lembke, A. (2002). The status of evidence-based guidelines and algorithms in the treatment of depression. *Psychiatric Annals, 32,* 658–663.

DeRubeis, R. J., & Crits-Christoph, P. (1998). Empirically supported individual and group psychological treatments for adult mental disorders. *Journal of Consulting and Clinical Psychology, 66,* 37–52.

DeRubeis, R. J., Gelfand, L. A., Tang, T. Z., & Simons, A. D. (1999). Medication versus cognitive-behavioral therapy for severely depressed outpatients: Meta-analysis of four randomized comparisons. *American Journal of Psychiatry, 156,* 1007–1013.

Dieserund, G., Roysamb, E., & Kraft, O. (2001). Toward an integrative model of suicide attempt: A cognitive psychological approach. *Suicide and Life Threatening Behavior, 31,* 153–158.

Dimidjian, S., & Dobson, K. (2003). Processes of change in cognitive therapy. In M. Reinecke & D. Clark (Eds.), *Cognitive therapy across the lifespan: Evidence and practice* (pp. 477–506). Cambridge, England: Cambridge University Press.

Dixon, W., Heppner, P., & Anderson, W. (1991). Problem-solving appraisal, stress, hopelessness, and suicide ideation in a college population. *Journal of Counseling Psychology, 38,* 51–56.

Dixon, W. A., Heppner, P. P., & Rudd, M. D. (1994). Problem-solving appraisals, hopelessness, and suicide ideation: Evidence for a mediational model. *Journal of Counseling Psychology, 41,* 91–98.

Dobson, K. S. (1989). A meta-analysis of the efficacy of cognitive therapy for depression. *Journal of Consulting and Clinical Psychology, 57,* 414–419.

Dobson, K. S., & Dozois, D. (2001). Historical and philosophical bases of the cognitive-behavioral therapies. In K. Dobson (Ed.), *Handbook of cognitive-behavioral therapies* (2nd ed., pp. 3–39). New York: Guilford Press.

Drake, R., & Cotton, P. (1986). Depression, hopelessness, and suicide in chronic schizophrenia. *British Journal of Psychiatry, 148,* 554–559.

Elkin, I., Shea, M. T., Watkins, J. T., Imber, S. D., Sotsky, S. M., Collins, J. F., et al. (1989). National Institute of Mental Health Treatment of Depression Collaborative Research Program: General effectiveness of treatments. *Archives of General Psychiatry, 46,* 971–982.

Ellis, T., & Ratliff, K. (1986). Cognitive characteristics of suicidal and nonsuicidal psychiatric patients. *Cognitive Therapy and Research, 10,* 625–634.

Evans, J., Williams, J. M. G., O'Loughlin, S., & Howells, K. (1992). Autobiographical memory and problem-solving strategies of parasuicidal patients. *Psychological Medicine, 22,* 399–405.

Evans, K., Tyrer, P., Catalan, J., Schmidt, U., Davidson, K., Dent, J., et al. (1999). Manual-assisted cognitive-behaviour therapy (MACT): A randomized controlled trial of a brief intervention with bibliotherapy in the treatment of recurrent deliberate self-harm. *Psychological Medicine, 29,* 19–25.

Farberow, N. (1981). Assessment of suicide. In P. McReynolds (Ed.), *Advances in psychological assessment* (Vol. 5., pp. 124–190). San Francisco: Jossey-Bass.

Fawcett, J., Scheftner, W., Clark, D., Hedeker, D., Gibbons, R., & Coryell, W. (1987). Clinical predictors of suicide inpatients with major affective disorders: A controlled prospective study. *American Journal of Psychiatry, 144,* 35–40.

Fawcett, J., Scheftner, W., Fogg, L., Clark, D., Young, M., Hedeker, D., et al. (1990). Time-related predictors of suicide in major affective disorder. *American Journal of Psychiatry, 147*(9), 1189–1194.

Freeman, A., & Reinecke, M. (1993). *Cognitive therapy of suicidal behavior.* New York: Springer.

Fremouw, W., Callahan, T., & Kashden, J. (1993). Adolescent suicidal risk: Psychological, problem-solving, and environmental factors. *Suicide and Life-Threatening Behavior, 23,* 46–54.

Freud, S. (1927). Mourning and melancholia. In E. Jones (Ed.), *Collected papers* (Vol. 4, pp. 137–156). London: Hogarth Press.

Gaffan, E. A., Tsaousis, I., & Kemp-Wheeler, S. M. (1995). Researcher alliance and meta-analysis: The case of cognitive therapy for depression. *Journal of Consulting and Clinical Psychology, 63,* 966–980.

Gibbons, J. S., Butler, J., Urwin, P., & Gibbons, J. L. (1978). Evaluation of a social work service for self-poisoning patients. *British Journal of Psychiatry, 133,* 111–118.

Gloaguen, V., Cottraux, J., Cucherat, M., & Blackburn, I. (1998). A meta-analysis of the effects of cognitive therapy in depressed clients. *Journal of Affective Disorders, 49,* 59–72.

Guze, S., & Robins, E. (1970). Suicide and primary affective disorders. *British Journal of Psychiatry, 117,* 437–438.

Hagnell, O., & Rorsman, B. (1980). Suicide in the Lundby study: A controlled prospective investigation of stressful life events. *Neuropsychobiology, 6,* 319–332.

Hawton, K., Arensman, E., Townsend, E., Bremner, S., Feldman, E., Goldney, R., et al. (1998). Deliberate self-harm: A systematic review of the efficacy of psychosocial and pharmacological treatments in preventing repetition. *British Medical Journal, 317,* 441–447.

Hawton, K., & Catalan, J. (1982). *Attempted suicide: A practical guide to its nature and management.* Oxford, England: Oxford University Press.

Hawton, K., McKeown, S., Day, A., Martin, P., O'Connor, M., & Yule, J. (1987). Evaluation of outpatient counseling compared with general practitioner care following overdoses. *Psychological Medicine, 17,* 751–761.

Hewitt, P., Flett, G., & Turnbull-Donovan, W. (1992). Perfectionism and suicide potential. *British Journal of Clinical Psychology, 31,* 181–190.

Hollon, S., Haman, K., & Brown, L. (2002). Cognitive-behavioral treatment of depression. In I. Gotlib & C. Hammen (Eds.), *Handbook of depression* (pp. 383–403). New York: Guilford Press.

Hoyer, G., & Lund, E. (1993). Suicide among women related to the number of children in marriage. *Archives of General Psychiatry, 50,* 134–137.

Ingram, R., Miranda, J., & Segal, Z. (1998). *Cognitive vulnerability to depression.* New York: Guilford Press.

Ivanoff, A., Smyth, N., Grochowski, S., Jang, S., & Klein, K. (1992). Problem-solving and suicidality among prison inmates: Another look at state versus trait. *Journal of Consulting and Clinical Psychology, 60,* 970–973.

Joiner, T., & Rudd, M. (1995). Negative attributional style for interpersonal events and the occurrence of severe interpersonal disruptions as predictors of self-reported suicidal ideation. *Suicide and Life Threatening Behavior, 25,* 297–304.

Keller, M., McCullough, J., Klein, D., Arnow, B., Dunner, D., Gelenberg, A., et al. (2000). A comparison of nefazadone, the cognitive-behavioral analysis system of psychotherapy, and their combination for the treatment of chronic depression. *New England Journal of Medicine, 342,* 1462–1470.

Klerman, G. (1987). Clinical epidemiology of suicide. *Journal of Clinical Psychiatry, 48,* 33–38.

Koerner, K., & Linehan, M. (2002). Dialectical behavior therapy for borderline personality disorder. In S. Hofmann & M. Tompson (Eds.), *Treating chronic and severe mental disorders: A handbook of empirically supported interventions* (pp. 317–342). New York: Guilford Press.

Kozak, C., & Gibbs, J. (1979). Dependent children and suicide of married parents. *Suicide and Life Threatening Behavior, 9,* 67–75.

Kreitman, N. (1988). Suicide, age and marital status. *Psychological Medicine, 18,* 121–128.

Lambert, M., & Davis, M. (2002). Treatment of depression: What the research says. In M. Reinecke & M. Davison (Eds.), *Comparative treatments of depression* (pp. 21–46). New York: Springer.

Lerner, M., & Clum, G. (1990). Treatment of suicide ideators: A problem-solving approach. *Behavior Therapy, 21,* 403–411.

Lesage, A., Boyer, R., Grunberg, F., Vanier, C., Morissette, R., Menard-Buteau, C., et al. (1994). Suicide and mental disorders: A case-control study of young men. *American Journal of Psychiatry, 151,* 1063–1068.

Lewinsohn, P., Rohde, P., & Seeley, J. (1996). Adolescent suicidal ideation and attempts: Prevalence, risk factors, and clinical implications. *Clinical Psychology: Science and Practice, 3,* 25–46.

Linehan, M. (1987). Dialectical behavior therapy: A cognitive-behavioral approach to parasuicide. *Journal of Personality Disorders, 1,* 328–333.

Linehan, M., Armstrong, H., Suarez, A., Allmon, D., & Heard, H. (1991). Cognitive-behavioral treatment of chronically parasuicidal borderline personality disorder. *Archives of General Psychiatry, 48,* 1060–1064.

Linehan, M., Camper, P., Chiles, J., Strosahl, K., & Shearin, E. (1987). Interpersonal problem-solving and parasuicide. *Cognitive Therapy and Research, 11*(1), 1–12.

Linehan, M., Chiles, J., Egan, K., Devine, R., & Laffaw, J. (1986). Presenting problems of parasuicides versus suicide ideators and nonsuicidal psychiatric patients. *Journal of Consulting and Clinical Psychology, 54,* 880–881.

Linehan, M., Heard, H., & Armstrong, H. (1993). Naturalistic follow-up of a behavioral treatment for chronically parasuicidal borderline patients. *Archives of General Psychiatry, 50,* 971–974.

Litman, R. (1990). Suicides: What do they have in mind. In D. Jacobs & H. Brown (Eds.), *Suicide: Understanding and responding* (pp. 143–156). Madison, CT: International Universities Press.

Maris, R., Berman, A., Maltsberger, J., & Yufit, R. (Eds.). (1992). *Assessment and prediction of suicide.* New York: Guilford Press.

McLeavey, B., Daly, R., Ludgate, J., & Murray, C. (1994). Interpersonal problem solving skills training in the treatment of self-poisoning patients. *Suicide and Life-Threatening Behavior, 24,* 382–394.

Mendelson, M. (1974). *Psychoanalytic concepts of depression* (2nd ed.). New York: Spectrum.

Metalsky, G., & Joiner, T. (1992). Vulnerability to depressive symptomatology: A prospective test of the diathesis stress and causal mediation components of the hopelessness theory of depression. *Journal of Personality and Social Psychology, 3,* 667–675.

Murphy, G. (1984). The prediction of suicide: Why is it so difficult? *American Journal of Psychotherapy, 38,* 341–349.

Murphy, G. (1985). Suicide and attempted suicide. In R. Michels (Ed.), *Psychiatry* (pp. 1–18). Philadelphia: Lippincott.

Nekanda-Trepka, C., Bishop, S., & Blackburn, I. (1983). Hopelessness and depression. *British Journal of Clinical Psychology, 22,* 49–60.

Neuringer, C. (1968). Divergencies between attitudes towards life and death among suicidal, psychosomatic, and normal hospitalized patients. *Journal of Consulting and Clinical Psychology, 32,* 59–63.

Neuringer, C., & Lettieri, D. (1971). Cognition, attitude, and affect in suicidal individuals. *Suicide and Life-Threatening Behavior, 1,* 106–124.

Orbach, I., Bar-Joseph, H., & Dror, N. (1990). Styles of problem-solving in suicidal individuals. *Suicide and Life-Threatening Behavior, 20,* 56–64.

Patsiokas, A., & Clum, G. (1985). Effects of psychotherapeutic strategies in the treatment of suicide attempters. *Psychotherapy, 22,* 281–290.

Pollock, L., & Williams, J. M. G. (1998). Problem-solving and suicidal behavior. *Suicide and Life-Threatening Behavior, 28,* 375–387.

Prezant, D., & Neimeyer, R. (1988). Cognitive predictors of depression and suicide ideation. *Suicide and Life-Threatening Behavior, 18,* 259–264.

Priester, M., & Clum, G. (1992). Attributional style as a diathesis in predicting depression, hopelessness, and suicide ideation in college students. *Journal of Psychopathology and Behavioral Assessment, 14,* 111–122.

Priester, M., & Clum, G. (1993). Perceived problem-solving ability as a predictor of depression, hopelessness, and suicide ideation in a college population. *Journal of Counseling Psychology, 40,* 79–85.

Reinecke, M. (2000). Suicide and depression. In F. Dattilio & A. Freeman (Eds.), *Cognitive-behavioral strategies in crisis intervention* (2nd ed., pp. 84–125). New York: Guilford Press.

Reinecke, M. (2002). Cognitive therapies of depression: A modularized treatment approach. In M. Reinecke & M. Davison (Eds.), *Comparative treatments of depression* (pp. 249–290). New York: Springer.

Reinecke, M., Ryan, N., & DuBois, D. (1998). Cognitive-behavioral therapy of depression and depressive symptoms during adolescence: A review and meta-analysis. *Journal of the American Academy of Child and Adolescent Psychiatry, 37,* 26–34.

Rich, C., Warsradt, G., Nemiroff, R., Fowler, R., & Young, D. (1991). Suicide, stressors, and the life cycle. *American Journal of Psychiatry, 148,* 524–527.

Rotheram-Borus, M., Trautman, P., Dopkins, S., & Shrout, P. (1990). Cognitive style and pleasant activities among female adolescent suicide attempters. *Journal of Consulting and Clinical Psychology, 58,* 554–561.

Roy, A., Segal, N. L., Centerwall, B. S., & Robinette, D. (1991). Suicide in twins. *Archives of General Psychiatry, 48,* 29–32.

Rudd, M. (2000). The suicidal mode: A cognitive-behavioral mode of suicidality. *Suicide and Life Threatening Behavior, 30,* 18–33.

Rudd, M., Joiner, T., & Rajab, M. (1996). Relationships among suicide ideators, attempters, and multiple attempters in a young-adult sample. *Journal of Abnormal Psychology, 105,* 541–550.

Rudd, M., Joiner, T., & Rajab, M. (2001). *Treating suicidal behavior.* New York: Guilford Press.

Rudd, M., Rajab, M., & Dahm, P. (1994). Problem-solving appraisal in suicide ideators and attempters. *American Journal of Orthopsychiatry, 64,* 136–149.

Rudd, M., Rajab, M., Orman, D., Stulman, D., Joiner, T., & Dixon, W. (1996). Effectiveness of an outpatient problem-solving intervention targeting suicidal young adults: Preliminary results. *Journal of Consulting and Clinical Psychology, 64,* 179–190.

Salkovskis, P., Atha, C., & Storer, D. (1990). Cognitive-behavioural problem-solving in the treatment of patients who repeatedly attempt suicide: A controlled trial. *British Journal of Psychiatry, 157,* 871–876.

Schotte, D., & Clum, G. (1982). Suicide ideation in a college population: A test of a model. *Journal of Consulting and Clinical Psychology, 50,* 690–696.

Schotte, D., & Clum, G. (1987). Problem-solving skills in suicidal psychiatric patients. *Journal of Consulting and Clinical Psychology, 55,* 49–54.

Smith, J., Mercy, J., & Conn, J. (1988). Marital status and the risk of suicide. *American Journal of Public Health, 78,* 78–80.

Solomon, A., & Haaga, D. (2003). Cognitive theory and therapy of depression. In M. Reinecke & D. Clark (Eds.), *Cognitive therapy across the lifespan: Evidence and practice* (pp. 12–39). Cambridge, England: Cambridge University Press.

Spirito, A., Overholser, J., & Hart, K. (1991). Cognitive characteristics of adolescent suicide attempters. *Journal of the American Academy of Child and Adolescent Psychiatry, 30,* 604–608.

Stolberg, R., Clark, D., & Bongar, B. (2002). Epidemiology, assessment, and management of suicide in depressed patients. In I. Gotlib & C. Hammen (Eds.), *Handbook of depression* (pp. 383–403). New York: Guilford Press.

Thase, M., Greenhouse, J., Frank, E., Reynolds, C., Pilkonis, P., Hurley, K., et al. (1997). Treatment of major depression with psychotherapy—pharmacotherapy combinations. *Archives of General Psychiatry, 54,* 1009–1015.

Turner, R., Korslund, K., Barnett, B., & Josiassen, R. (1998). Assessment of suicide in schizophrenia: Development of the Interview for Suicide in Schizophrenia. *Cognitive and Behavioral Practice, 5,* 139–169.

Van der Sande, R., Buskens, E., Allart, E., van der Graaf, Y., & van Engeland, H. (1997). Psychosocial intervention following suicide attempt: A systematic review of treatment interventions. *Acta Psychiatrica Scandinavica, 96,* 43–50.

Van der Sande, R., van Rooijen, E., Buskens, E., Allart, E., Haeton, K., van der Graaf, Y., & van Engeland, H. (1997). Intensive in-patient and community intervention versus routine care after attempted suicide: A randomized controlled intervention. *British Journal of Psychiatry, 171,* 35–41.

Wagner, B. (1997). Family risk factors for child and adolescent suicidal behavior. *Psychological Bulletin, 121,* 246–298.

Wetzel, R. (1976). Hopelessness, depression, and suicide intent. *Archives of General Psychiatry, 33,* 1069–1073.

Wilson, K., Stelzer, J., Bergman, J., Kral, M., Inayatullah, M., & Elliott, C. (1995). Problem-solving, stress, and coping in adolescent suicide attempts. *Suicide and Life Threatening Behavior, 25,* 241–252.

Yang, B., & Clum, G. (1996). Effects of early negative life experiences on cognitive functioning and risk for suicide: A review. *Clinical Psychology Review, 16,* 177–195.

CHAPTER 11

Voice Therapy: A Treatment for Depression and Suicide

Lisa Firestone

> *I could not sleep, although tired, and lay feeling my nerves shaved to*
> *pain & the groaning inner voice: oh, you can't teach, can't do anything.*
> *Can't write, can't think. . . . I cannot ignore this murderous self: it is*
> *there. I smell it and feel it, but I will not give it my name. . . .*
>
> *I have a good self, that loves skies, hills, ideas, tasty meals, bright*
> *colors. My demon would murder this self by demanding that it be a*
> *paragon, and saying it should run away if it is anything less.*
>
> From "Letter to a Demon" by Sylvia Plath
> (Hughes & McCullough, 1982, pp. 176–177)

Sylvia Plath's quote illustrates the three premises underlying the approach to understanding suicide and self-destructive behavior developed by Robert Firestone, clinical psychologist and theorist (R. Firestone, 1986, 1997a, 1997b; R. Firestone & Firestone, 1998). The first premise states that a division exists within all of us, as Plath so clearly expressed. There is a "good self" that is life-affirming, goal-directed, with specific desires and wants and priorities; and there is an inner demon, an antiself that is self-critical, self-destructive, and, at its ultimate extreme, suicidal. As Plath described it, her "demon" demanded perfection of her, and when she fell short, she thought she deserved to die for this failure.

The second premise of Firestone's approach, as reflected in the quote, involves the concept of the inner voice, or the language of the defensive process. His early investigations into the voice process demonstrated that self-destructive thoughts exist on a continuum, from mild self-critical thoughts, to thoughts of extreme self-hatred, and finally to actively suicidal thoughts. "You can't teach, you can't do anything. Can't write, can't think." These self-destructive thoughts lead to emotional pain, perturbation, and a desperation to escape, driving the suicidal process.

The third premise of his approach proposes that there exists a corresponding continuum of self-destructive behaviors that people engage in, directed by the voice process. In Plath's case, she isolated herself, alienated the people closest to her, and ultimately took her own life.

It was found that by accessing the negative thoughts that people are experiencing toward themselves, we can predict the self-destructive behaviors they are likely to engage in (R. Firestone & Firestone, 1996, 1998). In addition, R. Firestone has developed a treatment technique, voice therapy, for giving voice to this self-destructive process (R. Firestone, 1988, 1997a). The technique allows clients to identify the enemy within, understand its sources, recognize the impact it is having on their lives today, and learn to resist carrying out its dictates and act instead in their own self-interest.

In this chapter, I first discuss the basic tenets of R. Firestone's overall theoretical approach of *separation theory,* including the *fantasy bond,* or self-parenting process, and the voice process. Second, I describe the steps in voice therapy, a cognitive/affective/behavioral treatment approach. Finally, I present a hypothetical session to illustrate this methodology as applied in the treatment of an individual at risk for suicide.

THEORETICAL APPROACH

Separation theory represents a broadly based system of concepts and hypotheses that integrate psychoanalytic and existential views (R. Firestone, 1997a; R. Firestone, Firestone, & Catlett, 2003). The theory explains how emotional pain and frustration in the child's earliest relationships lead to defense formation and how these original defenses are reinforced as the developing child gradually becomes aware of his or her own mortality. In this approach, there is an emphasis on the exposure of destructive fantasy bonds (imagined connections with another person) as externalized in personal relationships or as internalized in the form of negative parental introjects (destructive thought processes or *voices*). According to R. Firestone (1997b):

Dissolution of these bonds and movement toward separation and individuation is essential for the realization of one's destiny as a fully autonomous human being. . . . A merged identity or diminished sense of self is a micro-suicidal[1] or even suicidal manifestation, as one no longer lives a committed, feelingful existence. (p. 182)

Separation as described here is very different from isolation, defense, or retreat; rather, it involves the maintenance of a strong identity at close quarters with others. Without a well-developed self system, people find it necessary to distort, lash out at, or withdraw from intimacy in interpersonal relationships. A defended life characterized by imagined fusion with another person or other people acts to limit a person's capacity for self-expression and self-fulfillment. Without a strong sense of self, life seems empty, meaningless, and without direction.

Inwardness[2] is a necessary ingredient for suicidal ideation to take control over an individual's behavior. The syndrome of inwardness is made up of the following dimensions: a tendency toward isolation, self-denial and withholding, withdrawal from favored activities and relationships, reliance on addictive substances or routines to relieve emotional pain, preference for seeking gratification in fantasy rather than in the real world, increased attitudes of self-hatred and cynicism toward others, and a lack of direction in life.

The dissolution of a fantasy bond or imagined connection with another person often leaves the inward, self-protective person feeling overwhelming psychological pain. This pain is not a response to the loss of the relationship, which may or may not have been close or fulfilling, but to the loss of the imagined fusion, the feeling of being whole by being merged with another person. Repressed pain from childhood and existential fears of aloneness and death are aroused. For example, the

---

[1] *Microsuicide* is a term that refers to behaviors, communications, attitudes, or lifestyles that are self-induced and threatening to an individual's physical health, emotional well-being, or personal goals (Firestone & Seiden, 1987).

[2] The term *inwardness* refers to a syndrome of specific personality traits and behavioral patterns that play a crucial part in all forms of psychopathology and that are especially evident in suicidal individuals. It is important to distinguish this syndrome from self-reflection, introspection, time spent alone for creative work or planning, meditation, and other forms of spiritual or intellectual pursuits (R. Firestone & Catlett, 1999; R. Firestone et al., 2003).

following statements were excerpted from the diary of a young woman who committed suicide. Here she reflects on her ambivalence about intimacy after feeling rejected by her boyfriend when he flirted with another girl:

> I have such a problem with loss. Fear of losing someone. Fear of loving someone. Fear of trusting someone. I feel so abandoned and unconnected with everyone, everyone. I feel like I'm going to die. . . . I did try reaching out again for the last time. People are so mean and selfish. I want to kill myself on my birthday. I have to.

What are the sources of pain and anxiety that disturb the individuation process, interfere with people's developing a strong sense of identity, and contribute to an inward, defended orientation toward life?

Origins of Psychological Pain

According to R. Firestone (1997a), there are two major sources of psychological pain and anxiety: (1) deprivation, rejection, and overt or covert aggression on the part of parents, family members, and significant others; and (2) basic existential problems of aloneness, aging, illness, death, and other facts of existence that have a negative effect on a person's life experience, such as social pressure, crime, economic fluctuations, political tyranny, and the threat of nuclear holocaust. *Interpersonal pain* refers to the frustration, aggression, and abuse an individual experiences in relationships, whereas issues of being, aloneness, and the fact of death fall into the category of existential pain. Firestone feels that it is important to integrate both psychoanalytic and existential systems of thought to achieve a better understanding of the conflict between life-affirming propensities and self-destructive tendencies operating within each individual.

Early Trauma

Each person experiences varying degrees of emotional pain in growing up. Even in ideal families, there is inevitable frustration, and most family constellations are less than ideal. Experiences of emotional deprivation, rejection, parental aggression, and intrusiveness necessitate the development of childhood defenses in order to cope with the interpersonal environment. The more that parents were deprived or rejected when they were children, the greater the impairment of their parenting functions, regardless of their love and concern for their offspring (Baumeister, Bratslavsky, Finkenauer, & Vohs, 2001; Fonagy et al., 1995; Main & Hesse, 1990; Main & Solomon, 1986; Sanders & Giolas, 1991; Siegel, 2001).

Felitti (2002) has called attention to the prevalence of emotional, physical, and sexual abuse in our society. Some of the most compelling evidence of the prevalence of abusive or dysfunctional child-rearing practices and their effects were reported by the Kaiser Foundation Health Plan investigation into adverse childhood experiences (ACE; Felitti et al., 1998). Questionnaires filled out by more than 17,000 patient members revealed "a powerful relation between our emotional experiences as children and our adult emotional health, physical health, and major causes of mortality in the United States" (Felitti, 2002, p. 44). Felitti et al. (1998) also reported that "23.5% of participants reported having grown up with an alcohol abuser . . . contact sexual abuse was reported by 22% of respondents" (p. 252), and "more than half of respondents (52%) experienced ≥ 1 category of adverse childhood exposure" (p. 249).

Under conditions of physical, emotional, or sexual abuse, the person to whom the child naturally turns to for care also becomes the frightening or punishing agent, and the child typically fails to develop a secure attachment (Main & Solomon, 1986). Witnessing violence between parents and/or being the victim of these abuses are perhaps the most serious forms of trauma that can occur in the life of a young child. Fear states aroused by these events can cause the brain to release certain toxins that change the structure of the brain and central nervous system, destroying cells and synapses that are responsible for the regulation of emotions and the development of compassion and empathy (Lyons-Ruth & Jacobvitz, 1999; Perry, 1997; Schore, 1994; Siegel, 1999; van der Kolk, McFarlane, & Weisaeth, 1996).

Psychological defenses formed as a reaction to interpersonal pain precede the child's growing awareness of death. They represent an adaptation to the parental climate and act as a psychological survival mechanism to maintain equilibrium. One defense mechanism or coping strategy that seems to be linked directly to suicide is dissociation (Briere & Runtz, 1987; Brown, Cohen, Johnson, & Smailes, 1999; Chu & Dill, 1990). *Dissociation* is a person's ability to detach from his or her body, to watch things happen to the self, rather than the experience of being the one perpetrated on. Early abuse, particularly sexual abuse, appears to facilitate the development of this defensive maneuver. Unfortunately, this may pave the way for later self-destructive behavior and higher suicide risk (van der Kolk, 1996).

The Impact of the Evolving Knowledge of Death on the Child's Defenses

The point in the developmental sequence when the child first discovers death is the critical juncture where his or her defense system, developed to cope with interpersonal pain, crystallizes and shapes his or her future (R. Firestone et al., 2003). Thereafter, most people accommodate to the fear of death through the withdrawal of energy and emotional investment in life-affirming activity and close, personal relationships. In renouncing real satisfaction, they rely increasingly on internal gratification, fantasies of fusion, and painkillers. The fantasy of suicide can provide a sense of triumph over death, that is, of taking control over your destiny (Fierman, 1965; Maltsberger, 1999; Orbach, 2002).

Defenses provide a method of escaping psychological pain at the expense of varying degrees of obliteration of personality and personal experience. Unfortunately, defenses cannot selectively cut out emotional pain without seriously interfering with other functions. They act to dull awareness, distort perceptions, deaden emotional responses, and eventually lead to an overall deterioration in the quality of life. These distorted perceptions often result in persons seeing themselves and the world through a negative filter, which contributes to suicide risk. Moreover, detaching from themselves and their life sets the stage for suicidal behavior.

The Basic Defense System

R. Firestone asserts that the basic defense is the fantasy bond, originally an imagined connection with the mother or primary caregiver that the infant develops to protect itself against pain, anxiety, and frustration (R. Firestone, 1984). This illusion of fusion provides partial gratification of the infant's basic needs and reduces painful tension states. Infants have a natural ability to comfort or soothe themselves by using images and memories of past feeding experiences to ward off the anxiety of being temporarily separated from their mother and to help diminish feelings of hunger and frustration (R. Firestone, Firestone, & Catlett, 2002). The fantasy bond is created to deal with the intolerable pain and anxiety that arise when the infant is faced with excessive frustration. This anxiety can be far more devastating to the infant than the frustration itself and at times may be experienced as a *threat of annihilation,* a very primitive anxiety that was described by Winnicott (1958). An illusion of being connected to the primary parenting figure thus becomes a substitute or compensation for the love and care that may be missing in the infant's environment. The degree to which the child, and later the adult, comes to rely on fantasies of fusion largely depends on the degree of deprivation and trauma he or she suffered early in life.

People have a natural tendency to resort to psychological defenses to reduce or eliminate primitive pain and anxiety states. Ironically, core defenses or imagined connections with other people that are erected by children early in life to protect themselves from a toxic environment and from painful aspects of the human condition can eventually become more damaging than the original trauma (R. Firestone, 1997b). In other words, defenses that initially function as a survival mechanism later act to limit their life.

The Self-Parenting Process

The fantasy bond is a manifestation of a process of parenting self both internally in fantasy and externally by using objects and persons in the environment. The result is a pseudo-independent posture of self-sufficiency—a fantasy that the individual can take care of himself or herself without needing others. The child experiences a false sense of self-sufficiency or omnipotence because he or she has introjected an image of the "good and powerful" mother or primary caretaker. Unfortunately, at the same time, the child must also necessarily incorporate the corresponding self-image of the "bad and helpless" child. This introjected parental image takes on the significance of a survival mechanism in the child's mind. The process of parenting oneself is made up of two components, each of which takes on its unique character from the introjection and internalization of parental attitudes and responses in the process of growing up in a specific interpersonal environment (R. Firestone, 1984, 1985, 1997a).

The self-nourishing or self-soothing component is made up of behaviors that dull or numb painful feelings: originally thumb-sucking, stroking a blanket, nail-biting, and later elaborated in adult life to eating disorders; addiction to cigarettes, alcohol, and other drugs; compulsive masturbation; praising and coddling oneself; vanity; and an impersonal, self-feeding, habitual style of sexual relating. The self-nurturing component includes any behavior that is engaged in for the purpose of cutting off feelings. Even constructive behaviors, such as exercise, can be used in this way. The self-punishing component includes self-critical thoughts, guilt reactions, warnings, prohibitions, and attacks on self, which are all examples of the punitive aspect of parental introjects. This excerpt from the diary of the same young woman who committed suicide illustrates the internalization of the abusive parenting she experienced at the hands of a schizophrenic mother and an alcoholic father:

> I've got to make it end tonight!! I HATE MYSELF SO MUCH. I'VE TRIED to learn how to love myself . . . but I can't because people always want more than me. God, I wish I could torture myself—not subtly but viciously. I feel so sick. I CAN'T TAKE ANYMORE!! Please God Help Me!

Fantasies of fusion and self-parenting systems act as painkillers to cut off feeling responses and impede the development of a true sense of self. The end product of this progressive dependence on self-nourishing patterns is a form of psychological equilibrium achieved at the expense of genuine object relationships. Defended individuals seek equilibrium over actualization; that is, they are willing to give up positive, goal-directed activity to maintain internal sources of gratification.

The Voice Process

The voice process can be thought of as a secondary defense. The voice is defined as a well-integrated, discrete antiself system—an alien point of view that is an overlay on the personality at the core of an individual's maladaptive behavior. Our research (L. Firestone, 1991; R. Firestone & Firestone, 1998) has demonstrated that people are able to readily identify the content of their self-critical, self-destructive thoughts or voices when they verbalize them in the second person, that is, as though another person were addressing them (in the form of statements *toward* themselves rather than statements *about* themselves). They often get to deeper core beliefs about themselves that they were not fully aware of, but which govern a great deal of their behavior. Suicidal individuals have awareness of the voices they are experiencing, as evidenced by those who have conducted interviews with suicide attempters (Heckler, 1994; Michel & Valach, 2001). For example, this excerpt is drawn from Michel and Valach's work:

> It was so that there were so many thoughts and they had such a power over me that I developed the feeling that I would really go mad. I then said to myself that I didn't want my children to end up with a disturbed mother and that they would have to come to see me in a psychiatric hospital, but that they should rather have no mother at all, then. This was very strong, rather something else, dead or unconscious or I don't know what. I also thought that I would tell my sister that if I ended up as a vegetable they should switch off the machines, because I didn't want that my children or my relatives would have to suffer because I was nuts. This, too, I felt very strongly. It was so that there were so many thoughts and they had such a power over me that I developed the feeling that I would really go mad.
>
> Actually, I wanted to flee from these thoughts, not from the too heavy demands but from the many thoughts because they made what they wanted. I couldn't live with them any longer. I wanted to kind of kill them.
>
> In the evening I was very agitated. My sister had a terrace to which the door was open, and I thought that the door should be closed, because I had the feeling that I was like being pushed out through this door. And always this thought—you can't live with the children if you end up in a psychiatric hospital. It seems that I also spoke to my mother on the phone and she said something about suicide and that I shouldn't harm myself, but somehow it didn't reach me. And my daughter said something but I couldn't concentrate and I thought it would be best if nobody said anything because I couldn't follow any more.
>
> And then—I can't remember what happened after that. They said that I got up and walked straight out to the terrace and jumped over it as if this had always been clear to me. My sister saw me in the last moment and asked what I was doing and in that moment I jumped.

The voice alternately builds up and tears down the self and provides ostensibly rational reasons for self-denial, isolation, and avoidance of others. It functions as an antifeeling, antibody process, wherein people live primarily in their heads, cut off from their emotions and bodily sensations. Even so-called positive voices of approval and self-affirmation are indications that people are removed from themselves and treating themselves as objects. This emotional distance from the self is a key element in the suicidal process. You have to be removed from yourself to kill yourself. Suicide is diametrically opposed to our animal instinct to survive at all costs. The following excerpt from an interview with a woman who made a serious suicide attempt illustrates this point:

> **Client:** I know it doesn't look appetizing, but it works well, and then I tried at first here (upper lower arm) and it did not hurt. Then I watched how it was bleeding, and it was nothing particular. And then I cut myself in the strategic places (wrist) and put the arm into water and watched the rings, which was pretty. I was more or less simply watching myself. In the previous months when I was feeling so low after the breakdown of the relationship with my boyfriend, I had often looked at myself from outside, like now while I was cutting myself.
>
> **Interviewer:** The way you tell it, it sounds as if you were separated from your feelings.
>
> **Client:** Yes, completely. I was watching myself even then. I know it sounds schizophrenic, but it was like that, "it's simply bleeding now." And then I cut again. I cut three times and then once more . . . and then, suddenly, I was not outside of myself any more.
>
> **Interviewer:** Then you were what?
>
> **Client:** Not outside of myself any more. It was this last deep cut and it really did not look nice any more and I knew that if I did not do anything, I would die. As stupid as it sounds.

In summary, psychological defenses are subject to malfunction in a manner that is analogous to the body's physical reaction to pneumonia. The presence of organisms in the lungs evokes cellular and humoral responses that meet the invasion, yet the magnitude of the defensive reaction leads to congestion that is potentially dangerous to the person. In this disease, the body's defensive reaction is more destructive than the original assault. Similarly, defenses that were erected by the vulnerable child to protect himself or herself against a toxic environment eventually become more detrimental than the original trauma. In this sense, people's psychological defenses formed under conditions of stress become the core of their self-destructive propensities and impact their risk of committing suicide.

The Core Conflict

As a result of forming defenses early in life, all people exist in conflict between an active pursuit of goals in the real world and a defensive reliance on self-gratification. An individual who chooses to cultivate life and lead an honest and undefended lifestyle will experience both the joy and pain of his or her existence. In contrast, the defended person's attempt to block out pain neutralizes the life experience and deprives the individual of life's enrichment. To the extent that individuals succumb to a defensive posture, form addictive attachments and habit patterns, and choose an inward self-protective life, their adjustment will suffer, and it is unlikely that they will approach their potential. Retreat to an increasingly inward posture represents, in effect, a form of controlled destruction of the self. Anything that threatens to disturb an individual's solution to the core conflict arouses fear. Descending into this process more and more and withdrawing investment from real life often creates the necessary conditions for suicide.

Movement in any direction, either a retreat further into fantasy and self-parenting or movement toward external goal-directed behavior, is accompanied by anxiety. The rise in anxiety results in both aggressive and regressive reactions. An individual's defensive reaction to the basic conflict is determined, to a considerable degree, by the amount of pain experienced early in life and the type of defense mechanism he or she adopted to deal with it. Overwhelming experiences from the perspective of the helpless child lead to an inability to tolerate and deal effectively with pain. Suicidal people, while heterogeneous in many ways, have in common a lack of pain tolerance and a lack of effective (non-self-destructive) coping strategies to deal with pain. In essence, they cannot tolerate psychological pain and are desperate to get out of it, and, because they lack healthy strategies for alleviating pain, they often resort to self-destructive actions.

The Self and Antiself Systems

Destructive parental introjects that are represented by the voice lead to an essential dualism within the personality. This "division of the mind" reflects a primary split between forces that represent the self and those that oppose or attempt to destroy the self. These propensities can be conceptualized as the *self system* and the *antiself system*. The two systems develop independently; both are dynamic and continually evolve and change over time (see Figure 11.1).

The *self system* consists of the unique characteristics of the individual including his or her biological, temperament, and genetic traits; the harmonious identification with parents' positive qualities and strivings; and the ongoing effects of experience and education. Parents' genuine selves, as demonstrated in lively attitudes, positive values, and an active

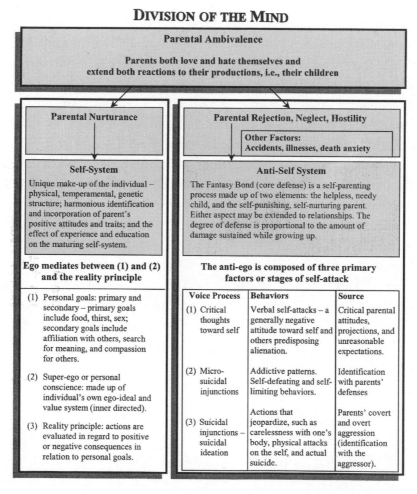

DIVISION OF THE MIND

Parental Ambivalence

Parents both love and hate themselves and extend both reactions to their productions, i.e., their children

Parental Nurturance	**Parental Rejection, Neglect, Hostility**
	Other Factors: Accidents, illnesses, death anxiety
Self-System Unique make-up of the individual – physical, temperamental, genetic structure; harmonious identification and incorporation of parent's positive attitudes and traits; and the effect of experience and education on the maturing self-system.	**Anti-Self System** The Fantasy Bond (core defense) is a self-parenting process made up of two elements: the helpless, needy child, and the self-punishing, self-nurturing parent. Either aspect may be extended to relationships. The degree of defense is proportional to the amount of damage sustained while growing up.

Ego mediates between (1) and (2) and the reality principle

(1) Personal goals: primary and secondary – primary goals include food, thirst, sex; secondary goals include affiliation with others, search for meaning, and compassion for others.

(2) Super-ego or personal conscience: made up of individual's own ego-ideal and value system (inner directed).

(3) Reality principle: actions are evaluated in regard to positive or negative consequences in relation to personal goals.

The anti-ego is composed of three primary factors or stages of self-attack

Voice Process	Behaviors	Source
(1) Critical thoughts toward self	Verbal self-attacks – a generally negative attitude toward self and others predisposing alienation.	Critical parental attitudes, projections, and unreasonable expectations.
(2) Micro-suicidal injunctions	Addictive patterns. Self-defeating and self-limiting behaviors.	Identification with parents' defenses
(3) Suicidal injunctions – suicidal ideation	Actions that jeopardize, such as carelessness with one's body, physical attacks on the self, and actual suicide.	Parents' covert and overt aggression (identification with the aggressor).

Figure 11.1   Divisions of the mind. Copyright © 2004 by the Glendon Association.

pursuit of life, are easily assimilated into the self system through the process of identification and imitation and become part of the child's developing personality.

The *antiself system* refers to the accumulation of destructive internalized cynical or hostile voices that represent the defensive aspect of the personality. These negative parental attitudes cannot be assimilated because they are against the self. Therefore, they exist as an alien point of view. As stated previously, the defensive process is influenced primarily by interpersonal pain reinforced and compounded by the suffering inherent in the human condition. People tend to protect the defensive apparatus at the expense of limiting their real lives and goal-directed activities. They tend to exist in a state of defensive equilibrium.

The antiself system has three primary factors or levels of self-attack. The first level consists of critical thoughts leading to inwardness and low self-esteem, thoughts promoting self-denial and isolation as well as cynical, hostile attitudes toward others. The second level of self-attacks consists of thoughts that encourage indulgence in addictive behaviors followed by thoughts of self-recrimination. The third level includes thoughts that represent the full spectrum of self-annihilation, from psychological suicide (hopelessness, thoughts urging the removal of self from significant others), thoughts associated with giving up priorities and favored activities, injunctions leading to self-mutilation, and actual physical suicide including suicide plans and suicide injunctions.

The thoughts at level three seem to stem from parents' covert or overt aggression (in other words, the anger the parents covered over or acted out). At this serious level, the person has become identified with the punishing parent and has taken on that anger toward himself or herself. In the process, the child idealizes the parent, seeing the parent as good or powerful; in internalizing the parent's anger, the child perceives himself or herself as bad and weak. Identifying with the powerful parent functions to partially relieve the child's terror in relation to being at the mercy of an out-of-control parent (Ferenczi, 1929). As Fairbairn (1952) commented in writing about the defense of identifying with the aggressor: "It is better to be a sinner in a world ruled by God than to live in a world ruled by the Devil" (pp. 66–67). This level represents an internalization of the parent at the parent's worst—not the parent as he or she was every day, but the angry parent at those times of extreme stress when the parent "lost it." The child now unleashes that anger toward himself or herself.

For example, the following are excerpts from the diary of a young woman who committed suicide:

> I sit here with my untamed piano, untamed mind, untamed heart, with the music I only know, within myself. My mother is alive! Screaming viciously, laughing viciously, Jekyll and Hyde. Mommy Dearest.

Individuals are reluctant to recognize the essential division within their personalities because they are afraid to realize how distorted their thinking is or feel that they cannot trust their own thoughts. They attempt to deny this fracture by identifying negative traits predisposed by the antiself system as their own. As a result, they tend to compromise their essential point of view, their aliveness, spontaneity, and individuality and move in the direction of the prescriptions of the voice, as noted in this excerpt from the same young woman's diary:

> I see how my interests & drives as a child have honestly disappeared. It all makes me very angry. There are a lot of things & people to blame for this. I never picked my circumstances. . . . Besides, who in their right mind would actually choose to live where I did—honestly now—come on. Anyway, it is all taking so long. I've changed things on a bit—let them dangle—or better yet myself in limbo. It's not very healthy.
>
> But then, what is always going on inside me? I can feel so damn restless and irritable talking about it. Obsessing aimlessly. It's ridiculous. But mainly I have inner fears and abuses. Things I do to myself. I act out horrible ways with myself. I act very unconstructive. Whether it's lying to people, or stealing, or being cruel by hurting my body. Whether it's all the helplessness I had to accept—lack of control which both of these were imperative factors.

People worry that if they recognize hostile or suicidal inclinations in themselves, they will be more likely to act them out. The reverse is true: Becoming aware of unconscious negative attitudes toward self and others allows greater mastery of your life. In voice therapy sessions, the destructive introjects surface and the full profile or the various dimensions of the enemy within can be identified and understood. This enables clients to resist defensive behavior patterns and self-destructive tendencies and helps them to take control over destructive behavioral manifestations of the antiself system.

The Continuum of Negative Thought Patterns

The extent to which people act out self-limiting, self-destructive behaviors is related to the intensity of and frequency with which they experience negative thoughts. As noted earlier, self-attacks or voices vary along a continuum from mild self-critical thoughts to vicious self-attacks and thoughts urging self-harm. Severely depressed or suicidal clients characteristically become exhausted and listless in struggling against self-destructive urges and self-abusive thoughts. Furthermore, they often lack the means of determining an accurate view of self and cannot differentiate an objective assessment from the current negative view of themselves. The specialized techniques of voice therapy help depressed clients learn to make this important distinction. They provide the opportunity for individuals to identify and separate from negative views of themselves and to strengthen their own point of view, thereby regaining feeling for themselves and a more positive, realistic view of self.

Excerpts from this same diary:

> This life is so empty—didn't even get a quick fix this time—just uneasiness and emotional eruption. I felt like I died—all my dreams died—felt like a different person—completely isolated from other selves in other parts of my life—still feel that way now—feel dirty now—not only because I was abused when I was young, but because I abuse myself now—mutilate, destroy, manipulate, lie, control (sickens).

As described at the beginning of this chapter, three hypotheses about self-destructive behavior were derived from data gathered in R. Firestone's early investigations into the voice process:

1. A conflict exists within each individual between life-affirming tendencies to actively pursue goals in the real world and self-limiting, self-protective, and self-destructive propensities that are related to seeking gratification primarily through fantasy processes.

2. Thoughts opposed to the self vary along a continuum of intensity from mild self-reproach to strong self-accusations and suicidal ideation.

3. Self-destructive behavior exists on a parallel continuum ranging from self-denial; self defeating behaviors, that is, behavior contrary to the individual's goals; accident-proneness; substance abuse; and eventually to direct actions that cause bodily harm, with suicide representing an acting out of the extreme end of the continuum (R. Firestone, 1988, 1997a, 1997b).

Based on these premises, it was logical to conclude that an assessment of an individual's self-destructive thoughts could be utilized to predict future self-destructive behavior. This led to the development of the *Firestone Assessment of Self-Destructive Thoughts* (FAST; R. Firestone & Firestone, 1996) to provide an accurate estimation of an individual's self-destructive and suicide potential.

VOICE THERAPY METHODOLOGY

Voice therapy is a method developed by R. Firestone for uncovering core defenses that directly affect the acting out of self-destructive behavior patterns. It was found in early investigations that by exposing negative thoughts and their antecedents, individuals were able to alter their self-concept in a positive direction, experience relief of symptoms, and feel more in control of their behavior (R. Firestone, 1988).

The ultimate goal of therapy is to help clients move away from compulsive, self-limiting lifestyles so that they can expand their lives and tolerate more gratification in reality. The hope is to help clients achieve a free and independent existence, remain open to experience and feelings, and maintain the ability to respond appropriately to both positive and negative events in their lives. To this end, the process of identifying the voice and the associated feelings of hatred toward self, combined with corrective strategies of behavioral change, significantly expand the client's boundaries and bring about a more positive sense of self.

Overview of the Three Components of Voice Therapy

Voice therapy consists of three components:

I. The process of eliciting and identifying negative thought patterns and releasing the associated affect.

II. Discussing insights and reactions to verbalizing the voice.

III. Changing self-destructive behaviors regulated by the voice through the collaborative planning and application of appropriate corrective experiences.

Voice therapy is not interpretive or analytical in the sense that clients form their own conclusions as to the sources of their destructive thinking.

The first step of voice therapy involves identifying the contents of the client's negative thought process and facilitating the release of the associated affect. Articulating the self-attacks in the second person facilitates the process of separating the client's own point of view from the hostile thought patterns that make up an alien point of view toward self. Before articulating the voice, most clients generally accept their negative thoughts as true evaluations of themselves and implicitly believe them. In addition, these thoughts dictate much of their behavior in a manner that undermines their true goals in life.

The process of identifying the voice can be approached intellectually as a primarily cognitive technique or approached more dramatically using cathartic methods. In both procedures, the client attempts to identify self-criticisms and self-attacks and learns to restate negative thought patterns in the second person as voices experienced from the outside. In the latter technique, there is an emphasis on the release of the affect accompanying the voice attacks on the self. In this abreactive method, the client is asked to amplify his or her self-attacks and express them more emotionally, with instructions to, "Say it louder," "Really feel that," or "Let go and say it the way you really hear it."

In our early studies, clients and subjects frequently adopted this style of expression of their own volition. When asked to formulate their negative thoughts in the second person, they spontaneously began to speak louder and with more intensity of feeling. With this release of emotions, valuable material was revealed. Often, clients would pause for a few seconds after saying their initial self-attacks and then go to a much deeper level and bring out core negative beliefs about themselves.

In the second step, clients discuss their spontaneous insights and their reactions to verbalizing the voice. They then attempt to understand the relationship between their voice attacks and their self-destructive behavior patterns. They subsequently develop insight into the limitations that they impose on themselves in everyday life functions. The insights also give clients an understanding of where their thoughts originated so that they can develop compassion for themselves. This step is important in that it helps clients account for their limitations and self-defeating behaviors. The approach does not attribute blame to parents or other family members. Parents are not malicious people; they generally wish the best for their children. But they, too, suffered varying degrees of emotional pain and frustration in *their* formative years. To the extent that they remain unaware of the ways they may have been mistreated, they tend to unintentionally reenact this form of maltreatment in interactions with their children. This step in the therapeutic process helps clients recognize that events in their childhood contributed to the formation of their distorted beliefs and other forms of destructive thinking.

The third step involves the process of initiating behavioral changes that expand individuals' boundaries and expose misconceptions about themselves. Since the procedures of voice therapy challenge core defenses and an individual's basic self-concept, collaborative interventions that effect changes in an individual's behavior are a necessary part of any effective therapeutic procedure. The potential for therapeutic progress is not merely a function of identifying negative thought patterns and uncovering repressed material; indeed, personal growth ultimately must involve constructive behavioral changes that oppose self-limiting or self-destructive patterns and lifestyles.

Corrective experiences bear a direct relationship to the maladaptive behavior patterns that are influenced and controlled by the client's negative cognitive processes. The therapist and client identify the specific behaviors regulated by the voice that are self-destructive and constricting, and both participate in formulating ideas about altering routine responses and habitual patterns of behavior. Corrective suggestions are arrived at through a collaborative effort and are in accord with clients' personal goals and ambitions. Taking the action always represents personal risk in the sense of increased vulnerability, breaking with psychological defenses that protected the individual from experiencing painful emotions. Altering negative self-image and core defenses invariably arouses an individual's anxiety and generates a temporary intensification of self attacks. Clients need to be educated that initially acting against the voice will arouse voice attacks, trying to get the person back in line. If they can tolerate the anxiety and stick with the behavior, these attacks will subside and the person will have less compulsion to act on these voices.

Applying the Techniques of Voice Therapy

The therapist's first task is to establish a therapeutic relationship that is conducive to working together. The therapeutic alliance or relationship provides empathic support and establishes an expectation of collaboration. This sets the stage for the application of voice therapy techniques in clinical practice.

Step I: Introducing Voice Therapy to the Client

The principal technique of voice therapy is the verbalizing of the individual's negative thoughts in the second person format. This methodology is important for two reasons:

1. This is the form in which most people think critically about themselves or experience internal dialogue (the voice is a kind of intrapsychic communication wherein people carry on internal conversations or dialogues with themselves as though another person were talking to them, advising, accusing, and enticing them in ways that are self-defeating and often self-destructive).

2. This technique usually brings out considerable affect, leading to important emotional and intellectual insight. The release of feelings provides the "hot emotional environment" needed for changing core beliefs (Samoilov & Goldfried, 2000; Westen, 2000).

Assessment and Development of a Focused Treatment Strategy

The *Firestone Assessment of Self-Destructive Thoughts* (FAST) can be used to establish a therapeutic focus. The FAST is a self-report questionnaire consisting of 84 items drawn equally from 11 levels of self-destructiveness (see Table 11.1). The FAST asks clients to endorse how frequently they experience negative thoughts on a five-point Likert-type scale. Using information about the specific items and levels that clients endorse as being experienced, the therapist can direct his or her interventions toward those areas in which clients are experiencing the most distress.

Table 11.1   Continuum of Negative Thought Patterns

Levels of Increasing Suicidal Intention	Content of Voice Statements
Thoughts that lead to low self-esteem or inwardness (self-defeating thoughts):	
1. Self-depreciating thoughts of everyday life	*You're incompetent, stupid. You're not very attractive.* *You're going to make a fool of yourself.*
2. Thoughts rationalizing self-denial; thoughts discouraging the person from engaging in pleasurable activities	*You're too young (old) and inexperienced to apply for this job. You're too shy to make any new friends, or* *Why go on this trip? It'll be such a hassle. You'll save money by staying home.*
3. Cynical attitudes toward others, leading to alienation and distancing	*Why go out with her (him)? She's cold, unreliable; she'll reject you. She wouldn't go out with you anyway. You can't trust men (women).*
4. Thoughts influencing isolation; rationalizations for time alone, but using time to become more negative toward oneself	*Just be by yourself. You're miserable company anyway; who'd want to be with you? Just stay in the background, out of view.*
5. Self-contempt; vicious self-abusive thoughts and accusations (accompanied by intense angry affect)	*You idiot! You bitch! You creep! You stupid shit! You don't deserve anything; you're worthless.*
Thoughts that support the cycle of addiction (addictions):	
6. Thoughts urging use of substances or food followed by self-criticisms (weakens inhibitions against self-destructive actions, while increasing guilt and self-recrimination following acting out)	*It's okay to do drugs, you'll be more relaxed. Go ahead and have a drink, you deserve it. (Later) You weak-willed jerk! You're nothing but a drugged-out drunken freak.*
Thoughts that lead to suicide (self-annihilating thoughts):	
7. Thoughts contributing to a sense of hopelessness, urging withdrawal or removal of oneself completely from the lives of people closest	*See how bad you make your family (friends) feel. They'd be better off without you. It's the only decent thing to do—just stay away and stop bothering them.*
8. Thoughts influencing a person to give up priorities and favored activities (points of identity)	*What's the use? Your work doesn't matter any more. Why bother even trying? Nothing matters anyway.*
9. Injunctions to inflict self-harm at an action level; intense rage against self	*Why don't you just drive across the center divider? Just shove your hand under that power saw!*
10. Thoughts planning details of suicide (calm, rational, often obsessive, indicating complete loss of feeling for the self)	*You have to get hold of some pills, then go to a hotel, etc.*
11. Injunctions to carry out suicide plans; thoughts baiting the person to commit suicide (extreme thought constriction)	*You've thought about this long enough. Just get it over with.* *It's the only way out!*

Any combination of the voice attacks listed above can lead to serious suicidal intent. Thoughts leading to isolation, ideation about removing oneself from people's lives, beliefs that one is a bad influence or has a destructive effect on others, voices urging one to give up special activities, vicious self-abusive thoughts accompanied by strong anger, voices urging self-injury and a suicide attempt are all indications of high suicide potential or risk. Copyright © 1996 by The Glendon Association.

Administering the FAST can be beneficial as a first step in voice therapy for two reasons. First, it allows the clinician to gain direct access to voices that are governing clients' self-destructive actions. The FAST thereby provides direction for interventions. Second, the FAST alerts clients to the presence of specific negative cognitions and brings those cognitions more fully into clients' conscious awareness so that they can work on them in therapy.

The Intake Interview   As in most therapy approaches, in the intake interview or first session, the therapist explores with the client the specific problem or problems that brought him or her to treatment. Often, this exploration provides an opportunity for the therapist to inquire about the methods the client has traditionally used in coping with problems. This line of inquiry also helps to build rapport and establish the therapeutic alliance. An informal review of personal history and recent events can increase the therapist's awareness of clients' overall feeling state and typical ways of thinking about themselves, others, and events in life.

In general, when a client begins the session with a complaint related to his or her presenting problem, the therapist would ask, "When did you start feeling this way?" The client might describe an event that he or she believes signaled the onset of the problem. The therapist would then inquire: "What do you think you were telling yourself about this event?" The client would go on to discuss his or her thoughts related to the event.

For example, a client reveals: "I feel terrible. I'm out of work and I can't find a job. I feel like I can't do anything right. I feel like such a failure."

The therapist would respond: "Try to say that as though you were talking to yourself."

The client might respond: "What do you mean?"

The therapist would then say: "Like, '*You can't do anything right. You're such a failure.*'"

Another client relates how he asked a woman for a date and was turned down. The therapist would ask: "What were you telling yourself about being turned down?" The client at this point might say, "I was telling myself that I'm not very attractive. I'm not very interesting. Women don't like me very much." The therapist would suggest that the client

say the same statements as though he were talking to himself, for example, "*You're* not attractive. *You're* not interesting. No woman would
ever like *you*."

In another example, a client discloses that she was hurt by a criticism
from someone. The therapist would ask, "What really bothered you
about the criticism? What really got to you? Was there a certain part of
it? A certain word?" In cases where people respond to criticism in a dramatically negative manner, it is not the content that causes the pain but
the fact that the negative feedback happens to correspond to specific
self-critical, self-attacking thoughts already existing within the person.
The therapist then says, "What did it make you think to yourself?" After
the client relates the thoughts, the therapist says, "Now try to put these
thoughts in the second person—as though someone were talking to you."

When clients put their thoughts in this form, strong feelings often
emerge in which the tone is transformed from flat, matter-of-fact statements to a more expressive, emotional verbalization. It has been found
that, as clients express the voice in this format, they usually have their
own momentum and keep the words and feelings going on their own initiative. The therapist simply offers encouragement with statements such
as, "Say it louder." "Don't hold back." "Let go." "Say it how you're really
hearing it."

Many clients come by this method naturally, on their own, without
needing much encouragement from the therapist. They sense the emotion behind specific thoughts and spontaneously express it along with
the content. Others who are more inhibited in expressing themselves
need support and permission to not hold back their feelings while reveal-
ing their voices. Verbalizing the voice dramatically and releasing the associated feelings often uncover core beliefs previously unknown to the
client. The voice is made up of conscious and partially unconscious
thought processes that emerge during the feeling release segment of the
session. As noted previously, clients sometimes become silent after verbalizing their initial self-attacks, the thoughts that are in their conscious
awareness. This pause may last for several seconds. The therapist needs
to remain quiet and listen patiently as other, partly conscious thoughts
emerge. These thoughts often represent the client's basic negative beliefs or core schema.

With the release of deep emotion, the client often experiences a
sense of relief on a physical level. The pent-up aggression toward self is

relieved, along with a great deal of body tension. This can relieve some of the perturbation and psychic pain the suicidal person is experiencing.

In clinical studies, it was observed that assuming an angry, attacking posture in relation to parental attitudes and prohibitions was less effective than initiating behavioral change and was frequently counterproductive.

Therapist's Responses to Client's Expression of Feeling   There are a number of responses that therapists should both use and avoid:

- Therapists should not attempt to interrupt or stop a client's expression of feeling or show by their responses that they believe that strong emotions are somehow dangerous. If the therapist shows alarm or tries to reassure or quiet the client, the client will feel more tentative in relation to expressing strong feelings in the future. Clients will get the message that their feelings are bad, dangerous, or overwhelming. Therapists must have a tolerance for their own emotions to effectively use techniques that access strong emotions.

- Therapists should not become unduly alarmed if clients express suicidal ideation or injunctions to mutilate themselves while in the process of saying their voice. After clients say their voice and discuss their insights and feelings, the therapist should then inquire about the seriousness and possible intent of carrying out such actions. When clients are able to talk openly about these feelings, it is less likely that they will act on them.

- Therapists should indicate that they believe the expression of feeling can be beneficial in reducing symptoms, in clients recovering feeling for themselves, and in helping clients gain insight into the connection between self-attacks and destructive behaviors that they are acting out in their lives.

- Therapists should encourage clients to express feelings more freely if they perceive the client is holding back. For example: "Try just letting go." "Let it all out," and so on.

- Many therapists tend to intervene with comments, questions, or interpretations prematurely, thereby interrupting the client's flow of free associations, feelings, or insight development. In voice therapy sessions, especially when strong feelings are being expressed, it is important to permit clients to remain silent if they want, to close their eyes and contemplate thoughts and feelings that are emerging into consciousness, to gather courage for the full expression of feelings perhaps never before expressed out loud to anyone. Therapists need to be comfortable with strong emotions and trust that they are not inadvertently communicating to clients a fear that their emotions can get out of control.

Step II: Discussing Insights and Reactions to Verbalizing the Voice

Following the verbalization of the voice and the expression of the accompanying affect, the therapist can help clients identify their dysfunctional core beliefs that govern their lives and provide the basic rationale for self-defeating and self-destructive behavior. Often, these beliefs emerge as clients express the anger and sadness associated with the verbalization of the voice.

Following the emotional release, often clients spontaneously develop insight into the origin of their negative thought processes. Clients can be encouraged to identify the connection between their destructive thoughts and important events in their everyday lives. This connection between past and present needs to be clearly made because it allows clients to develop compassion for themselves. Clients also examine the relationship between their self-attacks and the types of behaviors they engage in that are self-limiting or self-destructive. Questions designed to draw out the client are kept to a minimum because clients are generally eager to communicate their newly formed insights to the therapist. However, in some cases, the therapist may need to make inquiries about clients' feelings and thoughts after they have finished verbalizing the contents of their voices.

Questions such as the following can be posed: "What were you feeling just then?" "When did you start having thoughts like that about yourself?" Or, questions can be asked that challenge negative views that are clearly uncharacteristic of the client: "Where do you think you got an idea like that?" "Why do you think you feel like that about yourself?" "Where do thoughts like that come from?"

Inquiries that focus clients' attention on the connection between their thoughts and behaviors are also appropriate during the discussion phase of the session. Questions leading to this type of insight can be stated, including: "Looking back over the past week, what would you say you typically do when you're listening to a voice like that one?"

The few statements that the therapist does make need not be interpretative. For example, instead of the therapist saying, "That sounds just like your father, the way you described your father" (a psychoanalytic interpretation), he or she might say, "Who does that remind you of when you're saying these negative thoughts that way?"

One man summed up his insights after a powerful session where previously unconscious material became available to him: "These voices sound just like my father. He always told me that I'd never amount to anything, that I was going to grow up to be a ditch-digger. Now here I am, 35 years old, failing at one job after another because I've listened to that voice—his predictions. It's like the voice is a self-fulfilling prophecy to prove that my father was right about me."

Step III: Corrective Suggestions

The techniques described in Steps I and II challenge clients' major character defenses, their self-concept, and their core beliefs. The next step consists of initiating behavioral changes that expand clients' sense of self, the real self. This step allows clients to overcome imagined limitations based on their misconceptions about themselves. Many clients come to therapy with a confused sense of their own identity. These clients are frightened of challenging these labels and definitions even though they reflect an unrealistic and often unfavorable self-image. They must learn to cope with the fear and the disorientation that comes with the exploration of a more positive identity. The process of accepting a changing identity rather than a fixed one disrupts an individual's psychological equilibrium. For this reason, corrective suggestions that challenge a client's rigid self-concept and open up new experiences play an important part in personal growth.

In the process of helping clients discover their unique points of identity and increase their sense of self (that is, allowing the self system to emerge and take precedence over the antiself system), the therapist needs to be alert to body language and other behavioral cues (increased rate of speaking, eye contact, a fleeting smile, or light in their eyes) indicative of any person or anything that might have special meaning for them. Subsequently, by their responses, they can encourage clients to increase their participation in such activities, projects, or friendships and in the process take chances, reach out to others, or be more open to new experiences.

Corrective suggestions for behavioral change derive from the types of negative prescriptions clients have discovered for themselves. The ideas are not directives or strategies imposed by the therapist, but are usually initiated by clients based on their identification of specific destructive thoughts that control specific behaviors that they desire to change. The motivation for attempting to alter self-defeating behaviors comes from the client, who envisions new or different behaviors and activities as an "answer" to the dictates of his or her voice.

In using this approach, therapists encourage clients to explore alternatives and possibilities as equals; both client and therapist contribute corrective ideas that apply to the unique circumstances of each case. The therapist should approach the collaborative effort with compassion and a nonjudgmental attitude when clients indicate that they are afraid to undertake basic changes.

Although initially collaborating on the suggestion as an equal partner with the therapist, clients may subsequently deny their point of view and project the desire to change onto the therapist and perceive the therapist as having a stake in their progress. For example, clients may come to believe that the therapist is telling them how to run their lives or accuse the therapist of making decisions for them.

It is important for the therapist to avoid becoming overly invested in clients' acting on the corrective suggestions in order to preclude clients from polarizing against the suggestion; for example, playing out one side of themselves (the antiself) while the therapist is taking on the other side (the self). Therapists need to accept clients as they are, without having a stake in "changing them" in the disrespectful or prescriptive sense of the word. This will reduce clients' opportunities to polarize in this manner. Instead, the therapist can investigate with clients voices that arise and interfere with carrying out the corrective suggestions. Failures become opportunities to learn more about clients' voices and how they operate.

Collaboration to Change Specific Behaviors   Perhaps the most simple and straightforward examples of the use of corrective suggestions are those that relate to substance abuse. Implementing a suggestion that breaks a self-nourishing habit pattern is often a first step toward change on a deep character level. Although it is difficult for alcoholics, heavy drug users, or clients with eating disorders to maintain the resolution to alter their addictive patterns throughout the course of treatment, it is necessary for a successful prognosis.

In spite of this dilemma, a therapist of strong character, concerned and sensitive, can establish a preliminary contract with the client on this issue and act as a transitional object to alleviate the anxiety aroused by giving up the addiction. Early on, the therapist points out, in nonevaluative terms, the serious consequences of the client's addiction. It is important that clients *not* relate to their behavior as a moral issue, but that they become aware, on a feeling level, of the harm they are inflicting on themselves through the continued use of substances. The therapist's warmth, independence, and maturity are essential in gaining and holding clients' respect and trust so that they will continue to be motivated to give up the addiction. Controlling addictive behavior leaves clients vulnerable to the painful feelings they have been suppressing yet opens the way for potential cure.

Most clients find it difficult to give up symbolic substitutes for the love and care they felt they missed as children. They are reluctant to break into the self-parenting process in which they have been symbolically feeding and caring for themselves to preserve a sense of security and self-sufficiency. Many clients have revealed voices that tell them to isolate themselves. In such cases, the corrective suggestion would be to discourage time spent alone, encourage communication with a friend, and help the client schedule activities in a social context. The therapist can suggest to clients that they change seemingly simple actions such as eating lunch alone at the office, shopping alone, or avoiding socializing on the weekends.

When treating a suicidal client, the therapist should be especially alert to any tendencies toward isolation. Isolation provides the space for self-destructive voices to increase and gain control. Individuals' self-attacks decrease when they are in the company of friends or family, people more congenial toward them than they are toward themselves. Many suicidal individuals report that when they sought out isolation, their self-destructive voices increased, specifically suicidal ideation. In general, clients report a decline in voice attacks when in the company of other people.

Clients also report voices that cause them to hold back or withdraw emotional and behavioral responses from others (withholding) and pleasure and enjoyment from themselves (self-denial). This behavior is often held back because of clients' critical attacks on themselves. Having been thwarted as children in their attempts to express love, they now tell themselves when they feel generous, "They don't want (need) anything from you!" "He won't like your gift," or "What did she ever do for you, so why should you do anything for her?" Having been taught as children that it is selfish to want things, they now tell themselves: "You don't deserve anything. You're greedy, always thinking of yourself. You always want things your own way." Some make a virtue of self-denial and see it as constructive: "You don't really need to go on that trip. Think how much money you'll save by staying home and working!" In listening to the voice and following its injunctions, people deny themselves the excitement and enjoyment they could feel in their work and personal lives.

Corrective suggestions in voice therapy can be applied to a wide range of fears, from a fear of public speaking to those of being close to another person. In many cases, these clients are listening to self-attacks related to the activity or situation that they are afraid of. Before therapy, their behavior has been in accordance with their voice; that is, they have been acting on their fears and have generally become demoralized in relation to the goals they want to pursue. Verbalizing the voices that operate to paralyze clients' actions can facilitate changes in attitudes that allow them to challenge their fears. By understanding the roots of their fear, they can develop the courage to initiate corrective suggestions to move toward situations that were previously too threatening.

Corrective Suggestions for Suicidal Clients   For clients who are unusually depressed or facing a suicidal crisis, establishing a strong therapeutic relationship and trust is essential. Even then, evaluation of the client's ego strength is necessary before considering which specific techniques or suggestions will be used and in which order. After rapport has been achieved, the therapist can begin to help the client identify his or her self-destructive thinking and suicidal ideation. With more seriously disturbed or suicidal clients, a cognitive approach is usually introduced first; cathartic methods can be used at a later stage of treatment when the client's ego is stronger and acting out is more under control.

With depressed or suicidal clients, voice therapy methods are particularly useful in separating attitudes of hopelessness and helplessness from a more realistic or hopeful view. Suicidal clients are ambivalent about taking their own lives, often up to the last minute. Therefore, any technique, suggestion, or therapeutic statement that supports the self system and the client's desire to live is helpful and perhaps potentially life-saving. At the same time, therapists should avoid making any suggestion or interpretation that would support the antiself system, such as guilt-provoking statements, "How could you think of doing this to your wife and children?"

The therapist needs to be sensitively alert to *any* communication that would provide a clue as to activities or relationships that are potentially meaningful to the client. For example, therapists can attempt to identify an activity that was at one time of special interest to the client or a relationship that held special meaning and support the client's reinvolvement in such activities or relationships.

Corrective suggestions directed toward altering self-destructive behaviors that lie along the continuum (Table 11.1) should be employed, including:

- Discouraging time spent alone, encouraging communication with a friend, and helping clients schedule activities in a social context.

- Helping clients pursue activities in which they have invested any modicum of energy and excitement.

- Discouraging substance abuse or any other addictive patterns and encouraging the client to substitute activities and relationships that are real and constructive.

- Helping clients struggle through increased voice attacks and painful anxiety states involved in renewing personal contact with friends and family—in this context, simply being cognizant that they are attacking themselves is a valuable technique that intrudes on voice attacks that suicidal or depressed clients experience.

- Encouraging clients to recognize the anger involved in passive-aggression (holding back from others) and helping them maintain generous attitudes and at the same time develop the capacity for accepting kindnesses and generosity from others.

- Helping clients to discover that which they find to be most meaningful in life—a person, a cause, a raison d'être (R. Firestone, 1997b).

---------------------------------- Amelia: A Case Study ----------------------------------

Case Description and Analysis

Diagnostic Picture

DSM-IV Diagnoses: Axis 1, 296.31-2, Major Depressive Disorder, recurrent, mild to moderate; Axis II, 301.83, Borderline Personality Disorder; Axis III, no known physical ailments; Axis IV, break-up of a relationship, 3 major ones, financial problems, occupational problems; Axis V, GAF, 30 (at her lowest points), 90 (at her highest points).

Case History

At intake, Amelia presented herself in an open, talkative manner. She was attractive and looked younger than her 22 years. She cried frequently as she spoke. She stated that she was referred by the counseling center at her college. She reported that she had called them many times in suicidal crisis, and they felt she could benefit from ongoing psychotherapy.

Her presenting problem was depression, which she believed stemmed from childhood physical and sexual abuse. She was experiencing a low mood, fits of crying, problems sleeping, difficulty concentrating, lack of energy, and suicidal ideation. She reported a history of one suicide attempt at age 16, when she took pills. No medical treatment was sought for this attempt. The attempt was precipitated by a fight between Amelia and her parents.

Amelia reported that her current suicidal ideation centered around the breakup of a two-year relationship with a boyfriend. She reported feeling homicidal toward him as well as suicidal. She described an incident where they struggled over a knife, and she expressed being unsure of whether she wanted to hurt him or herself. The relationship had been intense, and it was her first sexual relationship.

Family History

Amelia grew up in a family composed of her mother, father, older brother, and much younger sister. She described her parents as having emigrated from an eastern European country and having very Old World values and ideas. Her parents ran a shop below their home, and she and her brother were expected to work in the shop after school and on vacations and holidays. She described her father as stern and hard-working. She described her mother as warm and more accessible, taking care of everyone. The family played music together and performed at ethnic festivals. They were actively involved in their church and attended regularly.

Amelia reported frequent beatings by her parents throughout her childhood. She felt her parents imposed Old World restrictions and would not allow her to do what most Americans her age were allowed to do. She reported getting around this by lying to them about her whereabouts and activities. Her parents were supporting her going to college and were apparently generous with her financially. Amelia worked as a policewoman while she was attending school, which also brought in a considerable amount of income.

Amelia reported that the beatings stopped when she was 16, when her high school coach found out and confronted her parents. She also reported sexual abuse by an older man down the street. This was a one-time incident. Amelia said her father also touched her inappropriately when she was younger, but that he had stopped this when she got older. She reported attempting to protect her younger sister and asking her if her father did these things to her as well.

Amelia was alienated from her older brother, who had also received beatings from her parents. Her strongest apparent attachment was to her younger sister, toward whom she felt protective.

At the time of intake, Amelia lived with her mother, father, and younger sister.

Psychiatric and Psychological History

Amelia denied ever having sought or obtained psychological or psychiatric care previously, except for the calls to the campus counseling center.

Initial Treatment Plan

The initial focus of treatment was on reducing Amelia's risk for suicide and on targeting her symptoms of depression. A psychiatric referral was made, and Amelia was prescribed Prozac. An antisuicide contract was established, where she would call if she was feeling suicidal. Initially, Amelia called often, and I made myself available for these calls throughout the course of treatment. We discussed her suicidal ideation directly and explored the flaws in her thinking processes. The focus was on the cognitions and feelings she was experiencing that were contributing to the development and maintenance of her depression. Later we addressed these thoughts directly with the techniques of voice therapy.

I worked on establishing trust and rapport with Amelia and attempted to be supportive. We also focused on the other side of her ambivalence about suicide, on her reasons for living. Amelia expressed a strong desire to move to New Zealand, a place she had visited on a student project, and where she felt she could establish a better life. This dream was life-sustaining for her, and we discussed steps she could take to achieve this goal. She reported that her parents objected to this goal, and her motivations in relation to them were mixed. She wanted to get back at them, hurt them, yet she wanted to maintain a close bond with them.

Ongoing Treatment and Case Conceptualization

Amelia's personality style and manner of coping contributed to the fact that her life seemed to be a series of crises. Her frequent difficulties in relationships were often brought about by behaviors she engaged in, such as manipulation, lying, promiscuous sexual activity, drinking too much, overspending, and acting out vengeful behaviors. Examples of these include lying about being pregnant to manipulate her boyfriend back into the relationship, lying to her parents about going on a trip with girl-friends when she was with her boyfriend, cruising for men with her best friend when she was supposedly in the committed relationship, not taking her Prozac so she could go out drinking, spending too much money on credit cards, stalking ex-boyfriends, and reporting her friend to the INS when she felt her boyfriend was paying too much attention to the friend.

Amelia's relationships with men were intense, difficult, and turbulent. She went through two major breakups during the course of our treatment. The first relationship was rekindled (by her pregnancy lie) but tumultuous before a final blow-up where she revealed her many sexual infidelities. Next, she became seriously involved with a married man at her place of work.

Her female friendships were also intense and unstable. She had one particularly close friend she had known since childhood and who had a similar background. They seemed to have similar personality styles.

Coworker relationships were also difficult. She often felt she was the victim of the gossip in her places of work, a fact that was often precipitated by her affairs with men in these settings and her unpredictable acting-out behaviors.

Amelia's base of social support was often in a state of flux. At times, she was close to a friend, her family (especially her sister), or a man, but at other times she quickly became distant or at odds with these same people as a result of her behavior. Many self-precipitated crises also occurred in the work setting. She was fired or let go over incidents with coworkers, sometimes leaving her financially strapped. Often her work environments became very tense.

Amelia did have periods of high functioning, where she moved forward in her life and achieved goals. She applied for and completed a highly competitive school program. She also entertained dreams of moving to New Zealand and took steps toward this goal. When Amelia set her mind to it, she could accomplish many difficult tasks. Although she struggled with employment opportunities, she sought and obtained a series of jobs.

I administered the FAST to Amelia, as I was concerned about her suicide risk and wanted to focus my treatment plan on the areas where she was experiencing the most distress. Amelia scored high on the suicide intent scale, the substance abuse scale, and suicide ideation level. From the test results, I had direct information about her negative thoughts toward self or voices, so I could address these with her in sessions.

I also assessed Amelia's ego strength, particularly her ability to experience strong emotion and not dissociate or become overwhelmed. Amelia demonstrated ego strength in a number of ways despite her diagnostic picture. She had a great deal of personal drive and had accomplished many tasks that required sustained focus and stamina. Amelia's dissociative tendencies were not evident in her interactions in therapy but could be deduced from her recounting of outside interactions. For example, she worked in settings where she was exposed to tragic situations and was able to "remove herself" from gory situations and not react emotionally. Amelia's relationships were strained, but she did maintain long-term connections with others. She also evidenced a strong self system in some aspects. She had interests and pursued activities that she enjoyed. Amelia was bright, as indicated by her academic achievements and could also be quite likeable. She had strong feelings for her younger sister, toward whom she felt protective and motherly.

Mock Voice Therapy Session

Therapist: So you have indicated on the FAST that you experience a lot of negative thoughts toward yourself, with a serious degree of intensity. I was wondering if it might be helpful to address these thoughts directly.

Amelia: I'm not sure what you mean. Do you mean we should talk about the things from the FAST test? Like about how I sometimes feel worthless or that life feels pointless? Or thoughts about killing myself?

Therapist: Yes, exactly. Why don't you start with any negative thoughts you have had this week or even today.

Amelia: Well, mostly I've been feeling bad about things with Mike recently. I feel really insecure and angry a lot of the time, and I'm not sure what to do with it. Like this morning, I tried to call him first thing, but he didn't answer. I left a message, and he still hadn't called back by the time I left this afternoon. It kind of makes me crazy thinking about it. When I was driving over here, I started thinking things about what if something had happened to me and he didn't call me back and then he found me hurt or dead, and wouldn't he be sorry then? Then he'd really feel like a bastard. The thought was actually compelling. But it was also compelling in another way, like that if he hasn't called me back after six hours, he really doesn't care about me anyway. He doesn't love me, I'm not worth anything, he wouldn't even care if I *was* dead. Maybe no one would care. Is that what you mean?

Therapist: Yes, exactly. But now I want you to try saying those thoughts as though another person were saying them to you, about you. So instead of saying, "He doesn't like me," try saying "He doesn't like you." Or instead of "Nobody cares about me," say "Nobody cares about you." See what I mean?

Amelia: Yes, I think so. Like "He doesn't even care enough about you to call you back. He doesn't love you." Like that?

Therapist: Yes. Just let the thoughts flow.

Amelia: Okay. "See, he doesn't care about you. He's just like all the rest of them. You're such a fool for thinking he gives a damn about you. You're such a stupid fool. No one cares about you." [crying, pause]

Therapist: Try to really let go. You might as well say it all, get all of the feelings out.

Amelia: [loud voice] *"You don't matter to anyone. No one gives a damn if you're alive or if you're dead. You're worthless! You're nothing. Maybe you should just kill yourself. You'd be better off dead, you worthless bitch!"* [pauses, crying] *"Then see how he feels! Then he'll know how bad he hurt you. That'll really show him. That'll get him. That'll show him! The bastard!"*

Therapist: That seemed to make you sad.

Amelia: Yeah. That was so weird, like suddenly someone else was talking through my mouth. Sometimes I think things like that, but this felt like someone else was yelling them at me. And the thing is, that's how it feels, like there's someone in my head telling me these things. Not to be a fool, not to trust anyone, that I need to stand up for myself or I'm just a stupid jerk, that I am a stupid jerk.

Therapist: Try saying those thoughts as if someone else were talking to you.

Amelia: *"You're such a stupid jerk! You think the world is a good place? Well, not for someone like you, you dumb girl. You are just trouble and pain to everyone.* [pause] *I can't wait for you to die. Everyone will be better off! You should just die, you stupid girl! Why don't you just die? Why don't you just kill yourself?"* [crying loudly]

Therapist: [after waiting for the full experience of her emotions] Where do you think that way of thinking about yourself came from?

Amelia: That was very powerful. I felt so sad and so full of rage. It's like it wants me to die. When I was talking, yelling those things, I really felt the rage toward myself, like I deserved to be dead. The amount of anger I felt really surprised me and scared me. It was almost like my father was hitting me and yelling at me. Or my mother.

They both used to hit on me a lot. Sometimes I was afraid they wouldn't stop and they would actually kill me. It's like they wanted to kill me. They wanted me dead. It's like they are the ones yelling at me, telling me I should die. [sad, crying]

Therapist: That makes you sad.

Amelia: I never really thought about how they felt toward me. I never realized how my own feelings that I should die might come from them, and not from me. I don't really want to die. I like being here. It made me sad to realize that maybe that's not me. Maybe I'm not so terrible.

Therapist: How are these thoughts affecting your life now?

Amelia: Yes. Sometimes it feels like the only way to get rid of the pain is to kill myself, like I'd be killing the pain, stopping the hatred. But then that makes me angry, too. I get angry and start hating everyone—thinking everyone hates me. I don't want to die, but I'm so angry! I want to hurt because I feel hurt.

Therapist: Why don't you try to express some of those thoughts as a voice, as if someone else were talking to you?

Amelia: *"You are such a fool! He's just jerking you around. Can't you see that? You think he cares a bit about you? You're only good for one thing, and once he's done with you, you're out of his mind. He's just using you, you know. He doesn't care if you're around, except to be his housekeeper and his whore. You are so stupid, so dumb. Such a fool!"* [yelling] *"You're not even smart enough to live! And he's just a stupid bastard like the rest of them. Only hurting you all the time. Using you all the time. You need to show him how bad he is. Get him back! You need to make him hurt!"*

Therapist: [after a pause for the emotions to be spent] How are these thoughts coming together in your mind?

Amelia: Well, I don't know if that's really how I feel or if it's my mother. I mean, Mike is an asshole a lot of the time, and that hurts my feelings, makes me mad. Then I want to lash out, and I feel justified. But also I think some of those thoughts are my mother's. She was always the victim of my father, his house servant. She waited on him hand and foot, took care of him, but all the time resented it. And all the time thought he was a helpless baby, like he was so lame he couldn't take care of himself and so that was her job. And she acted like she was somehow better than him, even though she acted like his slave. I get angry at Mike when I think he's acting like I should take care of him, and that makes me mean to him. But also I get angry when he's not around. Then I want him to suffer. I think killing myself would be the ultimate revenge on him. On them. I want them to suffer.

Therapist: But at your own expense. Hurting yourself to get back at Mike or your parents is not exactly taking your side.

Amelia: Yes, I guess you are right. It's much more sane to move forward and do things for myself than to lash out by hurting myself. But at those moments when I'm into thinking that way, I'm not thinking about myself. My world narrows and I'm only thinking about him, what I want him to feel, how I want to make him suffer. It's like I don't exist in those thoughts, like my body is just a vehicle I can use to get back at him. Not like my body is myself. [Sad, crying] That made me sad to say that.

Therapist: To realize your body is yourself?

Amelia: Yes, to feel connected to myself.

Therapist: How do you feel after letting out some of those feelings?

Amelia: I feel so much clearer. I don't really want to hurt myself, or Mike. I feel almost a physical sense of relief, like I just finished swimming a hundred laps. My body is more relaxed. Also the pain and agitation I was feeling are gone. My mind is quieter.

Therapist: Let's talk about what you can do this week, actions you can take that would be in your self-interest, instead of actions based on those destructive thoughts.

Amelia: Like not sitting around obsessing about how Mike has hurt me and how I can hurt him back?

Therapist: Yes. It might help to make a plan of action. When those thoughts come up, what could you do instead of being alone and losing yourself in them?

Amelia: Well, I could leave my room and see if there's anyone else to hang out with—my sister. Also, maybe I could leave the house and try to do more things with friends.

Therapist: Okay, that sounds good. Now, having said those feelings, you may feel some anxiety this week, especially if you don't give in and allow yourself to ruminate about all of Mike's shortcomings. So if you do, don't be surprised, and feel free to call me. Going against these thoughts will initially make them louder, like a parent yelling at you to get back into line, but if you can keep resisting them and don't do what they are telling you to do, in this case isolating yourself and spending hours thinking about Mike, you will begin to relax and feel better. The thoughts will fade into the background almost like a parent who gets tired of nagging. Also, it might help to journal about any negative thoughts that come up this week, and then we can talk about them in our next session.

Amelia: Okay. I feel so much better than when I got here. I really feel positive, but I also feel like there's a lot more there. I want to keep talking about this.

Discussion

In introducing voice therapy to Amelia, I began by asking her about the items she had endorsed on the FAST. Would she say these thoughts out loud as though someone else were saying them to her?

She felt awkward at first, but then got into a flow with it, saying more than she realized was there. The anger and rage associated with those thoughts started to surface, and I encouraged her to let out this rage, say it louder, let the feelings out. After verbalizing a stream of voices, she paused, and then very destructive core beliefs about herself and others surfaced. Her rage was directed at herself and at others that she felt betrayed, hurt, or used by. These expressions were followed by sadness and pain, a mournful feeling. It pained her to realize how vicious her tirades against herself were. She spontaneously expressed insights about the origin of these thoughts. She traced them back both to specific interactions with her parents when they were enraged at her and she felt they wanted her to die and leave them alone, and also to a general feeling she picked up from them that she was a burden, not a child they wanted.

She was also able to connect both the thoughts toward herself and those toward others as being related to her self-destructive behavior and disrupted relationships. She realized that the acting-out behaviors she was engaged in, such as lashing out at others, were driven from a point of view that was hostile toward herself and bent on her destruction. These forces kept her from sustaining a relationship, first by directing her to be suspicious and attacking of her partner and then by belittling her for failing in the relationship and confirming that she would never be loved, that she was unlovable and better off dead. Her suicidal thoughts came from a desire to "punish the man who had betrayed her" but she became aware that she was ultimately hurting herself with this attitude and endangering her own life.

As Amelia voiced her self-attacks in the following sessions, her suicidal impulses wielded less power over her and she began to feel relief. I also addressed behavioral changes she might want to make, actions she could take that would go against the voice and would be in her self-interest. For instance, when she felt the impulse to attack her partner, she would control her behavior, keeping in mind her goals for the relationship and the behaviors that would reflect those goals.

We discussed other healthy strategies she might adopt for coping with her feelings, in particular her anger, so that she could keep her behavior in line with the goals she wanted to achieve in life, that is, maintain the relationship, keep her job, and so on.

Amelia also needed to address her substance abuse problem of binge drinking. This obviously self-destructive behavior pattern also led to additional behaviors while intoxicated that were counter to her personal goals. Once we achieved a reduction in Amelia's suicidal thoughts, we addressed the issue of her substance abuse directly.

By identifying the voices that could precipitate her use of substances, Amelia was able to recognize the type of thinking that would get her into trouble, acting against her personal goal of staying sober. Once she identified these thought patterns and connected them with her father's pattern of "drinking away his pain," she was able to catch herself falling into this pattern and begin to avoid situations where she was more likely to drink and to make better choices for herself. She came to feel more comfortable expressing the emotions she had been trying to suppress and began dealing with them in a more constructive manner. Strong feelings of wanting arose as she gave up this defense against feeling, this self-soothing pattern of behavior. Amelia felt more vulnerable and began to take chances on getting her needs met in interpersonal relationships rather than leading a self-soothing style of existence. There were struggles as she went through this process, but she gradually developed an ability to be open to expressing her wants and seeking gratification in her real life as opposed to fantasy.

FURTHER CONSIDERATIONS

Separation theory makes a significant contribution to our understanding of people's self-destructive behavior and the suicidal process. It provides a developmental perspective and allows us to understand the basis of self-destructive behavior. In addition, an understanding of the voice process provides a window into the mind of the suicidal individual. It allows us to assess suicide risk and target our interventions to effectively intervene in the suicidal process. Voice therapy provides us with a methodology for addressing the underlying forces driving the suicidal process directly. Bringing these voices out into the open allows clients to start to separate this overlay on the personality from a more realistic view of themselves, other people, and the world. It allows them to subject these thoughts to a realistic evaluation, loosening their hold on the person's behavior. Accessing the strong emotions that accompany these thoughts allows these persons to change core beliefs about self and develop compassion for themselves and others.

The overall goal of this type of psychotherapy is to help clients come to terms with painful feelings and frustration that cause them to retreat to an inward, self-nurturing pattern and self-destructive behaviors. The essential therapeutic task with suicidal individuals is to support the development of their self system, which involves helping them become aware of their ongoing desires, priorities, and sense of meaning in life so that they are better able to pursue what they want and need directly and become more willing to take the chance on being vulnerable to the realities of life. The therapist's goal should be to help these individuals to live more in the real world than depend on fantasy, to have real gratification and meaning in life, and to reach their personal potential.

REFERENCES

Baumeister, R. F., Bratslavsky, E., Finkenauer, C., & Vohs, K. D. (2001). Bad is stronger than good. *Review of General Psychology, 5,* 323–370.

Briere, J., & Runtz, M. (1987). Post sexual abuse trauma: Data and implications for clinical practice. *Journal of Interpersonal Violence, 2,* 367–379.

Brown, J., Cohen, P., Johnson, J. G., & Smailes, E. M. (1999). Childhood abuse and neglect: Specificity and effects on adolescent and young adult depression and suicidality. *Journal of the American Academy of Child and Adolescent Psychiatry, 38,* 1490–1496.

Chu, J. A., & Dill, D. L. (1990). Dissociative symptoms in relation to childhood physical and sexual abuse. *American Journal of Psychiatry, 147,* 887–892.

Fairbairn, W. R. D. (1952). *Psychoanalytic studies of the personality.* London: Routledge & Kegan Paul.

Felitti, V. J. (2002). The relation between adverse childhood experiences and adult health: Turning gold into lead. *Permanente Journal, 6*(1), 44–47.

Felitti, V. J., Anda, R. F., Nordenberg, D., Williamson, D. F., Spitz, A. M., Edwards, V., et al. (1998). Relationship of childhood abuse and household dysfunction to many of the leading causes of death in adults: The Adverse Childhood Experiences (ACE) study. *American Journal of Preventive Medicine, 14,* 245–258.

Ferenczi, S. (1929). The unwelcome child and his death-instinct. *International Journal of Psycho-Analysis, 10,* 125–129.

Fierman, L. B. (Ed.). (1965). *Effective psychotherapy: The contribution of Hellmuth Kaiser.* New York: Free Press.

Firestone, L. (1991). The Firestone voice scale for self-destructive behavior: Investigating the scale's validity and reliability (Doctoral dissertation, California School of Professional Psychology, 1991). *Dissertation Abstracts International, 52,* 3338B.

Firestone, R. W. (1984). A concept of the primary fantasy bond: A developmental perspective. *Psychotherapy, 21,* 218–225.

Firestone, R. W. (1985). *The fantasy bond: Structure of psychological defenses.* Santa Barbara, CA: Glendon Association.

Firestone, R. W. (1986). The "inner voice" and suicide. *Psychotherapy, 23,* 439–447.

Firestone, R. W. (1988). *Voice therapy: A psychotherapeutic approach to self-destructive behavior.* Santa Barbara, CA: Glendon Association.

Firestone, R. W. (1997a). *Combating destructive thought processes: Voice therapy and separation theory.* Thousand Oaks, CA: Sage.

Firestone, R. W. (1997b). *Suicide and the inner voice: Risk assessment, treatment, and case management.* Thousand Oaks, CA: Sage.

Firestone, R. W., & Catlett, J. (1999). *Fear of intimacy.* Washington, DC: American Psychological Association.

Firestone, R. W., & Firestone, L. (1996). *Firestone Assessment of Self-Destructive Thoughts.* San Antonio, TX: Psychological Corporation.

Firestone, R. W., & Firestone, L. (1998). Voices in suicide: The relationship between self-destructive thought processes, maladaptive behavior, and self-destructive manifestations. *Death Studies, 22,* 411–443.

Firestone, R. W., Firestone, L., & Catlett, J. (2002). *Conquer your critical inner voice: A revolutionary program to counter negative thoughts and live free from imagined limitations.* Oakland, CA: New Harbinger Publications.

Firestone, R. W., Firestone, L., & Catlett, J. (2003). *Creating a life of meaning and compassion: The wisdom of psychotherapy.* Washington, DC: American Psychological Association.

Firestone, R. W., & Seiden, R. H. (1987). Microsuicide and suicidal threats of everyday life. *Psychotherapy, 24,* 31–39.

Fonagy, P., Steele, M., Steele, H., Leigh, T., Kennedy, R., Mattoon, G., et al. (1995). Attachment, the reflective self, and borderline states: The predictive specificity of the Adult Attachment Interview and pathological emotional development. In S. Goldberg, R. Muir, & J. Kerr (Eds.), *Attachment theory: Social, developmental, and clinical perspectives* (pp. 233–278). Hillsdale, NJ: Analytic Press.

Heckler, R. A. (1994). *Waking up, alive: The descent, the suicide attempt, and the return to life.* New York: Ballantine Books.

Hughes, T., & McCullough, F. (Eds.). (1982). *The journals of Sylvia Plath.* New York: Ballantine Books.

Lyons-Ruth, K., & Jacobvitz, D. (1999). Attachment disorganization: Unresolved loss, relational violence, and lapses in behavioral and attentional strategies. In J. Cassidy & P. R. Shaver (Eds.), *Handbook of attachment: Theory, research, and clinical applications* (pp. 520–554). New York: Guilford Press.

Main, M., & Hesse, E. (1990). Parents' unresolved traumatic experiences are related to infant disorganized attachment status: Is frightened and/or frightening parental behavior the linking mechanism. In M. T. Greenberg, D. Cicchetti, & E. M. Cummings (Eds.), *Attachment in the preschool years: Theory, research, and intervention* (pp. 161–182). Chicago: University of Chicago Press.

Main, M., & Solomon, J. (1986). Discovery of an insecure-disorganized/disoriented attachment pattern. In T. B. Brazelton & M. W. Yogman (Eds.), *Affective development in infancy* (pp. 95–124). Norwood, NJ: Ablex.

Maltsberger, J. T. (1999). The psychodynamic understanding of suicide. In D. G. Jacobs (Ed.), *The Harvard Medical School guide to suicide assessment and intervention* (pp. 72–82). San Francisco: Jossey-Bass.

Michel, K., & Valach, L. (2001). Suicide as goal-directed action. In K. Van Heeringen (Ed.), *Understanding suicidal behaviour: The suicidal process approach to research, treatment and prevention* (pp. 230–254). Chichester, England: Wiley.

Orbach, I. (2002, March). *The role of dissociation and bodily experiences in self-destruction.* Paper presented at the 2nd AESCHI Conference, "Understanding and Interviewing the Suicidal Patient," Aeschi, Switzerland.

Perry, B. D. (1997). Incubated in terror: Neurodevelopmental factors in the "cycle of violence." In J. D. Osofsky (Ed.), *Children in a violent society* (pp. 124–149). New York: Guilford Press.

Samoilov, A., & Goldfried, M. R. (2000). Role of emotion in cognitive-behavior therapy. *Clinical Psychology: Science and Practice, 7,* 373–385.

Sanders, B., & Giolas, M. H. (1991). Dissociation and childhood trauma in psychologically disturbed adolescents. *American Journal of Psychiatry, 148,* 50–54.

Schore, A. N. (1994). *Affect regulation and the origin of the self: The neurobiology of emotional development.* Hillsdale, NJ: Erlbaum.

Siegel, D. J. (1999). *The developing mind: Toward a neurobiology of interpersonal experience.* New York: Guilford Press.

Siegel, D. J. (2001). Toward an interpersonal neurobiology of the developing mind: Attachment relationships, "mindsight," and neural integration. *Infant Mental Health Journal, 22,* 67–94.

van der Kolk, B. A. (1996). The complexity of adaptation to trauma: Self-regulation, stimulus discrimination, and characterological development. In B. A. van der Kolk, A. C., McFarlane, & L. Weisaeth (Eds.), *Traumatic stress: The effects of overwhelming experience on mind, body, and society* (pp. 182–213). New York: Guilford Press.

van der Kolk, B. A., McFarlane, A. C., & Weisaeth, L. (Eds.). (1996). *Traumatic stress: The effects of overwhelming experience on mind, body, and society.* New York: Guilford Press.

Westen, D. (2000). Commentary: Implicit and emotional processes in cognitive-behavioral therapy. *Clinical Psychology Science and Practice, 7,* 386–390.

Winnicott, D. W. (1958). *Collected papers: Through pediatrics to psychoanalysis.* London: Tavistock.

CHAPTER 12

Dialectical Behavior Therapy

David Lester

We saw in Chapter 7 that the classic systems of psychotherapy have rarely devoted an in-depth discussion to psychotherapy for suicidal individuals. The lone exception is cognitive therapy, and Chapter 10 presented a discussion of the application of cognitive therapy to suicidal behavior.

However, two new systems of psychotherapy have appeared in recent years that have specifically explored their application to suicidal behavior. Voice therapy is presented in Chapter 11, and this chapter presents the other system, dialectical behavior therapy.

Dialectical behavior therapy (DBT) was developed by Marsha Linehan, who originally cast the system as *cognitive-behavioral treatment* (Linehan, 1993a). However, the wide acceptance of Aaron Beck's cognitive therapy (Beck, Rush, Shaw, & Emery, 1979), which has been described as "the single most influential cognitive approach" (Todd & Bohart, 1999, p. 345), perhaps influenced a change of name to distinguish DBT from Beck's system of therapy. In addition, not all commentators view DBT as a cognitive therapy. Todd and Bohart (1999), for example, view DBT as a postmodern behavior therapy and label Linehan as a radical behaviorist.

Dialectical behavior therapy has been widely disseminated and has become very popular. Although some commentators have noted that the empirical base for the effectiveness of DBT is slim (Swenson, 2000), the empirical base is comparable (if not superior) to that for other systems of psychotherapy. Swenson suggests that DBT's popularity is a result of the sound principles and strategies it proposes and the integration of several theoretical orientations that "reflect the Zeitgeist of today's mental health community" (p. 87).

In this chapter, we review the basic principles of DBT, explore the application of DBT to suicidal clients, and then examine the reasons for its popularity.

DIALECTICAL BEHAVIOR THERAPY: A BRIEF DESCRIPTION

In her initial presentation of DBT, Linehan (1993a) focused on therapy for women with a borderline personality disorder (BPD) who engaged in repeated deliberate self-harm (including attempted suicide). Clients with BPD show dysregulation in the areas of emotions, thoughts, behavior, and interpersonal relationships, and these are the problems that DBT seeks to remedy.

Dialectical behavior therapy is, therefore, intimately involved with a particular psychiatric diagnosis, the syndrome of BDP, a linkage not present in other systems of psychotherapy. Other systems of psychotherapy may focus on particular problems. For example, Gestalt therapy may be best suited for people who overemphasize rational thinking and underemphasize both emotions and input from their bodies and from the environment. However, linking a system of psychotherapy to a psychiatric diagnosis raises the question of whether the system is useful for clients with any other of the many psychiatric diagnoses and, furthermore, what will happen if the psychiatric diagnostic system is changed dramatically.[1] Clinicians are exploring the application of DBT to other syndromes (e.g., depression), and the linkage between DBT and BPD may become less pronounced in the future.

Because DBT is intimately linked to BPD, it is important to examine what Linehan sees as the basic characteristics of such clients.

Characteristics of Borderline Personality Disorder

Borderline personality disorder clients are characterized by emotional dysregulation, interpersonal ineffectiveness, intolerance of distress, and

---

[1] A minority of psychologists and psychiatrists are highly critical of the present psychiatric diagnostic system authorized by the American Psychiatric Association. For example, it is based on descriptive clusters of symptoms rather than causes, making it very different from the medical diagnostic system. In addition, for present purposes, the definition of *borderline* has undergone tremendous changes since it was first formulated, and there is no reason to suppose that it might not undergo changes in the future.

poor self-management; and the goal of DBT is to ameliorate these problems. Linehan described the problems facing BPD clients as involving three dilemmas (Linehan, 1993a, p. 67):

1. *Emotional vulnerability versus self-invalidation:* BPD clients are emotionally sensitive and experience intense emotions, which last for a long time. Linehan compares BPD clients with burn patients. Just as severely burned patients have no skin to cover their flesh, BPD clients have no emotional skin to protect them from painful emotions.

In self-invalidation, BPD clients invalidate their experienced emotions and turn to others to reflect what they should be feeling. These clients often do not label their emotions correctly, and they come to distrust their emotional experience as a guide to action.

The dilemma, therefore, is that BPD clients experience intense emotions to the slightest stimulus, yet do not trust these emotions as guides to decision making. Borderline personality disorder clients are not sure whom to blame for their problems (themselves or others) and whether they *cannot* control their behavior or whether they are *unwilling* to do so. The dilemma for the therapist is that trying to induce change in the client reinforces the self-invalidation. Yet, communicating sympathy for the client reinforces the emotional vulnerability and increases the client's hopelessness. The therapist must validate the client's experiences *and* help the client change.

2. *Active passivity versus apparent competence:* Borderline clients tend to approach the problems that they encounter passively and helplessly, and they demand that others (including the therapist) provide solutions for them. On the other hand, borderline clients appear to be competent and able to cope with their problems, at least in situations other than that causing the crisis. This inconsistency can easily lead the therapist into expecting the client to have competencies and to be able to generalize them from one situation to another, blaming and rejecting the client when he or she does not do so.

3. *Unrelenting crises versus inhibited grieving:* Finally, many borderline clients experience a series of unrelenting crises. They endure chronic stressors and experience continual stress that overwhelms them. Since this state of affairs can interfere with constructive treatment, DBT involves regular group therapy sessions in which skills are taught. Not only does the group setting make it easier for clients to deal

with lack of attention to their crises, but also the therapists can more easily avoid being drawn into these crises.

Many crises involve loss of some kind, and borderline clients avoid the full experience of the painful emotions that accompany such loss. Rather, they inhibit their grief and avoid grieving, often accompanying this with acting-out behaviors such as drinking, driving fast, or spending money. It is important to help borderline clients reencounter the losses and traumas of their life and experience and express their grief.

The Essence of Dialectical Behavior Therapy

Linehan's presentation of DBT differs considerably from the presentation of most of the major systems of psychotherapy. Dialectical behavior therapy provides a complete, systematic manual for the conduct of *psychotherapy.* It is a comprehensive guide to all phases of psychotherapy, covering even the rules for setting up a clinical practice (with advice on collecting fees), establishing a therapeutic relationship (including the use of written contracts and ethical rules such as no sexual contact between the therapist and the client), and the importance for therapists of consultation with peers and supervisors. Thus, it is difficult to identify in what ways DBT differs from other systems of psychotherapy.

There are three areas of interest for discussion: (1) the philosophical orientation of DBT, (2) the targets or goals for the therapist using DBT, and (3) the specific techniques to use to achieve each of the goals or targets of DBT.

The Philosophical Orientation of Dialectical Behavior Therapy

The philosophical orientation of DBT involves one major and two minor components. The major component is that DBT is a cognitive-behavior therapy. Dialectical behavior therapy is eclectic in that it uses tactics from both cognitive therapy and behavior therapy, which have been proposed by a variety of therapists. Tactics taken from Albert Ellis's rational-emotive therapy (Ellis, 1973) and Aaron Beck's cognitive therapy (Beck et al., 1979) are mentioned explicitly. However, some cognitive and behavior tactics receive little or no attention. For example, DBT does not appear to use aversive conditioning.

Furthermore, since DBT is a cognitive-behavior therapy, tactics from systems of psychotherapy such as Gestalt therapy and psychoanalysis are not suggested although DBT is not averse to clients' using ancillary resources such as Alcoholics Anonymous. Thus, it is possible (although not mentioned in Linehan's book) that a client could be encouraged to attend sessions with therapists offering alternative tactics. (Alcoholics Anonymous, for example, uses techniques similar to those used in reality therapy.)

Dialectical behavior therapy is a long-term therapy (at least when used to treat clients with BPD). Linehan suggests a year as the minimum, but she expects that clients will be in therapy for several years as a rule. Dialectical behavior therapy requires attendance at weekly (or more) individual therapy sessions and, in addition, group therapy sessions that focus on the development of problem-solving skills. It is recommended that the group leader(s) be different from the client's individual therapist.

The two minor orientations are *dialectics* and Zen Buddhism.

Linehan uses the word *dialectics* a great deal in her presentation of DBT, and the term appears in a variety of contexts. One major dialectic is that the therapist must accept and validate clients' behavior while insisting that clients change their behavior (Linehan, 1993a, p. 19). This does not seem dissimilar to the orientation of most systems of psychotherapy. For example, Carl Rogers accepts clients unconditionally while having the goal of inducing change. Albert Ellis, in his rational-emotive therapy, accepts clients while seeking to change their cognitive styles. Dialectical behavior therapy, however, makes this particular dialectic explicit and central to the therapy.

Sometimes, *dialectic* takes on other meanings. For example, Linehan (1993a, p. 124) notes that clients often think dichotomously (a "dialectical behavior pattern"), and DBT seeks to move the clients to a more balanced response. Here, then, *dialect* replaces a more commonly used cognitive therapy term, *dichotomous thinking*.

The use of the word dialectical in DBT is, perhaps, distracting. It serves to label the system of therapy in a way that distinguishes it from other systems at least in name, but it does not imply major differences in the tactics used by the system. It appears to be more of a marketing tool than a fundamental change in cognitive-behavior therapy. Dialectical behavior therapists, however, would object to this characterization of DBT because they view the dialectic orientation as central to DBT.

Zen Buddhism is introduced into DBT because Linehan uses exercises to encourage "mindfulness," exercises to develop core skills. The tactics are meditation skills: (1) learning to observe and describe, (2) being non-judgmental and focusing on the present, and (3) focusing on the current activity.

This orientation is distracting. Zen is open to many interpretations, and Linehan's interpretation of Zen is dissimilar to other interpretations of Zen. Linehan's interpretation ignores, for example, the four noble truths[2] and the ways in which Alan Watts (1961) and Jay Haley (1971) interpret Zen philosophy. Watts and Haley are explicit in seeing psychotherapy as a game, similar to that played by Zen masters, in which clients who are "one-down," try to get "one-up" on the therapist until they give up the effort, quit therapy, and go on with their lives. This is not the philosophical orientation of DBT. Rather, DBT includes several meditation tasks, some of which are compatible with some versions of Zen Buddhism.

The Techniques of Dialectical Behavior Therapy

Before discussing the specific therapeutic tactics for dealing with these clients, Linehan proposes a general framework for therapy, including assessment, data collection on the current problem behaviors, precise operational definition of the targets for the therapy, a collaborative relationship between client and therapist, commitment to the goals of treatment, and application of the therapeutic techniques (Linehan, 1993a, p. 19). This framework, although not made explicit by all systems of psychotherapy, could apply to any system.

The goals of DBT are to help the client achieve emotional regulation, interpersonal effectiveness, tolerance of distress, and self-management. Again, this set of goals is compatible with other systems of therapy, although these other systems may not explicitly articulate the goals. In particular, the goals are almost identical to those used in traditional stress management (Lester, Leitner, & Posner, 1983, 1984).

---

[2] The four noble truths are: (1) Life is mainly suffering, (2) Suffering is caused by desire for the wrong things, (3) The way to extinguish suffering is to extinguish desires, and (4) The way to extinguish desire is to follow the eightfold path.

It is possible here to give only examples of the techniques of DBT. We look, therefore, in some depth at the training in interpersonal effectiveness skills. The training manual for therapists contains ten handouts and three homework sheets for this component. The material contains a great deal of information, listing things such as the goals of interpersonal effectiveness, factors reducing interpersonal effectiveness, and myths.

Some of the material is identical to rational-emotive therapy. The myth, "I can't stand it if someone gets upset with me," is changed to, "I can stand it if . . ." Clients are taught, "I can insist on my rights and still be a good person," a position that is found in standard assertiveness training. Homework assignments are given, such as going to the library and asking the staff for assistance in finding a book, inviting someone to dinner, and paying for a small item with a large-denomination dollar note. One of the homework assignments has clients observe and describe an interpersonal situation they encounter, using a standard format, much in the same way as cognitive therapists have clients keep a record of the ABCs involved when they feel depressed or angry.[3]

There are no new or innovative techniques introduced in this (or other) skills section. Rather, what Linehan has done is to compile and organize a well-designed module that incorporates all of the possible cognitive and behavioral tactics that a therapist might use to improve the interpersonal skills of clients. Therapists following this module would provide a *standardized* group therapy session and thus would resemble one another much more than group therapists in general resemble one another.

The guidelines for the individual psychotherapy, which accompanies the skills-training group therapy sessions, are not as thoroughly planned out and described. However, checklists are provided for each issue. For example, the chapter on the core strategy of validation provides checklists for emotional, behavioral, and cognitive validation strategies, and, in addition, cheerleading strategies. The emotional validation strategies checklist includes items such as, "T [therapist] listens with a nonjudgmental and sympathetic attitude to emotional expression of P [patient],"

---

[3] A = Antecedent event, B = the irrational thought that followed this event, and C = the emotional (or behavioral) consequence. Clients are encouraged to write down a rational thought to replace the irrational thought and then to examine the new emotional consequence.

and some forbidden items such as, "T criticizes P's feelings." These sound very much like typical Rogerian person-centered guidelines.

Again, therefore, what distinguishes DBT is not the tactics themselves, but rather the thorough and comprehensive compilation and ordering of the tactics and guidelines. As a final illustration, Swenson (2000) noted that, to get the client to commit to the treatment, the therapist can use "six change-oriented commitment strategies to generate a 100% commitment, but balances that push with a genuine acceptance of whatever commitment can be secured" (p. 90). If one tactic does not work, there are five more to try.

APPLICATION OF DIALECTICAL BEHAVIOR THERAPY TO SUICIDAL CLIENTS

Linehan (1993a, 1999) addresses the problem of suicidal clients specifically. As before, she provides a thoroughly comprehensive sets of guidelines for dealing with suicidal clients, but there seem to be few new or innovative tactics proposed. She presents commonly known information on risk factors for suicide, and her Suicidal Behavior Strategies Checklist contains items such as discussing alternative solutions versus tolerance, reinforcing nonsuicidal responses, validating the client's pain, instructing the client not to commit suicide, generating hopeful statements and solutions, coaching the client in obtaining medical treatment, and so on. (Dialectical behavior therapy does introduce an explicit hierarchical approach, in which safety is the first priority, to be followed by other goals once the initial goals are met.)

DISCUSSION

As noted in the introduction to this chapter, commentators have cast DBT as a postmodern behavior therapy or radical behavior therapy (Todd & Bohart, 1999). This approach is based on a criticism of traditional behavior therapy as a collection of techniques with little theoretical cohesion and an acceptance that therapists must consider private behaviors (e.g., thinking and feeling), childhood determinants of adult behavior, and genetic influences. For postmodern behaviorists, treatment must also be idiographic, that is, tailored for the individual inhabiting a particular social context. For example, what functions as a reinforcer may vary from person to person, and a skill that is to be learned has to function in that person's situation.

There are many variants of postmodern behavior therapy aside from DBT. For example, Hayes and his colleagues (Hayes, Strosahl, & Wilson, 1999) have developed acceptance and commitment therapy (ACT). In ACT, the therapist encourages the client to accept and experience disturbing thoughts and feelings. Trying to avoid them may lead to self-defeating behaviors, but they can be placed in a different context (reconceptualized). Clients learn to distinguish between themselves and their thoughts and feelings: "I am having the thought that I am stupid" versus "I am stupid."

Functional analytic psychotherapy (FAP), proposed by Kohlenberg and Tsai (1991), seeks to develop an intense relationship between the client and therapist and to use the natural reinforcers present in the therapy session, the genuine responses of the therapist (e.g., "I feel close to you when you say that") rather than arbitrary reinforcers (e.g., praise from the therapist). Therapists using this system pay attention to what they call clinically relevant behaviors and, when improvement occurs in these behaviors, reinforce the improvements immediately in the session. Therapists also observe their own behavior as it evokes or improves the clinically relevant behaviors, and they modify their behavior so that they encourage improvement.

All of these therapies, including DBT, borrow heavily, but creatively, from other systems of psychotherapy, so they are more readily integrated into the classical systems of psychotherapy.

A search of PSYCINFO in July 2003 for "dialectical behavior therapy" identified 170 entries, indicating that this system of therapy has attracted widespread interest and stimulated many applications. For example, DBT has been applied to depression (Lynch, Morse, Mendelson, & Robins, 2003), eating disorders (Safer, Telch, & Agras, 2001), substance abuse (Dimeff, Rizvi, Brown, & Linehan, 2000), posttraumatic stress disorder (Becker & Zayfert, 2001), dissociative behavior (Wagner & Linehan, 1998), emotion dysregulation (McMain, Korman, & Dimeff, 2001), domestic violence (Fruzzetti & Levensky, 2000), delinquents (Trupin, Stewart, Beach, & Boesky, 2002), and sex offenders (Quigley, 2000). It has also been extended to other formats for psychotherapy, including group therapy (Telch, Agras, & Linehan, 2000) and family therapy (Miller, Glinski, Woodberry, Mitchell, & Indik, 2002).

It is noteworthy that many of these reports focus on clients with BDP who also show these other behaviors (e.g., anorexia, drug abuse, or dissociative symptoms). Thus, it appears that DBT remains best suited for clients with BPD. In the present context, therefore, it is important in future research and practice to explore the effectiveness of DBT with suicidal clients who have other personality disorders or other disorders (e.g., major depressive disorders or schizophrenia).

Although DBT has been used with suicidal clients, especially those with BPD, it does not appear to provide techniques specifically designed for suicidal clients. The section in Linehan (1993a, pp. 468–495; see also Linehan, 1999) provides only general (but useful) guidelines for dealing with suicidal clients. For example, the Suicidal Behavior Strategies Checklist includes items such as "T removes or gets P to remove lethal items" and "T maintains position that suicide is not a good solution." However, dialectical behavior therapy is one of the few therapies to demonstrate empirically a reduction in suicide-related outcomes such as rehospitalization for suicidality.

Swenson, Torrey, and Koerner (2002) note that the best training for conducting DBT is a 10-day intensive workshop for practitioners. As noted previously, the training manual (Linehan, 1993b) includes detailed instructions on how to conduct the skills-training component, complete with handouts, discussion points, and advice on when and how to give clients breaks during the group therapy sessions. This detailed structure goes far beyond the training manuals for other systems of psychotherapy and may give reassurance to novice therapists (as well as to those managing mental health facilities).

Furthermore, the proposal to have long-term, simultaneous individual and group therapy for clients, focusing on different issues and led by different therapists, seems to be an excellent arrangement for clients, especially chronically suicidal clients with personality disorders. It is important, however, for the therapists involved to meet regularly to discuss the clients with whom they are working and to coordinate their therapeutic goals and tactics. Time and financial constraints may, however, make such intensive treatment difficult to arrange these days when there is pressure for short-term treatments such as medication and brief crisis intervention, perhaps supplemented by short-term cognitive therapy.

Despite these reservations, DBT is one of the few systems of psychotherapy to focus on suicidal clients. As such, it merits our attention and may prove to be useful for therapists who encounter suicidal clients (especially those with BPD) in their clinical practice.

REFERENCES

Beck, A. T., Rush, A. J., Shaw, B. F., & Emery, G. (1979). *Cognitive therapy of depression.* New York: Guilford Press.

Becker, C. B., & Zayfert, C. (2001). Integrating DBT-based techniques and concepts to facilitate exposure treatment for PTSD. *Cognitive and Behavioral Practice, 8,* 107–122.

Dimeff, L., Rizvi, S. L., Brown, M., & Linehan, M. M. (2000). Dialectical behavior therapy for substance abuse. *Cognitive and Behavioral Practice, 7,* 457–468.

Ellis, A. (1973). *Humanistic psychotherapy.* New York: Julian.

Fruzzetti, A. E., & Levensky, E. R. (2000). Dialectical behavior therapy for domestic violence. *Cognitive and Behavioral Practice, 7,* 435–447.

Haley, J. (1971). *The power tactics of Jesus Christ and other essays.* New York: Avon.

Hayes, S. C., Strosahl, K. D., & Wilson, K. G. (1999). *Acceptance and commitment therapy.* New York: Guilford Press.

Kohlenberg, R. J., & Tsai, M. (1991). *Functional analytic psychotherapy.* New York: Plenum Press.

Lester, D., Leitner, L., & Posner, I. (1983). Stress and its management for police officers. *Police Journal, 56,* 324–329.

Lester, D., Leitner, L., & Posner, I. (1984). Stress and its management for police officers. *Police Journal, 57,* 31–35, 193–196, 254–156.

Linehan, M. M. (1993a). *Cognitive-behavioral treatment of borderline personality disorder.* New York: Guilford Press.

Linehan, M. M. (1993b). *Skills training manual for treating borderline personality disorder.* New York: Guilford Press.

Linehan, M. M. (1999). Standard protocol for assessing and treating suicidal behaviors for patients in treatment. In D. G. Jacobs (Ed.), *The Harvard Medical School guide to suicide assessment and intervention* (pp. 146–187). San Francisco: Jossey-Bass.

Lynch, T. R., Morse, J. Q., Mendelson, T., & Robins, C. J. (2003). Dialectical behavior therapy for depressed older adults. *American Journal of Geriatric Psychiatry, 11,* 33–45.

McMain, S., Korman, L. M., & Dimeff, L. (2001). Dialectical behavior therapy and the treatment of emotion dysregulation. *Journal of Clinical Psychology, 57,* 183–196.

Miller, A. L., Glinski, J., Woodberry, K. A., Mitchell, A. G., & Indik, J. (2002). Family therapy and dialectical behavior therapy with adolescents. *American Journal of Psychotherapy, 56,* 568–584.

Quigley, S. M. (2000). Dialectical behavior therapy and sex offender treatment. *Dissertation Abstracts International,* 60B, 4904. Antioch University.

Safer, D. L., Telch, C. F., & Agras, W. S. (2001). Dialectical behavior therapy adapted for bulimia. *International Journal of Eating Disorders, 30,* 101–106.

Swenson, C. R. (2000). How can we account for DBT's widespread popularity? *Clinical Psychology, 7*(1), 87–91.

Swenson, C. R., Torrey, W. C., & Koerner, K. (2002). Implementing dialectical behavior therapy. *Psychiatric Services, 53,* 171–178.

Telch, C. F., Agras, W. S., & Linehan, M. M. (2000). Group dialectical behavior therapy for binge-eating disorder. *Behavior Therapy, 31,* 569–582.

Todd, J., & Bohart, A. C. (1999). *Foundations of clinical and counseling psychology.* Prospect Heights, IL: Waveland Press.

Trupin, E. W., Stewart, D. G., Beach, B., & Boesky, L. (2002). Effectiveness of dialectical behaviour therapy program for incarcerated female juvenile delinquents. *Child and Adolescent Mental Health, 7,* 121–127.

Wagner, A. W., & Linehan, M. M. (1998). Dissociative behavior. In V. M. Follette, J. I. Ruzek, & F. R. Abueg (Eds.), *Cognitive-behavioral therapies for trauma* (pp. 191–225). New York: Guilford Press.

Watts, A. (1961). *Psychotherapy east and west.* New York: Random House.

CHAPTER 13

The Widening Scope of Family Therapy for the Elderly

Joseph Richman

This chapter presents theoretical and therapeutic principles of family therapy in the treatment of the suicidal elderly. Family therapy is the treatment of choice for suicidal people. It is valuable because often family members have become enmeshed in the conflicts and pressures associated with suicidal behavior. Family members are valuable in the healing process because the family system possesses blocked forces of love and caring that can be released through the therapy process. The goals of such an approach can result in an enriched and satisfying life for the suicidal person and increased satisfaction and well-being for the entire family.

The premise of this chapter is that suicide is based on a crisis, often the last in a series of crises. Therefore, this chapter also discusses the development and fate of these crises and the role of the family in their resolution and cure. The modern crisis concept was formulated by Gerald Caplan (1964), who defined a *crisis* as an event or problem for which the person's usual coping methods and defenses do not work.

Man is a social animal whose activities are based on an unspoken and usually unconscious set of social roles, rules, and regulations. It is in the family that the social roles by which we live are learned and handed down to future generations. That touches on a major reason for family therapy: A family problem is often precipitated when a change in one person, who becomes the patient, affects the entire family system, requiring a change in the other family members. One such crisis may occur after a positive session in individual psychotherapy. The family may then take steps to restore the status quo, the result being a setback in which the patient gets worse—the negative therapeutic reaction. Family therapy is one response to the resulting crisis.

THE FAMILY IN THE PSYCHIATRIC EMERGENCY ROOM

Beginnings are important. The first experiences of family therapy may determine the family's attitudes toward therapy, whether accepting or rejecting. My first experiences with suicidal patients and family therapy took place unexpectedly, before I received the necessary training and education for either. In 1965, after 17 years as a clinical psychologist, I was assigned to the psychiatric emergency room of Jacobi Hospital where I interviewed patients for assessment, diagnosis, and disposition.

Early in my assignment, I saw a 59-year-old wheelchair-bound man, who had savagely slashed his arms and legs in a suicide attempt. After being cleared by the medical team, he was brought into the psychiatric emergency room where I saw him. I asked the patient what happened.

"I don't want to live this way," he said. "I have been trapped in this wheelchair for years. I can't walk because I have a spinal tumor, which is benign but inoperable, and I'm in constant pain. I have terrible arthritis, which is agonizing. I have stomach ulcers and diabetes, and the diet for one makes the other worse. Would you want to live this way?"

I sympathized with this gentleman and his seemingly rational decision to commit suicide. After arranging for his hospitalization, I called in his son, who had been waiting patiently, to notify him of his father's hospitalization. His son was eager to talk but presented a very different picture. He described his father as a tyrant who bullied his children and dominated his wife and the entire family with his illness. On this particular day, there was a huge family argument, which ended abruptly when the wife and three children walked out. The father made his suicide attempt during his resulting state of frustration and rage.

By happenstance, the development of my skills in family therapy coincided with the parallel development of my skills in treating suicidal patients. I discovered that one individual's story or point of view is not necessarily the whole story. It is necessary to hear all sides.

After my experience, first with the patient and then with his son, I kept a record of every patient I interviewed in the psychiatric emergency room. The majority came in with a relative or close friend. My interviews soon included seeing the patient and relatives first separately and then together in a family interview.

Eventually, I saw some of the patients for more than one interview. The first case took place shortly after I saw that unfortunate man in a wheelchair. It involved a woman in her mid-40s, whom I saw with her husband. A crucial event had occurred several years before. The couple was visiting the husband's family with their 7-year-old son. Their son locked himself in an abandoned refrigerator in an empty lot and died of asphyxiation. The husband blamed his wife, turned away from her, and flamboyantly began an affair with another woman. In retaliation, she did the same with another man. She became pregnant and had a son, who is now the same age as the first child when he died. She had made many suicide attempts since the death of her first son.

I had the couple return twice to the psychiatric emergency room. The husband continued his irrational blaming of his wife for their son's death. She expressed remorse at having a son from another man. Her husband replied, "I can't blame you for that. After all, I was the one who started it." His wife visibly relaxed and said, "I am so glad to hear you say that." Both partners agreed that there was no further need for treatment.

For the next 35 years as I routinely saw patients with their families, I realized that the first requirement was to listen to all sides, without preconceptions. However, practice alone without a theoretical background was not enough. I also joined the Family Therapy Training Institute at the Bronx Psychiatric Center and read the literature on family therapy. The founders of the contemporary family movement were skillful and well trained in the foundations of the basic theory and practice of therapy. They were also courageous men and women in the face of opposition from the prevailing individual tradition.

SOME CONTEMPORARY PIONEERS

The contemporary family therapy movement began in the late 1940s, one of the first practitioners was John Bowlby (1949). Its momentum increased in the 1950s and has never ceased. The findings and recommendations of groundbreakers such as Ackerman, Minuchin, Bowen, Whitaker, and many others focused on the family, the context, and the current situation in therapy. Their views are as valuable today as they were then.

These early teachers of family therapy were well prepared in their professional backgrounds, whether medicine, psychology, or social work. They did not have to be told that proper education and training are essential. As Ackerman (1958) said, "To do therapy without a conceptual framework is like playing in the dark. It may be fun at first, but very soon it leads to mounting anxiety and disorganization" (p. 278). He also saw the interactions and communication processes of the family to be largely unconscious.

Ackerman ran a monthly workshop at the Family Training Unit of the Bronx Psychiatric Center, which I attended. I was particularly impressed by his skill as a teacher and his ability to work in widely different family situations.

Salvador Minuchin was a teacher and therapist with a positive approach to the family. "In effect," he said, "I turn other family members into cotherapists, making the larger unit the matrix for healing" (Minuchin, 1974, p. 121). Minuchin was also a pioneer in the use of relabeling: "A reconceptualization of the symptom in interpersonal terms can open new pathways for change" (p. 155).

Murray Bowen emphasized the difference between what he called "the static concept" of personality as purely individual in contrast to the family-oriented view that we understand the functioning of one person in relation to others (Bowen, 1978, p. 29). His personal approach was based on the meanings of closeness and distance and, rather unexpectedly, humor. "The right emotional distance for the therapist is a point between seriousness and humor, where he can shift either way to facilitate the process in the family" (p. 229). He saw the disturbed family as consisting of "an undifferentiated ego mass." Therefore, a primary goal of Bowen's therapy was the differentiation of one's self from the family. Minuchin (1974) developed a similar concept, which he called "enmeshment."

The family can best be understood as a system that is more than the sum of its members. Disturbed communication feature is present. The most prominent disturbed communication feature is an extreme secretiveness, combined with how "they," the outside world, perceives them, the "family." This covering up of what is actually going on often makes a suicide unexpected and shocking.

Another communication feature that contributes to family discord is the process of *triangling,* described by Bowen (1978). The most frequent result is that one member of the family becomes furious at the person who has been reported as doing or saying something disparaging or hurtful. The therapeutic goal, therefore, is to increase communications that are direct instead of triangled, open rather than concealed, and honest instead of devious. Family therapy is the most effective means for achieving this goal.

The family suicidal system includes the forms of nonverbal communication that are the basis of the "family unconscious" (Richman, 1996). The nonverbal communications may also be positive. For example, the mere fact that the family members appear for a session is a pleasant surprise to some suicidal patients. More than one such patient has commented, "Now I see that you care."

While acknowledging the importance of the past, the focus is on the present. Family therapy is effective because the family is influential at all ages, and its influence continues into the old age of its members.

FAMILY THERAPY AND THE ELDERLY

In 1971, I joined a newly formed geropsychiatric clinic at Jacobi Hospital, and I spent the next 18 years in intensive work with the elderly, with a special interest in suicidal patients. Many of their situations required a widening use of different family therapy approaches.

None of the early family therapy thinkers and practitioners focused particularly on the elderly, but their contributions applied to all ages. My studies and treatment of the suicidal elderly have been presented in several books and papers, representative examples of which are found in the references at the end of this chapter.

The work of Erik Erikson (1950) is essential for those working with the elderly. Erikson presented what he called a psychosocial-psychoanalytic description of development. It is a comprehensive process that goes through various stages, beginning at birth and continuing to the very end of life. Erikson called the crises and tasks of the last two stages of development "generativity versus stagnation" and "ego integrity versus despair." They became the major theoretical focus of my therapy with older patients.

A crisis may take place resulting from a normal change in development, a "maturational event," as it was called by Kappenberg (1994, p. 8). It may represent a family developmental lag, where a change is necessary in an individual with whom the family is intimately involved, but the task of moving to the next stage is too anxiety provoking.

Robert Butler's (1963) influential paper on "the life review" is consistent with Erikson's theory of development. Butler hypothesized an individual's need to review his or her life experiences and make sense of them. The positive results of a life review, with the help of therapy, indicate that old age can truly become what Robert Browning in his poem "Rabbi Ben Ezra" called "The last for which the first was made."

However, the social bias against the aged has been a major impediment to providing the emotionally disturbed elderly with the help they need. A typical example was provided by John Leonard (2002) in a review of *You Shall Know Your Own Velocity,* by David Eggers. Leonard approvingly quotes a conclusion by the author: "The only infallible truth in our lives is that everything we love in life will be taken from us" (Leonard, p. 9). That is an attitude that can cultivate despair; it is not one to live by. It is true that everything comes to he who waits, death among other things. It is also true that, if we did not know of death, we would not be appreciative of life. You might as well relax, be patient, and find meaningful things to do in the interim.

Social attitudes are imbued with ambivalence, and being old is sometimes admired and envied and yet also sometimes seen as undesirable. That attitude is also true of the elderly themselves. My son-in-law, Marvin, phoned and sang "Happy Birthday," on my 84th birthday. I thanked him and said, "84 is just a birthday, 85 is a milestone." "What do you want when you are 85?" "To be 86," I replied.

The positive response to psychotherapy by elderly patients and the degree to which they benefit from treatment is unknown, ignored, or misunderstood by many therapists and counselors. They are not aware that elderly people form positive relationships, benefit from treatment, and welcome the opportunity to talk to someone who listens and understands. Psychotherapy particularly fits the need of the elderly to make sense out of their lives, what Butler (1963) called the "life review."

The value of family crisis intervention was demonstrated by a research study by Langsley and Kaplan (1968). A team of therapists compared patients in a psychiatric emergency room who were seen in family therapy instead of hospitalization with matched patients who were hospitalized. The family therapy patients did as well as the hospitalized ones and, in a follow-up, they needed less hospitalization or return visits to the emergency room.

INTRODUCTION TO THE CLINICAL EXAMPLES

The elderly play different roles in family therapy—from the identified patient to a key figure in the family or the catalyst who may not be directly involved in family therapy. All of these appear in the following examples.

The Effect of One Family Session during Ongoing Therapy

A change in the family system can occur as the result of one family therapy session, even when the patient is in individual and group treatment. The following example was presented, in part, from a different point of view in Richman (1995).

Mr. S was a retired stand-up comedian in his late 70s who suffered from a variety of serious medical conditions, including emphysema and heart disease. He was referred to the geropsychiatric clinic by his physician, who periodically became furious with Mr. S. For example, the patient knew how to irritate his throat, after which he would go to the emergency room and be hospitalized. His annoyed internist would then discharge him the next day. He was referred with the diagnosis of depression and seen both in couples therapy with his wife and in a geriatric group with predominantly depressed patients.

He used a great deal of humor during therapy, but, for a comedian, he was remarkably negative with a need to undermine treatment by all possible means. His humor was hostile and divisive. For example, the group therapy members always arrived early and socialized. By the time I entered the room, their mood was cheerful and relaxed. One day, however, the group was silent and angry. One woman pointed to Mr. S and said, "He called you King Kong." Mr. S looked pleased although his hostility had alienated him from the rest of the group.

Mr. S and his wife had three daughters, all of whom lived out of state. I had tried to arrange a family session but with no success. One day all three were available. A family session was arranged, and it became the turning point. The eldest daughter was the family member to whom the parents turned for acknowledgment and approval. At the end of the session, she remarked, "I thought therapy meant that you had to dig up all the dirt that takes place in life and talk about it. But it appears that it isn't, and I think it will be good for my parents to be in treatment."

At the next group session, Mr. S declared, "I know what's wrong with me and that there is no hope. I can only go downhill, and I know what the end is." The other group members tried to cheer him up and suggested alternative attitudes. He skillfully "proved" they were wrong.

Sara, one of the group members, said, "You should be more positive." He replied, "I'm positive my condition is hopeless." The group was taken aback by his pun, and no one could respond. I finally turned to Sara and said, "You would be a great straight man." The ghost of a smile passed Mr. S's lips.

I then asked Sara how she was. "I just want to die, that's all," she said. Mr. S was shocked, as we all were, and said, "We all love you. You don't have to feel that way." He then regaled her with a multitude of one-line jokes, such as, "Once upon a girl, there was a time."

Following the session, his attitude changed to being positive, socially cohesive, and loving. There was also a significant improvement in Mr. S's medical and psychiatric condition concomitant with his more positive attitude. That one family meeting transformed his destructive wit into cohesive humor. In that respect, the change resembled an incident in one of William Shakespeare's plays.

Four hundred years ago in "Love's Labour's Lost" (Shakespeare, 1957/ 1598), Shakespeare described a method for turning negative wit into therapeutic humor. The heroine, Rosaline, gave her lover, Biron, who was noted for his hostile wit, an assignment: "To remove the worm from your heart." She asked him to spend every day for a year visiting the severely and terminally ill and, during each visit, he was to make them laugh. Biron agreed (pp. 158–159).

Like Biron, who followed the wishes of his beloved to change his hostile wit to the positive use of humor, Mr. S followed the prescription of his beloved oldest daughter to cooperate in psychotherapy. The family session transformed his humor into a therapeutic instrument.

The Effect of One Home Visit

Joan was 19 years old, the youngest of five children, and the only one who did not graduate from high school or college. She was "the family loser." She was brought home by her boyfriend one evening high on drugs. Her "friend" pushed her in through her parents' door and said, "Here, you take her. I've had enough." An enormous family argument ensued, culminating in her suicide attempt. She was hospitalized and, after discharge, referred to me. I saw her, alternating individual and family therapy.

The parents and her four siblings resisted treatment, both for themselves and for Joan, although one result was her enrolling for training to become a physician's assistant. They insisted that she quit her training, however, and remain at home under lock and key 24 hours a day to prevent her taking drugs.

The family's resistance was adamant until a home visit that allowed the inclusion of Joan's grandmother, a lively Irish immigrant who was the matriarch of the family. She immediately responded favorably to family therapy. After that, psychotherapy progressed fruitfully. Joan graduated as a physician's assistant and continued to work successfully.

Before the home visit, the family was not able to accept the changes that would be required in the entire family by Joan's becoming independent. Consequently, she was treated as a sick person, as seen in her drug addiction, rather than a person. However, Joan's mother may have been more involved than it seemed on the surface. She was the one who suggested and arranged the home visit. When her elderly but feisty mother, the family matriarch, approved of therapy, it gave permission for the entire family to participate. The one family session transformed a family that was going nowhere in therapy into a cohesive unit that worked together to the benefit of Joan, who continued to be successful in her career.

The parents also became more autonomous. For the first time in years, the parents went on a vacation alone, something they had been afraid to do, supposedly because Joan could not be trusted without their constant surveillance. Therapy ended when Joan married and had a child.

A Suicide Pact: One Couple and One Family Session

Mr. C was a 77-year-old retired teacher who was in individual therapy. His therapist asked me to see him after he confided to the therapist his plans to commit suicide. I saw Mr. C and his wife for one session and then the family, including all the children, for one more session.

The meeting with the couple began with the expression of loss and mourning and the belief that their joint suicide was the only solution. The husband explained that when their last son left the house, "I was left all alone."

"Didn't you have your wife?" I asked.

"We are so much one," he replied, "that it is like being alone." His wife agreed.

"How do you think the children will take it, losing both parents at once?" I asked.

Both questions were efforts at relabeling in order to present alternatives to suicide. Mrs. C was responsive. "I never thought of that," she said, her first self-statement.

The family meeting that followed a week later also presented an alternative to the patient's feeling that he had been abandoned, with the assurance by the couple's children that their parents were loved and would not be abandoned. The husband then returned to his individual treatment, no longer suicidal. The major problem was the belief that the striving for autonomy by the offspring was a loss for the parents, a result that occurs when the parents have not attained autonomy. The relatively quick resolution was related to both the timing of a family intervention at the time of a suicidal crisis and the availability of a therapist experienced in the treatment of suicidal patients and families.

When One Family Session May Not Be Enough

Statistically, it is found that married men who have experienced the loss of a wife are more subject to suicidal impulses and behavior than women. With the right timing, a bereaved spouse is particularly responsive to family interventions. The family meetings often find that more than the loss of a spouse is involved.

I saw a 75-year-old man for intake who was brought into treatment by his daughter after he expressed the wish to join his wife after she died.

During the session, he tearfully described how devastating the loss had been. After airing his grief, he realized that he could not commit suicide and leave his daughter even more bereft. Although that was an example of a single successful family visit, the daughter seemed more distraught than her father, and I therefore recommended five more sessions.

Death as a Catalyst

Paula G was a 16-year-old adolescent who slashed her arms and legs so savagely that several hours of surgery were required. She was hospitalized for two weeks on the psychiatric ward of the hospital and discharged into my care. Before her discharge, I saw her parents as a couple. The precipitant of her suicidal act was her grandmother's death, which precipitated a series of events in the family, including the separation of her parents, with Paula being pressured to choose whom to live with. The culmination was her serious suicide attempt.

I saw the family for four weekly sessions. I saw each member of the family separately during the first half-hour and the entire family for the second half-hour. Paula was a highly intelligent, sensitive, and mature girl who eagerly responded to the opportunity to consider her suicidal act and its meaning.

During the third session, Mrs. G expressed her shock and surprise at Paula's suicidal act. "I told you, 'What's the use of living?'" Paula replied. "I thought that was just an expression," replied the mother. I decided that an interpretation of the situation in which Paula had been placed was in order, with humor to make it palatable. I was reminded of a joke, which I shared with them:

> An Irish magician retired after many successful years on stage and television. He met a friend whom he informed of his retirement. "Whatever happened to your assistant in your famous act where you sawed a woman in half?" asked the friend. "Oh, she retired, too," said the magician, "and is living in Belfast and Dublin."

Mrs. G was the only one who laughed at the joke. She seemed to understand the impossible situation in which they had placed their daughter. In the fourth session, the mother announced that she was giving up her apartment and returning to the family.

A Developmental Lag in the Family

Some families dread the change that is often required when a family member becomes mentally or physically ill. They insist, therefore, on maintaining an outmoded status quo as when, in this example, an elderly woman is treated as if she were a trouble-making adolescent. I respect and accept the traditions of the family and the tenacity of family bonds. My goal is to increase individual competence by working with the family and with individuals when called for.

Miriam W was a 68-year-old woman who attempted suicide after her only son died of a heart attack. I saw her with her sister because other family members were too busy. Her sister said that Miriam could not live with any of her relatives. Miriam was saddened by the news, but said she was arranging to move in with a female friend. Her sister ordered her not to because the family disapproved of the friend. She spoke to Miriam as though she was a rebellious adolescent whose efforts at autonomy and independence were getting her into bad company.

I saw Mrs. W during my early investigations into suicidal patients, but she was not my patient. Had she been my patient, I would be understanding of the family members who feel upset and unable to deal with the patient's situation, and I would work to reduce their anxiety. I would also schedule some individual sessions to help Mrs. W mourn for her son, deal with her current situation, and encourage her to continue making autonomous decisions.

Feeling Loved Overcomes the Death Wish

A social worker called, asking if I could see Mrs. Sally V, a 79-year-old woman who had just been hospitalized after a serious suicide attempt. The precipitant was the sudden death of her 50-year-old daughter. I saw her in the hospital with her son, his wife, and the two grandchildren. Mrs. V was an angry woman, especially because she wanted to die and resented being revived. I offered to see her in family therapy, but only if she agreed. I suggested that she think it over. She agreed and was seen for two years in family and individual therapy.

At our first outpatient session with the family, Mrs. V was a lively and outspoken woman who reassured the family that she would not commit suicide, but she added that she still wanted to die. Her family commented on her reaching the ripe old age of 79. They were astonished when she admitted that she was really 80, not 79. Eighty meant she was old. The negative significance of aging was also the dominant theme in her two years of psychotherapy. Becoming old meant primarily the loss of independence.

A session with her 50-year-old son present was a turning point. Mrs. V was obsessed, as she usually was, about becoming ill and unable to care for herself. "When that happens, I want you to pull the plug," she said to me. I turned to her son and asked, "How would you feel if your mother became feeble and helpless, and you had to take care of her?" He replied, "I would want you to pull the plug."

The session went on to other topics. Toward the end, I commented to her son, "You are still very young. You might find that feeding and taking care of your mother is not so distasteful when you become a few years older." Her son completely agreed. "After all," he said, "I never had that experience, and I don't know what I would really do." At the end of the session, Mrs. V lagged behind while her son went for the car and said, "I have such a good feeling."

In a later meeting, her son recalled how he loved his mother when he was a child. "I remember that, when I was 3 years old, you were my life." From that point on, Mrs. V lost her wish to die and no longer obsessed about becoming disabled and helpless. Therapy ended a year later when she entered a senior residence.

Mrs. V's acute suicidal state and subsequent almost fatal attempt was based primarily on the disturbed behavior of family members who could not cope with her bereavement. Her mourning was actually a more appropriate response to the death of her daughter than that of her daughter's children. The result, after her serious suicide attempt, was a positive breakthrough with her son and a decrease in her death and illness preoccupations.

Thursdays with Howie

The greatest loss, perhaps, is that of the self in the face of a terminal or life-threatening illness. However, it is rarely only the self with whom the terminally ill patient is concerned.

The patient was Howard C, a 60-year-old man, who phoned at the recommendation of a friend to whom he had confided his intention to commit suicide. He had a history of cancer, which had now spread to many organs of his body. Despite being on antidepressant medication for months, he remained depressed and suicidal. There was no reason to live, he said, "because there is no time to do anything." As a result, he and his wife had collapsed into a state of mutual hopelessness. He was seen in a combination of individual and couple therapy with his wife, Emily.

In the first session, we discussed what he could do, had he the time, and how he wanted to be remembered. He responded favorably to the suggestion that he could achieve both goals by writing an "ethical will" for his children and others, setting forth his values and recommendations for the good life.

In the second session, he brought in his ethical will, a 10-page summary of his life, with an emphasis on his failures and frustrated ambitions, although he had in fact been a successful professional. The task encouraged a discussion of his life review that provided a sense of continuity among the past, present, and future, and a reassuring sense that something vital in his life would live on after him.

After the first session, he felt less stress but more anger. He expressed resentment at some of the doctors he had seen who had not been helpful. I "agreed," and added, "As they say, the patient was at death's door, but the doctor pulled him through." Mr. C laughed heartily. The couple resumed their social life and contacts with their family members, and he became significantly less suicidal.

Mr. C then requested more individual sessions. At one individual session, I intuitively read a sonnet by Shakespeare, where the poet longs for death, "Except that to die I would leave my love alone." Mr. C responded emotionally. "That's it! Emily said she can't live without me. What will happen to her?"

Meanwhile, Mr. C and his wife became much calmer and were enjoying their life and activities together. Death was placed in the distance, in favor of life. At the end of one session, I said to Mr. C, "I'll see you next Thursday, if I live." He finished that old joke with, "and if not, I'll see you Friday."

Shortly after, Mr. C's condition worsened, and therapy had to be discontinued. I spoke to him by phone, and he repeated that he was most concerned about his wife. She was becoming more upset and helpless. I spoke to her by phone and advised her to show Mr. C how competent she was, able to take care of herself and of him, too—a form of coaching of the wife of a dying husband that has been found to be helpful (Richman, 1981, 2000).

In our last call, Mr. C said, "I wanted to die and came very close to doing something." "Everything happens for the best," I said. "Can you imagine a way that would be better for you?"

He said "Yes. We [he and Emily] have become closer." He continued to express great admiration of his wife, her competence and caring, and what a relief he felt. His final words were to repeat that he is not afraid to die and could now do so without worrying.

EMOTIONAL INTENSITY IN FAMILY THERAPY WITH THE SUICIDAL ELDERLY

The family is where the strongest emotions are felt and expressed, in humor as well as life. My daughter Ellen and I were discussing the popularity of *Harry Potter* and *The Lord of the Rings*. Ellen said, "I prefer murder and mayhem" (meaning mystery stories). "Me, too," I said, "That's why I'm interested in families."

The extreme intensity of emotions that occurs in families breaks through in family therapy with suicidal people, with a mixture of anxiety, despair, and anger that can be very distressing. It took many months during my early intensive family work with the suicidal before I was able to deal therapeutically with my feelings. But as Ackerman (1966) said, "The emotions aroused in a therapist as he confronts a troubled family offer specific cues to the shared currents of feeling among the family members" (p. 110). Listening without interfering until I felt ready to deal with the feelings made the difference. I began to understand that these outbursts represented a plea to the therapist for help. When the emotional intensity rises, I now know that the patient and family will do well. The therapist helps by taking steps to diffuse the tension and turn it into a therapeutic situation. Under other circumstances, the intensity of the rage can be dangerous.

One of the most therapeutic responses is to treat the expression of rage as a positive event. It is positive because it is genuine and because it can become understandable to the family members, including the patient. The interpretation is that the family reacts with such intensity

because they feel helpless and at wits' end, seeing suicide as the only solution. Recognizing that they are dealing with a problem that they feel is
insoluble, I add, "All we need to do is find out what the problem is and
how to deal with it." These statements are usually met with universal
agreement. I then arrange for another family session, and the family
leaves with a significant reduction in the suicide-based tension.

The unexpected turmoil of feelings at a most primitive level is also
aroused in the supposedly objective therapist, an event known as the
countertransference. It often makes it difficult for the therapist to respond
therapeutically, which is why so few clinicians turn to family therapy
when treating suicidal patients. The two most frequent "wrong" reactions
are trying to change the subject or remaining quiet when some response is
needed to cool it. Remaining quiet can be seen as abandonment.

THE UNDESIRABLE OUTCOME OF A
NONTHERAPEUTIC FAMILY SESSION

One undesirable outcome can be the rejection of family therapy by patients who could otherwise benefit from such treatment.

A woman phoned me, agitated and upset and asking for help: "But not
family therapy. My mother tried to commit suicide and was hospitalized.
Her doctor saw the whole family, and my mother spent the whole time
accusing me, saying that it was because of me she wanted to kill herself.
The doctor just sat there."

The blaming and scapegoating described by this distraught woman was
the communication of a situation that the family could not deal with. The
resulting frustration leads to the buildup of anger, helplessness, and hopelessness to the breaking point. A suicidal attempt can be the beginning of
cure in the hands of a competent, well-trained therapist who knows what
has to be done and how to do it.

A cognitive factor is also involved. For the participants to deal with a
conflict, the situation must not be too emotional. The goal of the family
meeting is, "Come, let us sit down and reason together," but the family
therapy participants must first let off steam. Shouting, cursing, accusing,
and blaming can be very therapeutic as a start, but it can be deadly if the
session ends with those feelings still present. The best interventions

occur after the rage, despair, and agitation have been aired. As Mark Twain said, "When angry, count to ten; when very angry, swear" (quoted in Esar, 1962, p. 182). The expressed anger, helplessness, and hopelessness can become the beginning of a cure.

I believe that family therapy with suicidal clients should be a specialty within the general field of family therapy. Ideally, there should be adequate education, training, and knowledge, and much direct family therapy experience with suicidal patients.

The Vital Importance of Problem Recognition

I was asked to see an elderly grandmother, whose 19-year-old grandson had committed suicide. He had come to the emergency room with his chief complaint of anxiety. The interviewer told him to call the mental hygiene clinic and make an appointment. The young man left the emergency room, went to the roof of the apartment house where he and his grandmother lived, and jumped to his death.

This incident is typical. In this example, the presenting complaint covered up the real one. A suicide during therapy, where all seemed to be going well on the surface, is often based on the same oversight. The message to therapists is clear: A seemingly trivial problem may cover up a more important and life-threatening one. It is more difficult for that to occur if there are family sessions, at least from time to time.

CONCLUDING REMARKS

My first contacts in the psychiatric emergency room involved the integration of family therapy and suicidal crisis intervention. In that setting, it quickly became apparent that family therapy could turn a family that felt helpless and hopeless into a caring and constructive unit. The fundamental theoretical basis is the realization that people do not live in a social vacuum. The family context must be considered, as well as the larger social context. They are part of the suicidal situation and can determine the fate of the suicidal person.

The elderly in family therapy usually play one of three roles—as the patient, as a key figure in the family, or as a catalyst. In each case, the elderly person can help realize the goal of therapy—to allow the emergence of the family's resources for recovery. As a general rule, families possess forces of love and caring that may have been buried but that can emerge in family therapy.

Each of the 11 suicidal situations presented in this chapter was an example of the widening scope of family therapy. Therapy with the terminally ill is another example of the widening scope of palliative treatment, including individual and group, as well as family therapy.

Psychotherapy can play a major role in the proper treatment of severely ill and terminally ill patients and their families, which can also include those in hospices. It is fortunate that the question of heroic measures and futile or inappropriate medical treatment do not exist in hospices. Although people go there to die, hospice patients are alive, and many are oppressed by unfinished problems. They should be treated in the light of the latest developments in palliative care. (See the papers on "Psychotherapy with the Terminally Ill," by Caffrey, 2000; Greenstein & Breitbart, 2000; and Richman, 2000.)

Most of my patients take a variety of medications while in psychotherapy. I have often arranged for medical examinations and treatment and maintained contact with their physicians. The same is true of contact with social agencies, hospitals, nursing homes, and other institutions. (Examples of the widening scope of family therapy, from the emergency room, the outpatient clinic, the inpatient wards, to home visits, and how the atmosphere of each setting affected the therapy are presented in Richman, 1986, 1993.)

All therapists should be familiar with the principles of understanding and treating the suicidal elderly, combined with the principles of family therapy. This means that physicians and other health professionals should be trained to recognize and deal with the communication of suicidal intent. Even if they are not assigned the patient, they may be involved.

Sally V, for example, whose case was presented earlier, went to her family doctor asking for sleeping pills because she had insomnia. The doctor gave her the pills, enough for a lethal dose, which she used in her almost fatal suicide attempt. She said she expected the doctor to question her about the reason for her sleeplessness, and she was surprised when he did not.

Ageism, the negative perception of aging, is prominent among the suicidal aged. In our first family meeting, Sally V's children spoke of her being 79. She replied, "I'm 80, but I never told anybody." The difference between 79 and 80 may seem slight, but it depends on its meaning and attribution. A great importance is often attributed to the decades. It is as though "decade" were pronounced "decayed." The fear of becoming helpless and unable to take care of themselves is universal among the elderly. Part of the positive adjustment to aging is to know when it is rational and desirable to adjust to increased dependency and accept help.

An example can be seen in the film *Harold and Maude*. Maude was a happy, healthy, and lively 79-year-old, who killed herself when she became 80, for no apparent reason other than the meaning of that decade.

Rather than suicide, Maude should have sought treatment with an experienced geriatric therapist. That can take place more easily when the training of all therapists includes familiarity with family therapy and the treatment of the suicidal, including the suicidal elderly. Education of the public in recognizing the danger signs and learning where to obtain help is equally important. That applies, too, to the many homicides, especially within the family, which are often based on the same interpersonal dynamics as suicides.

In December 2002, the television program *Sixty Minutes* had a segment about Andrea Yates, a mother in Texas who cold-bloodedly and systematically drowned her five children in the bathtub. The husband blamed psychiatry for not doing enough. I do not believe him. After his wife had a "postpartum depression with psychotic features," the couple decided to have another child. They did so despite the psychiatrist's warning that another child would almost certainly result in another psychotic depression. The wife also discontinued her medication, including Haldol and an antidepressant.

The state asked for the death penalty. I felt frustrated by society. Execution and blaming are not the answer. Instead, this tragic story and others involving suicide and homicide have an educational message for society and leaders—institute measures for the courts, the legal professions, and leaders in Congress to educate the public about what can be done to prevent such tragedies.

In conclusion, it is not possible for a therapist to tell when he or she has saved a life, for the suicidal person in therapy may have survived without professional help. However, it is possible to tell whether the family as well as the patient have found a greater richness and meaning in life, and that makes the therapeutic effort worthwhile.

REFERENCES

Ackerman, N. W. (1958). *The psychodynamics of family life.* New York: Basic Books.

Ackerman, N. W. (1966). *Treating the troubled family.* New York: Basic Books.

Bowen, M. (1978). *Family therapy in clinical practice.* New York: Aronson.

Bowlby, J. (1949). The study and reduction of group tensions in the family. *Human Relations, 2,* 123–128.

Butler, R. N. (1963). The life review: An interpretation of reminiscence in the aged. *Psychiatry, 26,* 65–76.

Caffrey, T. A. (2000). The whisper of death: Psychotherapy with a dying Vietnam veteran. *American Journal of Psychotherapy, 54,* 519–530.

Caplan, G. (1964). *Principles of preventive psychiatry.* New York: Basic Books.

Erikson, E. (1950). *Childhood and society.* New York: Norton.

Esar, E. (Ed.). (1962). *Dictionary of humorous quotations.* New York: Paperback Library.

Greenstein, M., & Breitbart, W. (2000). Cancer and the experience of meaning: A group psychotherapy program for people with cancer. *American Journal of Psychotherapy, 54,* 486–500.

Kappenberg, R. P. (1994). Family crises. In R. A. Corsini (Ed.), *Encyclopedia of psychology* (Vol. 2, pp. 8–9). New York: Wiley.

Langsley, D. G., & Kaplan, D. M. (1968). *The treatment of families in crisis.* New York: Grune & Stratton.

Leonard, J. (2002, November 10). Review of *You shall know your own velocity,* by David Eggers. *New York Times Book Review,* 9.

Minuchin, S. (1974). *Families and family therapy.* Cambridge, MA: Harvard University Press.

Richman, J. (1981). Marital psychotherapy and terminal illness. In A. S. Gurman (Ed.), *Questions and answers in the practice of family therapy* (pp. 445–449). New York: Brunner/Mazel.

Richman, J. (1986). *Family therapy for suicidal people.* New York: Springer.

Richman, J. (1993). *Preventing elderly suicide: Overcoming personal despair, professional neglect, and social bias.* New York: Springer.

Richman, J. (1995). The life saving function of humor with the depressed and suicidal elderly. *Gerontologist, 35,* 271–273.

Richman, J. (1996). The family and unconscious determinants of suicide in the elderly. In A. A. Leenaars & D. Lester (Eds.), *Suicide and the unconscious* (pp. 206–216). Northvale, NJ: Aronson.

Richman, J. (2000). Introduction: Psychotherapy with terminally ill patients. *American Journal of Psychotherapy, 54,* 482–485.

Shakespeare, W. (1957). *Love's labour's lost: The London Shakespeare* (pp. 159–261). New York: Simon & Schuster. (Original work published 1598)

CHAPTER 14

Group Therapy and Suicide

Robert R. Fournier

> *The challenge is to be where the patient is—a place where, under*
> *ordinary circumstances, we would not choose to go. But in a sense,*
> *this is our obligation, our responsibility. . . . We must be able to see*
> *death in its darkest moments to make it possible to see the light.*
>
> (Jacobs, 1989, p. 341)

This chapter attempts to integrate knowledge about suicide for group practice in a manner that will be beneficial for the clinical practitioner, suicidologist, and interested reader. Also included in this work is a proposed method for suicide education that prioritizes healthy adaptation in life and may be included in any and all group practice.

Suicide is a phenomenon that is repulsive to most, welcomed by some, grieved by many, and discussed by few. Suicide, it is argued, is a powerful event and behavior that affects not only the dying, but also the living. Those who grieve a loved one lost by suicide, suicide survivors, become captive victims to the haunting residue of pain and suffering that suicide brings to life. In clinical practice, suicide is a powerful force for a worker's necessary reckoning, regardless of practice method, including individual and group psychotherapy.

Group work takes many forms, including that of the popular, walk-in peer support groups, such as Alcoholics Anonymous. This chapter focuses on professionally facilitated group psychotherapy. For a broader and more in-depth understanding of group psychotherapy, you may wish to explore from the perspective of others who have developed a greater expertise or vocational regard in this area (Yalom, 1995). My underlying philosophy for understanding suicide (and life) is based on existential phenomenology (Van Kaam, 1966), with a personal and professional value for the role of spirituality (Fournier, 1999) and psychological trauma (Fournier, 2002), within the context of clinical psychology and social work (Fournier, 1990).

Group psychotherapy provides a significant method for problem solving. It may be used as a sole method of treatment or combined with other treatment methods, such as individual psychotherapy. Groups can be for better or worse, depending on many factors, including the influence of the worker or group leader, the participants, the group structure, and the group process. The group presents an opportunity for a person to "place (her or his) subjective view in context," within the objective social world in which we all live (Carroll, Bates, & Johnson, 1997, p. x). Groups may permit greater flexibility of roles than in individual psychotherapy, encourage mutual support for "enabling empowerment," "make the (person's) past public" to promote the personal discovery of meaning in life, and, generally, "approximate the state of the human being in a natural setting" (van der Kolk, 1987, pp. 163–165). In addition, groups may "promote a sense of shared plight" and provide a trusting and safe social atmosphere for self-disclosure, skill development, and problem solving (Campbell, 1989, p. 603).

HISTORICAL BACKGROUND

The phenomenon of suicide has not been accepted and often contraindicated in the practice of group psychotherapy (Richman & Eyman, 1990, p. 147). Suicide has been viewed primarily as a problematic factor that interferes with successful group work, disturbing equilibrium of process and purpose, and increasing the risk for harm to the group participants and the group leader(s). Those who are seriously suicidal are almost always prohibited from group participation because they are considered by group leaders to be excessively burdensome, intrusive, and potentially dangerous, that is, as undesirables:

> Deeply depressed suicidal patients . . . are often too retarded to use the group . . . they do not receive the very specialized attention they require (except at enormous expense of time and energy to other group members); furthermore, the threat of suicide is too taxing; too anxiety provoking for the group members to manage. (Yalom, 1985, p. 231)

The previous quote is not to be interpreted as a critique of its author, but rather as a sign of how the potency of suicidal behavior and our inability to effectively treat it has led to its stigmatization as an "undesirable" in group therapy. Essentially, suicidality has become a fear factor, a hot potato, a phenomenon that, due to ignorance and perceived threat to personal integrity, elicits in the professional worker a survival response, such as avoidance, denial, withdrawal, immobilization, and/or even attack.

A paucity of research exists concerning the relationship between suicide and group psychotherapy. Most texts on group therapy give little attention to the phenomenon of suicide, some ignoring it completely. Unfortunately, this disregard leaves group leaders not only ill-prepared for addressing the phenomenon of suicide in group work, without practical information and guidelines, but also potentially fearful of its behavioral expression among group participants. Ironically, it is argued, such a fearful view may promote avoidance and ignorance, increasing rather than decreasing the risk for despair and suicide. The research that does exist concerning suicidology and psychotherapy, including group psychotherapy, provides us with some helpful suggestions to reduce our fear, invite interest, and weigh the value for group psychotherapy.

First and foremost, a change of mind or a more realistic and positive regard for the phenomenon of suicide is recommended, a regard that moves away from the nearsighted historical view. Those who are suicidal, it is argued, are individuals who are not alien from us, but rather a significant, accessible step away. To be suicidal does not make a person crazy or insane, not passive recipients of some diseased state, and not our enemy. Suicidal persons are persons who "feel isolated, . . . not understood, . . . trying to convey their misery" to others (Jacobs, 1989, p. 331), that is, they are in need of help from others, inclusion rather than exclusion from the world in which they and we live. Indeed, their very moment of despair, their suicidal moment, may be viewed as the ultimate request for inclusion or intimacy with life (Fournier, 1987).

Effective leadership is considered to be an important factor for successful group work with suicide.[1] The effective group leader is a stabilizing

---

[1] The phrase "with suicide" is used in this chapter as an abbreviated reference to group work concerning the phenomenon of suicide, including suicide bereavement and risk or vulnerability for suicidal behavior.

force (Jacobs, 1989, p. 340), an existential social worker with knowledge about suicide, practical resources, and philosophical issues (Shneidman, 1993). Effective group leaders use themselves passionately and empathically to connect with others throughout the group experience, helping others realize the personal worth "that he or she matters," and provide affirmation "that he or she is understandable" (Jacobs, 1989, pp. 331, 335). Nothing, it is argued, feels worse or more alienating from life than to not be understood, except perhaps to not feel loved. The group leader helps group participants appreciate and internalize the basic belief that they have meaning and worth in life, or a reason for living. For the effective group leader, work concerning suicide transcends the traditional temporal view of suicide as synonymous with a specific suicidal crisis or suicidal moment and becomes situated in the *every moment*. Such a reframing view of suicide as a movement of an individual's life toward premature death rather than a mere final moment enables the group leader to help participants understand not only the suicidal crisis but also the potential for suicide and the greater underlying issue of the participant's commitment to life (Fournier, 1987).

Apart from a change of perspective and effective leadership, the group itself is considered to have an essential role in work with suicide. The psychotherapy group is a powerful social force that creates a (unique) atmosphere of understanding, one that may explore intimately and intersubjectively the often ignored or misunderstood reality of many life events and experiences, including suicide. It is within the group, through the interaction of all participants, that problems are solved and well-being is promoted. The action of the group becomes the real-life place where participants may learn to view suicide as connected or related to life rather than as excluded from it. For example, group participants may learn to view suicide as related to the normal stress or pressure experienced by us all (Fournier, 2002; Richman & Eyman, 1990, p. 151). Pain and suffering may be viewed as normative experiences in everyday life, often undesirable, yet sometimes desirable for accomplishing a worthy life goal, such as in athletic training. As such, pain and suffering can come to be perceived as important factors in life, needing to be understood, managed to the best of a person's ability, and possessing potentiality for furthering personal meaning and purpose in life (Frankl, 1963). By this appreciative and empowering action, the group reverses the trend of isolation and withdrawal common to suicidality by establishing feelings of belonging and providing "an immediate source of nutriment, support, and renewed relationships" (Farberow, 1968, p. 331). Many consider this working through of interpersonal relationships as the "unique therapeutic value" of a group (Van der Kolk, 1987, p. 166).

The group, it is argued, plays another valuable role in suicide work, that is, as a resource and testing ground for the development of well-being. Group participants may help one another to discover and develop coping resources for responding effectively to stressful life events and enhancing well-being (Fournier, 2002). A group that includes this work may learn to address willingly the fundamental or existential life issues that we tend to avoid or deny or otherwise regard as undesirable. For example, by confronting what may be called the "unlived life" (Yalom, 2002b, p. 316) that persons experience with death anxiety, guilt, aloneness, depression, loss, confrontation with mortality, victimization, irresponsibility, and despair, participants may learn to understand better their own identity, relatedness to life, and relatedness to suicide. Group processing of these issues may lead to enhancement of meaning and purpose in life and avoidance of suicidality (Frankel, 2002, p. 215).

LEADERSHIP DISPOSITION

Successful group work is determined, in large part, by the group leader's preparation for this experience. A brief discussion of noteworthy factors for leader preparation for successful group work with suicide follows.

Being a Good Clinical Worker

There is no substitute for the use and dynamic development of sound clinical skills in individual and group practice, especially in interviewing, assessing, and treating risk for harm. It is uncomfortable enough dealing with the phenomenon of suicide without adding issues of being unprofessional or inappropriate as a therapist. Education, supervision, and consultation are essential. In addition, becoming a good person and living a healthy way of life are part and parcel of successful clinical work. Without a doubt, personal well-being is important, for it is our self, our personality, that is manifested to others as an ideal reference, including our beliefs, values, attitudes, ways of thinking, moods, and behavior. Group work, it is argued, creates an atmosphere of greater exposure of the leader to others than in individual work, a true testing of your metal, so to speak. What the leader reveals is influential, for better or worse, and total objectivity or neutrality is merely an illusion.

Being an Unassuming Presence

Genuine understanding of self and others enables effective therapeutic action. The opposite is also true—lack of understanding of self and others impedes effective action, risking harm. Many times I have made mistakes by assuming I knew the answer or meaning of something rather than gathering further information to confirm it as a fact or as a difference of opinion. Ego and preconceived notions may get in the way of authentic understanding. With suicide, the need to know the person's real, unique explanation and meaning is paramount.

Stress from working with suicide is a factor that impedes the leader's ability to genuinely understand. The significant facade of the suicidal person—call it impairment in reality (Friedman, 1989, p. 387), a narcissistic investment (Maltsberger, 1986), or other—emits a stressful force that influences others, including the group leader. This presented facade elicits a significant physiological, cognitive, and emotional response by the group leader. This response may be manifested in one or a combination of many ways, some of which may include fear, anxiety, anger, confusion, disgust, frustration, and/or denial. Behavioral responses are also common, including social distancing or withdrawal; avoidance; excessive personal involvement or rescuing; overreaction or hysterics; underreaction from disbelief, denial, or ignorance; and physical pain or immobility.

This influential power projected onto the group leader may be understood as related to the suicidal person's drive to escape suffering and alleviate pain (Shneidman, 1993). The remedial solution to the group leader's personal distress is to learn to transcend this facade of the suicidal other by seeking genuine understanding. A dynamic appreciation of the unique value and meaning of each human being (Fournier, 1999) means standing under this presented facade, looking to all its facets, all its angles, to the best of your ability. As to suicidal ideation, it is necessary to ask always for clarification, for it is not our life but that of the other that may be at risk. "What are the thoughts you are having about suicide? What orients you toward death or contributes to your thinking about suicide? What keeps you alive or gives you reason to live? What do you believe in or value in life?" More than a few persons have described to me their pretending to not be at risk for harm so they will be discharged from hospitalization, thereafter to be as suicidal as before, if not more so. The group leader's ability to understand this pretending and to view the reality that lies beneath it may be the difference between life and death.

Appreciating the Multidimensionality of Suicide

A significant mistake for understanding suicide, an error common among persons in the media, is to assume the existence of one reason or one cause for a suicide. Perhaps this erroneous assumption relates to the natural human need to know what is in our life, so we can identify threats, maintain control and equilibrium, and continue to survive. Unfortunately, this myopic view may be expected to impair assessment of risk for suicide and, therefore, detract from successful treatment. A multidimensional perspective for understanding suicide is paramount, including appreciation of biological, psychological, social, and spiritual dimensions that constitute the malaise of suicidality (Shneidman, 1993, p. 137). Seeing the whole picture is essential. This includes understanding not only the precipitating factors that led to the act, but also the physical, psychological, social, and spiritual factors that were recently or remotely, directly or indirectly, contributory.

Developing a Life-Affirming Perspective

To be effective, the group leader must integrate himself or herself with the phenomenon of suicide in practice. The leader's own personal, lived-out perspective in life is intimately aligned with her or his understanding of suicide. As with other potent human phenomena, the phenomenon of suicide challenges the group leader to integrate personal beliefs with practice, while maintaining an openness to the uniquely lived-out life of each group participant. The leader's strength and courage provides stability and strength for purposeful and effective action, overcoming personal fear and inviting group participants to feel safe and confident. In practice, flexibility of method is needed to free us to do what we can to understand not only the hurt but also the "problem that is trying to be solved" by the individual (Shneidman, 1993, p. 151). Beyond group practice, it is argued, the group leader must uphold an attitude and belief that life is meaningful and purposeful, that is, as actually and/or potentially valuable and worthy of being lived to its natural end (Fournier, 1999), this being no more important than when the individual is threatened with imminent nonbeing (Frankel, 2002, p. 224).

Being Willing and Dedicated in Suicide Work

As with any vocation or passionate endeavor, group work with suicide requires a personal commitment of love and work (Menninger, 1966, p. 390). Perhaps it is this commitment that is the most significant factor for creating successful group work with suicide. And, even with this commitment, work with suicide is never easy. Benefits to the group leader for this work are mostly intangible, including the personal satisfaction that he or she has contributed to improving and/or saving the life of another human being. Much is required. Time and energy are expended by the group leader, willingly and as needed. The group leader must accept risk as a fact of life, the risk that suicide may occur and that suicidal behavior and bereavement will occur, with all its physical, psychological, social, and spiritual consequences. Legal, ethical, and moral tensions and the potentiality for problems related thereto are to be anticipated. Courage is needed to ask about suicide in all its facets, to learn to discuss the discomfort of this phenomenon comfortably. Knowledge and experience is required to formulate and develop effective methods for intersubjective understanding, intervention, prevention, and bereavement work. Witnessing and/or sharing in the life of another who learns to live well and love life after suicidality may be the greatest benefit to the group leader, a road less traveled, yet one filled with many little miracles (Peck, 1978). As in any profession, it takes a dedicated, special person to do the job well.

PLANNING AND DEVELOPMENT

How we prepare and organize a group will determine its process and development and even help us predict outcome. Available literature about suicide and group therapy provides us with some information for effective group treatment. Some helpful suggestions for preparation for effective group work with suicide follow.

Create a Treatment-Constructive Group Atmosphere

A constructive atmosphere is one in which the group experiences power through self-mastery and action. Powerlessness expresses helplessness and victimization, leading to violence, including despair and suicide (May, 1972). A constructive group experiences real meaning and purpose in life, validating one another's interests, ideas, needs, beliefs, dreams, and goals. As previously mentioned, learning to view suicide as inclusive of the world versus alienated from it as a challenging problem to be faced versus as an illness to be suffered facilitates understanding and well-being. The constructive group is a real family, fostering growth in the self and in relationships to the world. Avoid a treatment-destructive atmosphere that "shrouds the group in feelings of heaviness and hopelessness" (Dub, 1997, p. 333). The destructive group atmosphere produces powerlessness and acts without attention to the real-life issues, creating a facade that may allow or foster suicide among its participants. Such may be the underpinnings of contagiousness of suicidal behavior that may foster the total destruction of a group's integrity.

Process Suicide in a Continuous Fashion

It is important for the group leader and group participants to realize that understanding reasons to live and commitment to life instruct us about vulnerability to despair and suicide. Avoid an intervention-only group experience with perpetual suicidal crises. This is burdensome and potentially oppressive and/or damaging to the group. The one exception to this guideline is the group that has as its exclusive purpose confronting those in suicidal crises, a specialized work that requires specialized knowledge and experience, such as advanced level group work with suicide.

In a group, the relationship of the participants to suicide may take many forms, including actor, witness, bereaved loved one, and/or serious or casual thinker about life and death. Prevention of suicidal crises is facilitated by understanding the participants' life perspectives and their problem solving for stressful life situations or events. Many important issues for group discussion relate to affirmation of life and vulnerability to suicide, including self-mastery and victimization, responsibility and lack of responsibility, hope and hopelessness, success and failure, love and hate, intimacy and isolation, and acceptance and blame.

This expansive group work prevents death by suicide from becoming *the* option. Talking about thoughts and ideas about living openly provides an opportunity to explore not only personal beliefs and opinions but also relationships with others and the environment (Buelow, 1994, p. 167). For those experiencing the loss of a loved one by suicide, this group processing will also "provide time and approval for grieving" (Buelow, p. 163). In addition, ongoing group action helps to lessen or eliminate risk of future contagion of suicidality if a suicide occurs among participants.

Know Your Tolerance

Knowing limits and maintaining boundaries are part and parcel of the professional work of any clinician. The group leader's confrontation with suicide and the risk or the possibility of suicide is burdensome. To reduce risk for burnout or personal loss of well-being, the group leader needs to be willing to dispel the delusional notions of "curing" another or "mastering death" (Jacobs, 1989, p. 331). As a group leader, one does what one can do, no more. Among other things, the effective group leader learns when to say no, including times when he or she can do no more, must seek consultation, must take a break, or must stop completely. The following suggestions may help leaders achieve and maintain well-being for effective group work with suicide (Dlugos & Friedlander, 2001):

1. Create and uphold boundaries between personal and professional life.
2. Use leisure activities to provide personal relief from group work.
3. Reframe problems in group: Turn obstacles into challenges.
4. Use diverse activities in group work to provide freshness and energy.
5. Continually seek feedback from group participants, peers, superiors, consultants, and others.
6. Accept and use responsibility wisely and assertively.
7. Develop and experience a strong sense of spirituality.

8. Develop high levels of personal accomplishment.

9. Develop a loving regard and openness to everyday life experiences.

Plan and Organize Wisely

Consider selection, purpose, and process in planning a group. Selection and screening of group participants are important. It is the obligation of the group leader to meet individuals who are interested in group participation to discuss the planned program, their personal needs, and the expected benefit and cost of treatment. Determining suitability for the group depends on many factors, many beyond space for discussion herein. A good pregroup evaluation is very important to help the leader to know who will be in the group, including the presenting problems; the personality types; reasons for attendance; personal expectations; factors of vulnerability to suicide and suicide history; situational life stressors, present and past; history of trauma or hurt; interpersonal and social history; and degree of commitment to life. Persons at serious risk for harm should be excluded from starting in a group until stabilized, unless the nature of the group is focused on this acutely distressed population, such as with a crisis intervention or inpatient psychiatric group. In determining acceptance for group participation, it is also helpful for leaders to consider factors associated with group dropout, such as situational crises; fear of social interaction; fear of self-disclosure; planned change of residence or geographical relocation; previous problematic experiences in group therapy; perception and understanding of the group experience; and inadequate orientation, interest, or motivation to the group (Yalom, 1970, p. 161).

Duration (short term or long term) is also an important consideration for group work with suicide. Short-term groups traditionally comprise 20 or fewer meetings, with the time for each meeting variable, often between one and three hours. Brief treatment with crisis situations or specific problem-solving issues is the usual focus in the short-term group. This group is often composed of persons in significant crisis or at significant risk of suicide, including those seriously thinking about it or having recently attempted it. The focus of intervention with this short-term group is "the reversal of this trend (away from a healthy life) and the reestablishment of feelings of belonging" in life (Farberow, 1968, p. 328).

Short-term groups prove an "immediate source of nutriment, support, and renewed relationships" (Farberow, p. 331). This gift giving makes it difficult for suicidal persons to deny the seriousness of their disturbed state, and facilitates the formative work of developing a commitment to life (Farberow, p. 331). The group leader's role is to be active and directive, confronting varied concerns, including acting-out behavior; the constant demand for nurturance; imminent risk for suicide; anger, guilt, and self-blame; risk for contagion of suicidality to other group participants; and the seemingly ever-present tension between wanting to live and wanting to leave life or die.

Long-term groups offer a different focus and challenge. Whereas short-term groups must focus on very specific problems and seek solutions within a short time framework, longer running groups have greater latitude, including a greater potential for in-depth exploration and understanding. The long-term group may discuss varied issues, including dependence and the need for self-mastery, personality formation, philosophy of life, meaningful investment in life, and intimacy with others. Significant suicidal preoccupations are repeatedly explored and understood, with intervention focusing on "altering self-destructive tendencies" (Comstock & McDermott, 1975). The group leader's role is as a guide or facilitator rather than as an actor, helping participants understand through group interaction the underlying dynamics related to suicide and stress in life, clarifying needs and motivations, and facilitating healthy change (Farberow, 1968, p. 334).

Another noteworthy factor for group work with suicide is the use of a cotherapist or coleader. This is strongly suggested, although not always feasible, especially in today's managed-care world. Group work is emotionally draining to the therapist and often involves acting-out and identification behavior by the participants that may be more easily diluted with the help of another leader (Comstock & McDermott, 1975; Farberow, 1968). If a cotherapist is not possible, group leader expertise and well-being are best reviewed frequently, with the use of introspection, supervision, consultation, and peer or other supportive methods.

Setting is another significant factor for group work with suicide—institution inpatient or community outpatient location. In the institutional setting, there is a need to counteract the powerlessness of persons in this setting and plan, as may be appropriate, for effective follow-up outside the institution. The institutional setting is usually one in which a person is removed or displaced from a normative routine and physical setting or home. The institutional setting usually presents an odd and awkward world for the group participant, one that must be recognized as such by the group leader. It is a physical place where few, if any, would choose to be. For example, in a psychiatric institution, doors are often locked to prevent unauthorized exit and entrance. Persons become patients and medicated or otherwise sedated for stabilization, some becoming out of control, unable to manage their mood, thinking, behavior, or even body functioning—a scary experience for patient, staff, and visitor.

The institutional setting creates a strict regulation of scheduling and programs to meet its needs, including stability and order, with compensation for anticipated loss of control; compliance with the demands and dictates of insurers and program directors; optimal allocation of time and space for identifying and treating patients' presenting problems; and discharge planning for helping patients return to a normative and acceptable, not-at-risk-for-harm behavior and lifestyle.

Risk for harm to self or others is often not only a primary reason for institutional admission but also an ongoing concern. The role of significant others may also be expected to affect group work in the institutional as well as in a community setting, contributing or not to understanding and social support. Whether myth, wishful thinking, oversimplification of the obvious, or some other reason, loved ones and friends frequently perceive the person in the institutional setting as safe, protected from harm, and either "all right" or better. In a similar fashion, loved ones and friends may consider a person leaving the institution to be not only safe but also healthy, having been cured from all of his or her ills. Risk for suicide does not terminate as a result of hospitalization and, in some cases, risk may be greater after discharge than before admission.

In the community setting, the person usually lives at home and commutes to the group, remaining within a normal life routine. In the community setting, the challenge for the group leader is to become aware of the participant's life situation, including life stressors, social support, everyday routine, and work and recreational habits. The protection and structure of the institution is absent, and the group leader must ensure that the group participants are fundamentally safe and secure in their environmental world. Issues of housing, finances, relational support, work, and recreation are important for the development of well-being. It is in this context that the group leader may most intimately take on the operational role of a social worker. To some extent, the group leader also may serve as a pseudo-parent as he or she explores group participants' life situations and circumstances, helping all to help themselves or be helped by others.

Incorporate an Understanding of Suicide Bereavement

The valuable, albeit painful, experience of those who have lost loved ones by suicide is sometimes paid the least attention by group leaders. For those so bereaved, their own group experience is often fruitful and empowering. Those who lead these suicide bereavement groups become intimately aware of the importance of life and the role of suicidal potential and behavior for thwarting well-being and generating hurt and suffering. Often, these survivor groups facilitate a greater intimacy with life among participants, thereby preventing suicide and even creating a survivor mission to help others adapt successfully after the loss. Why not learn from the experience of these bereaved to help those at risk for suicide? It is argued that the group leader working with suicide will benefit significantly in facilitating suicide prevention by understanding this bereavement and teaching the group participants about it. Understanding the suffering that we may impose on others and empathizing with their painful journey of healing may help us to avoid similar victimization, move away from our self-centered facade, and become sensitive and more aware of situations and circumstances that may produce this hurt, learning how to pause or think twice before acting, or to humble ourselves to seek help from others rather than act on impulse.

AN EDUCATIONAL MODEL FOR GROUP PRACTICE

Introducing suicide to a group is a daunting and anxiety-provoking task. Even if not dedicated to suicide work, it is argued that all group leaders have a responsibility to teach about and discuss suicide with group participants. Understanding prevention, crisis intervention, and postvention (i.e., suicide bereavement) for the promotion of well-being is relevant to this educational work. Somewhat akin to introducing the issue of adoption to adoptees, the challenge of addressing the prevention of suicide in the group involves learning when and how to and returning to the discussion again and again over time. Initially, dedicating one or a series of group meetings as a workshop to focus specifically on suicide may be helpful. Thereafter, ongoing dialogue about relatedness to suicide and commitment to life may be initiated and facilitated by the group leader, as may befit group participants' life experience and life reflection. Once the group knows that suicide is a speakable topic, comfortable to the group leader(s), and open for discussion, taboo and ignorance may be transcended, enabling spontaneous and intimate self-disclosure about living and dying. As very young children, we learn in our family that, if it's okay to ask, we ask; if we're not allowed to ask, we don't ask.

What follows are some valuable elements for inclusion in suicide education in group. These elements, based on the aforementioned discussion, may be perceived as significant ingredients for introductory and continuous group discussion. All are intended as a helpful guide for group leaders in the development of their own creative application for education and processing of the phenomenon of suicide.

Developing a Base for Understanding Life

The group leader's presentation and utilization of a basic approach for understanding suicide is a valuable first step for suicide education. Such an approach may be expected to provide a common ground on which the group participants may explore their own understanding and learn how to promote well-being. No matter what approach is used by the group leader as base for group work, it must be general enough to permit appreciation of each participant's unique subjective view of life and specific enough to help guide all participants in a practical, life-fostering fashion toward well-being.

One suggested approach includes use of a stress and coping model for explaining life and suicide. A theoretical model that emphasizes healthy adaptation in life may help group participants learn about the connection of suicide to life, rather than its historical view of being alienated from it. Discussing the natural role of stress in life and the resources and strategies for coping when stress becomes intolerable may help group participants relate personally to the extraordinary stress of despair, enabling practical problem solving.[2]

Suicide statistics lend support for this perspective, teaching us that most persons do not want to die through suicide, but rather wish to escape from a stressful pain and suffering that seems intolerable and unmanageable. Suicide may be understood as a powerful attempt to express the powerlessness of a stressful life situation, a desperate attempt to seek meaning, purpose, and belonging in life.

Defining Suicide

Presenting a clear and practical definition of suicide is an important second step in suicide education. Completion of this educational step may help group participants avoid unnecessary confusion about meaning and facilitate a healthy focus for problem solving. One of the dangers facing health care professionals in suicide work comes from too narrowly defining suicide, viewing it as synonymous with imminent or right-at-this-moment risk. The group leader may reframe the definition of suicide as more inclusive of a developing, maladaptive behavior toward premature death, a movement toward suicide, rather than merely a last-ditch moment of despair. Such a broadened definition may enable group participants to consider their own behavior in life, their own relatedness to suicide, in a more acceptable and less threatening manner, including their identification of factors that are preventive of suicide and those that may create vulnerability.

Society has a controversial and apparently contradictory view of suicide—for or against, rational or irrational. How to deal with this dilemma in the group? Some professionals do argue that suicide may be a meaningful experience in life (Werth, 1996). Throughout human history, suicide has presented a personal, social, and moral dilemma to all. My belief is that working with suicide in group would not be life-fostering

---

[2] Stress is often misunderstood and distorted in meaning in today's world. The media often portray stress as undesirable and bad, *always* something to be eradicated or destroyed—an impossible task and an erroneous assumption. For a deeper understanding of this proposed model for suicide work in groups, see the literature on stress. Helpful references may be found in my doctoral work (Fournier, 1997). Shneidman (1993) speaks often of perturbation as the disturbing stress that influences a person to become suicidal.

for participants without a basic focus on suicide prevention and a basic view of suicide as maladaptive. Although the understanding and expression of each group participant's subjective perspective of suicide is important and must be facilitated, the group leader must manifest a life-fostering perspective.

If the group leader identifies and reinforces suicide as a healthy choice for an individual in life, this decision confounds group understanding and detracts from prevention work. This may be expected to disturb the group leader's ability and confidence in the group, especially concerning suicide prevention. Additional, potentially unsolvable and suicide-fostering arguments may become manifested in a group that is taught that suicide is acceptable. If it is healthy for him or her, then why not for all of us? If the group leader believes suicide is good, and we view the group leader as an ideal reference for life, then suicide must be good. It also may be argued that, practically speaking, insufficient research and knowledge exist today to help any group leader advocating suicide to define or treat suicide in the group in a manner that would help others to prevent premature or unnecessary death by suicide. The group leader who accepts this rational suicide perspective at this time is skating on very thin ice, with risk for disaster, with consequences multiplied in the group setting.

Teaching Fact from Fiction

Presenting facts about suicide to the group and dispelling myths and mistaken beliefs are essential for suicide prevention and promotion of well-being. This educational component may serve as a welcomed and refreshing step in suicide education, clearing the air of taboo, bringing participants up to snuff with the latest research findings and statistics, and raising curiosity and wonder about this phenomenon and its relatedness to themselves.

Myths about suicide continue to impair suicide prevention work, such as:

- Those who talk about suicide don't do it.
- Those who attempt suicide and fail are unlikely to try it again.
- Talking about suicide will increase the risk that a person will commit the act.

- If someone has decided to commit suicide, there's nothing that can be done about it.
- Suicide is inherited.

Presenting factual information to the group invites the group participants to confront their own beliefs about suicide and, as needed, modify their understanding to align with fact and a healthy life perspective.

Teaching Crisis Intervention

Teaching what constitutes risk for suicidal behavior and what to do about it are essential for the suicide education of group participants. Perhaps this area of consideration is most obvious to many, presented often as knowing the warning signs for suicide. Crisis intervention, however, must involve not only knowledge but also appropriate action. Although you may assume this is merely common sense, many bereaved loved ones have learned of these warning signs only in retrospect, after a loved one has committed suicide.

The literature about suicide abounds with information about crisis intervention, and the group leader is urged to learn more about this for effective group education. In short, the group leader's teaching of what to observe and how to respond may enable participants to achieve a heightened awareness of suicide, a reduced helplessness and greater confidence in ability to help, and a greater attunement to the stress and demands of everyday life.

Education about crisis intervention also may serve, to a great degree, as a means to deter or prevent future vulnerability or suicidal behavior among group participants. The greater the group awareness and empowerment for addressing suicide, the more participants may become dynamic experts, facilitating earlier and more productive discourse about suicide-related thoughts and ideas as they become manifested in the group. Such group processing about suicide may be expected to help the participants eliminate risk for suicide before it becomes actualized in behavior.

Understanding Suicide Bereavement

As was argued previously, introducing suicide bereavement to the group is invaluable for preventing suicide. Educating participants about the degree to which suicidal behavior has a profound, detrimental impact on others may help participants confront their own personal investment in life and invite those who may be at risk for suicide to come out of their own narcissistic "bell jar" (Plath, 1971) and become more realistic in their appraisal of themselves, others, and life.

Those who are suicidal are often unable to realistically view the suffering that their action will cause in the lives of loved ones, constricted in a world of pain and deluded or myopic in perspective of life, overflowing with negativity, self-blame, helplessness, hopelessness. With their pain overwhelming them, they often assume its removal via suicide will relieve others and improve their life. Although they may be accurate that any burden of care that they have imposed will be removed, they fail to see the value and importance of their presence in life and the pain of its absence. Life may be better off for survivors, but not because the loved one is gone. To the contrary, life becomes better off for survivors because they choose the same commitment that is available to the suicidal loved one, that is, to choose life and recommitment to it in a manner that permits growth and development of well-being. An important issue for discussion in suicide education within the group is that risk for suicide itself may be significant for many following the suicide of a loved one. In a dissertation study of 509 persons who lost a loved one by suicide, results indicated that 131 or 26% of the survivors sampled had since the suicide death seriously contemplated suicide, and 73 or 15% of the survivors, at some time in their life, had attempted suicide (Fournier, 1997).

CONCLUDING REMARKS

Group psychotherapy may be an awesome and unique experience for suicide prevention and promotion of well-being. Group therapy is not the only method for treatment of suicidality, nor should it be viewed as such. Much of what pertains to group work with suicide is relevant also to other treatment modalities, such as individual and family psychotherapy. Groups, however, present a unique environment for understanding and dialoguing about suicide and life. In groups, there are many reactions to any one issue, providing a rich tapestry of personal perspectives for formulating and developing a healthy commitment in life, including prevention of suicide (Yalom, 2002b, p. 50). Regardless of its nature or objective, all groups can and should address suicide, presenting this phenomenon as a part of human life and human vulnerability. Such a dynamic action in groups, it is argued, is essential for facilitating well-being and preventing suicide. To not address this potent phenomenon is a risk considered too great, one that offers few, if any, second chances.

REFERENCES

Buelow, G. (1994). A suicide in group: A case of functional realignment. *International Journal of Group Psychotherapy, 44,* 153–168.

Campbell, R. J. (1989). *Psychiatric dictionary* (6th ed.). New York: Oxford University Press.

Carroll, M., Bates, M., & Johnson, C. (1997). *Group leadership: Strategies for group counseling leaders.* Denver, CO: Love.

Comstock, B. S., & McDermott, M. (1975). Group therapy for patients who attempted suicide. *International Journal of Group Psychotherapy, 25,* 44–49.

Dlugos, R. F., & Friedlander, M. L. (2001). Passionately committed psychotherapists: A qualitative study of their experiences. *Professional Psychology: Research and Practice, 32,* 298–304.

Dub, F. S. (1997). The pivotal group member: A study of treatment-destructive resistance in group therapy. *International Journal of Group Psychotherapy, 47,* 333–353.

Farberow, N. (1968). Group psychotherapy with suicidal persons. In H. L. P. Resnick (Ed.), *Suicidal behaviors: Diagnosis and management* (pp. 328–340). Boston: Little, Brown.

Fournier, R. R. (1987). Suicidal movement: An addiction to death or an invitation to spiritual formation. *Studies in Formative Spirituality, 8,* 175–185.

Fournier, R. R. (1990). Social work, spirituality, and suicide: An odd mix or a natural blend. *Social Thought, 16*(3), 27–35.

Fournier, R. R. (1997). *The role of spiritual well-being as a resource for coping with stress in bereavement among suicide survivors.* Ann Arbor, MI: Dissertation Services.

Fournier, R. R. (1999). Spirituality as a resource for suicide prevention: A response to a fellow suicidologist. *American Journal of Pastoral Counseling, 2*(1), 49–74.

Fournier, R. R. (2002). A trauma education workshop on posttraumatic stress. *Health and Social Work, 27,* 113–124.

Frankel, B. (2002). Existential issues in group psychotherapy. *International Journal of Group Psychotherapy, 52,* 215–231.

Frankl, V. E. (1963). *Man's search for meaning.* New York: Pocket Books.

Friedman, R. S. (1989). Hospital treatment of the suicidal patient. In D. Jacobs & H. N. Brown (Eds.), *Suicide: Understanding and responding* (pp. 379–402). Madison, CT: International Universities Press.

Jacobs, D. (1989). Psychotherapy with suicidal patients: The empathic method. In D. Jacobs & H. N. Brown (Eds.), *Suicide: Understanding and responding* (pp. 329–343). Madison, CT: International Universities Press.

Maltsberger, J. T. (1986). *Suicide risk: The formulation of clinical judgment.* New York: New York University Press.

May, R. (1972). *Power and innocence.* New York: Norton.

Menninger, K. (1966). *Man against himself.* New York: Harcourt, Brace & World.

Peck, M. S. (1978). *The road less traveled.* New York: Simon & Schuster.

Plath, S. (1971). *The bell jar.* New York: Harper & Row.

Richman, J., & Eyman, J. R. (1990). Psychotherapy of suicide: Individual, group, and family approaches. In D. Lester (Ed.), *Current concepts of suicide* (pp. 139–158). Philadelphia: Charles Press.

Shneidman, E. S. (1993). *Suicide as psychache.* Northvale, NJ: Aronson.

Van der Kolk, B. A. (1987). *Psychological trauma.* Washington, DC: American Psychiatric Press.

Van Kaam, A. (1966). *The art of existential counseling.* Wilkes-Barre, PA: Dimension Books.

Werth, J. L. (1996). *Rational suicide?* Washington, DC: Taylor & Francis.

Yalom, J. D. (1985). *Theory and practice of group psychotherapy.* New York: Basic Books.

Yalom, J. D. (1995). *Theory and practice of group psychotherapy* (4th ed.). New York: Basic Books.

Yalom, J. D. (2002a). *The gift of therapy: An open letter to a new generation of therapists and their patients.* New York: HarperCollins.

Yalom, J. D. (2002b). Religion and psychiatry. *American Journal of Psychotherapy, 56,* 301–316.

PART THREE

Special Issues

CHAPTER 15

Easing the Legacy of Suicide

David Lester

Since death is inevitable, we should perhaps reevaluate our designation of death from suicide as an undesirable act (Lester, 2003). Faced with the alternatives of, for example, a person dying in pain as his or her body slowly shuts down in the end stages of a terminal cancer versus a dignified self-chosen death from suicide several months earlier, it is clear that suicide may not always be irrational, immoral, or a "bad" choice. It may, indeed, on occasions, be a good death, a euthanasia.

In the past, only an occasional existentialist would argue that a suicidal act was appropriate. For example, Binswanger (1958), in his analysis of the suicide of Ellen West, argued that her existence had become "ripe" for its death and that her suicide was one of the rare authentic acts of her existence. (It is possible to criticize Binswanger for his analysis of the case; see Lester, 1971; Rogers, 1961.)

The cathartic effect of a nonfatal attempt at suicide has been noted (Farberow, 1950), and suicidal behavior can be seen as a useful and helpful approach to crises. For example, Farber (1962) has described a certain kind of person for whom the idea of suicide is a solution to any difficulty that might occur in life. Such people respond to a crisis by saying to themselves that, if things get worse, they will kill themselves. Although Farber condemned such an attitude, it may be a useful mechanism for dealing with depression and apathy. When depression descends on these people, rather than becoming morose and apathetic, they are able to say to themselves: "If things get worse, I'll kill myself." They can then proceed to cope with the crisis. The suicidal ideation provides them with a possible escape in the future, which thereby energizes them for the present.

Suicidal behavior (ideation, threats, and attempts) may also be effica-cious in changing the environment of the individual in a favorable way. However, I have gone further by viewing even completed suicide in a pos-itive light (Lester, 2003).

COUNSELOR-ASSISTED SUICIDE

Having a loved one commit suicide is extremely traumatic. Research evidence indicates that survivors of suicide attempts experience greater guilt, receive less social support, and feel more of a need to understand why the death occurred (Calhoun, Selby, & Selby, 1982). The emotions experienced include relief, anger, and depression; the cognitive reac-tions include shock, disbelief, and denial; the behavioral reactions in-clude smoking, drinking, and sleep disturbances; interpersonal reactions include changes in the interpersonal contacts and the type of communica-tion; and the physical reactions include illness and mortality. For exam-ple, Brent et al. (1992) found evidence for significant psychopathology, especially depression and posttraumatic stress disorder symptoms, six months after the suicide of a friend or acquaintance.

A suicidal death is traumatic for the survivors, partly because often it is unexpected and sudden. Although the suicidal person may have given cues to the impending suicide (Robins, Gasner, Kayes, Wilkinson, & Murphy, 1959), some suicides do not give cues, while in other cases the significant others do not decode these cues accurately. The suddenness of the death leaves the survivors with unfinished business—issues and con-flicts that are unresolved and expressions of affection that went unsaid.

Furthermore, in many cases, survivors are traumatized by being the ones who discover the body (McDowell, Rothberg, & Koshes, 1994). In a few cases, the suicide may take place in the presence of significant others. In some cases, there is great hostility on the part of the suicide, and the act of suicide serves to satisfy both a wish to die and a desire to punish the significant other by forcing him or her to witness the trauma of the death, creating an extremely unpleasant memory for the survivor. The following is a typical case:

> A 28-year-old female, who had been sexually abused as a child and who suf-fered from chronic low self-esteem, was having marital and financial prob-lems (she quit paying the household bills and did not tell her husband). She

called her husband at work one day and asked him to come home for lunch, telling him that she had a surprise for him. As he entered the house, she walked up to him and shot herself in the head with a .38 pistol. (McDowell et al., 1994, p. 218)

In other cases, the witness to the suicide may be a friend or acquaintance who is uninvolved in the dynamics of the suicide:

A 22-year-old male with a history of alcohol abuse and marital problems was depressed over a recent breakup with his girlfriend. . . . As he was riding with a friend in the other individual's car, they were discussing his problems. He asked his friend to give him his gun. When the friend handed a .32 pistol to him, he calmly put it to his head and shot himself. (McDowell et al., 1994, p. 219)

Even if the suicide is not witnessed, the body of the suicide is often discovered by significant others, who thereby are left with a very unpleasant visual memory of their loved one (Lester, 1994).

Survivors of suicides can often benefit from counseling. There is an active group of survivors in the American Association of Suicidology, and groups of survivors across America meet for support and counseling. In addition, many families go into counseling after a significant other commits suicide, and those who do not sometimes regret not doing so. Susan White-Bowden (1985) divorced her husband, but her husband refused to accept the finality of the divorce. In November 1974, he came to her house, tried to persuade Susan to continue their marriage and, when she refused, went upstairs in her house and shot himself. Susan had three children, two daughters and a son, Jody, age 14. Susan did not share her feelings with the children after this trauma, nor did she consider counseling for the family. She tried to act as if everything was fine—she labeled herself as "Susie Sunshine." By the age of 17, Jody had shown some behavior problems (vandalism at school and driving while high on marijuana), and, after his girlfriend broke up with him and refused to get back together, Jody went home and shot himself. In retrospect, Susan realized that she should have taken the family for counseling after the suicide of her husband.

Some suicidal people kill themselves after a long period of consideration, accompanied by a cumulative succession of losses, chronic depression, alcohol abuse, or medical illness. Their significant others may be aware of this process but often are at a loss for how to cope. It is not easy living with a person with chronic problems, and the significant others would benefit from support and counseling for themselves.

More and more in recent years, some of these suicidal people are seeking assisted suicide. In most instances, since physicians can provide the preferred means for suicide, namely, painless medications, these people consider physician-assisted suicide. Yet the decisions made by these individuals are often opposed by loved ones, and the problems of obtaining the medications and taking them in a way that ensures that there will be no legal consequences for the survivors make the process unpleasant. The suicide may be left alone, the survivors anxious, and the decision inadequately discussed by those involved.

For example, when Betty Rollin (1985) helped her mother, who was suffering from painful cancer and who refused further painful treatments, to commit suicide, Betty could find no assistance from physicians in America. A friend gave her the name of a physician in the Netherlands who told her and her husband how to arrange her mother's death. They obtained Nembutal, officially for insomnia, and her mother took it while Betty and her husband sat with her. However, Betty and her husband then left so they would not be there when her mother died to avoid being accused of causing her mother's death. Her mother was found dead the next day by the daytime maid.

In this context, I suggested those contemplating physician-assisted suicide could benefit from counseling (Lester, 1995). In the following section, I briefly review the proposals I made in that article.

COUNSELING THE ASSISTED SUICIDE

A good counselor should not have biases in favor of or opposed to certain options (Lester, 1995). A marriage counselor should not want to save every problem marriage or to break up every problem marriage. A good counselor first helps the couple decide what they want and then helps the couple to achieve their goal, whether it be marriage or divorce.

The same then is true for suicide. A counselor must first help the client decide what the client wants. If the client decides to opt for continued living, the counselor must help the client improve his or her life. If the client, however, opts for death, the counselor must help the client achieve this in the best possible way, including suicide if this is the choice of the client.

Much of the writing and debate on assisted suicide focuses on the morality, legality, and rationality of the act. Discussions of moral issues are fine for academics, but assisted suicide can be judged to be moral or immoral depending on the criteria applied, and I have rarely seen anyone change his or her opinion about the morality of assisted suicide as a result of intellectual debate. The illegality of assisted suicide, opinions about which are undergoing a change as various courts pass their opinions on this issue, has not deterred physicians in the past from assisting suicide (Quill, 1993) and, should physician-assisted suicide be legalized under some circumstances, it will probably increase in frequency.

I have discussed the rationality of suicide at length, examining a variety of criteria for judging suicide to be rational or irrational (Lester, 1993), but perhaps two of my observations will suffice here. First, our behavior is often irrational by certain criteria, yet such irrationality is not used to argue against our making other choices. For example, it would be easy to discover irrationality in the decisions that most of us have made when deciding to marry. I failed to see why we expect decisions over dying and death to be any more rational than the earlier decisions we have made in our lives. Second, counselors all too easily judged their clients' thinking to be irrational without any proof that it is. In criminal trials, a person is presumed innocent until proven guilty; in cognitive therapy, on the other hand, a person is presumed irrational until proven rational. I have known people who said that they would *never* find a partner or that they would *always* be unhappy, who indeed were correct, despite the fact that a cognitive therapist would have judged them to be thinking irrationally at the time (Ellis, 1973).

I outlined the steps that a counselor might follow in counseling a suicidal person (Lester, 1993). The first is to actively listen (Gordon, 1970), as advocated by person-centered therapists. The client must be encouraged to explore his or her desires, thoughts, and emotions, so that the client and the counselor are fully aware of the client's current psychological situation. Second, the counselor should explore the suicidogenic factors in the client's life—what stressors (e.g., physical illness, financial problems), psychiatric problems (e.g., depression), and interpersonal problems (e.g., living alone or in conflict) exist—and to what extent these can be ameliorated if the client is willing to try.

The third step is to discuss options. The presence of a severe illness does not argue for or against suicide. Treatment is possible as well as refusing treatment or suicide. For example, Abbie Hoffman tried lithium for his bipolar depressive disorder but disliked the side effects and discontinued it. He tried Prozac and Valium instead, but eventually committed suicide (Jezer, 1992). Had Hoffman been able to discuss these decisions with a counselor, he might have been better informed and made the same or different choices, but counseling might have helped him make these choices.

Decisions can be changed (Lester, 1993). A decision to undergo treatment can be reversed; a decision to commit suicide can, up to a certain point, be revised. Direct-decision therapy (Greenwald, 1973) provided a good framework for this type of counseling, because direct-decision therapy does not take a moral stance with respect to client behavior. Rather, it assists clients in examining their decisions, evaluating the positive and negative sides of each decision, and making an informed decision. The therapist's role is to help clients accomplish their goal once they have made a particular decision.

This approach raises the question of the extent to which a counselor can and should take a morally neutral stance. Perhaps a counselor can take a morally neutral stance over abortion, divorce, or suicide, issues for which there are widely differing opinions held by substantial segments of the population. But what about sexual behavior with children or terrorist activity? Societies have laws, and breaking the laws has consequences for those who break them. Child molesters and terrorists are punished, typically with long prison sentences, and clients who engage in such behaviors should be made aware of the consequences. Counselors may be required by laws to report such individuals to the criminal justice authorities, unless they are protected by laws governing confidentiality, and, again, clients should be made aware of these procedures.

To illustrate these dilemmas, Greenwald (1973) presented the case of a pedophile he treated. The client was motivated to modify his behavior so that he did not contravene the law. With Greenwald's help, he decided to become involved only with women over the age of 18, but to seek

Easing the Legacy of Suicide   343

those who had bodies that were relatively immature in appearance (that is, resembled the bodies of young adolescents). He also decided to ask his partners to modify their bodies to further resemble adolescents (for example, by shaving off their pubic hair). However, he decided to *not* seek psychotherapy to change his sexual interests.

Thus, for behaviors that are illegal, counselors have a duty to point out to clients the consequences for those who violate the laws. A moral stance on the part of the counselor is not necessary in such situations. For situations counter to the counselor's own moral position and with which he or she feels uncomfortable, referral of the client to another counselor would seem to be appropriate.

THE ROLE OF SIGNIFICANT OTHERS

In this process, there is obviously a role for the significant others. They have desires, thoughts, and emotions, too, which could be explored with the assistance of a counselor. The communication patterns between the suicidal person and the significant others may have also been less than complete and honest. Each party may have been affected by anger, anxiety, and depression in their attempts to talk to one another. Each member of the network would benefit both from individual sessions with the counselor and from family therapy. Thus, when the decisions are made, all members of the family can feel that they were heard, they played an important role in the discussion, and the decision was appropriate. The surviving members of the family will still experience grief and perhaps other emotions after the suicide but less intensely since some of these feelings will have been worked through before the death.

The suicidal death will not be a surprise to the survivors; it will be arranged so that handling the deceased will not be traumatic for them, and the process itself can be transformed from a traumatic and shocking event into a uniting and healing ceremony.

A good example of this process comes from the Netherlands, reported by Diekstra (1995). Mr. L had cancer and no more than six months to live. He was a retired civil servant, an authoritative and stubborn man, with a defeatist attitude toward life. His wife was informed of his prognosis first and communicated this to her husband, after which he declared that he wished to end his life with medications. He felt that his life was useless, and he feared dependence on physicians, burdening his wife with nursing, and the degeneration of his body.

One of his sons was a physician but refused to get involved with his father's decision. Mr. L's general practitioner refused to provide medications but said that he would withhold treatment, for example, if Mr. L caught pneumonia. The other family members did not object to Mr. L's suicide, but Mr. L's wife thought that it was too soon for him to die. Their relationship was still rewarding, and she saw that her husband could still enjoy aspects of life, at least for a while. She did not want him to live until the cancer killed him, but she also feared that her husband might try to kill himself by other, more violent methods if he was not provided with medication, a situation that she would find traumatic.

Mr. L's wife, at Diekstra's suggestion, told her husband that she thought it was too early for him to die and that she would miss him if he died at that moment. He was pleased to hear this and glad that he was still needed. He agreed to postpone the decision, but he wanted assurance that he would be given the medication when the appropriate time arrived. He was given this assurance, and he lived for two more months.

Diekstra noted that, apart from simply providing the man with the necessary medication for suicide, the counselor acknowledged the acceptability of Mr. L's request and mobilized communication within the family, getting the wife and children involved. Mr. L came to feel less anxious and agitated, and he was able to participate more constructively in the life of his family for the two months he survived. The process improved the quality of life for both Mr. L and for his family.

Diekstra notes that "assisted suicide" means more than providing the medications necessary for death. It can involve providing technical information on means for committing suicide, removal of obstacles (e.g., release from an institution), giving advice on precautions and actions (e.g., making a will), and remaining with the person until the very end. We might add that it should involve counseling of the client and the significant others by a counselor who is sensitized to the issues involved.

CONCLUDING REMARKS

It is obvious that we are all going to die. When asked, most people say that they want to die quickly, painlessly, and in their sleep. Few of us will.

Most of us will die slowly, in pain, and in unpleasant surroundings. If we think about this event now, we have time to plan our dying and our deaths. We can decide to which treatments we will or will not consent, whether we want to donate organs, how the funeral will be conducted, and whether we want to be buried or cremated.

We can also work to change the society so that dying becomes a more pleasant process, as many have done by establishing hospices and by training medical and mental health professionals to deal with the dying more compassionately. Suicidal deaths need not be excluded from these considerations. Alfred Nobel, founder of the Nobel Prizes, proposed many years ago that a luxurious institute be built on the French Riviera overlooking the Mediterranean Sea where people could go to commit suicide in beautiful surroundings (Seiden, 1986; Sohlman, 1962).

Fanciful though Nobel's vision may be, even some suicidal deaths today could be conducted with more dignity, more compassion, and more family integration through counselor-assisted suicide.

REFERENCES

Binswanger, L. (1958). The case of Ellen West. In R. May, E. Angel, & H. F. Ellenberger (Eds.), *Existence* (pp. 237–364). New York: Basic Books.

Brent, D. A., Perper, J., Mortiz, G., Allman, C., Friend, A., Schweers, J., et al. (1992). Psychiatric effects of exposure to suicide among the friends and acquaintances of adolescent suicide victims. *Journal of the American Academy of Child and Adolescent Psychiatry, 31,* 629–640.

Calhoun, L. G., Selby, J. W., & Selby, L. E. (1982). The psychological aftermath of suicide. *Clinical Psychology Review, 2,* 409–420.

Diekstra, R. F. W. (1995). Dying in dignity. *Psychiatry and Clinical Neurosciences, 49*(Suppl. 1), S139–S148.

Ellis, A. (1973). *Humanistic psychotherapy.* New York: Julian.

Farber, L. (1962). Despair and the life of suicide. *Review of Existential Psychology and Psychiatry, 2,* 125–139.

Farberow, N. L. (1950). Personality patterns of suicidal mental hospital patients. *Genetic Psychology Monographs, 42,* 3–79.

Gordon, T. (1970). *PET: Parent effectiveness training.* New York: Wyden.

Greenwald, H. (1973). *Direct decision therapy.* San Diego, CA: Edits.

Jezer, M. (1992). *Abbie Hoffman.* New Brunswick, NJ: Rutgers University Press.

Lester, D. (1971). Ellen West's suicide as a case of psychic homicide. *Psychoanalytic Review, 58,* 251–263.

Lester, D. (1993). The logic and rationality of suicide. *Homeostasis, 34,* 167–173.

Lester, D. (1994). Bereavement after suicide by firearm. In D. Lester (Ed.), *Suicide '94* (pp. 12–13). Denver: American Association of Suicidology.

Lester, D. (1995). Counseling the suicidal person in the modern age. *Crisis Intervention and Time-Limited Treatment, 2,* 159–166.

Lester, D. (2003). *Fixin' to die: A compassionate guide to committing suicide or staying alive.* Amityville, NY: Baywood.

McDowell, C. P., Rothberg, J. M., & Koshes, R. J. (1994). Witnessed suicides. *Suicide and Life-Threatening Behavior, 24,* 213–223.

Quill, T. E. (1993). Doctor I want to die. Will you help me? *Journal of the American Medical Association, 270,* 870–873.

Robins, E., Gasner, S., Kayes, J., Wilkinson, R. H., & Murphy, G. E. (1959). The communication of suicidal intent. *American Journal of Psychiatry, 115,* 724–733.

Rogers, C. R. (1961). The loneliness of contemporary man as seen in the case of Ellen West. *Annals of Psychotherapy, 2,* 94–101.

Rollin, B. (1985). *Last wish.* New York: Simon & Schuster.

Seiden, R. H. (1986). Self-deliverance or self-destruction? *Euthanasia Review, 1*(1), 48–56.

Sohlman, R. (1962). Alfred Nobel and the Nobel Foundation. In H. Schuck (Ed.), *Nobel: The man and his prizes* (pp. 15–72). Amsterdam: Elsevier.

White-Bowden, S. (1985). *Everything to live for.* New York: Poseidon.

CHAPTER 16

Coping with Suicide in the Schools: The Art and the Research

Antoon A. Leenaars, David Lester, and Susanne Wenckstern

Childhood and adolescent problems in health have been an increasing concern the past few centuries. In 1910, Sigmund Freud and his colleagues identified numerous problems in young people's mental health, highlighting suicide (Friedman, 1910/1967). By the 1960s, up to 30% of youth were identified as displaying some pathology or maladjustment (Glidewell & Swallow, 1969), with current rates being even higher and about 1% to 3% labeled as serious (Durlak, 1995). Schools are obvious environments to provide a community's response since these institutions are designed to support a child's and adolescent's development and to address the problems of young people through programs (e.g., sex and AIDS education, drinking and driving, and suicide prevention).

Suicide is an important mental health and public health problem worldwide (Diekstra, 1996; World Health Organization, 2002). Adolescents, and even children, commit suicide (Pfeffer, 1986; World Health Organization, 2002). An even greater number of youths attempt or seriously think about suicide as the solution to their life's difficulties (Berman & Jobes, 1991; Lester, 1993). As was stated at the turn of the past century by Freud and his colleagues (Friedman, 1910/1967), schools and communities must respond (Leenaars & Wenckstern, 1990a).

The rationale for beginning a suicide prevention program in schools (see Leenaars & Wenckstern, 1999) includes:

1. The sheer numbers of suicides and suicidal behaviors in youth worldwide.

2. The large number of unhappy youth, many of whom are depressed. Kazdin (1990) reported that only 10% to 30% of youths needing clinical help receive that care (and that is in one Western country). It can, therefore, be asked, "How many additional suicidal youths are not identified as at risk?"

3. There is a possible suggestibility or imitation factor and subsequent contagion effect in suicidal behavior. (Leenaars, 1985; Martin, 1998).

4. Schools are asking for assistance. Thus, it would be appropriate that the most knowledgeable professionals (educators, psychiatrists, psychologists, etc.) assist.

5. The survivors of suicide need assistance. Many youths in our schools are, in fact, traumatized by the suicide of their peers (Leenaars, 1985).

In conclusion, there is a rationale for suicide prevention in schools (as there is for AIDS education, etc.). The important question is not whether we do it, but how we do it (Leenaars et al., 2001). In the next section, we briefly comment on a comprehensive approach to suicide in youth and then address the main issue of how to do it by presenting a review of the art and of the current research on the topic. As to the latter, as practitioners, we believe that scientific research should guide any effective response to mental health and public health problems.

PREVENTION/INTERVENTION/POSTVENTION

The classical approach to the prevention of mental health and public health problems is that of Caplan (1964), who differentiated between primary, secondary, and tertiary prevention. The more commonly used concepts today for these three modes of "ventions" are prevention, intervention, and postvention, respectively. Caplan's view still provides a sound model for a community response to suicide in youth. Briefly, the three modes of a comprehensive response are as follows:

1. *Prevention* relates to the principle of good mental hygiene in general. It consists of strategies to ameliorate the conditions that lead

to suicide—to do something before the event occurs. Preventing suicide is best accomplished through primary prevention, primarily through education. Young people (and their gatekeepers) must be educated about suicide. Such education—given that suicide is a multidimensional malaise—is enormously complicated.

2. *Intervention* relates to the treatment and care of a suicidal crisis or suicidal problem. Secondary prevention is doing something during the event. Suicide is an event with biological, psychological, interpersonal, sociocultural, and philosophical/existential aspects (a perspective consistent with an ecological model of health; World Health Organization, 2002). Because suicide is not solely a medical problem, many people can serve as lifesaving agents. Nonetheless, professionally trained people (psychologists, psychiatrists, social workers, psychiatric nurses, crisis workers, etc.) continue to play the primary roles in intervention. Thus, although equally true for postvention, intervention in schools calls for the development of community linkages, a hallmark of a public health response.

3. *Postvention,* a term introduced by Shneidman (1973), refers to things done after the event has occurred. Postvention deals with the traumatic aftereffects in the survivors of a person who has committed suicide (or in those close to someone who has attempted suicide). It involves offering mental health and public health services to the bereaved survivors. It includes working with all survivors who are in need—children, parents, teachers, and so on.

Next, we outline the art in more detail, followed by the research on each *vention.*

PREVENTION

Prevention relates to the principle of good mental hygiene in general. In schools, this means education. This is in keeping with the general aim of schools, in fact, to educate our youth.

A current popular formulation about suicide is that suicide is simply caused by an external event or *stress,* such as rejection by a friend or the influence of a popular singer's lyrics. Although there is often a situational factor in suicide, there is much more, for example:

A 16-year-old was found dead in a car, having died of carbon monoxide poisoning. People were perplexed, "Why did this young person, from an upper middle-class family, kill himself?" The parents found out that his girlfriend had rejected him on the day of his suicide. That was the reason: When a young person gets rejected and is so in love, he may kill himself. A few friends and his teachers knew that he had been having problems in school: That was the reason. A few others knew that his father was an alcoholic and abusive: That was the reason. His physician knew that he had been adopted and had been recently upset about that. She knew the real reason. And others knew . . . .

The youth himself or herself is equally often blinded by a single event. Here we are speaking about lethal suicidal people. The teenager who is about to put a bullet through his head with his father's gun or the teenager who is about to take her mother's prescription pills, at the moment of decision, may be the least aware of the essence of the reasons for doing so. The adolescent's conscious perception is a critical aspect. Yet, to simply accept that perspective is not only simplistic, but may well be suicidogenic (i.e., destructive and iatrogenic). The pain simply makes it impossible for the young person to give a complete and accurate recitation of the event. Suicide is complex—more complicated than the child's or adolescent's conscious mind is aware of.

Regrettably all too often, adults—including parents, teachers, medical doctors, and psychologists—are willing to share in the misconception. Myths are, in fact, widespread and have gone as far as stating: "Suicide is normal." Suicide is not normal. It is an indication of major pathology (King, 1997). To have stated otherwise—as occurred in the late 1970s and 1980s—was not only a pitfall but also a disservice to prevention efforts. Next, we look at what we have learned about sound suicide prevention in schools over the past few decades.

Appendix A presents excerpts from a suicide prevention workshop for school staff, "Helping Your Suicidal Student."

Prevention: School-Based Programs

One of the problems in evaluating school suicide prevention programs is that the programs differ greatly in design and have very different goals. In a survey of school programs, Malley, Kush, and Bogo (1994) found that schools reported the following types of programs:

1. Written formal policy statements on suicide
2. Written procedures for dealing with at-risk students
3. Staff in-service training
4. Mental health professionals at the school
5. Mental health teams at the school
6. Suicide prevention materials for distribution to parents
7. Suicide prevention materials for distribution to students
8. Suicide reference materials for distribution to school counselors
9. Psychological screening programs to identify students at risk for suicide
10. Mental health counseling for students at risk for suicide
11. Classroom discussions
12. Suicide prevention training for school counselors
13. Suicide prevention training for teachers
14. Postvention program after student suicides

Shaffer, Garland, Gould, Fisher, and Trautman (1988) have also noted that school-based programs can aim to heighten awareness of the problem, promote case finding, provide staff and pupils with information about mental health resources, and improve adolescents' coping abilities. As a result, many different criteria have been used to evaluate school-based suicide prevention programs, and there appears to be no uniformity forthcoming.

Helping Peers

Kalafat and Gagliano (1996) found that, after exposure to the curriculum that they designed, students were more likely to seek adult help if a peer was suicidal, and they showed greater concern for a suicidal peer. Kalafat and Elias (1994) also found that students exposed to their curriculum developed more positive attitudes toward suicidal peers and were more likely to respond to them in a helpful manner as compared to students not exposed to the curriculum.

Abbey, Madsen, and Polland (1989) found that their curriculum for undergraduates led to more appropriate helping responses to suicidal peers.

Ciffone (1993) found that students who were given a suicide prevention curriculum developed a more positive attitude toward suicidal people and were more likely to seek help for suicidal peers and for themselves as compared to students who did not take the program.

Johnson (1985) found that students who were given a suicide prevention program were more likely to approach a teacher on behalf of a suicidal peer or for themselves after taking the curriculum than before taking it. Nelson (1987) found that students who attended a suicide prevention curriculum indicated that they would be more helpful to suicidal peers after the program than they would have been before the program.

Shaffer and his colleagues (1990; Shaffer, Garland, Vieland, Underwood, & Busner, 1991) found that students taking a suicide prevention curriculum showed an increase in helpful reactions and responses to a possible suicidal peer than those not taking the course. They did not, however, develop more positive attitudes toward seeking help for general mental health problems as compared to those not taking the course.

Knowledge about Suicide

Kalafat and Elias (1994) found that students exposed to their curriculum acquired greater knowledge about suicidal behavior than those not exposed. Abbey et al. (1989) gave a program to undergraduate students and found an increase in accurate knowledge about suicide. Nelson (1987) reported that his students also had more accurate knowledge after a suicide prevention program and were better able to recognize suicidal clues in others than they did before the program. Only 4% of the students thought that the program was not helpful for preventing suicide.

Johnson (1985) found that teachers given a curriculum on suicide prevention acquired more knowledge than they had before and developed a more positive attitude toward suicidal individuals.

Spirito, Overholser, Ashworth, Morgan, and Benedict-Drew (1988; Overholser, Hemstreet, Spirito, & Vyse, 1989) found that a suicide awareness curriculum increased the students' knowledge about suicide and improved their own coping strategies as compared with students not taking the curriculum.

Shaffer and his colleagues (1990; Shaffer et al., 1991) found that a suicide prevention curriculum increased the students' knowledge about suicide (although the researchers did not adequately report the scores and tests of statistical significance). The students taking the program also showed an increase in knowledge about treatment resources.

Lowering Suicidal Risk

Orbach and Bar-Joseph (1993) found that students exposed to their curriculum experienced an improvement in self-reported suicidal tendencies, ego identity, and coping, but not in hopelessness, as compared with students not exposed to the curriculum. No students reported feeling harmed by the program.

Eggert, Thompson, Herting, and Nicholas (1995) ran a program for high school students at high risk for suicide and found no significant differences in their suicidal risk behaviors, depression, and hopelessness as compared with those not in the program. All groups improved whether they were in the program or not.

INTERVENTION

Intervention relates to the treatment and care of a person in a suicidal crisis or a suicidal problem (Leenaars, 2004; Leenaars, Maltsberger, & Neimeyer, 1994). Many people, including those in schools, can serve as life-saving agents. Nonetheless, professionally trained people, often outside the schools, continue to play the primary roles in intervention.

Misconceptions are rife, not only about suicide, but about treatment of suicidal people. Often there are overly simplistic solutions, in part, because of the myth that suicide is due only to stress. Even in youth, the common consistency in suicide and suicidal behavior is not the precipitating event but complex coping patterns (Shneidman, 1985). Suicidal youth are in unbearable pain, weakened, and unable to cope with the demands of life (Leenaars & Wenckstern, 1994). Therefore, the mere focus on suicide as a result of stress grossly underestimates the pathology that these young people face (King, 1997) and is instrumental in the subsequent lack of help. The truth is that these young people need long-term, multifaceted services, not short-term counseling and other naive solutions (Leenaars, 2004).

Although professionals (e.g., psychiatrists, psychologists) have a central role in the treatment of suicidal youth, others have an equally valuable role. Parents, in fact, can make a critical contribution if they are on the side of life (Richman, 1990). Not only should the parents be included in our interventions, but also siblings, friends, teachers, schoolmates, priests, elders, and doctors—anyone who serves, directly or indirectly— to nullify the pain. Intervention demands a community response (World Health Organization, 2002).

The search for a singular, universal, simplistic response to suicide in youth is a chimera, an imaginary and nonexistent conceptual fabrication. Prescribing only medication as a cure-all is, for example, such a chimera. The search for a simple response is a foolish and unrealistic fancy.

Unfortunately, researchers have not adequately studied intervention in schools. Only a few studies have appeared in the literature; they are described in the following sections.

Intervention: Crisis Teams in Schools

Zenere and Lazarus (1997) trained crisis interveners for each school in the Dade County (Florida) public schools and examined the changes in suicidal behavior in the schools. After the teams were in place, there was a decrease in both completed suicide and attempted suicide but not suicidal ideation. However, the evaluation design was not methodologically sound. A better design would have placed the teams in only half the schools for several years and then added the teams to the remaining schools later.

Intervention: Counseling and Peer-Group Interventions

Randell, Eggert, and Pike (2001) evaluated the effects of two brief school-intervention protocols to students who were assessed as at risk (e.g., high school dropouts) in grades 9 to 12 in seven high schools. The first group received a brief intervention by counselors, using a computer-assisted assessment of risk and protective factors. The second group received the counselor program, with an additional 12 peer-group sessions. After the interventions, students in both experimental groups and a control group showed a decrease in suicide risk behaviors, with little differences between groups. The fact that a nonintervention (control) group showed a decrease in risk raises questions about what is being measured. Despite confusing results, the experimental groups did show greater increases in some factors such as problem solving. Furthermore, the study was a school-based prevention trial but did not sample clinical groups, suggesting the need for field replication.

POSTVENTION

Postvention refers to actions done after a suicide, attempted suicide, or any trauma that has occurred (Shneidman, 1981). Postvention deals with the traumatic aftereffects in the survivors. School systems, within the context of their communities, are an especially critical force in such endeavors with our children and teens (Centers for Disease Control, 1988; Leenaars & Wenckstern, 1998).

Suicide is a trauma for the survivors, a view already held by Freud in 1917 (Freud, 1917/1974b) and supported by research (e.g., Gleser, Green, & Wignet, 1981; Terr, 1979; Wilson, Smith, & Johnson, 1985). There are many diverse, unusual traumatic events such as serious crimes, homicides, accidents, and disasters. Suicide is also outside the range of usual human experience and, like other traumas, evokes "significant symptoms of distress in most people" (Leenaars, 1985; Shneidman, 1985).

Traumatic stress disorder refers to those natural behaviors and emotions that occur during a catastrophe. Figley (1985) defined posttraumatic stress disorder (PTSD) "as a set of conscious and unconscious behaviors and emotions associated with dealing with the memories of the stressors of the catastrophe and immediately afterwards," although by no means do all or even most survivors exhibit the necessary characteristics to be labeled as having a PTSD. Posttraumatic stress disorder is best seen as a heuristic label because it approximates the reactions in survivors of suicide and other trauma in our schools and communities (Leenaars, 1985). In addition to the existence of a recognized stressor, symptoms in a posttraumatic reaction may include reexperiencing the trauma (e.g., recurrent recollections, recurrent dreams, feelings that the event is reoccurring), numbing of responsiveness and a reduced involvement with the external world (e.g., diminished interest, detachment, constricted affect), and various other symptoms (e.g., depression, grief, hyperalertness, sleep disturbance, survivor guilt, problems in memory/ concentration, avoidance of events that evoke recall, intensification of symptoms by events that symbolize events) (American Psychiatric Association [APA], 1980; Freud, 1926/1974a; Janoff-Bulman, 1985).

Adjusting to a suicide, or any trauma or catastrophe, is remarkably difficult, with possible positive and negative responses (Freud, 1939/1974c). Freud saw remembering, repeating, and reexperiencing as positive, and forgetting, avoidance, phobia, and inhibition as negative.

Negative reactions are regrettably all too common in many victims after a suicide (and other traumas), even in adults who are to guide our youngsters, such as principals and psychologists. A common response is to deny it: "Don't talk about it; after all, talking about suicide causes suicide." We firmly believe, as has been so well documented with Vietnam veterans in the latter part of the past century, that this approach only exacerbates a trauma. However, as Wilson et al. (1985) have pointed out, it is important for us to see that the victims of a suicide may be caught in a no-win cycle of events:

> To talk about the powerful and overwhelming trauma means risking further stigmatization; the failure to discuss the traumatic episode increases the need for defensive avoidance and thus increases the probability of depression alternating with cycles of intensive imagery and other symptoms of PTSD. (Wilson et al., 1985, p. 169)

Posttraumatic stress disorder was initially intended as a description of a reaction to trauma for adults (APA, 1980). However, Eth and Pynoos (1985) have presented convincing arguments for applying PTSD to children and adolescents. There are, in fact, amazing commonalities in how children respond to various unusual traumatic events (Leenaars & Wenckstern, 1990b). In response to such observations, the APA (1987) has clarified its definition to include children and teens.

The response to suicide and trauma in school must be complex. Postvention is multifaceted and takes a while—from several months to the end of life, but certainly more than three or six hours (Leenaars & Wenckstern, 1998). Posttraumatic stress disorder work is multifaceted. More comprehensive discussion of the strategies for postvention are presented elsewhere (Leenaars, 1985; Leenaars & Wenckstern, 1990b, 1996, 1998; Wenckstern & Leenaars, 1990, 1993). Essential aspects of such programs include, at least, consultation, crisis intervention, community linkage, assessment and counseling or psychotherapy, education, liaison with the media, and follow-up. These approaches need to defuse the aftershocks and not add to the hysteria (Callahan, 1996; Goldney & Berman, 1996).

Appendix B presents excerpts from a suicide postvention workshop, "Suicide Postvention in Schools: Practical Applications."

Next, we present the only study that approaches the topic of postvention, although it is not really postvention. The study by Hazell and Lewin

(1993) is on debriefing. We have argued since 1980, when the senior author (AL) did his first postvention, that debriefing is not sufficient
postvention. Be that as it may, this is what we have learned.

Debriefing after Adolescent Suicides

Hazell and Lewin (1993) explored whether an hour and a half of group
counseling, sometimes called *debriefing,* helped students who were selected by the staff for the counseling. Counseled students did not differ
from those not counseled eight months later on measures of depression,
suicidality, or substance abuse, although the measures lacked validation.
Furthermore, a group meeting of 90 minutes is not good postvention,
raising doubts about Hazell and Lewin's study.

EVALUATION

A number of studies have attempted to evaluate the programs in
schools—what principals think, what experts think, and so on. Next we
present these studies.

Evaluation: What Do the Principals Think?

Miller, Eckert, DuPaul, and White (1999) sent secondary school principals
a description of one of three possible school-based suicide prevention programs to evaluate. The principals preferred both the curriculum-based
program (a two-hour teaching segment for all students during relevant
classroom periods) and the staff in-service training program (a two-hour
program for staff before the start of the school year) over the schoolwide
student screening program (in which a suicide potential form was distributed to all students, after which those with high scores would be interviewed by school psychologists). Clearly, for a school-based suicide
prevention program to work, it must receive the support of the staff of
the school.

Evaluation: The Opinions of Experts

Eddy, Wolpert, and Rosenberg (1987) asked 15 experts on youth suicide
to rank various preventive measures for their usefulness. Although there
was a wide variation in the experts' rankings, school-based screening
ranked third—equal with improved treatment, but behind restricting access to firearms and identifying high-risk youth.

Evaluation: An Ecological Study

Garland, Shaffer, and Whittle (1989) surveyed 115 agencies that implemented a school-based curriculum program for students, and they reported the number and proportion of adolescents exposed in each state. Lester (1992) compared these numbers with the changes in the suicide rate of 15- to 19-year-olds in the states. Student participation in the programs was associated with a detrimental effect on state teenage suicide rates. However, Lester found that state government initiatives in addressing youth suicide were associated with a beneficial impact on state teenage suicide rates.

Evaluation: Negative Effects

Occasional studies have reported negative effects from school-based programs. Spirito and his colleagues (1988; Overholser et al., 1989) found that their suicide awareness program increased the hopelessness scores of male students, but not female students, although they observed many more positive effects than this one negative effect. Shaffer et al. (1990) and Shaffer et al. (1991) found that students participating in their suicide prevention program were more likely to see suicide as a solution to problems after the course, especially male students and Black students. They also found that 7% of the students found the program "upsetting." In particular, Shaffer and his colleagues found that students who had previously attempted suicide were more negative about the program for their friends (but not themselves) than students who had never attempted suicide (although the majority of both groups were positive about the program), and the attempters were more likely to report knowing someone who was upset by the program. The attempters were also more likely to state that the program had made it more difficult for them to deal with friends' problems. It is likely, based on the data in Shaffer's study, that these attempters did not like the fact that their friends learned that they were troubled and might be suffering from psychopathology. Further, although for all students there was an increase in accurate knowledge about suicide and a more positive attitude toward seeking help, these effects were not found for the small subgroup (7% of the sample) who had previously attempted suicide.

CONCLUDING REMARKS

Suicide is a major mental health problem and public health problem in our youth. Prevention/intervention/postvention is needed, and schools are an obvious setting to provide such a comprehensive response within an ecological model of response (Leenaars, 2003; World Health Organization, 2002). More study and discussion are, however, needed. What are the critical issues in prevention in schools? What are the myths? Are our suggestions the myths? There are many other issues. We must ask at least the following questions:

- Do we agree that suicide is a problem?
- Are the school and community and society supportive about trying to solve the problem?
- Can we agree on the minimal strategies in prevention, intervention, and postvention?
- What are the ideal approaches?
- What should be the standard of care in schools? Are they the same, different, and/or unique as compared with other settings (e.g., hospitals)?
- What community linkages are needed—minimal and ideal—with schools?
- What a priori system entry issues must be addressed? Should "vention" efforts be mandatory?
- How do we evaluate the cost-effective component (if this is important) of our education programs?
- How can we increase the ability to assess suicide risk? What instructions, skills, and so on, are needed by school personnel to begin to screen people at risk for suicide (or violence)?
- What interventions are effective with youth? Do we have any data that psychotherapy, medication, and so on helps?
- How can we utilize means restriction more?
- What are the essential features of postvention in schools? At the very least, it appears to include the following: consultation, crisis intervention, community linkage, assessment and counseling or psychotherapy,

education, liaison with media, and follow-up. What aspects are minimal? Ideal?

- How does postvention in schools differ from grief counseling? How is it similar?
- How do we evaluate our "vention" efforts?
- Finally, are there any suicidogenic effects in our "vention" efforts? If so, how are they addressed and measured?

Research is needed on these topics. Regrettably, the research to date is sparse, except in prevention. We can conclude that prevention programs have been effective. There is no reason to listen to the voice of some, who have attempted to stop these efforts. Prevention works. This review of the evaluation research on school suicide prevention programs leads to the following further conclusions:

1. School suicide prevention programs increase knowledge about suicide in the participants.
2. School suicide prevention programs increase the probability that students will respond appropriately and helpfully to suicidal peers.
3. The negative impact of the programs is infrequent and appears to be minor.

A major thrust in the future will have to be greater clarity in the focus of prevention/intervention/postvention efforts and better training in this area as the social issues facing young people change (e.g., the current debate about euthanasia and assisted suicide). One final conclusion in this review is that research on intervention and postvention has been lacking. There is, in fact, nothing on postvention. The sheer numbers of young people at risk worldwide requires that this be remedied. We need not only sound prevention efforts but also intervention and postvention—and, with the memory of Columbine, postvention is a must. Who can forget the young people's anguish captured by live television in our living rooms? Postvention is needed to address suicide, homicide, and trauma in our schools. More research, however, is necessary because we need to be more effective in preventing suicide. Science should guide our practice in schools.

APPENDIX A _____

Suicide Prevention: Some Extracts
of a Workshop

HELPING YOUR SUICIDAL STUDENT

What can we do? What can you, as teachers, administrators, and other school staff do? In most cases, something can be done to save a young life. Shneidman (1985) has made a very important observation regarding this concern, namely that about 80% of suicides provide clues to their imminent suicide. Regrettably, the clues to suicide are usually not responded to before the act, and sometimes they are not even seen or heard. I have heard very frequently, "I didn't think he'd do it" or "I know she said that she was going to kill herself, but she had said that before." It follows that education about the facts of suicide would help us to prevent suicide. Most people would agree that the best prevention is primary prevention (preventing suicide from ever occurring), and primary prevention involves, among other things, education. It is important to teach which clues should be looked for, what can be done, and what help is available. . . .

PREVENTION: SOME OBSERVATIONS

Concept of Death

Do children understand death? Pfeffer's (1986) research suggests that they do, although perception of death differs depending on the age of the child. Young children (approximately at age 7) see death as temporary; everything is seen as alive and vulnerable to death. Children around age 10 see death as personified and temporary and that an outside agent causes death. By the time the child is a young adolescent, say 13, he sees death as final and realizes that internal biological processes cause death. Yet, even older teenagers may sometimes misunderstand the finality of

_____

From a workshop entitled "Helping Your Suicidal Student" (copyright A. Leenaars, used with permission).

death. For example, Jim, a 16-year-old suicidal individual, was referred to me because of a crisis he was having at home. He wanted to punish his parents and stated, "I'll teach my dad a lesson when I kill myself. Then, he'll learn a lesson." Of course, such reasoning is not logical. Jim could not know what his father's reaction to his death would be. Jim's ideas were based on a denial of what death really means. Teenagers (and adults too) often have an unrealistic concept of death (and also of life). Sometimes, people believe that somehow after they are dead they will actually continue to live in the hereafter. Thus, adolescents have a concept of death but it may be different from an adult's. Incidentally, Pfeffer has shown that intense fantasies about death may be an early warning sign of suicidal risk in youth. . . .

PREVENTION: CLUES TO SUICIDE

We need to be aware of which behaviors are potentially predictive of suicide. Unfortunately, to date there is no definitive list of behaviors. Two concepts that may be helpful here are lethality and perturbation. Lethality refers to the probability of a person killing him/herself, ranging from low, to moderate, to high. Perturbation refers to subjective distress, also ranging from low, to moderate, to high. Both lethality and perturbation can be useful concepts when assessing suicidal risk. It is important to note that one can be perturbed (agitated, distressed and so on) and not suicidal. Lethality kills, not perturbation. Perturbation is relatively easy to evaluate; lethality is not. My own experience with teachers, parents, clergy, and family doctors is that lethality is best assessed by a professional who is experienced in this area (such as a psychiatrist, psychologist, or social worker). But, it is important that everyone be aware of these concepts so that they can not only recognize the clues that point to potential suicidal behavior, but also differentiate the severity of risk (to the best degree possible by each individual). The following list cites important clues that point to suicidal potentiality:

1. *Previous attempts:* Although it is obvious that one has to attempt suicide in order to commit it, it is equally clear that the event of attempting suicide need not have death as its objective. It is useful to think of the attempter, sometimes referred to as a parasuicide or as

a self-injurer, and the completer as two different parts of overlapping populations: one is a group of those who attempt suicide, a few of whom go on to commit suicide, and the other is a group who commit suicide, a few of whom may have previously attempted to kill themselves. A great deal has to do with the lethality of the action. The ratio between suicide attempts and completions in the general population is about 8 to 1; 1 committed suicide for every 8 attempts (although countries differ in this ratio; some are as low as 4 to 1). However, in teenagers some studies report a rate of 50 to 1, even 100 to 1. No such data are yet available for children.

A previous attempt is a good clue to the possibility of future attempts, especially if no assistance is obtained after the first attempt, but not all attempters go on to attempt again (or kill themselves). However, all too frequently such behavior is not taken seriously. I recall a very depressed 11-year-old girl who cut her wrists at school. The principal's response was merely, "She is just trying to get attention." What an extreme way to get attention! The girl was moderately lethal and highly perturbed, and required considerable intervention.

2. *Verbal statements:* The attitude is often negative toward individuals who make verbal threats of suicide. Suicidal threats are frequently seen as only attempts to get attention. This attitude results in writing off and ignoring the behavior of a person who is genuinely perturbed and potentially suicidal. Also, it is a well-documented fact that questioning a person about possible suicidal behavior will not increase the chance that they will commit suicide. The important question is, "Why has this person chosen this particular way of getting attention when there are so many other ways?" Examples of direct verbal statements from young people are: "I'm going to kill myself" or "I want to die." More indirect examples are: "I am going to see my (deceased) mother" or "I always knew that I'd die at an early age."

3. *Cognitive clues:* The single most common state of mind of a suicidal person is known as constriction. There is tunnel vision, in other words a narrowing of the mind's eye. There is a narrowing of the range of perceptions, opinions or options that occur to the person.

The person frequently uses words like "only," "always," "never," and "forever." Examples of this in young people are the following: "No one will ever love me. Only Mom loved me"; "John was the only one who loved me"; "My teacher will always be that way"; and "Either I'll kill my brother or myself."

4. *Emotional clues:* The child or teenager who is suicidal is often highly perturbed. He is disturbed, anxious, and perhaps agitated. Depression, as already noted, is frequently evident (King, 1997). Suicidal teenagers are often very angry and hostile and may feel boxed in, rejected, harassed, and unsuccessful. A common emotional state in most suicidal people is hopelessness/helplessness. Hopelessness frequently reveals itself in statements such as: "Nothing will change. It will always be this way." The helplessness can sound like this, "There is nothing I can do. There is nothing my teacher can do."

5. *Sudden behavioral changes:* Changes in behavior may also be predictors of suicide. Both the outgoing individual who suddenly becomes withdrawn or isolated, and the normally reserved individual who suddenly becomes outgoing and thrill seeking may be at risk for suicide. Such changes are of particular concern when a precipitating painful event has occurred. Poor performance in school such as sudden failure may be an important clue. Making final arrangements like giving away a CD collection, a favorite watch, or other possessions may be ominous and should be recognized as a possible warning sign to teachers. A sudden preoccupation with death, such as reading and talking about death, may also be a clue. Constructive discussion of this topic as a class project may be helpful, however, for the individual and his/her classmates, since peers are often the first to hear this kind of information.

6. *Life-threatening behavior:* I recall a 9-year-old boy who killed himself. He previously had been seen leaning out of an open window of his apartment, and, at another time, playing with a gun. A 17-year-old teenager died in a single car accident on an isolated road after having had several similar accidents following his mother's death. Self-destructive behavior is not rare. Often alcoholism, drug addiction,

mismanagement of physical disease, and auto accidents should be seen for what they might be—suicidal clues. Farberow (1980) has called this, "the many faces of suicide." Here are a number of questions one should consider: Why did the young child, knowing that the gun was loaded and despite his parents' warnings, play with it? Why did the teenager drive so fast on a slippery wet road when he knew that for the past three months his brakes had been bad? Why did a person, knowing the dangers of cocaine use, continue to use it and get hooked? I am not suggesting that these young people intentionally want to die; yet, their behavior made them as "good as dead."

7. *Suicide notes:* Like prior suicide attempts and verbal statements, suicidal writings that suggest suicidal ideation are important clues, but, unfortunately, they are often read and ignored by the reader. Such writings are very rare in young children, but more common in adolescents (although most adolescents who kill themselves do not leave a suicide note). Art work, diaries, music, and other personal documents can be seen as similar expressive clues. I remember one suicide note stating, "I finally completed something I've always wanted to do. I removed the guilt from every person. . . . PS: Happy Father's Day."

Below are a number of genuine suicide notes. They are presented here not merely as a clue but to give you a better understanding of the subjective frame of mind of young people who actually kill themselves:

1. Single male, age 13:

   I know what I am doing. Annette, I found out. Ask Carol. I love you all.

2. Single female, age 16:

   Dear Mother & Dad,

   Please forgive me. I have tried to be good to you both. I love you both very much and wanted to get along with you both. I have tried. I have wanted to go out with you & Dad but I was always afraid to ask for I always felt that the answer would be no. And about Bill, I want to dismiss every idea about him. I don't like any more than a compassion, for a while I thought I did not no more, in fact, I am quite tired of him, as you know, I get tired of everyone after a while.

And mother, I wish you hadn't called me a liar, and said I was just like Hap. as I'm not. It is just that I am afraid of you both at times, but I love you both very much.

> So long
>
> Your loving daughter
>
> That will always
>
> love you
>
> Mary

P.S. Please forgive me. I want you to, and don't think for one minute that I haven't appreciated everything you've done.

I would also like to offer one last writing, a suicidal expression, not a suicide note. It was written by an 11-year-old girl (of high perturbation, but low lethality) who was contemplating suicide. She wrote the following to her teacher:

Hi hows your day going? I hope fine. I've been trying hard in french real hard Mrs. T. I know what im going to say isnt your problem but I just needed to tell someone my feelings I can't keep it in. I hate living I want to die no one understands why I cant explain why. I wish I wasn't born why did it hapen to me why did God make me. I'm frightened to get my tests signed even when good ones. I'm scared of failing. No-one really cares any way your a nice friend, special. I hope you have a nice future. The best I really like you and sometimes im afraid to live scared—I want to kill myself but I can't do it cause its against the law. I'll go to the oppisite of heaven. I really like you and want to say your a great friend. I love my family alot also. I love you. other kids think im a baby writing notes. If it weren't for my stupid eyes I wouldn't be as ugly. I don't understand why im so ugly. I'm not feeling sorry for myself I'm just telling how I feel inside. I don't want to pass cause I want to stay here with you. Sorry if I buged you or took up your time.

I hate life.

P.S. you probably can't read my writing

What is important here is that the teacher responded to the girl. I have other notes where teachers, parents, and others responded; these young people are alive because these adults did something, they got help. Although not all young people leave notes or show other clues, most do and what is important is that we respond—do something effective! . . .

APPENDIX B _____

Suicide Postvention: Some Extracts from a Workshop

SUICIDE POSTVENTION IN SCHOOLS: PRACTICAL APPLICATIONS

Postvention refers to those actions done after a trauma, such as suicide, has occurred (Shneidman, 1981). Postvention deals with the traumatic aftereffects in the survivors. School systems, within the context of their communities, are an especially critical force in such endeavors with our children and teens (Centers for Disease Control, 1988).

Adjusting to suicide or any trauma is remarkably difficult. Freud (1939/1974c) distinguished between positive and negative effects, after a trauma. He saw remembering, repeating, and reexperiencing as positive, which is opposite of the more typical denial approach. Forgetting, avoidance, phobia, and inhibition were described by Freud as negative. These are, however, common responses in many victims after a suicide (and other traumas), even in adults who are to guide our youngsters, such as principals, psychologists, and so on. A common response in the past and present is to deny it: "Don't talk about it; after all, talking about suicide causes suicide." We firmly believe, as has been so well documented with Vietnam veterans, that this approach only exacerbates the trauma. However, as Wilson et al. (1985) have pointed out, it is important for us to see that the victims of a suicide may be caught in a no-win cycle of events. They note the following:

To talk about the powerful and overwhelming trauma means risking further stigmatization; the failure to discuss the traumatic episode increases the need for defensive avoidance and thus increases the probability of depression alternating with cycles of intensive imagery and other symptoms of PTSD (p. 169).

We need to help survivors work through the trauma. We need to foster positive adjustive strategies to the trauma and for future response. . . .

_____

Postvention is not simple. Postvention efforts essentially represent a synthesis of educational strategies (being fostered by such associations as the American Association of Suicidology, the Canadian Association for Suicide Prevention, the International Association for Suicide Prevention); consultative intervention (see Goodstein, 1978); crisis intervention (see Farberow, 1967; Hoff, 1984; Leenaars, 1991, 1994, 2004; Leenaars, Maltsberger, & Neimeyer, 1994; Leenaars & Wenckstern, 1994; Parad, 1965; Shneidman, 1980, 1985); and a few strategies related to trauma response in general (see Figley, 1985; Lifton, 1969; Lindemann, 1944; World Health Organization, 2002) and postvention strategies in specific (see Shneidman, 1981). These efforts, furthermore, should be placed within an interactional-system frame (for example, see Watzlawick, Beavin, & Jackson, 1967) or ecological model (World Health Organization, 2002), or more simply called, a community approach to public health and mental health problems. By way of further introducing points on postvention: (1) Postvention programs are enormously demanding of resources, while our economic times are constraining efforts (Maltsberger, 1994); (2) Postvention programs include some generic aspects, although modifications will be necessary depending on such factors as time, situation, and nature of the suicide or trauma (Wenckstern & Leenaars, 1998).

PRINCIPLES OF POSTVENTION

1. *In working with survivor victims of suicide, it is best to begin as soon as possible after the tragedy, within the first 24 hours if that can be managed.*

   Consultation and networking between all concerned personnel at a school and in a community (e.g., administrator[s], teachers, mental health professionals, under the direction of a postvention coordinator) are critical at this time. Response must be as prompt as possible; waiting even 24 hours can exacerbate the situation. It is important to compile and share accurate, reliable information about the event as it becomes known. This is desirable to combat hysteria, which often mounts when misinformation, frequently of a sensational nature, proliferates. In these early moments of postvention, it is imperative to strive to establish clear lines of structure and communication as quickly and efficiently as possible. . . .

2. *Resistance may be met from the survivors; some—but not all—are either willing or eager to have the opportunity to talk to professionally oriented persons. . . .*

3. *Negative emotions about the decedent (the deceased person) or about any trauma—irritation, anger, fear, shame, guilt, and so on—need to be explored, but not at the very beginning. Timing is so important. . . .*

4. *The postventionist should play the important role of reality tester. He/she is not so much the echo of conscience as the quiet voice of reason. . . .*

5. *One should be constantly alert for possible decline in health and in overall mental well-being, especially suicide risk. . . .*

6. *Needless to say, pollyannish optimism, or banal platitudes should be avoided. . . .*

7. *Trauma work is multifaceted and takes a while—from several months to the end of life, but certainly more than 90 minutes. . . .*

Trauma work is multifaceted and we can offer here only a few highlights of such efforts. More comprehensive discussion of the strategies for postvention is presented elsewhere (Leenaars, 1985; Leenaars & Wenckstern, 1990b, 1996, 1998; Wenckstern & Leenaars, 1990, 1993).

STRATEGIES FOR POSTVENTION

Here is a brief summary of essential aspects of postvention with regard to basic strategies:

1. Consultation

Discussion, coordination, and planning are undertaken at every phase, beginning with school administration and then followed by school staff, and by other involved individuals, such as students and parents, under the direction of the postvention coordinator, that is, a mental health expert who takes charge and provides structure. Community personnel may need to be included during every sequence of the process, depending on the evaluation of the mild-moderate-severe level of the traumatic event (Goodstein, 1978; World Health Organization, 2002). Concurrent peer consultation and review among professional staff who are involved in the postvention program (postvention team) are undertaken to review the plans that were implemented and to plan or coordinate further action. For example, a flexible contingency plan must be preplanned to allow for alternative actions, if needed. Territorial problems between school and community (and their own internal politics) need to be addressed since often these are the very elements that raise the traumatic levels of the event.

2. Crisis Intervention

Emergency or crisis response is provided, using basic problem-solving strategies. We believe that students and staff of the local school(s) are likely to need support in response to a suicide trauma. It is crucial not to underestimate the closeness of relationships or the intensity of reactions of individuals who might be experiencing posttraumatic reactions (Caplan, 1964; Farberow, 1967; Hoff, 1984, 1990; Leenaars, 1994, 2004; Leenaars et al., 1994; Leenaars & Wenckstern, 1990a; Shneidman, 1981).

3. Community Linkage

Since it is imperative that survivors of suicide be provided with the appropriate support, we assist these individuals to obtain such services. Educational systems need to develop a linkage system or network to aid in making referrals to the appropriate community services and to exchange information and coordinate services with appropriate community services as needed. Such a network is central to responding to a trauma and should be predefined. No individual or system can address all the needs, a problem that is especially evident in contracted service. Being familiar with and updating local community resources before a traumatic event such as suicide occurs, for example, knowing which agency or service to contact and preferably the name of the contact person, is highly recommended (e.g., police, ambulance, hospital emergency). In the case of culturally different students, having a directory on hand listing local cultural centers and names of translators, with preestablished communications, may be not only very helpful but also a necessity.

4. Assessment and Counseling

Evaluation and therapy are provided as needed or requested by the postventionists or the school administrator, for example, the principal or his or her designate. Assessment, as we already noted, is complex but can be approximated (Leenaars, 1995; Maris, Berman, Maltsberger, & Yufit, 1992). Therapy almost always will include psychotherapy (Leenaars, 2004). Psychotherapy is equally complicated and, contrary to current efforts, often must be long term—and in many cases, will call for a multicompact approach, such as medication and hospitalization. Adolescents at risk are often suffering long-term pain that has undermined their ability to cope. We strongly believe since our first postvention effort that once students are identified, the treatment should be primarily individual, not only in groups. Groups may serve the initial task of response to a shared trauma, but the student in need should be referred to a therapist for scheduled appointments as soon as possible (a psychiatrist, psychologist, social worker, or some other professionally trained person). One needs to defuse the aftershock, not add to the hysteria (Callahan, 1996; Goldney & Berman, 1996). An outline for psychotherapy has been presented elsewhere (Leenaars, 1994, 2004; Leenaars et al., 1994).

5. Education

Information about suicide and its prevention (e.g., clues, myths, causes, what to do, where to go for help) is provided through discussion, seminars, workshops, and small assemblies/classes (30 people) at the school and within the community (Leenaars & Wenckstern, 1990a). This aspect of the program, based on the current literature, is oriented toward prevention. As a final note, educational programs should be undertaken after the aftershocks are normalized, not as part of the early crisis intervention.

6. Liaison with the Media

Information about suicide in the form of publicity, especially that which tends to sensationalize or glamorize the suicide, should be avoided (Martin, 1998). It is not and should not be the school's responsibility to provide information about the actuarial details of the suicide, as any trauma, to the media. This falls within the jurisdiction of the police department, coroner's office, or other authorities. However, our experience has shown us that (1) a media spokesperson for the school must be appointed at the outset of the crisis and (2) this role should be filled by the postvention coordinator and not by a school administrator (e.g., the principal). Not only does this ensure the accuracy and consistency of information being given out, but most important, it ensures that this information is being provided by someone who understands the postvention procedures and positive impact of the program. It is the procedures and their impact that should be emphasized to the media, not the trauma itself.

7. Follow-Up

Periodic follow-ups are undertaken with the school administrators, school staff, and mental health professionals. A formal final consultation and evaluation is provided several months after the suicide to facilitate a formal closure to the program. Our experience has shown that such consultations and reviews should be supportive in character (e.g., "What did we do?"; "What helped/didn't help?"; "What other things might we have considered?"). Aggressive and overly critical reviews (e.g., "Did you _____?" "Why did/didn't you do _____?") are of little help. A supportive approach from the first contact to follow-up is most helpful, although we should not eschew constructive feedback. Every attempt is made to let all concerned know that the postventionists are available on request for follow-up if the need arises. Obviously, debriefing is not the only aspect of these strategies, such a view is too limited, nor is it scientifically sound to evaluate the impact of suicide by, for example, a paper and pencil follow-up of one group, for example, students, of such endeavors.

It is, thus, obvious that work in postvention should last more than six sessions (of who knows what). To limit it to one session, such as debriefing, is even more absurd. . . .

REFERENCES

Abbey, K. J., Madsen, C. H., & Polland, R. (1989). Short-term suicide awareness curriculum. *Suicide and Life-Threatening Behavior, 19,* 216–227.

American Psychiatric Association. (1980). *Diagnostic and statistical manual of mental disorders* (3rd ed.). Washington, DC: Author.

American Psychiatric Association. (1987). *Diagnostic and statistical manual of mental disorders* (3rd ed., rev.). Washington, DC: Author.

Berman, A., & Jobes, D. (1991). *Adolescent suicide: Assessment and intervention.* Washington, DC: American Psychological Association.

Callahan, J. (1996). Negative effects of a school suicide postvention program: A case example. *Crisis, 17,* 108–115.

Caplan, G. (1964). *Principles of preventive psychiatry.* New York: Basic Books.

Centers for Disease Control (CDC). (1988). Recommendations for a community plan for the prevention and containment of suicide clusters. *MMWR, 37*(Suppl. No. S-6). Washington, DC: Author.

Ciffone, J. (1993). Suicide prevention. *Social Work, 38,* 197–203.

Diekstra, R. (1996). The epidemiology of suicide and parasuicide. *Archives of Suicide Research, 2,* 1–29.

Durlak, J. (1995). *School-based prevention programs for children and adolescents.* Thousand Oaks, CA: Sage.

Eddy, D. M., Wolpert, R. L., & Rosenberg, M. L. (1987). Estimating the effectiveness of interventions to prevent youth suicide. *Medical Care, 25*(12, Suppl.), S57–S65.

Eggert, L. L., Thompson, E. A., Herting, J. R., & Nicholas, L. J. (1995). Reducing suicide potential among high-risk youth. *Suicide and Life-Threatening Behavior, 25,* 276–296.

Eth, G., & Pynoos, R. (1985). *Post-traumatic stress disorder in children.* Washington, DC: American Psychiatric Press.

Farberow, N. (1967). Crisis, disaster, and suicide: Theory and therapy. In E. Shneidman (Ed.), *Essays in self-destruction* (pp. 373–398). New York: Science House.

Farberow, N. (Ed.). (1980). *The many faces of suicide.* New York: McGraw-Hill.

Figley, C. (Ed.). (1985). *Trauma and its wake.* New York: Brunner/Mazel.

Freud, S. (1974a). Inhibitions, symptoms and anxiety. In J. Strachey (Ed. and Trans.), *The standard edition of the complete psychological works of Sigmund Freud* (Vol. 20). London: Hogarth Press. (Original work published in 1926)

Freud, S. (1974b). Introductory lectures in psychoanalysis. In J. Strachey (Ed. and Trans.), *The standard edition of the complete psychological works of Sigmund Freud* (Vol. 16). London: Hogarth Press. (Original work published in 1917)

Freud, S. (1974c). Moses and monotheism. In J. Strachey (Ed. and Trans.), *The standard edition of the complete psychological works of Sigmund Freud* (Vol. 23). London: Hogarth Press. (Original work published in 1939)

Friedman, P. (Ed.). (1967). *On suicide.* New York: International University Press. (Original work published in 1910)

Garland, A., Shaffer, D., & Whittle, B. (1989). A national survey of school-based, adolescent suicide prevention programs. *Journal of the American Academy of Child and Adolescent Psychiatry, 28,* 931–934.

Gleser, G., Green, B., & Wignet, C. (1981). *Buffalo Creek revisited: Prolonged psychosocial effects of disaster.* New York: Simon & Schuster.

Glidewell, J., & Swallow, C. (1969). *The prevalence of maladjustment in elementary schools.* Chicago: University of Chicago Press.

Goldney, R., & Berman, A. (1996). Postvention in schools: Affective or effective? *Crisis, 17,* 98–99.

Goodstein, L. (1978). *Consulting with human service systems.* Menlo Park, CA: Addison-Wesley.

Hazell, P., & Lewin, T. (1993). An evaluation of postvention following adolescent suicide. *Suicide and Life-Threatening Behavior, 23,* 101–109.

Hoff, L. (1984). *People in crisis.* Menlo Park, CA: Addison-Wesley.

Hoff, L. (1990). Crisis intervention in schools. In A. Leenaars & S. Wenckstern (Eds.), *Suicide prevention in schools* (pp. 123–134). Washington, DC: Hemisphere.

Janoff-Bulman, R. (1985). The aftermath of victimization: Rebuilding shattered assumptions. In C. Figley (Ed.), *Trauma and its wake* (pp. 15–35). New York: Brunner/Mazel.

Johnson, W. (1985). Classroom discussion of suicide. *Contemporary Education, 56,* 114–117.

Kalafat, J., & Elias, M. (1994). An evaluation of a school-based suicide awareness intervention. *Suicide and Life-Threatening Behavior, 24,* 224–233.

Kalafat, J., & Gagliano, C. (1996). The use of simulations to assess the impact of an adolescent suicide response curriculum. *Suicide and Life-Threatening Behavior, 26,* 359–364.

Kazdin, A. (1990). Psychotherapy for children and adolescents. *Annual Review of Psychology, 41,* 21–54.

King, C. (1997). Suicidal behavior in adolescence. In R. Maris, M. Silverman, & S. Canetto (Eds.), *Review of suicidology* (pp. 61–95). New York: Guilford Press.

Leenaars, A. (1985). Suicide postvention in a school system. *Canada's Mental Health, 33,* 29–30.

Leenaars, A. (1991). Suicide notes and their implications for intervention. *Crisis, 12,* 1–20.

Leenaars, A. (1994). Crisis intervention with highly lethal people. *Death Studies, 18,* 341–360.

Leenaars, A. (1995). Clinical evaluation of suicide risk. *Japanese Journal of Psychiatry and Neurology, 49*(Suppl. 1), 561–568.

Leenaars, A. (2000, November). Helping your suicidal student. Workshop first presented January 1980 and numerous meetings. Windsor, Canada.

Leenaars, A. (2003, September). *Examples of effective public health strategies in suicide prevention.* Plenary presented at the International Association for Suicide Prevention Conference, Stockholm, Sweden.

Leenaars, A. (2004). *Psychotherapy with suicidal people.* Chichester: Wiley.

Leenaars, A., Maltsberger, J., & Neimeyer, R. (Eds.). (1994). *Treatment of suicidal people.* London: Taylor & Francis.

Leenaars, A., & Wenckstern, S. (Eds.). (1990a). *Suicide prevention in schools: Practical applications.* Washington, DC: Hemisphere.

Leenaars, A., & Wenckstern, S. (1990b). Post-traumatic stress disorder: A conceptual model for postvention. In A. Leenaars & S. Wenckstern (Eds.), *Suicide prevention in schools* (pp. 173–180). Washington, DC: Hemisphere.

Leenaars, A., & Wenckstern, S. (1994). Helping lethal suicidal adolescents. In D. Adams & E. Deveau (Eds.), *Threat to life, dying, death and bereavement: The child's perspective* (pp. 131–150). Amityville, NY: Baywood.

Leenaars, A., & Wenckstern, S. (1996). Postvention with elementary school children. In C. Corr & D. Corr (Eds.), *Handbook of childhood death and bereavement* (pp. 265–283). New York: Springer.

Leenaars, A., & Wenckstern, S. (1998). Principles of postvention: Applications to suicide and trauma in schools. *Death Studies, 22,* 357–391.

Leenaars, A., & Wenckstern, S. (1999). Suicide prevention in schools: The art, issues and pitfalls. *Crisis, 20,* 132–142.

Leenaars, A., & Wenckstern, S. (2000, November). Suicide postvention in schools: Practical applications. Workshop first presented December 1985 and numerous meetings. Windsor, Canada. Copyright, A. Leenaars & S. Wenckstern.

Leenaars, A., Wenckstern, S., Appleby, M., Fiske, H., Grad, O., Kalafat, J., et al. (2001). Current issues in dealing with suicide prevention in schools: Perspectives from some countries. *Journal of Educational and Psychological Consultation, 12,* 365–384.

Lester, D. (1992). State initiatives in addressing youth suicide. *Social Psychiatry and Psychiatric Epidemiology, 27,* 75–77.

Lester, D. (1993). *The cruelest death: The enigma of adolescent suicide.* Philadelphia: Charles Press.

Lifton, R. (1969). *Death in life.* New York: Vintage.

Lindemann, E. (1944). Symptomatology and management of acute grief. *American Journal of Psychiatry, 101,* 141–148.

Malley, P. B., Kush, F., & Bogo, R. J. (1994). School-based adolescent suicide prevention and intervention programs. *School Counselor, 42,* 130–136.

Maltsberger, J. (1994). Calculated risk taking. In A. Leenaars, J. Maltsberger, & R. Neimeyer (Eds.), *Treatment of suicidal people* (pp. 195–205). Washington, DC: Taylor & Francis.

Maris, R., Berman, A., Maltsberger, J., & Yufit, R. (1992). *Assessment and prediction of suicide*. New York: Guilford Press.

Martin, G. (1998). Media influence to suicide: The search for solutions. *Archives of Suicide Research, 4,* 51–66.

Miller, D. N., Eckert, T. L., DuPaul, G. J., & White, G. P. (1999). Adolescent suicide prevention. *Suicide and Life-Threatening Behavior, 29,* 72–85.

Nelson, F. L. (1987). Evaluation of a youth suicide prevention school program. *Adolescence, 88,* 813–825.

Orbach, I., & Bar-Joseph, H. (1993). The impact of a suicide prevention program for adolescents on suicidal tendencies, hopelessness, ego identity, and coping. *Suicide and Life-Threatening Behavior, 23,* 120–129.

Overholser, J. C., Hemstreet, A. H., Spirito, A., & Vyse, S. (1989). Suicide awareness programs in the schools. *Journal of the American Academy of Child and Adolescent Psychiatry, 28,* 925–930.

Parad, H. (Ed.). (1965). *Crisis intervention.* New York: Family Service Association.

Pfeffer, C. (1986). *The suicidal child.* New York: Guilford Press.

Randell, B., Eggert, L., & Pike, K. (2001). Immediate post intervention effects of two brief youth suicide prevention interventions. *Suicide and Life-Threatening Behavior, 31,* 41–61.

Richman, J. (1990). Family therapy with suicidal children. In A. Leenaars & S. Wenckstern (Eds.), *Suicide prevention in schools* (pp. 159–170). Washington, DC: Hemisphere.

Shaffer, D., Garland, A., Gould, M., Fisher, P., & Trautman, P. (1988). Preventing teenage suicide. *Journal of the American Academy of Child and Adolescent Psychiatry, 27,* 675–687.

Shaffer, D., Garland, A., Vieland, V., Underwood, M., & Busner, C. (1991). The impact of curriculum-based suicide prevention program for teenagers. *Journal of the American Academy of Child and Adolescent Psychiatry, 30,* 588–596.

Shaffer, D., Vieland, V., Garland, A., Rojas, M., Underwood, M., & Busner, C. (1990). Adolescent suicide attempters. *Journal of the American Medical Association, 264,* 3151–3155.

Shneidman, E. (1973). *Suicide* (Vol. 21, pp. 383–385). Chicago: Encyclopedia Britannica.

Shneidman, E. (1980). *Suicide thoughts and reflections.* New York: Human Science Press.

Shneidman, E. (1981). Postvention: The care for the bereaved. In E. Shneidman (Ed.), *Suicide thoughts and reflections* (pp. 157–167). New York: Human Sciences Press.

Shneidman, E. (1985). *Definition of suicide.* New York: John Wiley & Sons.

Spirito, A., Overholser, J., Ashworth, S., Morgan, J., & Benedict-Drew, T. (1988). Evaluation of a suicide awareness curriculum for high school students. *Journal of the American Academy of Child and Adolescent Psychiatry, 27,* 705–711.

Terr, L. (1979). Children of Chonchilla: Study of psychic trauma. *Psychoanalytic Study of the Child, 34,* 547–623.

Watzlawick, P., Beavin, J., & Jackson, D. (1967). *Pragmatics of human communication.* New York: Norton.

Wenckstern, S., & Leenaars, A. (1990). Suicide postvention in a secondary school. In A. Leenaars & S. Wenckstern (Eds.), *Suicide prevention in schools* (pp. 181–195). Washington, DC: Hemisphere.

Wenckstern, S., & Leenaars, A. (1993). Trauma and suicide in schools. *Death Studies, 17,* 253–266.

Wenckstern, S., & Leenaars, A. (1998). Suicide postvention: Cultural issues. In A. Leenaars, S. Wenckstern, I. Sakinofsky, R. Dyck, M. Kral, & R. Bland (Eds.), *Suicide in Canada* (pp. 309–321). Toronto: University of Toronto Press.

Wilson, J., Smith, W., & Johnson, S. (1985). A comparative analysis of PTSD among various survivor groups. In C. Figley (Ed.), *Trauma and its wake* (pp. 142–173). New York: Brunner/Mazel.

World Health Organization. (2002). *World report on violence and health.* Geneva: Author.

Zenere, F. J., & Lazarus, P. J. (1997). The decline of youth suicidal behavior in an urban, multicultural public school system following the introduction of a suicide prevention and intervention program. *Suicide and Life-Threatening Behavior, 27,* 387–403.

CHAPTER 17

Helping College Students Cope with Suicidal Impulses

Morton M. Silverman

Since the 1990s, campus student suicides have aroused much public interest and concern because the act itself is perceived to be a rejection of all that university life strives to be for bright and ambitious young adults. Campus student suicides also raise questions about how truly ideal and idyllic campus communities are and to what extent they really differ from the general society as a whole. These events raise questions about the comprehensive missions of institutions of higher education, the extent to which campuses are harbingers of more general societal problems, and the degree to which campuses are expected to function *in loco parentis* (Silverman, 1993).

There is no more painful disruption of the rhythm of campus life than that of a student suicide. Such an event brings to a halt the daily patterns of teaching, research, and scholarship that define university life, as well as bringing into question individual concerns about vulnerability, safety, security, and destiny. Hence, from a community perspective, student suicides engender questions of prevention, protection, and promotion that have relevance to similar settings where large numbers of late adolescents and young adults are found on a daily basis (e.g., high schools, summer camps, military bases, military deployment locations).

Despite the apparent significance of this cause of death for this age range, suicide on campuses remains a very poorly understood phenomenon, shrouded by inconsistent findings derived from noncomparable studies. With approximately 14 million students currently enrolled in American colleges and universities, this problem deserves careful review because it may well shed light on ways and means of approaching the problems of young adult suicides in other contexts and communities. As relatively well-defined institutions and environmental settings, campuses are natural laboratories for the introduction of testable hypotheses about disease prevention and health promotion.

College students (predominantly 17 to 23 years old) and graduate students (mainly 24 to 34 years old) remain a neglected population in terms of accurate epidemiological health surveys (Patrick, Grace, & Lovato, 1992). Suicide prevention programming that addresses specific risk factors is lacking for these two groups in part because they straddle the conventional reporting categories (15 to 19, 20 to 24, 25 to 29, etc.) traditionally used to identify behavioral health risk factors. The early survey studies of Schwartz and Reifler (1980, 1988) were unable to answer many of the epidemiological questions associated with completed suicide in this population, leaving unaddressed the identification of modifiable risk factors (Silverman, 1993).

Although there is a growing literature on the factors (psychological, biological, sociocultural, and environmental) that might contribute to suicidal behaviors and completions among college and university students, public attention has mainly focused on the rates themselves (Silverman, 1993; Silverman, Meyer, Sloane, Raffel, & Pratt, 1997). The inquiries generated by campus officials and professionals always begin with concerns about how many and how often. The literature on parasuicidal behaviors (threats, gestures, attempts, failed completions) in young adults is large and diverse, yet any serious attempt to synthesize the findings is marred by major inconsistencies in definitions, methodologies, and reporting techniques (Berman & Jobes, 1991; Maris, Berman, Maltsberger, & Yufit, 1992; O'Carroll et al., 1996; Silverman, 1993). Before a campus can develop effective preventive intervention programming to address the critical factors linked to the range of suicidal behaviors, the basic questions of "how many" and "how often" must first be answered.

SUICIDE RATES

The Big Ten Student Suicide Study was undertaken from 1980 to 1990 to determine the suicide rates on Big Ten university campuses (Silverman et al., 1997). This longitudinal, multisite study reports on the largest number of campus student suicides in a single continuous study (10 years inclusive), using standardized data collection instruments, homogeneous campuses, comparable student populations, and monitoring for the critical variables of age, gender, race, country of origin, academic class status, method of suicide, time of suicide, and history of prior contact with campus mental health facilities. This study was the most comprehensive attempt to report on the incidence of suicides in undergraduate and graduate school populations by age, gender, and race.

The study design attempted to address many of the statistical and epidemiological flaws identified in previous studies of campus student suicides (Silverman, 1993). The 10-year study collected demographic and correlational data on 261 suicides of registered students at 12 midwestern campuses. The largest number of suicides for both males and females was in the 20- to 24-year-old age group (46%) and among graduate students (32%). The overall student suicide rate of 7.5 per 100,000 was one-half of the computed national suicide rate (15.0 per 100,000) for a matched sample by age, gender, and race. Despite the overall lower suicide rate, the analyses revealed that students 25 and over (regardless of their student class status) have a significantly higher risk than younger students. Although women have rates roughly half those of men throughout their undergraduate years, graduate women have rates not significantly different from their male counterparts (graduate women 9.1 per 100,000 and graduate men 11.6 per 100,000), raising concerns about older female graduate students who may be out of synch with their classmates.

The age range of 17 to 19 years of age accounted for 31% of the females and 25% of the males on campus, whereas this age range comprised only 9% of the female suicides and 14% of the male suicides, respectively. The 20- to 24-year-olds accounted for 48% of the females and 50% of the males on campus, as well as 49% of the female suicides and 45% of the male suicides. However, for the age range of 25 to 29 years, the respective numbers were 10% of the females and 14% of the males on campus, corresponding to 22% of the female suicides and 23% of the male suicides. In fact, 39% of all female suicides occurred among graduate students, who comprised only 19% of female students overall.

The study suggested that there is, in fact, a higher suicide rate (compared to national rates) in those female students who are in their mid to late 20s and older, compared to those female students who would normally be pursuing undergraduate degrees (ages 18 to 23). The data suggested that, for females, the suicide rate is below the national rates during the first two years of college life, about even during the junior and senior years, and above the national rates during the graduate school years. It appears as though there is a continuous transition toward increased suicidal behavior as female students grow older. This surely suggests that university counseling services and other student support services should target the graduate student female population as one where the risk for suicide is higher than in the normative undergraduate population, as well as the older female student who may be returning to campus to pursue undergraduate or graduate studies later in her life.

Although suicide probably is a low base rate phenomenon on college and university campuses, current surveys suggest that suicidal ideation and life-threatening behaviors may be more common.

SUICIDAL IDEATION

Suicidal ideation in college-age students is not uncommon. In 1995, the Centers for Disease Control and Prevention (CDC) conducted the first-ever National College Health Risk Behavior Survey (NCHRBS) among 5,000 college students (CDC, 1997). They found that 11.4% (11.8% females; 10.9% males) reported having seriously considered attempting suicide during the 12 months preceding the survey, and 7.9% (7.5% female; 8.2% male) had made a suicide plan.

Five years later, the American College Health Association (ACHA) conducted the Spring 2000 National College Health Assessment (NCHA), which, along with other health indicators, measured depression, suicidal ideation, and suicide attempts among 15,977 college students on 28 campuses (ACHA, 2001). Its findings were comparable to the CDC's NCHRBS conducted in 1995, finding that 9.5% had seriously considered suicide within the past school year (Kisch, Leino, & Silverman, in press).

In 2001, the CDC conducted its biennial Youth Risk Behavior Survey (YRBS) among a representative national sample of high school students, grades 9 to 12. The students reported that 19% had seriously considered attempting suicide during the 12 months preceding the survey and

14.8% had made a suicide plan. Among 12th graders, 16.4% (18.9% female; 11.4% male) reported seriously considering attempting suicide and 12.2% making a suicide plan. Among 11th graders, 18.9% reported seriously considering attempting suicide, and 15.2% reported making a suicide plan (CDC, 2002). Undoubtedly, a number of these students currently are enrolled at two-year and four-year colleges.

Hence, suicidal ideation in adolescence and young adulthood is not reported as being so unusual. It is easy to dismiss the presence of ideation as being "within normal limits" and not psychopathological or pathognomonic of more serious underlying psychological or emotional disturbance. If understood as a static or chronic state, we might choose to dismiss its presence as a true harbinger of future problems because only approximately 1.4% of the general population dies by suicide per year. I would strongly caution against such perspectives.

Suicidal ideation is one of only nine criteria used to arrive at the diagnosis of major depressive episode (American Psychiatric Association, 1994). Suicidal ideation is not an uncommon symptom or consequence and is found in other major psychiatric disorders, including substance abuse, schizophrenia, bipolar illness, social phobia, and borderline personality disorder.

The main concern needs to be in understanding the context in which the ideation occurs. The who, what, when, where, why, and how of the circumstances that engendered the ideation are critically important to know and explore. For example: Who was present? What was said? What happened? When did it start? Where were you when the thought occurred? Why now? How did you deal with it? Did you act on it? Would you act on it next time? Was it associated with other injury risk behaviors? (Barrios, Everett, Simon, & Brener, 2000). In addition, it is important to know about the character of the ideation: Was it serious? Pervasive? Fleeting? Disturbing? Distressing? Comforting? Relieving? Familiar? Logical? Paranoid? Also, it is very helpful to inquire about the progression of the idea: Did it go from a thought to a wish, desire, or intent? Did it go from a thought to a plan? Is it an idea that is still in the retrievable background (for now or for the future)?

One approach to responding to and managing suicidal ideation is to address the underlying etiological factors: affective disorder, substance

abuse, poor social skills, poor problem-solving skills, personality disturbance, and so on. An additional approach is to teach the appropriate
skills and perspectives to prevent these thoughts from emerging at times
when the student is not psychologically, cognitively, or emotionally prepared to manage them safely.

SUICIDE ATTEMPTS

In 1995, 1.7% of college students (ages 18 to 24 years) reported attempting suicide one or more times during the 12 months preceding the CDC
survey. Of note is that only 0.4% reported that the suicide attempt required medical attention. One interpretation is that the reported suicide
attempts are not life threatening because the majority did not require
medical attention. However, it is also possible that these were serious attempts that were deliberately not brought to medical attention for fear of
hospitalization, notification to parents or school officials, expulsion
from school, or medical leave from college (CDC, 1997; Brener, Hassan,
& Barrios, 1999).

The ACHA survey found that 1.5% of college students surveyed had
attempted suicide within the past school year. Among those who reported
a suicide attempt, 0.5% reported suicide attempts on three or more occasions (ACHA, 2001). In 2001, 8.8% of high school students reported attempting suicide one or more times during the 12 months preceding the
survey (11.2% female; 6.2% male). Among 12th graders, 5.5% (6.5%
female; 4.4% male) reported a suicide attempt one or more times during
the preceding 12 months. For 11th graders, it was 8.3%. Only 1.6% reported that the suicide attempt required medical attention (CDC, 2002).

A recent study by Hawton, Zahl, and Weatherall (2003) investigated
the risk of suicide after a documented episode of deliberate self-harm.
The risk of suicide in the first year of follow-up for all the patients studied was 0.7%, which was 66 times the annual risk of suicide in the general population. The risk after five years was 1.7%, 2.4% at 10 years,
and 3.0% at 15 years. Of note is that for all the 10- to 24-year-olds in the
study, the risk of suicide in the first year after an episode of deliberate
self-harm was 0.3%, 0.7% at 5 years, 1.3% at 10 years (2.5% for males
ages 10 to 24 years), and 1.8% at 15 years (3.2% for males ages 10 to 24

years). They conclude that reduction in the risk of suicide following deliberate self-harm must be a key element in national suicide prevention strategies.

As with suicidal ideation, it is essential to understand the context of the attempt to better understand its intent (and the likelihood of lethality). For example: Was the attempt designed to end the individual's life? Was it a cry for help? Was it instrumental in nature (a behavior to accomplish some specific end that was not intended to be self-destructive/lethal)? Did the attempt involve lethal methods? Does the individual have knowledge of lethal means—amounts, dosages, accessibility, time frames, and so on? Is there a pattern to the behavior?

OTHER SELF-INJURIOUS BEHAVIORS

Not all self-injurious behaviors are self-destructive or intended to be self-destructive (although they may, by accident or miscalculation, have that result). Suicidologists have struggled for years with classifying behaviors such as chronic alcohol abuse, eating disorders (anorexia), and tobacco use as being self-destructive because the public has a fairly good understanding that such behaviors have a high likelihood of early morbidity and mortality. In addition, other risk-taking behaviors might include bungee jumping, freestyle rock climbing, driving without a seatbelt, driving while under the influence of alcohol, and not wearing a helmet while riding a motorcycle. These have a slightly different character to them, albeit also with a potential death wish flavor to them. In between these two sets of behaviors, we might put unprotected sexual activity, cutting, homemade tattoos, sexual promiscuity, and illicit drug experimentation. These behaviors are not perceived to be imminently lethal (having instead unforeseen long-term health risks), although some of them can be acutely lethal if miscalculations are made.

Most observers of these behaviors (commonly seen in the late adolescent and young adult populations) believe that they reach the plateau of being suicidal only if and when there is an explicit or strongly implicit presence of an intention to die. Nevertheless, some of these behaviors may be comorbid in suicidal individuals or may be the early warning signs of future, more self-destructive behaviors. For sure, such indicators need to be understood and put into an appropriate developmental framework.

STRESS

Over 40 years ago, some researchers speculated that college campuses provide opportunities for the development and exacerbation of stress disorders, including suicidal behaviors that are consequences of perceived or real stress (Seiden, 1966). These researchers suggest that parental pressures to succeed and economic pressures to successfully complete a course of education and training in shorter periods of time may contribute to increased stress.

You might argue that most undergraduates are, for the most part, under little stress and pressure to provide for their own daily needs. Even if they are being supported by student loans, they often perceive the day of reckoning as so far off in the future as not to be immediately important. We would predict, then, that the pressures would begin to increase for juniors and seniors, for they see that the decisions they have made and are making, the grades they receive, and the relationships they enter are going to carry over into what follows their college experience. They are beginning to adopt a work-world mentality and adapt to a mature role.

Depending on the relative level of financial support awarded to an entering graduate student, this sequence of mounting pressures might not become significant until the later years of graduate study. However, graduate students are trying not only to carry on an adult life (perhaps with a significant relationship, children, or responsibilities for their parents) but also to learn and carry on an academic life. Those who experience a setback in an important relationship or in their student work are more likely to be weighed down by the consequences that the setback will have for current and future relationships and work. For the younger student, there are always new opportunities, new relationships to be found. This may remain true for the older student, but that is not the way it is often perceived. As a consequence, we would expect a differential in the way younger and older students approach setbacks, face realities, and select ways of responding and coping.

As students age, they may well perceive the college (and university) experiences differently and hence respond to the challenges and stresses by using different strategies and coping mechanisms. Even if all the resources that are traditionally available on university campuses remain constant for all students, older students may access them differently, if at all. This suggests that universities might well consider developing new and targeted intervention programs for older students—both at the undergraduate and graduate level.

Attention should be paid to the older returning undergraduate and graduate students who must make major life transitions and accommodations in order to return to university life in pursuit of education and training. For them, returning to school appears to be a major life stressor. The financial and personal investment in their future, coupled with the sacrifices made to reenter this environment, may place them at increased risk for subsequent suicidal behavior.

PROTECTIVE FACTORS

A discussion of risk factors associated with suicidal behaviors appears elsewhere in this book. While risk factors and even warning signs are often known and shared with the public, protective factors are not as appreciated. Why are suicide rates on college campuses, for the most part, less than the comparable national figures matched for age and sex?

College campuses provide more readily available student support services, including easy (and low cost) access to health services and mental health services. In addition, college campuses provide a more supportive peer and mentor environment than can be easily and safely found in the general community. We cannot dismiss the importance of peer support, peer companionship and compatibility, and ready availability and accessibility of numerous student support services and personnel on most American campuses. The range of support includes coaches, professors, residential advisors and staff, career and placement experts, university health service professionals, student guidance counselors, educational skills counselors, campus ministries, clinical therapists, nurses, wellness counselors, physicians, clinical psychologists, social workers, student activities professionals, deans of students, and other administrators whose careers are devoted to nurturing healthy minds and healthy bodies. Similar personnel and environments are not so readily available to young adults in settings outside academia.

However, this raises a theoretical question about the possible halo effect associated with being an active participant in the ecology of campus life. What might be the protective benefits of being exposed on a daily basis to the ambience of a campus environment? How long does the halo last? What might be the essential ingredients that comprise the halo? Is it an interactive process between able participant and receptive environment? These and other related issues deserve further thought and research.

A decrease in the overall suicide rate among university students may be due to the general campus prohibitions on the availability and use of firearms, the careful monitoring and control for the abuse of alcohol, the state prohibition on the possession and use of illicit drugs, the clear message of the purpose of a college and graduate school education (i.e., the advancement of an individual's career, the enhancement of skills and knowledge, and the opportunities for personal growth and development), and the relative degree of protection from the hassles of day-to-day life that may occur in nonacademic settings. Promoting healthy behaviors and protecting students from health risks are some of the preventive interventions that we can offer to college students.

THE ROLE OF GATEKEEPERS

On a college campus, there are a plethora of gatekeepers who have daily contact with students, including faculty, academic tutors, academic advisors, deans of students, student affairs staff, coaches, trainers, dining staff, residential hall staff, campus ministers, bus drivers, police and campus security staff, and fraternity and sorority advisors.

These individuals are usually adept at recognizing and discerning inappropriate demeanors and behaviors in college students. For the most part, these individuals have spent their working lives in and around the college campus environment and often have a very sophisticated set of criteria to determine when a student may be displaying unusual behavior or expressing ideas and desires that are not within the norm. The majority of students on campus are in touch with a number of these individuals on a daily basis. Hence, it makes sense to turn to these individuals to provide initial assessment and intervention for students who may be in the early phases of distress. It also seems appropriate to include parents as potential allies in being observers and significant others to monitor the health and welfare of students on campus. Furthermore, students themselves can be taught to be good observers and interveners, and they can learn how to be friends and caretakers for their friends and peers.

Gatekeepers can play important roles in the early identification of potential risk behaviors and individuals at risk. Publicizing risk factors, warning signs, and protective factors for major psychiatric disorders (including anxiety, depression, eating disturbances, and substance abuse), violence, aggression, and self-destructive behaviors can serve to raise awareness and educate the campus. Knowing some of the common signals of distress contributes to a supportive and caring environment. Teaching basic skills in approaching distressed students can help individuals feel more in control of situations that may arise as well as assist in addressing disruptive behaviors and patterns. These intervention skills and guidelines include:

- Assessing safety and danger
- Remaining calm, supportive, and interested
- Avoiding escalation by being nonconfrontational and not intimidating (or humiliating)
- Asking direct questions
- Remaining objective and nonjudgmental
- Knowing your limits

The final piece—referral techniques, skills, and knowledge—is critical to ensuring that the distressed student receive appropriate clinical assessment. Gatekeepers need to know under what circumstances and how to convey concern to a student that a referral is needed (and should be acted on). In general, students should be referred for professional counseling if and when their problems have compromised their ability to function academically, personally, or socially, or to find and take pleasure in life. Gatekeepers need to know available emergency resources; how to access these resources; how to make contact with on-call administrators and clinicians; the location of clinics, hospitals, and emergency rooms (and hours of availability); and what arrangements are available to get students to these locations. Systems need to be developed to provide feedback to gatekeepers to ensure that they maintain their skills and judgment.

ASSESSMENT, INTERVENTION, AND TREATMENT

In the 1990s, there were major advances in the assessment, treatment, and management of psychological disturbances and psychiatric disorders in adolescents. Consequently, it is fair to say that more students are currently attending colleges today who, 20 years ago, might not have been able to manage the stresses and strains of college life because their underlying psychopathology and/or learning disorders were not under sufficient control to allow them to function as students. As discussed by Jobes (2000), a number of theorists and clinical researchers have increasingly examined multiple cognitive, behavioral, and affective underpinnings of suicidal states, asking important research questions with clear implications for clinical practice. Over the past decade, we have seen an increasing emphasis on the phenomenology of suicide. What do suicidal individuals feel, think, and ultimately respond to when they get psychologically stuck in a state of acute crisis? How and when does suicidal thinking cognitively break down? How do people get trapped in psychological spaces where their need for escape becomes overwhelming?

Clinical Assessment

The assessment of a student who presents with suicidal ideation, suicidal impulses, a history of a current/past suicide attempt, or other self-injurious behaviors (e.g., cutting or risk-taking behaviors) must first document risk factors, warning signs, and protective factors. Such an assessment must include a full biopsychosocial investigation. The paradigm that seems to be most inclusive is that of the five axes of the *DSM-IV* (American Psychiatric Association, 1994). The assessment entails exploring the categories on all five axes. Axis I covers signs and symptoms of the major psychiatric disorders and dysfunctions, including those with the highest association to life-threatening behaviors (i.e., schizophrenia, major depressive disorder, bipolar disorder, substance use and abuse, and anxiety disorders).

Axis II includes the personality disorders (especially borderline personality disorder, which is associated with self-destructive behaviors).

Axis III includes other medical disorders (especially chronic pain syndromes and other central nervous system disorders associated with suicidal behaviors). Axis IV includes current environmental and life stressors, such as interpersonal problems, financial problems, and adjustment problems. Axis V is an overall (global) assessment of functioning that ranks individuals along a continuum from fully functional to those requiring hospitalization.

As part of the assessment process, ask a series of questions that specifically address suicidal ideation, intent, planning, and access to means. Other questions should address risk factors, warning signs, protective factors, and health promotion factors. Many such inventories exist, and no one set of questions is necessarily more comprehensive or diagnostic than another. However, it is necessary to be sure that the clinician is able to satisfy his or her concerns about and make a full assessment of the student's:

1. Reasons for living

2. Reasons for dying

3. Sense of hope

4. Sense of a future

5. Circumstances that led to prior self-destructive thoughts and behaviors

6. Likelihood that past circumstances will not repeat themselves in the present (or future), by noting the similarities or differences between the current situation and past situations that involved self-destructive behaviors

7. Capacities/capabilities to influence the current situation in a positive, health-protective manner

8. Reasons for being a student at this time

9. Judgment and insight into current and/or chronic problems

10. Likelihood of the development of a therapeutic relationship and present evidence of mutual trust and respect

11. Involvement with alcohol and other drug use or abuse that can alter cognitive functioning (reality testing, information processing, judgment)

12. Imminent versus chronic risk for self-destructive thoughts and behaviors

13. Presence of support network and its level of involvement acutely and ongoing

14. Prior exposure to suicidal behavior (family, friends, etc.)

15. Social skills (ability to ask for/seek help: peer pressure resistance)

16. Cognitive skills (problem solving)

17. Current and past use or abuse of over-the-counter and prescription medications

18. Clinical judgment as to relative risk for ongoing and future suicidal behaviors

19. History of impulsivity/aggression

20. Sleep patterns and sleep hygiene

21. Past and present acting-out behaviors—sexual promiscuity, binge drinking, binge eating/purging

22. Instrumental messages related to past/current suicidal behaviors

23. Psychological messages of past/current suicidal behaviors

24. Interpersonal messages of past/current suicidal behaviors

25. Support networks—family (parents, siblings, others), friends, significant others, religious, athletic, and so on

26. Modifiable versus nonmodifiable risk factors

In addition, emphasize on the quality of the interaction (level of cooperation/anger/confrontational style; eye contact; verbal interchange; ability to track the dialogue; level of distress/anxiety; appearance).

Crisis Intervention

There is only one goal of crisis intervention: The patient must remain physically safe and alive until the crisis situation has resolved. Therefore, extraordinary means of maintaining safety and stability are sometimes necessary, including voluntary or even involuntary inpatient hospitalization. Various authors have discussed at length the range of responses that make up what we generally associate with crisis intervention with suicidal youth (Berman & Jobes, 1991; Jobes & Berman, 1991). For example, these responses typically include protection from self-harm using the following types of crisis interventions:

- Restricting access to means of death
- Decreasing the patient's interpersonal isolation
- Removing or decreasing agitation, anxiety, sleep loss
- Structuring the treatment (e.g., increasing number of sessions)
- Working on problem-solving skills
- Providing accessibility and availability to patient
- Creating future linkages
- Negotiating the maintenance of safety and the development of a contingency plan
- Use of inpatient hospitalization in cases of clear and imminent suicide risk (Cimbolic & Jobes, 1990; Jobes & Berman, 1993).

Often, the acute suicidal crisis is produced by a unique synergy of intrapersonal, environmental, social, and situational variables. Because young adults may respond to life crises with suicidal behaviors, clinicians must be prepared to face the immediate tasks of assessing possible and imminent self-harm behavior while concurrently protecting against that possibility. These tasks must often be accomplished under conditions of incongruent expectations and goals. Suicidal people tend to defy the health professional's expectation that fostering and maintaining life is a shared goal of patient and doctor (Hoff, 1984). Suicidal individuals, especially adolescents and young adults, are invariably brought to treatment by others under conditions of acute distress. Thus, working with depressed and suicidal people can be a frightening and difficult undertaking. Indeed, the assessment, treatment, and general management of an acute suicidal crisis are among the most difficult challenges faced by any mental health professional, despite attempted suicide being one of the most frequently encountered of all mental health emergencies (Roberts, 1991).

Consistent with the commonly accepted definition of *crisis* (e.g., Slaikeu, 1990) is the notion that acute emotional upset, dysphoria, and the associated sense of urgency to act in a self-destructive and potentially life-ending way will usually subside with adequate time and protective constraints (e.g., hospitalization in cases of imminent danger). Underlying skill deficits in emotion regulation, distress tolerance, interpersonal dysfunction, impulsivity, problem distress tolerance, interpersonal dysfunction, impulsivity, problem solving, and related cognitive distortion and rigidity typically do not spontaneously remit. These issues and deficits usually require appropriate clinical intervention and targeted care (e.g., Rudd & Joiner, 1998).

It is well established that suicidal impulses and behaviors are largely temporal, transient, and situation-specific. Suicide intent is state dependent and tends to wax and wane. Empirical research indicates that most people who kill themselves give some form of prior warning and often desire an outcome other than the termination of their biological existence (Shneidman, 1993). The crisis clinician is thus in a pivotal, potentially life-saving, position. Accurate clinical risk assessment and appropriate interventions can literally make a life-or-death difference.

As described by Roberts (1991), clinicians may effectively respond to an individual in crisis by working through seven stages of intervention:

1. Assessing lethality and safety needs
2. Establishing rapport and communication
3. Identifying the major problems
4. Dealing with feelings and providing support
5. Exploring possible alternatives
6. Formulating an action plan
7. Providing follow-up.

Roberts' seven-stage model was developed to apply broadly to a range of crises, but it is clearly applicable to specific interventions with suicidal young adults.

Training in suicidal crisis intervention and specific systems of crisis intervention has become increasingly popular in North America. For example, suicidologists in Calgary (Canada) have developed a very popular community gatekeeper training called Applied Suicide Intervention Skills Training (ASIST) (www.livingworks.ne). This particular crisis intervention approach is taught in intensive training workshops emphasizing role playing among ordinary community gatekeepers who may be uniquely positioned to intervene with a suicidal person (e.g., ministers, priests, or rabbis; police officers; or school personnel). Similarly, Paul Quinnett has developed the question, persuade, and refer (QPR) approach, which is designed to train community gatekeepers to help someone in a suicidal crisis using action steps (www.qprinstitute.com).

Principles of Treatment

Treatment is predicated on the clinical assessment and diagnosis of past and current problems or concerns. Nevertheless, independent of diagnoses, certain key elements need to be in place for treatment to be possible:

1. Mutual trust, respect, and honesty
2. Potential for the development of a common language/vocabulary
3. Clear expectations/understanding of acceptable behavior
4. Identification and transmission of multiple emergency contacts and protocols/procedures for emergency situations
5. Agreed on goals/outcomes
6. Agreed on understanding of obstacles, barriers, challenges to improvement/change
7. Frank discussion of past, current, and future clinical status—with an emphasis on undertreated and untreated conditions
8. Understood role of medications/psychological treatment/support/cognitive-behavior therapy
9. Current and future roles, functions, involvement of key players and significant others—friends, roommate(s), coaches, campus ministers, faculty, residential staff, academic staff, parents, friends, student health physicians, and so on
10. Skills to assess and manage impulsive thoughts and behaviors as well as aggressive tendencies
11. Potential for management of anxiety
12. Need for moderation (ideally, abstinence) of alcohol use
13. Abstinence from illicit drug use (especially marijuana, cocaine, heroin, LSD, and other mood-altering and hallucinogenic drugs)

14. Communicating side effects of prescription medications, especially in combination with any prescribed psychotropic medications

15. Management of sleep hygiene

16. Management of eating behaviors (diet, nutrition)

17. Management of exercise

18. Assessment of concentration and ability to focus as a student

19. Availability of options and feelings/concerns about medications, hospitalization, leave of absence, resources at home.

Treatment Strategies

A number of studies are now emerging that elucidate the psychology of suicide and suicidal behaviors, particularly in terms of hopelessness, the absence of future thinking, the lack of problem-solving skills, the tendency toward impulsivity, and the presence of psychological pain (Berman, Jobes, & Silverman, in press). These larger conceptual constructs are not necessarily diagnosis-specific (Jobes, 2003b; Henriques, Beck, & Brown, 2003; Salkovskis, 2001) and are suggesting new directions in clinical practice (Jobes, 2000, 2003a).

At the core of virtually every suicidal struggle is an intense need for escape and relief from psychological pain and suffering. At the center of many suicidal states is a fundamental relational struggle related to the presence or absence of certain key relationships and how those relationships are perceived by the suicidal individual. Jobes (2003b) believes that, increasingly, suicidal teens need contemporary asylum that may be better found in a well-formed and carefully monitored *outpatient* therapeutic alliance. Clearly, there are different kinds of suicidal young adults; a one-size treatment does not fit all (Rogers & Soyka, 2004). Suicidal teenagers often need a full range of interventions—psychotherapy, medication, engagement of peers, even spiritual and existential consideration. But more tailored and individualized interventions cannot be applied until we become more sophisticated about assessing, understanding, and conceptualizing different kinds of suicidal states.

Evidence-based research in the provision of mental health care has consistently shown that a combination of psychotherapy and medication is more efficacious than either approach by itself. Most suicidal patients can directly benefit from good psychotherapy that specifically helps them problem solve, cope, and develop a thicker and more resilient psychological skin.

Rudd, Joiner, Jobes, and King (1999) have pointed out that practice guidelines have emerged to direct the very nature of care provided and that directly affect the clinician's day-to-day work. Despite considerable disagreement as to their appropriateness, scientific foundation, and clinical utility, guidelines continue to emerge and will probably persist. Recently, the American Academy of Child and Adolescent Psychiatry released a "Practice Parameter for the Assessment and Treatment of Children and Adolescents with Suicidal Behavior" (Shaffer & Pfeffer, 2001), and the American Psychiatric Association (2003) has published "Practice Guidelines for the Assessment and Treatment of Patients with Suicidal Behaviors." Although not claiming to be authoritative, both documents have become must reading for those actively engaged in working with suicidal patients across the lifespan.

Rudd et al. (1999) have observed that:

> Changes in the nature of the psychotherapy delivery system have been particularly challenging for those clinicians treating suicidal patients. Others have documented the negative impact of managed care on the overall sense of well-being and satisfaction experienced by practitioners in today's mental health marketplace (Hersch, 1995; Sherman & Thelen, 1998). This problem is compounded by the complexity of clinical and practical demands presented by suicidal patients. With considerable restrictions in access to inpatient care or long-term psychotherapy, those clinicians and treatment centers that provide outpatient services to suicidal patients are left with no proven treatment alternatives (e.g., Maltsberger, 1993, 1994; Rudd & Joiner, 1998). (p. 438)

EMPIRICAL STUDIES OF TREATMENT

Much of the limited suicide treatment literature is not specific to the late adolescent and young adult suicidal patient. Indeed, outpatient treatment studies that target depressed adolescents generally exclude adolescents with suicidal behaviors (e.g., Kroll, Harrington, Jayson, Fraser, & Gowers, 1996; Wood, Harrington, & Moore, 1996). One clear exception to the tendency to exclude suicidal adolescents is Brent et al.'s (1997) comparison of individual cognitive-behavior therapy (CBT), systemic behavior family therapy (SBFT), and individual nondirective supportive therapy (NST) on adolescents' depressive symptoms, suicidality, and functional impairment. Results from their study indicated that CBT was more efficacious than SBFT or NST at reducing depression during the acute phase of treatment, although all three conditions showed significant reductions in suicidality and functional impairment. However, only 31% of the study participants had suicidal features, thus limiting the generalizability of these findings (Rathus & Miller, 2002).

There has been a great deal of focus on the *lack* of research in the treatment of suicidality (Hawton et al., 1998; Linehan, 1997; Rudd et al., 1999). For example, Linehan (1997) scrutinized all investigations that have included randomized clinical trials (RCTs) of psychosocial and behavioral interventions for treatment of suicidal behaviors (adults and adolescents). Remarkably, only 20 studies were found in the extant literature that randomly assigned individuals to treatment conditions (i.e., experimental treatment groups, treatment-as-usual groups, and control groups). Four of the 20 studies showed a significant effect for psychosocial interventions and another for pharmacotherapy. Prominent among the findings was that the psychosocial interventions were most effective with those at high risk for suicidal behaviors. Linehan concluded, however, that despite these results, it is still unclear how we might lower *completed* suicide. In contrast, more is known about *nonfatal* suicidal behaviors, where focused behavioral interventions appear to hold promise in reducing suicide attempts and other nonfatal suicidal behaviors.

As discussed by Rudd (2000), with fewer than two dozen studies in the world's literature that approach sound research criteria for randomness or control, we are still in our infancy in terms of pursuit of empirical research in this area. Both Linehan (1997) and Rudd (2000) have highlighted a central common problem in the scientific study of suicidality to date—namely, patient-subjects evidencing some form of suicidality (ideation, intent, prior or current attempt) are ordinarily and routinely *excluded* from clinical trial research (both medication and psychotherapy) because of their high-risk status.

MAJOR TREATMENT APPROACHES

A variety of major treatment approaches have been put forward in the literature for working with suicidal adolescents and young adults. My purpose here is not to provide an extensive review of these approaches.

Excellent reviews of many valid therapies (e.g., CBT, dialectical behavior therapy, psychodynamic psychotherapy) can be found in other chapters of this book. An emerging literature that relates to the treatment of late adolescent and young adult suicidal individuals is now available (Berman, Jobes, & Silverman, in press; Ellis & Newman, 1996; Jobes, 1995; Leenaars, Maltsberger, & Neimeyer, 1994; Linehan, 1993a, 1993b; Quinnett, 2000; Rudd, Joiner, & Rajab, 2001; Spirito & Overholser, 2003; Zimmerman & Asnis, 1995), including the pros and cons of conducting therapy over the Internet (Hsiung, 2002). Furthermore, there exists a literature on the standard of care in the assessment, treatment, and management of suicidal individuals (Bongar, 1992, 2002; Bongar et al., 1998; Gutheil, 1992; Simon, 1992). My purpose here is to simply highlight some key areas that, in my experience and from my perspective, relate specifically to the suicidal college student. These comments and emphases are not intended to be exhaustive or authoritative. However, they may be considered as clinical pearls relevant to therapeutic considerations when working with suicidal college students.

Psychodynamic Psychotherapy

Beyond theoretical and clinical discussions, there is, unfortunately, no direct empirical support for the specific efficacy of psychodynamic treatment of suicidal adolescents or young adults. While there is little dispute that, clinically and conceptually, psychodynamic theories have much to offer the practitioner and the patient, it is important to remember that, until data more clearly support the value of this type of therapy, some necessary caution about its potential usefulness and efficacy is in order (Berman et al., in press).

With this caution in mind, psychodynamic treatments for suicidal college students do have many compelling features. For example, treatments in the psychodynamic theoretical tradition tend to routinely emphasize the importance of development (e.g., Erikson, 1968), the impact of family relationships on personality development and the individual's ability to relate to others (e.g., Guntrip, 1968), the development of the self (e.g., Kohut & Wolf, 1978), and the central healing role of the clinical relationship (e.g., Freud, 1917/1957; Guntrip, 1968; Kohut, 1977).

While empirical data supporting psychodynamic approaches to adolescent and young adult suicide is unavailable, Jobes (1995) has concluded:

. . . a psychodynamic approach to the assessment, management, and treatment of suicidal adolescents can be quite effective . . . there is much in psychoanalytic tradition to help guide one's clinical interventions. Perhaps most important, beyond crisis-management, a psychodynamic approach to this clinical work holds the promise of actually treating (and resolving) the underlying causes of suicidality within in the young person. (p. 152)

Case Illustration I—Danielle

During her first year of college, Danielle was able to keep her bingeing and purging under control. Only once or twice did her roommates "catch" her throwing up in the dormitory bathroom. She felt that she had made a good adjustment to college and that she was able to make friends and have some fun, especially when it involved the presence of alcohol. However, she did not understand why her freshman roommates did not want to live with her the next year and why she continued to have "episodes" of feeling dysphoric, "out-of-sorts," negative, and "down" on herself. The more she looked to others for support, understanding, caring, and advice, the more she felt that her peers were rejecting her and losing interest in her stories. That is, until she met Brenda, an older student who shared similar experiences of growing up and similar struggles with often feeling hurt, unappreciated, misunderstood, and unattractive. Brenda dealt with her moments of feeling alienated and alone by cutting her thighs and upper arms with a razor blade. Danielle and Brenda formed a bond around their mutual feelings of distrust toward others. They particularly were wary of the college authorities who seemed to be focused on setting strict rules and regulations and not on letting students decide how best to do things for themselves. Danielle and Brenda decided to live together off-campus, because there would be less oversight and interference by the school authorities.

Sophomore year turned out to be a disaster. Brenda got a boyfriend and spent most of her free time with him. When he was around the apartment, he rarely paid any attention to Danielle. Brenda would fight with him, and their verbal yelling sometimes escalated into physical fights. Especially on these occasions, to try to contain her feelings and fears, Danielle would binge and purge. But the tension in the apartment didn't remit. As time went by, Danielle became more depressed and desperate. The combination of her depression and eating problems brought her to the attention of her academic advisor. Reluctantly, she agreed to go to the health service for a checkup. Her primary care physician diagnosed bulimia nervosa and referred her to the counseling service. Initially, she resisted going or admitting that she needed help. However, on careful clinical assessment, it became evident that Danielle had entertained the thought of suicide on more than one occasion. In fact, whenever she felt "ugly," "stupid," or "out of control," the idea of "ending it all" would cross her mind. Having seen Brenda's scars, Danielle fantasized what it would be like to cut herself and whether that would make her feel better or worse. She wondered if anyone would really miss her or whether any-one even cared that she had episodes of feeling so miserable that she just wanted to die. Her initial assessment also revealed a long-standing his-tory of conflict with her mother and older sister. It was also revealed that there was a family history of depression and a suicide in a maternal aunt.

Her psychotherapy was stormy, at best. Whenever there were periods of conflict in her life (with Brenda or with her parents) or episodes of self-doubt and despair (poor grades or social rejections), she would binge and purge and think about suicide. On more than one occasion, she reported hoarding pills in a shoebox placed under her bed—"in case I needed them." She also reported visiting sites on the Internet that dis-cussed how to die by suicide. Some of these sites she found "gory and disgusting," while others she found to be engaging, enticing, and sooth-ing. Her fascination with suicidal behaviors did not wane until she began to develop a better sense of herself and more respect for her ability to "hold my own" in different settings.

Her therapist maintained a consistent stance of caring, concern, and availability. The therapist routinely asked Danielle about her good days and her bad days and tried to explore with her what made the difference. They discussed the hassles of daily living, the problem with boys, and learning to feel comfortable in her own skin. They gingerly explored the observation that there is "no one right answer all the time" for a number of social interactions or even how to think about yourself. They dis-cussed her problems with her parents, her inability to always get what she wanted, and ways to cope with disappointments and rejections—and, for that matter, successes. With time, she began to move away from her fascination with Brenda's cutting behaviors and saw that she could "live inside myself" even when she felt threatened and unloved. She began to accept that others were not perfect either and that developing tolerance for self and others was a lifelong goal. As she learned, tested, modified, and adopted new coping skills for a range of interpersonal interactions, she gained a better respect for herself and her own ability to "control my emotions." Her treatment continued throughout her undergraduate career, allowing her to feel a part of the campus community and to progress academically. Leading up to graduation, the therapy focused on "next steps" and carefully identified those signs and symptoms that would signal the need for Danielle to pursue further treatment as new challenges confronted her in a different environment.

Problem-Solving Approaches

A variety of studies have emphasized the potential therapeutic worth of problem-oriented psychotherapy. Although an explicit problem-solving strategy is usually modified to fit with the particular person being helped, it generally follows a format that includes (Salkovskis, 2001):

1. Making a problem list
2. Prioritizing problems to be dealt with, not only on the basis of importance and impact but also on the basis of likely short-term effectiveness
3. Deciding on a range of possible solutions, usually involving an element of unconstrained brainstorming, in which the person is encouraged to consider freely any possible solution
4. Selecting a particular solution, often by systematically reviewing the pros and cons of the most likely solutions available
5. Breaking down the implementation of the chosen solution into smaller, more manageable steps
6. Anticipating and identifying obstacles to each step (including not only practical difficulties but also cognitive and emotional difficulties)
7. Systematically reviewing progress between steps before deciding whether to move on to the next step

Throughout this process, the importance of specificity in thinking about solutions and their implementation is emphasized. Thus, both problem-solving deficits and deficits in specificity of recall may be corrected by treatment. It also seems likely that problem solving has the effect of reducing hopelessness in people who have previously been unable to see any way out of what had seemed to be insoluble situations (Salkovskis, 1996).

Cognitive-Behavior Therapy

Cognitive-behavioral therapy (CBT; Beck, Rush, Shaw, & Emery, 1978, 1979) has deservedly gained repute as a primary treatment modality of choice with depressed and suicidal patients. This is especially true when depressive symptoms make introspection difficult. Depressed suicidal adults often experience negative cognitions about themselves, their environment, and their future. To this end, CBT has been shown to be an effective intervention for depressive symptoms (Clarke, Rohde, Lewinsohn, Hops, & Seeley, 1999).

The cognitive model of treatment strictly focuses on a number of cognitive deficits and the distorted and negative cognitions that are used by the patient. Cognitive therapy postulates three primary areas of maladaptive thinking for attention: (1) the *cognitive triad*—the idiosyncratic and negative view of self, experience, and future; (2) *schemas*—stable patterns of molding data or events into cognitions; and (3) *systematic errors* in thinking that establish and maintain a depressed mood and the hopelessness that Beck believes is "at the core of the suicidal wishes" (Beck et al., 1978, p. 151).

Brent has created a CBT treatment manual (Brent & Poling, 1997), modifying the approach of Beck and colleagues (1979) for depressed adolescents. The treatment is composed of 12 to 16 weekly sessions followed by a six-month booster phase of monthly or bimonthly sessions. Parents and adolescents receive a psychoeducational manual about mood disorders and their treatments. The active intervention is described as a collaborative "guided discovery" to monitor and modify automatic thoughts, assumptions, and beliefs (Brent, 1997). Since suicidal individuals are thought to often have difficulty in communicating and negotiating their needs and wishes (McLeavey, Daly, Ludgate, & Murray, 1994) and to frequently resort to passive avoidant coping strategies (Adams & Adams, 1991), Brent's treatment model encouraged more assertive and direct methods of communicating, as well as increasing the teenager's ability to conceptualize alternative solutions to problems (Shaffer & Pfeffer, 2001).

Brent's study provides no evidence of the efficacy of CBT for teenagers who had made a suicide attempt. This group of adolescents was not included in this study. However, the intervention was reported to be as effective as systemic family therapy and nondirective supportive therapy in reducing suicidal ideation in depressed adolescents during the 12- to 16-week treatment period (Brent et al., 1997).

Beck and his associates (Henriques et al., 2003) have recently developed a specific 10-session cognitive therapy intervention for adolescent and young adult suicide attempters. A novel element of the therapy is that the treatment can be applied to individuals exhibiting suicidal behavior regardless of psychiatric diagnosis. Another central philosophical element is the notion that the suicidal behavior is both understandable given the patient's frame of reference but ultimately disadvantageous to the patient.

The intervention owes much to the cognitive model of emotional disorders in general and depression in particular, as well as the large empirical literature linking hopelessness with suicidal behavior (e.g., Beck, Steer, Kovacs, & Garrison, 1985). In accordance with cognitive theory, the central feature of the intervention is the identification of proximal thoughts and associated core beliefs that were activated just before the patient's suicide attempt. With the particular cognitive components identified, cognitive and behavioral strategies are applied to help individuals develop more adaptive ways of thinking about their situation and more functional ways of responding during periods of acute emotional distress. The focus of the therapy is on reducing suicidal behavior, and key elements of the intervention include: (1) developing specific ways to address hopelessness and target suicidal behavior, (2) developing effective ways for engaging patients quickly in the treatment to reduce dropout, (3) increasing adaptive use of other health services, and (4) increasing the adaptive use of social support.

Rudd et al. (2001) have extended Beck's original theorizing about the "suicidal mode." Rudd et al. have written a treatment guide titled, *Treating Suicidal Behavior: An Effective, Time-Limited Approach*. This text is one of the first treatment manuals specific to suicide. These authors comprehensively and specifically present an initial theoretical model of suicidality, build a system of clinical assessment based on this model, which logically leads to a clinical approach for dealing with crisis intervention and symptom management, and then seamlessly evolves into a clinical treatment designed to eliminate suicidal behaviors through skill building and the development of enduring adaptive modes. This CBT approach is one of the first comprehensive efforts to conceptually target and treat suicidality within a cohesive and coherent theoretical model that directly shapes clinical assessment and treatment.

Dialectical Behavior Therapy

Dialectical behavior therapy (DBT; Linehan, 1993a, 1993b) is an evidence-based outpatient psychotherapy for chronically parasuicidal adults diagnosed with borderline personality disorder. *Parasuicide* is defined as acute, deliberate, nonfatal self-injury or harm that includes suicide attempts and nonsuicidal self-injurious behaviors (Linehan, 1993a). Suicidal behaviors are considered to be maladaptive solutions to painful negative emotions that also have affect-regulating qualities and elicit help from others.

This approach shares many features and procedures of cognitive-behavioral problem solving but is much more broadly based. Linehan identifies emotional dysregulation as a key factor that arises from biologically vulnerable patients being exposed at an early age to invalidating environments. The resulting affective instability then interacts with instability in behavioral, interpersonal, and cognitive domains to produce the pattern of reactions that are characteristic of such patients, including parasuicidal behavior.

Dialectical behavior therapy focuses on validation and empowerment, consistent with the philosophy of cognitive-behavioral approaches to Axis I disorders. In DBT, the therapist aims to help the patient to modulate his or her emotional reactions, to reduce the associated extreme behaviors, and to accept his or her own reactions. Problem solving is a core skills training strategy, supplemented by a range of ancillary treatments, supportive group sessions, and telephone consultations. There is a considerably greater emphasis on working on and with the therapeutic relationship (more in the style of cognitive than psychodynamic psychotherapy). Other core skills taught in DBT include mindfulness training, interpersonal effectiveness skills, and techniques designed to deal with psychological distress (including well-validated cognitive and behavioral techniques designed to deal with depression, anxiety, and posttraumatic stress). These techniques are applied in an integrated and formulation-driven way, adapted for use with this particular group of patients in ways that take their particular sensitivities into account (Berman et al., in press).

In a randomized clinical trial comparing DBT with treatment as usual, DBT was more effective in reducing suicide attempts, other parasuicidal acts, number of inpatient psychiatric hospitalization days, and anger, while improving social adjustment, treatment compliance, and treatment dropout rate (Linehan, Armstrong, Suarez, Allmon, & Heard, 1991).

Interpersonal Psychotherapy

The focus of interpersonal therapy (IPT) is on the link between the onset of depressive symptoms and the current interpersonal problems. The emphasis of change strategies is on the person's immediate personal context, his or her reaction to life events and current social dysfunction, and how these factors relate to symptom formation. No attempt is made to deal with more enduring aspects of personality. Having established links between interpersonal functioning and depressive symptoms, specific intervention strategies are used according to a detailed manual. This 12- to 16-week therapy focuses on the style and effectiveness of interpersonal interactions (Mufson, Moreau, Weissman, Klerman, 1993).

Interpersonal therapy may be a useful treatment for addressing the adolescent's use of suicidal behavior as a method of communicating anger, distress, or resolving conflict. The adolescent's ability to establish a therapeutic alliance and commit to informing the therapist about suicidal preoccupations and intent and going to an emergency service if necessary is central to IPT. However, there have been no published results of its specific effectiveness among suicidal youth, although IPT has been found to be effective in the treatment of depression (Mufson, Weissman, Moreau, & Garfinkel, 1999).

Comparisons of Problem-Solving, Cognitive-Behavior Therapy, Dialectical Behavior Therapy, and Interpersonal Therapy Approaches

According to Salkovskis (2001), an active psychological treatment needs to meet the following criteria if it is to have any chance of being successful in reducing the repetition rate of attempted suicide and diminishing the number of successful suicides:

1. It must help the patient to feel understood (including, but not confined to, the use of nonspecific therapy factors, such as empathy, genuineness, and nonpossessive warmth, and including aspects of patient empowerment).

2. The main focus of therapeutic efforts should be on factors understood through empirically grounded theory, to be generally involved in the experience and maintenance of intense and persistent distress in particular patient groups (including, but not confined to, those that meet criteria for particular diagnoses).

3. Therapy should be adapted to target the particular specific and idiosyncratic manifestations of the generally identified maintaining factors (i.e., the way in which the general maintaining factors affect the particular patient who the therapist is seeking to help).

4. Therapy should have been demonstrated to be more effective than a waiting list or treatment as usual.

Currently, only CBT with a problem-solving emphasis and DBT meet all of these criteria. Both standard cognitive therapy for depression and interpersonal therapy currently meet the first three criteria. Salkovskis (2001) observes that examination of the details of all four approaches suggests common elements in terms of:

1. Focus on the here and now

2. Attention to negative emotions as a guide to the appropriate focus of therapy

3. A major element of both problem-solving and skills training being included in the treatment package

4. The emphasis on engaging the person in an empathic, active, and collaborative therapeutic relationship to empower him or her to make changes to the current situation

Collaborative Assessment and Management of Suicidality

The collaborative assessment and management of suicidality (CAMS) approach to suicidality is a novel clinical protocol specifically designed to quickly identify and effectively engage suicidal outpatients in their own clinical care (Jobes, 2000, 2003a; Jobes & Drozd, 2004). The CAMS approach is intended to modify and change *clinician* behaviors in how they initially identify, engage, assess, conceptualize, make a treatment plan, and manage suicidal outpatients (Jobes, 2003b; Jobes, Luoma, Jacoby, & Mann, 1998).

The CAMS approach emphasizes a thorough and *collaborative* assessment of the patient's suicidality that ultimately leads to a problem-solving approach to treatment planning. In effect, the clinician and suicidal patient *coauthor* an outpatient treatment plan. The CAMS approach is specifically designed to form and launch a strong therapeutic alliance creating an effective and superior treatment trajectory (Jobes & Drozd, 2004). Thus, the heart of the CAMS approach is a strong therapeutic alliance where both parties work together to develop a shared phenomenological understanding of the patient's suicidality.

Use of the Suicide Status Form (SSF; Jobes, Jacoby, Cimbolic, & Hustead, 1997) is central to the CAMS protocol. The psychometric validity and reliability of SSF quantitative and qualitative assessments are discussed in depth elsewhere (Jobes & Mann, 1999). Within the CAMS protocol, the clinician asks permission to literally take a seat next to the patient to work together in the completion of the SSF assessment. The interactive assessment process is used to build the clinical partnership; what is learned through this assessment is then used to directly shape the outpatient treatment plan.

The CAMS approach conceptualizes the assessment and treatment of suicidal patients in a way fundamentally different from current conventional approaches (Jobes, 2000). Here the treatment focus and target is *suicidality,* independent of diagnosis. Through collaborative assessment and deconstruction of the patient's suicidality, key problems and goals naturally emerge; the key is for the clinician to see the world—and the seduction of suicide—through the eyes of the patient. Collaborative assessment leads to collaborative treatment planning that emphasizes a problem-oriented approach designed to reconstruct more viable ways of coping and living.

In this regard, certain aspects of CAMS are philosophically and strategically akin to aspects of Linehan's (1993a, 1993b) DBT and Beck's recent cognitive therapy approach to relapse prevention in suicide attempters (Henriques et al., 2003). However, CAMS is flexible and facilitates therapeutic work, independent of theoretical orientation or clinical techniques. The protocol does *not* usurp clinical judgment or autonomy, but does provide helpful front-end guidance on how to handle suicidality quickly and directly without getting into an adversarial struggle.

Thus, the CAMS approach integrates a range of behavioral, cognitive, psychodynamic, humanistic, existential, and interpersonal approaches to assessing, understanding, managing, and intervening with suicidality. Within the CAMS approach, there is a fundamental understanding that virtually all suicidality seen in patients represents some effort to cope or problem-solve, albeit a very dramatic and extreme form of coping/problem solving. From this perspective, clinicians must approach suicidality in an empathic, matter-of-fact, and nonjudgmental fashion. Ironically, the clinician's ability to understand the viability and attraction of suicide as a coping option seems to provide the essential glue for forming a strong therapeutic alliance where more adaptive methods of coping can be evaluated, explored, and tested. The use of CAMS, therefore, prompts early identification of suicidality, a thorough assessment of the risk, development of a suicide-specific treatment plan, clinical tracking, and documentation through treatment until suicidality resolves. The specific steps within the CAMS protocol are as follows:

1. Early identification of risk
2. Collaborative assessment using the SSF
3. Collaborative treatment planning
4. Clinical tracking of "suicide status" at each session using the SSF Suicide Tracking Form
5. Clinical resolution of suicide status

In summary, CAMS engages the suicidal patient differently than do conventional approaches, thereby creating a different treatment trajectory. This trajectory is fundamentally shaped by an enhanced therapeutic alliance forged in the shared pursuit of trying to assess and understand what it *means* for the patient to be suicidal and with that shared knowledge determining how that risk will be clinically managed. Given the challenges of clinical work with suicidality, increased concerns about malpractice liability, and the decreased use of inpatient hospitalization, CAMS may provide a promising new approach to effective clinical work with suicidal individuals on an outpatient basis (Jobes & Drozd, 2004).

PSYCHOPHARMACOLOGY:
GENERAL CONSIDERATIONS

Medications and medication management can play a role in the therapy of suicidal adolescents and young adults. While there is yet to be an anti-suicide pill, medication may be helpful in cases where the diagnostic condition and related symptoms can be therapeutically helped with the judicious use of certain medicines (Maris, Berman, & Silverman, 2000). This may be particularly true in a case where a needed level of symptom reduction allows for greater accessibility and success to cognitive, be-havioral, or verbal modes of clinical intervention. For example, antide-pressants, or more specifically, selective serotonin reuptake inhibitors (SSRIs), may be indicated should a major depressive disorder be diag-nosed (Goldblatt & Silverman, 2000).

One of the most exciting advances in understanding the genetic and bi-ological bases for suicidal behavior is Mann's proposed stress-diathesis model of suicide, which is based on research findings in neurobiology (Mann, 1998; Mann, Waternaux, Haas, & Malone, 1999). Basic neurobi-ological research about the role of neurotransmitters (e.g., serotonin, dopamine, and norepinephrine) in modulating brain function has led to the theoretical proposition that a vulnerability to suicidality may exist independently of those stressors (or risk factors) that have been corre-lated with suicidal behavior (especially psychiatric disorders such as mood disorders, schizophrenia, anxiety disorder, substance abuse disor-ders, and certain personality disorders). Mann proposes that there is a diathesis, or predisposition to suicidal behavior, that has distinct biolog-ical underpinnings. He contends that there are biological correlates of this diathesis for suicidal behavior as well as biological correlates of the stressors for suicidal behavior, such as major psychiatric disorders (Mann, 1998). Each of these two domains has different biological corre-lates leading to different therapeutic approaches (Maris et al., 2000).

Empirical evidence is mounting that the most common diagnostic condition related to suicide, major depression, is clearly associated with impaired serotonergic function involving different brain regions (predominantly the ventral prefrontal cortex), but is *independent* of the serotonergic abnormality associated with the vulnerability or diathesis for suicidal behavior (Mann & Arango, 2001). The familial transmission of the stressors (i.e., psychiatric illnesses) is independent of the familial transmission of the diathesis for suicidal behavior. Hence, these authors postulate that there are familial, and almost certainly genetic, factors related to the diathesis for suicidal behavior. The consequence of such genetic factors most likely is a biological abnormality or phenotype.

Decreased brain serotonin function (as measured by cerebrospinal fluid levels of 5-HIAA) has been found in suicidal patients, independent of their psychiatric disorders. Hopelessness, low self-esteem, social isolation, and inadequate control of aggressive impulses may be core symptoms of such individuals (Ahrens & Linden, 1996). Of note is that persons who exhibit aggressive, impulsive behavior toward others are also more prone to impulsive, aggressive, and suicidal behaviors (Verkes & Cowen, 2000). A long line of empirical research has established decreased brain serotonin function in mood disorders (especially major depressive disorder), which may explain why the majority of depressed individuals do not engage in suicidal behaviors and why only approximately 60% of individuals who complete suicide have a diagnosis of major depressive disorder at the time of their death.

Of all the available medications for the treatment of psychiatric disorders and dysfunctions related to suicidality, I wish to focus solely on antidepressants. (See Verkes & Cowen, 2000, for discussions of other psychopharmacological approaches to the treatment of suicidal individuals.) Some studies suggest that the use of antidepressants have lowered the suicide rates in clinical populations (Isacsson, Holmgren, Druid, & Bergman, 1997), although these studies need to be prospectively replicated and carefully controlled.

There are well more than 20 antidepressants on the market, only a few of which are SSRIs. Hence, global statements about causal mechanisms cannot be made because truly rigorous studies have not been undertaken that compare and contrast all the available medications with specific target symptoms. Furthermore, currently there is a controversy as to whether certain classes of antidepressants can be associated with the worsening, or even the emergence, of suicidal ideation or behavior in the early weeks of treatment (Breggin, 2003/2004; Mann & Kapur, 1991). In July 2003, both the FDA and its British equivalent, the Medicines and Healthcare Products Regulatory Authority (MHRA), published warnings about the use of paroxetine for those patients in the under-18 age group because of a possible increased risk of suicidal impulses. New data from various clinical trials showed episodes of self-harm and potentially suicidal behavior were between 1.5 and 3.2 times higher in patients younger than 18 taking the medication versus those receiving a placebo (American College of Neuropsychopharmacology, 2004).

There are reasons to believe that SSRIs might reduce suicidality because of their potential to reduce irritability, affective response to stress, hypersensitivity, depression, and anxiety (Leon et al., 1999). Selective serotonin reuptake inhibitors may be effective at reducing suicidal ideation (Isacsson et al., 1997). It remains speculative if SSRIs might specifically increase akathisia in children and adolescents. If they do, even in a very small percentage of patients, it would speak to the use of concomitant medications to address this side effect—at least during the initial phases of antidepressant medication treatment. Selective serotonin reuptake inhibitors remain the preferred psychopharmacological treatment for young adult depression, with caution that suicidal patients on SSRIs must be watched for any increase in agitation or suicidality, especially in the early phase of treatment (Montgomery, 1997).

When medications are prescribed, careful monitoring of their administration to the suicidal individual is essential. Dosage levels must be considered carefully and hoarding of pills by the patient prevented. Similarly, access to medications by a suicidal young adult must be severely limited. While medications may be essential in stabilizing and treating the suicidal young adult, all administration must be carefully monitored by a third party who can report any unexpected change of mood, increase in agitation, or emergency state or unwanted side effects, and who can regulate dosage (American Psychiatric Association, 2003; Shaffer & Pfeffer, 2001).

When the primary therapist is not a physician, but rather works with a physician who prescribes medication for referred patients, it is essential that interactive lines of communication remain open. The therapist should be familiar with the common dosages, properties, and effects, particularly side effects, of prescribed medications. Moreover, the clinician must be on top of the case and cognizant of all treatments provided to his or her patient. Those who provide concurrent treatments should be informed of significant changes in the patient's behavior, significant events threatening behavioral response, and any observed responses to medication (lack of compliance, side effects, etc.) that are perhaps not reported directly to the psychopharmacologist by the youthful patient or parents.

Both the patient-physician relationship and the therapist-physician relationship are critical to the successful implementation and maintenance of psychopharmacological treatments. Issues of transference and countertransference influence the degree to which patients are compliant with medications. Furthermore, transference and countertransference issues may also become significant in the relationship between therapist (nonphysician) and the physician (primary care physician or psychiatrist) charged with medicating the patient. Always be aware of these dynamics and discuss them on a regular basis. Open and frequent communication between and among therapist, physician (psychopharmacologist), patient, and the patient's support network is key to the success of the treatment.

HOSPITALIZATION

Given the various issues—including stigma, managed care constraints, and the significantly reduced numbers of available inpatient beds—the need for hospitalization, management while hospitalized, and postdischarge planning is tinged with medical-legal implications and liability issues for clinician, hospital staff, and hospital administration (Berman et al., in press).

The American Association of Suicidology (AAS; 2003) has recently developed specific recommendations for consideration prior to therapeutic passes, trial leaves, or discharge. These recommendations are appropriate for inpatient psychiatric units in general hospitals, psychiatric hospitals, and residential treatment centers. The AAS recommendations are not comprehensive treatment guidelines for suicidal persons and are not a substitute for the clinical decisions that arise from the treatment relationship. Moreover, empirical support for these recommendations is less than conclusive. However, based on the literature that does exist, and in the collective clinical experience of the AAS authors, these recommendations represent current best practices. These recommendations are subject to change as additional research is published and new knowledge gained.

Generally, trial leaves, passes, and discharges are transitions that necessarily result in a reduction in the level of monitoring of patients known to be at elevated risk for suicidal behaviors. Frequently, some or many clinical or environmental risk factors remain to at least some degree. Vulnerability to suicide may persist and may be exacerbated while the individual is on pass or leave or after discharge from an inpatient or residential setting. While the use of trial leaves and passes has declined significantly because of changes in the system of financing for inpatient care, they still warrant selective use but with an understanding that they require a careful balancing of risks and benefits. For patients at significant risk of suicide, risk may also be exacerbated during the period following discharge from an inpatient setting. That risk is most elevated in the month following discharge with about half of all postdischarge suicides occurring in the week following discharge (Appleby et al., 1999; Ho, 2003). It is also clear that patients do not always accurately self-report suicidal ideation to mental health professionals, increasing the importance of communication and coordination between families and the treatment team (Busch, Fawcett, & Jacobs, 2003).

The following case illustrates the beneficial use of a hospitalization when it is necessary to quickly assess an escalating set of behaviors and self-destructive perspectives. The hospitalization is but the beginning road to recovery for this student. Yet, a brief hospitalization can serve as the impetus for getting the help needed to address modifiable risk factors.

———————————— **Case Illustration II—Steve** ————————————

Steve was a 20-year-old biology major when he was first diagnosed with a learning disability. He had apparently been able to compensate for his learning deficits while in high school, but as the material became more difficult and the amount of memorization increased, Steve found that he was struggling more than expected. He knew that he would struggle academically in college because his older brother was in medical school and that was what it was like for him as well. However, he wasn't getting good enough grades to be pre-med and, no matter how much harder he tried, he still wasn't able to perform to his expectations.

Fortunately, he was identified as having an observable discrepancy between his aptitude and performance on classroom examinations by an academic tutor, and he was referred for testing. He was subsequently placed on medication, which helped him focus and perform better. However, Steve was worried about the implications of having a "learning disability." He feared that such a label would exclude him from being accepted into medical school. If accepted, he was concerned about whether he could succeed in medical school and beyond, if he was "disabled." He wondered whether anyone would want to marry him if he had "disabilities." He worried about whether a learning disability was genetic and whether he would be passing this on to his children. He worried that he would have to be on this medication for the rest of his life in order to "be myself." He worried about the long-term consequences of being on these stimulant medications. He decided that as long as the medications were working to keep him getting good grades, he'd "pay the price and worry about the consequences later."

Steve was a hard worker and an overachiever. He decided to take a preparatory course for the medical school entrance examinations. These Saturday courses were in addition to his part-time campus job, his full-time classes, his volleyball team practices, his daily exercise routine, his outdoors club participation, and his neighborhood volunteer activities. Steve's plate was pretty full. Having a social life was out of the question. Going to movies, watching Sunday afternoon football games, and reading novels were to be put off to some future time.

Disaster struck when Steve got back his first set of practice test scores. By his standards, he did very poorly. Not only was he unable to finish the exam, but the correct answers either didn't make sense to him or suggested that he hadn't done a good job of memorizing the material from his prior courses. After some brooding, he came to the conclusion that his "illness" was getting worse and that he would never be able to do well. He got very angry with himself for thinking that the medication was really of help to him and, therefore, decided to abruptly stop it. Over the next two days, as he brooded more, he became more despondent, irritable, agitated, and confused. In a fit of despair, he put a plastic bag over his head to see "what it would feel like to stop breathing and thinking—at least temporarily." He had not anticipated that as he became oxygen-deprived, he would lose control over his fine motor coordination—making the removal of the bag that more difficult. Fortunately, while he was struggling, a next-door dorm neighbor happened to walk past his room and look in through his open door. The plastic bag was quickly removed, and he was taken to the emergency room on campus. There he was assessed and, although he pleaded that he had not intended to die ("and couldn't upset his parents by having a psychiatric hospital-ization"—let alone something on his college record that the medical schools might see), a decision was made to admit him for observation and stabilization.

The brief hospitalization allowed Steve to be reassessed for the extent of his learning disabilities, and an adjustment was made in his medication. His level of impulsivity was assessed in light of the need for medications. Furthermore, his preoccupation with a negative self-image and fear of being "damaged" was identified as contributing to an underlying dysphoria and attendant need to be an overachiever. On discharge, he was referred to the campus student counseling service for ongoing medication monitoring, psychotherapy, and career counseling. With the help of his therapist, Steve came to accept his strengths and weaknesses as a student and as an individual. With time, he learned better academic skills and techniques that allowed him to perform better on examinations and to retain and retrieve information. A real breakthrough came when he was able to report feeling able to positively "take care of myself" and enjoy being a college student.

PRACTICE RECOMMENDATIONS

Rudd et al.'s (1999) review of the treatment literature was able to tentatively answer only a few of the most fundamental questions about the treatment of suicidality. Nevertheless, these authors provide a useful set of 28 practice recommendations that make intuitive and clinical sense. These recommendations represent a first-generation effort to develop empirically relevant considerations and provide a useful focus and organization about clinical treatment aspects pertaining to suicidal patients, including youth (Berman et al., in press):

Intervention

1. Intensive follow-up, case management, telephone contacts, or home visits may improve treatment compliance over the short term for lower risk cases.

2. Improved ease of access (i.e., a clearly stated crisis plan) to emergency services can potentially reduce subsequent attempts and service demand by first-time suicide attempters.

Treatment

3. Intensive follow-up treatment following an attempt is most appropriate and effective for those identified as *high risk*. High risk is indicated by multiple attempts, psychiatric history, and diagnostic comorbidity.

4. Short-term cognitive-behavioral therapy that integrates problem solving as a core intervention is effective at reducing suicidal ideation, depression, and hopelessness over periods of up to one year. Such brief approaches do not appear effective in reducing attempts over enduring time frames.

5. Reducing suicide attempts requires longer term treatment and treatment modalities that target specific skill deficits such as emotion regulation, poor distress tolerance (e.g., impulsivity), anger management, interpersonal assertiveness, as well as other enduring problems, such as interpersonal relationships and self-image disturbance.

6. High-risk suicidal patients can be safely and effectively treated on an outpatient basis if acute hospitalization is available and accessible.

Clinical Practice

7. When imminent risk does not dictate hospitalization, the intensity of outpatient treatment (i.e., more frequent appointments, telephone contacts, concurrent individual and group treatment) should vary in accordance with risk indicators for those identified as high risk.

8. If the target goal is a reduction in suicide attempts and related behaviors, treatment should be conceptualized as long term and target identified skills deficits (e.g., emotion regulation, distress tolerance, impulsivity, problem solving, interpersonal assertiveness, and anger management), in addition to other salient treatment issues.

9. If therapy is brief and the target variables are suicidal ideation or related symptomatology such as depression, hopelessness, or loneliness, a problem-solving component should be used in some form as a core intervention.

10. Regardless of therapeutic orientation, an explanatory model should be detailed identifying treatment targets, both direct (i.e., suicidal ideation, attempts, related self-destructive and self-mutilatory behaviors) and indirect (depression, hopelessness, anxiety, and anger; interpersonal relationship dysfunction; low self-esteem and poor self-image; and day-to-day functioning at work and home).

11. Use of a standardized follow-up and referral procedure (e.g., letters or phone calls) is recommended for those dropping out of treatment prematurely in an effort to enhance compliance and reduce risk for subsequent attempts.

12. The lack of definitive data about the efficacy of one approach over another should be reviewed with the patient as a component of informed consent.

Informed Consent

13. Provide informed consent pertaining to limits of confidentiality in relation to clear and imminent suicide risk and offer a detailed review of available treatment options, fees for service (both short and long term), risks/benefits, and the likely duration of treatment (especially for multiple attempters and those evidencing chronic psychiatric problems).

14. Provide an extended evaluation before specific treatment recommendations when patients present with more complex diagnostic issues or chronic suicidality.

Diagnosis

15. Evaluate for *DSM-IV* Axis I and Axis II diagnoses and document supporting symptomatology.

16. Provide diagnostic and symptom-specific treatment recommendations.

17. Routinely monitor, assess, and document a patient's initial and ongoing suicide risk and document interventions for maintaining outpatient safety until suicidality has clinically resolved.

18. For cases of chronic suicidality, monitor, assess, and document ongoing risk of suicidality and document interventions that address

the chronic nature of the suicidal preoccupations. It is important to note the chronicity of some symptoms (e.g., specific suicidal thoughts with a definitive plan), indicating factors that escalate risk (e.g., emergence of intent) versus those that diminish risk (e.g., lack of intent).

Treatment Duration

19. For acute crisis cases of suicidality (particularly in the presence of an Axis I disorder), provide a relatively short-term psychotherapy that is directive and crisis focused, emphasizing problem solving and skill building as core interventions.

20. For chronic cases of suicidality (particularly in the presence of an Axis II disorder), provide a relatively long-term psychotherapy in which relationship issues, interpersonal communication, and self-image issues are the predominant focus of treatment when crises have resolved.

Therapeutic Relationship

21. Develop a strong therapeutic alliance with the suicidal patient and make the clinical relationship central to the outpatient treatment plan (e.g., negotiating access, using the relationship as a source of safety and support during crises, and attending to the patient's sense of profound loneliness).

22. Monitor and respond to countertransference reactions to suicidal patients (particularly those who are chronically suicidal) and routinely seek professional consultation, supervision, and support for difficult cases.

Treatment Outcome Monitoring

23. Use a clearly articulated scheme for identifying, classifying, and discussing suicidal behaviors in treatment (such as that provided by O'Carroll et al., 1996).

24. Use a consistent approach to assessing treatment outcome, incorporating both direct (i.e., suicidal ideation, suicide attempts, and instrumental behaviors) and indirect markers of suicidality (i.e., markers of symptomatology, personality traits, or general level of day-to-day functioning).

25. Assess treatment outcome at predictable intervals, using psycho-metrically sound instruments to complement and balance patient self-report.

Specific Considerations for Treatment of Adolescents

26. Involve parents or guardians in the clinical assessment, treatment planning, and ongoing suicide risk assessment process. Acknowledge their helpful contributions and empower them to have positive influences in their roles as parents and caregivers.

27. Evaluate the parents' or caregiver's ability to fulfill essential parental functions such as the provision of food and shelter and the maintenance of a safe, nonabusive home environment for the suicidal adolescent. If there exists a concern about the adolescent's basic care and safety, address with parents or caregivers directly and notify protective services if appropriate.

28. Evaluate the parents' or caregiver's ability to fulfill other parental functions such as consistent limit setting with follow-through, healthy communication with the adolescent, and positive role modeling. Recommend treatment for severe, identifiable parental psychopathology and recommend interventions as needed to (1) assist and empower parents in fulfilling their supportive and limit-setting functions and (2) assist family members in improving their communication skills and relationships with one another.

THOUGHTS ON PROVIDING APPROPRIATE CARE

There are a number of policies and procedures that are important to follow to ensure that the standard of care is provided to all students seeking psychological help (Bongar et al., 1998). There exist full discussions of malpractice, negligence, and standards of care policies and procedures in the clinical outpatient setting that are too detailed to include here (Bongar, 2002; Maris et al., 2000).

The standard of care requires that the student deemed to be at risk for self-destructive behaviors receive special attention and be treated differently from his or her peers in terms of maintaining the sanctity of confidentiality over the dictates of a need-to-know response protocol. For example, concerted efforts are often spent to ensure that the student is provided with a safe and secure environment, and such situations often involve multiple levels of college administrative involvement. Key to the appropriate care of students at increased risk is the importance of full documentation and frequent consultation with peers. In addition, adhering to established policies and protocols is essential to ensuring the best care for the student. Being vigilant of and carefully monitoring changes in the student's environment and his or her relationship to the therapist and significant others are also essential.

CONCLUSION

As Rudd (2000, pp. 56–57) has concluded, there is adequate support in the existing scientific literature for the following:

1. Intensive follow-up treatment following an attempt is most appropriate and effective for those identified as high risk, as indicated by multiple attempts, psychiatric history, and diagnostic comorbidity.

2. Short-term CBT, integrating problem solving as a *core intervention,* is effective at reducing suicidal ideation, depression, and hopelessness over periods of up to one year. Such brief approaches do not appear effective at reducing attempts over much longer time frames.

3. Reducing suicide attempts requires longer term treatment and treatment modalities targeting specific skills deficits, such as emotion regulation, poor distress tolerance (e.g., impulsivity), anger management, and interpersonal assertiveness, as well as other enduring problems such as interpersonal relationships and self-image disturbance (i.e., personality disorders).

4. High-risk suicidal patients can be safely and effectively treated on an outpatient basis if acute hospitalization is available and accessible.

As Salkovskis (2001) has pointed out, only two focused psychotherapeutic approaches (CBT and DBT) have been found to be helpful with people at risk of attempting suicide, although risk factor research suggests that techniques of interpersonal psychotherapy may also prove helpful. One meta-analysis (Hawton et al., 1998) of randomized controlled clinical trials, in which repetition of deliberate self-harm—including attempted suicide—was an outcome measure, found a significant reduction in repetition of self-harm behaviors among patients participating in DBT. While these data are encouraging, there is a clear need for a great deal more research in this important area of study.

In summary, when treating suicidal college students, two overriding major themes seem to prevail. First, relatedness and attachment are central to both the etiology of suicidal problems, and relationships may prove to be pivotal to successful clinical outcomes. Thus, from beginning to end, treatment demands attention to issues of linkage, attachment, and relatedness, and the potential success of treatment is often largely dependent on these themes.

A second major theme is the therapist's need for a pragmatic, problem-solving, and strategic approach to treatment that takes into account idiographic aspects of each presenting case. A thorough understanding of the full range of helpful clinical strategies and techniques forms the clinician's treasure trove from which he or she may selectively draw and apply as deemed appropriate for optimal clinical care. Based on a careful and complete assessment of the suicidal adolescent, these multilayered clinical interventions and strategies can translate into effective treatment that leads to successful suicide prevention at the individual clinical level.

REFERENCES

Adams, M., & Adams, J. (1991). Life events, depression, and perceived problem-solving alternatives in adolescents. *Journal of Child Psychology and Psychiatry, 32,* 811–820.

Ahrens, B., & Linden, M. (1996). Is there a suicidality syndrome independent of specific major psychiatric disorder? Results of a split-half multiple regression analysis. *Acta Psychiatrica Scandinavica, 94,* 79–86.

American Association of Suicidology. (2003). *Recommendations for inpatient and residential patients known to be at elevated risk for suicide.* Washington, DC: American Association of Suicidology.

American College Health Association (ACHA). (2001). *National college health assessment: Aggregate Report Spring 2000.* Baltimore: American College Health Association.

American College of Neuropychopharmacology (ACNP). (2004). *Executive summary: Preliminary report of the task force on SSRIs and suicidal behavior in youth.* Washington, DC: American College of Neuropsychopharmacology.

American Psychiatric Association. (1994). *Diagnostic and statistical manual of mental disorders* (4th ed.). Washington, DC: Author.

American Psychiatric Association. (2003). Practice guideline for the assessment and treatment of patients with suicidal behaviors. *American Journal of Psychiatry, 160*(11, Suppl.), 1–60.

Appleby, L., Shaw, J., Amos, T., McDonnell, R., Harris, C., McCann, K., et al. (1999). Suicide within 12 months of contact with mental health services: National clinical survey. *British Medical Journal, 318,* 1235–1239.

Barrios, L. C., Everett, S. A., Simon, T. R., & Brener, N. D. (2000). Suicidal ideation among U.S. college students: Associations with other injury risk behaviors. *Journal of the American College Health Association, 48,* 229–233.

Beck, A. T., Rush, A. J., Shaw, B. F., & Emery, G. (1978). *Cognitive therapy of depression: A treatment manual.* New York: Guilford Press.

Beck, A. T., Rush, A. J., Shaw, B. F., & Emery, G. (1979). *Cognitive therapy of depression.* New York: Guilford Press.

Beck, A. T., Steer, R. A., Kovacs, M., & Garrison, B. (1985). Hopelessness and eventual suicide: A 10-year prospective study of patients hospitalized with suicidal ideation. *American Journal of Psychiatry, 42,* 559–563.

Berman, A. L., & Jobes, D. A. (1991). *Adolescent suicide: Assessment and intervention.* Washington, DC: American Psychological Association.

Berman, A. L., Jobes, D. A., & Silverman, M. M. (in press). *Adolescent suicide: Assessment and intervention* (2nd ed.). Washington, DC: American Psychological Association.

Bongar, B. (Ed.). (1992). *Suicide: Guidelines for assessment, management and treatment.* New York: Oxford University Press.

Bongar, B. (2002). *The suicidal patient: Clinical and legal standards of care* (2nd ed.). Washington, DC: American Psychological Association.

Bongar, B., Berman, A. L., Maris, R. W., Silverman, M. M., Harris, E. A., & Packman, W. L. (Eds.). (1998). *Risk management with suicidal patients.* New York: Guilford Press.

Breggin, P. R. (2003/2004). Suicidality, violence and mania caused by selective serotonin reuptake inhibitors (SSRIs): A review and analysis. *International Journal of Risk and Safety in Medicine, 16,* 31–49.

Brener, N. D., Hassan, S., & Barrios, L. (1999). Suicidal ideation among college students in the United States. *Journal of Consulting and Clinical Psychology, 67,* 1004–1008.

Brent, D. A. (1997). The aftercare of adolescents with deliberate self-harm. *Journal of Child Psychology and Psychiatry, 38,* 277–286.

Brent, D. A., Holder, D., Kolko, D., Birmaher, B., Baugher, M., Roth, C., et al. (1997). A clinical psychotherapy trial for adolescent depression comparing cognitive, family, and supportive therapy. *Archives of General Psychiatry, 54,* 877–885.

Brent, D. A., & Poling, D. (1997). *Cognitive therapy manual for depressed and suicidal youth* (Rev. ed.). Pittsburgh: University of Pittsburgh Medical Center, Western Psychiatric Institute and Clinic.

Busch, K. A., Fawcett, J., & Jacobs, D. G. (2003). Clinical correlates of inpatient suicide. *Journal of Clinical Psychiatry, 64,* 14–19.

Centers for Disease Control and Prevention. (1997, November 14). CDC surveillance summaries. *Morbidity and Mortality Weekly Report 46* (No. SS-6).

Centers for Disease Control and Prevention. (2002, June 28). Surveillance Summaries. *Mortality and Morbidity Weekly Report 51* (No. SS-4).

Cimbolic, P., & Jobes, D. A. (Eds.). (1990). *Youth suicide: Assessment, intervention, and issues.* Springfield, IL: Charles C. Thomas.

Clarke, G. N., Rohde, P., Lewinsohn, P. M., Hops, H., & Seeley, J. R. (1999). Cognitive-behavioral treatment of adolescent depression: Efficacy of acute group treatment and booster sessions. *Journal of the American Academy of Child and Adolescent Psychiatry, 38,* 272–279.

Ellis, T. E., & Newman, C. F. (1996). *Choosing to live: How to defeat suicide through cognitive therapy.* Oakland, CA: New Harbinger.

Erikson, E. (1968). *Identity: Youth in crisis.* New York: Norton.

Freud, S. (1957). Mourning and melancholia. In J. Strachey (Ed. & Trans.), *The standard edition of the complete psychological works of Sigmund Freud* (Vol. 14, pp. 237–260). London: Hogarth Press. (Original work published 1917)

Goldblatt, M. J., & Silverman, M. M. (2000). Psychopharmacological treatment of suicidal patients. In R. W. Maris, S. S. Canetto, J. L., McIntosh, & M. M. Silverman (Eds.), *Review of suicidology 2000* (pp. 140–148). New York: Guilford Press.

Guntrip, H. (1968). *Schizoid phenomena, object relations and the self.* Madison, CT: International Universities Press.

Gutheil, T. G. (1992). Suicide and suit: Liability after self-destruction. In D. G. Jacobs (Ed.), *Suicide and clinical practice* (pp. 147–168). Washington, DC: American Psychiatric Press.

Hawton, K., Arensman, E., Townsend, E., Bremner, S., Feldman, E., Golney, R., et al. (1998). Deliberate self harm: Systematic review of efficacy of psychosocial and pharmacological treatments in preventing repetition. *British Medical Journal, 31,* 441–447.

Hawton, K., Zahl, D., & Weatherall, R. (2003). Suicide following deliberate self-harm: Long-term follow-up of patients who presented to a general hospital. *British Journal of Psychiatry, 182,* 537–542.

Henriques, G., Beck, A. T., & Brown, G. K. (2003). Cognitive therapy for adolescent and young adult suicide attempters. *American Behavioral Scientist, 46,* 1258–1268.

Hersch, L. (1995). Adapting to health care reform and managed care: Three strategies for survival and growth. *Professional Psychology: Research and Practice, 26,* 16–26.

Ho, T. P. (2003). The suicide risk of discharged psychiatric patients. *Journal of Clinical Psychiatry, 64,* 702–707.

Hoff, L. A. (1984). *People in crisis: Understanding and helping.* Menlo Park, CA: Addison-Wesley.

Hsiung, R. C. (Ed.). (2002). *E-therapy: Case studies, guiding principles, and the clinical potential of the internet.* New York: Norton.

Isacsson, G., Holmgren, P., Druid, H., & Bergman, U. (1997). The utilization of antidepressants: A key issue in the prevention of suicide. An analysis of 5281 suicides in Sweden during the period 1992–1994. *Acta Psychiatrica Scandinavica, 96,* 94–100.

Jobes, D. A. (1995). Psychodynamic treatment of adolescent suicide attempters. In J. K. Zimmerman & G. M. Asnis (Eds.), *Treatment approaches with suicidal adolescents* (pp. 137–154). New York: Wiley.

Jobes, D. A. (2000). Collaborating to prevent suicide: A clinical-research perspective. *Suicide and Life-Threatening Behavior, 25,* 437–449.

Jobes, D. A. (2003a). *Manual for the collaborative assessment and management of suicidality—revised (CAMS-R).* Unpublished manuscript.

Jobes, D. A. (2003b). Understanding suicide in the 21st century. *Preventing Suicide: The National Journal, 2*(3), 2–4.

Jobes, D. A., & Berman, A. L. (1991). Crisis intervention and brief treatment for suicidal youth. In A. Roberts (Ed.), *Contemporary perspectives on crisis intervention and prevention* (pp. 53–59). Englewood Cliffs, NJ: Prentice-Hall.

Jobes, D. A., & Berman, A. L. (1993). Suicide and malpractice liability: Assessing and revising policies, procedures, and practice in outpatient settings. *Professional Psychology: Research and Practice, 24,* 91–99.

Jobes, D. A., & Drozd, J. F. (2004). The CAMS approach to working with suicidal patients. *Journal of Contemporary Psychotherapy, 34,* 73–86.

Jobes, D. A., Jacoby, A. M., Cimbolic, P., & Hustead, L. A. T. (1997). Assessment and treatment of suicidal clients in a university counseling center. *Journal of Counseling Psychology, 44,* 368–377.

Jobes, D. A., Luoma, J. B., Jacoby, A. M., & Mann, R. E. (1998). *Manual for the collaborative assessment and management of suicidality (CAMS).* Unpublished manuscript.

Jobes, D. A., & Mann, R. E. (1999). Reasons for living versus reasons for dying: Examining the internal debate of suicide. *Suicide and Life-Threatening Behavior, 29,* 97–104.

Kisch, J., Leino, E. V., & Silverman, M. M. (in press). Aspects of suicidal behavior, depression, and treatment in college students: Results from the Spring 2000 national college health assessment. *Suicide and Life-Threatening Behavior.*

Kohut, H. (1977). *The restoration of the self.* New York: International Universities Press.

Kohut, H., & Wolf, E. (1978). The disorders of the self and their treatment: An outline. *International Journal of Psycho-Analysis, 59,* 413–425.

Kroll, L., Harrington, R., Jayson, D., Fraser, J., & Gowers, S. (1996). Pilot study of continuation cognitive-behavioral therapy for major depression in adolescent psychiatric patients. *Journal of the American Academy of Child and Adolescent Psychiatry, 35,* 1156–1161.

Leenaars, A. A., Maltsberger, J. T., & Neimeyer, R. A. (Eds.). (1994). *Treatment of suicidal people.* Washington, DC: Taylor & Francis.

Leon, A. C., Keller, M. B., Warshaw, M. G., Mueller, T. I., Solomon, D. A., Coryell, W., et al. (1999). Prospective study of fluoxetine treatment and suicidal behavior in affectively ill subjects. *American Journal of Psychiatry, 156,* 195–201.

Linehan, M. M. (1993a). *Cognitive behavioral therapy of borderline personality disorder.* New York: Guilford Press.

Linehan, M. M. (1993b). *Skills training manual for treating borderline personality disorder.* New York: Guilford Press.

Linehan, M. M. (1997). Behavioral treatments of suicidal behaviors. In D. M. Stoff & J. J. Mann (Eds.), *The neurobiology of suicidal behavior* (pp. 302–328). New York: Annals of the New York Academy of Sciences.

Linehan, M. M., Armstrong, H. E., Suarez, A., Allmon, D., & Heard, H. L. (1991). Cognitive-behavioral treatment of chronically parasuicidal borderline patients. *Archives of General Psychiatry, 48,* 1060–1064.

Maltsberger, J. T. (1993). Problems in the care of suicidal patients. *American Association of Suicidology Newslink, 19,* 3–5.

Maltsberger, J. T. (1994). Calculated risk-taking in the treatment of suicidal patients: Ethical and legal problems. In A. A. Leenaars, J. T. Maltsberger, & R. Neimeyer (Eds.), *Treatment of suicidal people* (pp. 195–205). Washington, DC: Taylor & Francis.

Mann, J. J. (1998). The neurobiology of suicide. *Nature Medicine, 4,* 25–30.

Mann, J. J., & Arango, V. (2001). Neurobiology of suicide and attempted suicide. In D. Wasserman (Ed.), *Suicide: An unnecessary death* (pp. 29–34). London: Martin Duritz.

Mann, J. J., & Kapur, S. (1991). The emergence of suicidal ideation and behavior during antidepressant pharmacotherapy. *Archives of General Psychiatry, 48,* 1027–1033.

Mann, J. J., Waternaux, C., Haas, G. L., & Malone, K. M. (1999). Toward a clinical model of suicidal behavior in psychiatric patients. *American Journal of Psychiatry, 156,* 181–189.

Maris, R. W., Berman, A. L., Maltsberger, J. T., & Yufit, R. (Eds.). (1992). *Assessment and prediction of suicide.* New York: Guilford Press.

Maris, R. W., Berman, A. L., & Silverman, M. M. (2000). *Comprehensive textbook of suicidology.* New York: Guilford Press.

McLeavey, B. C., Daly, J. D., Ludgate, J. W., & Murray, C. M. (1994). Interpersonal problem-solving skills training in the treatment of self-poisoning patients. *Suicide and Life-Threatening Behavior, 24,* 382–394.

Montgomery, S. A. (1997). Suicide and antidepressants. *Annals of the New York Academy of Sciences, 836,* 329–338.

Mufson, L., Moreau, D., Weissman, M. M., & Klerman, G. L. (1993). *Interpersonal psychotherapy for depressed adolescents.* New York: Guilford Press.

Mufson, L., Weissman, M. M., Moreau, D., & Garfinkel, R. (1999). Efficacy of interpersonal psychotherapy for depressed adolescents. *Archives of General Psychiatry, 56,* 573–579.

O'Carroll, P. W., Berman, A. L., Maris, R. W., Moscicki, E. K., Tanney, B. L., & Silverman, M. M. (1996). Beyond the Tower of Babel: A nomenclature for suicidology. *Suicide and Life-Threatening Behavior, 26,* 237–252.

Patrick, K., Grace, T. W., & Lovato, C. Y. (1992). Health issues for college students. In G. S. Omenn, J. E. Fielding, & L. B. Love (Eds.), *Annual Review of Public Health, 1992, 13,* 253–268.

Quinnett, P. G. (2000). *Counseling suicidal people: A therapy of hope.* Spokane, WA: The QPR Institute.

Rathus, J. H., & Miller, A. L. (2002). Dialectical behavior therapy adapted for suicidal adolescents. *Suicide and Life-Threatening Behavior, 32,* 146–157.

Roberts, A. (Ed.). (1991). *Contemporary perspectives on crisis intervention and prevention*. Englewood Cliffs, NJ: Prentice-Hall.

Rogers, J. R., & Soyka, K. M. (2004). "One size fits all": An existential-constructivist perspective on the crisis intervention approach with suicidal individuals. *Journal of Contemporary Psychotherapy, 34*, 7–22.

Rudd, M. D. (2000). Integrating science into the practice of clinical suicidology: A review of the psychotherapy literature and a research agenda for the future. In R. W. Maris, S. S. Canetto, J. McIntosh, & M. M. Silverman (Eds.), *Review of suicidology, 2000* (pp. 47–67). New York: Guilford Press.

Rudd, M. D., & Joiner, T. E. (1998). The assessment, management, and treatment of suicidality: Towards clinically informed and balanced standards of care. *Clinical Psychology: Research and Practice, 30*, 437–446.

Rudd, M. D., Joiner, T. E., Jobes, D. A., & King, C. A. (1999). The outpatient treatment of suicidality: An integration of science and recognition of its limitations. *Professional Psychology: Research and Practice, 30*, 437–446.

Rudd, M. D., Joiner, T. E., & Rajab, M. H. (2001). *Treating suicidal behavior: An effective time-limited approach*. New York: Guilford Press.

Salkovskis, P. M. (1996). *Frontiers of cognitive therapy*. New York: Guilford Press.

Salkovskis, P. M. (2001). Psychological treatment of suicidal patients. In D. Wasserman (Ed.), *Suicide: An unnecessary death* (pp. 161–172). London: Martin Duritz.

Schwartz, A. J., & Reifler, C. B. (1980). Suicide among American college and university students from 1970–71 through 1975–76. *Journal of the American College Health Association, 28*, 205–209.

Schwartz, A. J., & Reifler, C. B. (1988). College student suicide in the United States: Incidence data and prospects for demonstrating the efficacy of preventive programs. *Journal of the American College Health Association, 37*, 53–59.

Seiden, R. H. (1966). Campus tragedy: A study of student suicide. *Journal of Abnormal Psychology, 6*, 389–399.

Shaffer, D., & Pfeffer, C. (2001). Practice parameters for the assessment and treatment of children and adolescents with suicidal behavior. *Journal of the American Academy of Child and Adolescent Psychiatry, 40*(7, Suppl.), 24S–51S.

Sherman, M., & Thelen, M. (1998). Distress and professional impairment among psychologists in clinical practice. *Professional Psychology: Research and Practice, 29*, 79–85.

Shneidman, E. S. (1993). *Suicide as psychache: A clinical approach to self-destructive behavior*. Northvale, NJ: Aronson.

Silverman, M. M. (1993). Campus student suicide rates: Fact or artifact? *Suicide and Life-Threatening Behavior, 23,* 329–342.

Silverman, M. M., Meyer, P. M., Sloane, F., Raffel, M., & Pratt, D. M. (1997). The big ten student suicide study: A 10-year study of suicides on Midwestern university campuses. *Suicide and Life-Threatening Behavior, 27,* 285–303.

Simon, R. I. (1992). Clinical risk management of suicidal patients: Assessing the unpredictable. In R. I. Simon (Ed.), *Review of clinical psychiatry and the law* (Vol. 3, pp. 3–66). Washington, DC: American Psychiatric Press.

Slaikeu, K. (1990). *Crisis intervention* (2nd ed.). Boston: Allyn & Bacon.

Spirito, A., & Overholser, J. C. (Eds.). (2003). *Evaluating and treating adolescent suicide attempters: From research to practice.* New York: Academic Press.

Verkes, R. J., & Cowen, P. J. (2000). Pharmacotherapy of suicidal ideation and behavior. In K. Hawton & K. van Heeringen (Eds.), *The international handbook of suicide and attempted suicide* (pp. 487–502). New York: Wiley.

Wood, A., Harrington, R., & Moore, A. (1996). Controlled trial of a brief cognitive-behavioral intervention in adolescent patients with depressive disorders. *Journal of Child Psychology and Psychiatry, 37,* 737–746.

Zimmerman, J. K., & Asnis, G. M. (Eds.). (1995). *Treatment approaches with suicidal adolescents.* New York: Wiley.

CHAPTER 18

Suicide Terrorism

Ariel Merari

By a strict definition, a suicide terrorist attack is an assault intended to achieve a political objective, performed outside the context of a conventional war, in which assailants intentionally kill themselves while killing others. The self-destructive element makes this form of terrorism substantially different in both its psychological foundations and potential consequences from other terrorist attacks that involve high risk for the perpetrators.

Suicide terrorism constitutes a political and strategic problem of considerable import. This observation seems obvious after the September 11, 2001, attacks in the United States. Yet, even before the attacks in New York and Washington, suicide attacks had, on some occasions, far-reaching political consequences. Attacks against American and French forces and diplomatic missions in Lebanon in 1983 resulted in the evacuation of the Multinational Force from that country. This step enabled the Syrian de-facto takeover of the country and had a vast influence on Lebanese domestic and international politics in the following years. In another arena, Palestinian suicidal terrorist attacks in Israel in 1996 resulted in a change of government and had a major deleterious impact on the Middle East peace process.

Suicide terrorist attacks attract much public interest and concern. This phenomenon has always been surrounded by mystery and fear. The fact that, unlike ordinary self-destruction, terrorist suicide has been murderous and often directed randomly against the population naturally augmented the feeling of danger and a need to understand it. In the

Thanks are due to Ms. Nasra Hassan, who conducted the interviews.

absence of empirical research on this phenomenon, the explanations offered have been speculative. The most common explanations emphasized
cultural factors. Islamic religious fanaticism has been particularly popular in this context (Hoffman, 1998; Israeli, 1997; Taylor, 1988). Taylor,
for example, included the analysis of suicidal terrorism in a chapter titled "Fanaticism." He found the roots of this behavior in the tradition of
the Assassins, and attributes suicidal terrorism to Shiite fanaticism in
particular: "The forces that gave rise to the Assassins remain and influence the Shi'ites today" (p. 109). And similarly: ". . . the behaviours
which we find so difficult to understand (suicide bombing, for example)
have their origins in the kind of religious practice which characterizes
Islamic fundamentalism, and especially shi'iteism" (p. 110). Taylor,
however, extended his explanation to political suicides in other societies,
including Western nations, such as the German RAF suicides in prison
in the 1970s, the Irish hunger strikes in the Maze Prison in 1980/1981,
and the Jonestown mass suicide in 1978. His broader explanation of this
phenomenon attributes it to social pressure and conformity that characterize certain societies: "Both contemporary Shi'ite society, and the
Japanese society of the time, show many attributes of intense control,
with restrictions on extra-societal influences. In many respects they are
as 'psychologically' closed as the prisons which sustained both the
Baader-Meinhof and the IRA suicides" (p. 120).

Israeli (1997) found the basic explanation of this phenomenon in the
Islamic frame of mind: "Turning to an Islamic frame of reference for a
definition, and perhaps a diagnosis, would then appear imperative if we
are to comprehend the underlying motives of this sort of unparalleled
mode of self-sacrifice" (p. 107). He did, however, maintain (with no
empirical evidence to support his claim), that personality factors also play
a role in the making of a suicide terrorist. Specifically, he speculated that
there are three common characteristics of suicide bombers: They are
young and have few life responsibilities; they are unsuccessful or are
shunned by their family and society, so that they feel isolated; and they
have low self-esteem. Suicide terrorists, according to Israeli, "may be
somewhat depressed and in search of easy solutions to their problems. Unsuccessful, perhaps self-despising, they find solace in becoming martyrs,
thus almost instantly and mythically transforming frustration into glory,
failure into victory and self-depreciation into public adoration" (p. 106).

Other explanations ascribed the phenomenon to indoctrination, even brainwashing, in the sense of persuading "uninformed youth" to commit suicide in the service of their advocated cause (Post, 2001). In an earlier study (Merari, 1990), I attributed politically motivated suicide, particularly cases of group suicide such as Masada (A.D. 73) and the Irish chain suicide of 1980/1981, to situational factors, notably group pressure, group commitment, and the influence of a charismatic leader, as well as to personality factors. These explanations are not entirely compatible with the factual evidence that has accumulated on suicide terrorism, which will be described later.

PREVALENCE

Several writers have maintained that suicide terrorism is an ancient phenomenon, claiming that it was used by groups such as the Jewish Sicarii of the first century and the Muslim *Hashashin* (Assassins) of the eleventh to thirteenth centuries (Atran, 2003; Schweitzer, 2001; Sprinzak, 2000). This claim is erroneous because these groups carried out attacks that involved high risk for the perpetrators, sometimes their almost sure death, but were not suicide in the strict sense of self-destruction. As much as recorded evidence is concerned, true suicide terrorist attacks, in which the attackers kill themselves while killing others, are a modern phenomenon. The first recorded case of a suicide terrorist attack was the car bombing of the Iraqi embassy in Beirut on December 15, 1981, although as a methodical terrorist tactic, these attacks were first used in Lebanon in 1983 by radical Islamic groups that later formed Hizballah. Since that time, this tactic has been espoused by many other groups around the globe, including eight groups in Lebanon (six of them Lebanese and two Palestinian), four Palestinian groups in Israel's occupied territories, two Egyptian groups, the Kurdish Labor Party (PKK), the Turkish Revolutionary People's Liberation Front (a left-wing group), Chechen rebels, the Tamil Tigers (LTTE), Islamic militant groups in Kashmir, al-Qaeda, a militant Islamic group in Morocco, and anti-American groups in Iraq. Most of these groups have carried out only a small number of suicide assaults. A few have embarked on a systematic campaign of suicide attacks as a central method in their armed struggle. The Tamil Tigers carried out nearly 170 suicide attacks from 1987 to

2000 (Gunaratna, 2000). Palestinian groups carried out 160 suicide attacks from 1993 through July 2003, nearly half of them perpetrated by Hamas. Nevertheless, as demonstrated by the September 11, 2001, events, the frequency of attacks is not the most important factor in creating the impact of suicide terrorism. Extremely large numbers of casualties result when the suicide method is coupled with other characteristics of the group, namely, the ability to acquire and use a large quantity of explosives (or other means of causing mass casualties), selection of densely populated targets, and smart planning that makes it possible for the group to devise original modes of attack and circumvent defenses.

PROFILE OF SUICIDE TERRORISTS

Psychological data on suicide terrorists of most groups has not been published. Since 1983, I have collected data on suicide terrorism around the globe from a variety of sources, using mainly media reports that included demographic and biographical details of suicides, sometimes based on interviews with the suicides' families. Valuable information was gained from interviews with jailed would-be suicides. Particularly useful as a basis for psychological autopsy was a systematic set of data on 34 of the 36 suicide Palestinian terrorists in the period of 1993 to 1998. These data were based on interviews with family members (parents and siblings) of the suicides.[1] Other data included interviews with persons who attempted to carry out suicide attacks but failed and with Hamas and Palestinian Islamic Jihad (PIJ) trainers of suicide bombers. Data on suicide terrorists in Israel after 1998 and on suicide attackers in Lebanon in the period of 1983 to 1989 (almost all suicide attacks in Lebanon took place within this time frame) are mainly based on media sources and include some demographic characteristic, as well as on interviews with jailed would-be suicides. These data, supplemented by information on other groups, are summarized next.

Demographic Characteristics

Age

The mean age of the Lebanese suicide bombers was 21, and the age range was 16 to 28. The mean age of the Palestinian suicides before the second intifada was 22, with a range of 18 to 38. The age range of the Palestinian suicides in the current intifada was somewhat broader (17 to 53), but the average remained the same—22. Two-thirds of them were between 18 and 23 years old. The age range of the female PKK suicides was 17 to 27 and the males 18 to 40. The mean age of the actual and would-be male suicides combined was 27 (Ergil, 2001). The age of LTTE suicides is younger, most of them under 15, as a matter of organization policy (Joshi, 2000). The age range of the al-Qaeda September 11 suicides was reported as 20 to 33 (Schweitzer & Shay, 2002).

Marital Status

Data for the Lebanese sample are lacking, but almost all of the suicides were single. In the 1993 to 1998 Palestinian sample, 31 (91%) were single (moreover, none of them was engaged to be married), and three were married (only one of them had children). During the second intifada (which started on September 29, 2000, and is still going on at the time of writing), the proportion of married suicide bombers remained below 10%. By the Palestinian Authority (PA) 1997 census, the median age at first marriage was 23 (Palestinian Central Bureau of Statistics, 1997). The fact that almost all suicides have been single may suggest that unmarried persons are more willing to volunteer for suicide missions. However, in the Palestinian case, it has also been the policy of the organizations to refrain from recruiting married persons for such missions. In a study of the demographic characteristics of Hizballah members killed in action (most of them were not suicides), Hurwitz (1999) found that only 45% of those whose marital status was known were single. Hurwitz notes, however, that Hizballah's leadership preferred to recruit unmarried youth, but this policy was incongruent with the Lebanese Shiite custom of marrying young. Martin Kramer (1991) also noted that the "window of opportunity" for recruiting a youngster by Hizballah for military activity was rather narrow, because the Lebanese custom of marrying young allows the organization only a few years for training and participation in operations. Thus, although the willingness to embark on suicide missions is presumably higher among young, unmarried persons, both marital status and age of the suicides seem to reflect mainly the policy of the terrorist group.

Gender

In the Lebanese case, 38 of the suicides were males and seven were fe-males (all of the latter were sent by secular groups). All of the Palestin-ian suicides before the second intifada were males, a result of the fact that until recently the Palestinian organizations that used suicide attacks were religious groups that objected to the use of women in combat mis-sions. During the second intifada, the secular groups of Fatah and the Popular Front for the Liberation of Palestine (PFLP) also espoused sui-cide attacks. These groups used women as well as men for suicide mis-sions. It is also noteworthy that left-wing Turkish and Kurdish groups, as well as the Tamil Tigers, have used women as often as men for suicide attacks. In the PKK, 11 of the 15 terrorist suicides from 1995 to 1999 were women (Ergil, 2001). In the LTTE, there is a special women sui-cide unit, called Birds of Freedom (Joshi, 2000), and about one-third of the suicide attacks have been carried out by women (Chandran, 2001; Schweitzer, 2001). Thus, the greater number of male suicides in the Lebanese and Palestinian cases reflects only the preference of religious Islamic groups.

Socioeconomic Status

Reliable data are available only for the Palestinian 1993 to 1998 sample. In this study, the economic level of the suicides' families was assessed by the interviewer on the basis of her extensive acquaintance with the living conditions of the Palestinians in the West Bank and the Gaza Strip. In general, the economic status of the Palestinian suicides' families is roughly a cross-section of Palestinian society in the Occupied Territo-ries. In the 1993 to 1998 sample, the 34 families were distributed as fol-lows: very poor, 12%; poor, 21%; lower middle class, 26%; middle class, 32%; upper class, 9%.

Education

The education level of the suicides at the time of their suicidal attack was higher than that of the general Palestinian society. Twenty-six per-cent of the suicides had at least partial university education. In compar-ison, according to the Palestinian Central Bureau of Statistics (2002) data, 11.9% of the general Palestinian population attained above a high

Table 18.1   Education Level of Palestinian Suicides and of the General Palestinian Population (Percent)

	Education					
	No Schooling	Partial Elementary	Elementary	High School	Partial University	Full University
Suicides	0	2.9	8.8	62	23.5	2.9
General population	10.5	29.2	25.3	23.0	11.9	11.9

school education. The distribution of the suicides' education level is shown in Table 18.1.

Refugees versus Nonrefugees

Whereas 21% of the Palestinian population in the Territories live in refugee camps (Arzt, 1997, p. 60; Shavit & Banna, 2001), before the second intifada they were responsible for 56% of the suicides, more than twice their proportion in the population. Thus, living in a refugee camp should be regarded as an important contributing factor to the likelihood of committing a suicide attack. This phenomenon is true for both the West Bank and the Gaza Strip. In each one of these regions, refugee camp residents are represented among the suicides at more than twice their share of the general population. Because no relationship has been found between economic status and participation in suicide attacks, the influence of being a refugee is, presumably, not due to the greater economic hardship associated with the refugee status. Rather, it probably reflects the greater militancy of refugees' descendents and the greater support for Hamas and Islamic Jihad among them.

Religion

Suicide attacks in Lebanon were initially carried out by the radical Shiite groups, which eventually formed Hizballah. For this reason, the phenomenon of suicide terrorism, especially the Middle East brand, has been associated in public perception with religious fanaticism. This notion also permeated academic writings. However, by 1986, it became clear that nearly two-thirds of the suicide attacks in Lebanon were carried out by secular groups (Merari, 1990).

Before the second intifada, suicide attacks by Palestinians were carried out only by militant religious groups (two-thirds of them by Hamas and one-third by the Palestinian Islamic Jihad). In the second intifada (al-Aqsa intifada), which started on September 29, 2000, and is still going on at the time of writing, two secular groups—Fatah and the PFLP—have also resorted to suicide attacks. By July 31, 2003, these two secular groups combined were responsible for 32% of the suicide attacks in the second intifada.

The conclusion that religious fanaticism is neither necessary nor a sufficient factor in suicide terrorist attacks gains further support from the fact that several nonreligious groups have resorted to this tactic. Thus, the Tamil Tigers (LTTE), the group that has carried out nearly 170 suicide attacks, more than any other single group, is composed of Hindus and motivated by nationalist-separatist sentiments rather than by religious fanaticism. Suicide attacks have also been carried out by Marxist (and, therefore, clearly nonreligious) groups such as the Kurdish PKK and the Turkish Revolutionary People's Liberation Front.

Revenge for Personal Suffering

Some observers have suggested that the suicides have been motivated by the wish to take revenge for suffering from the enemy that they had personally undergone (Fisk, 2001; Joshi, 2000). Whereas this explanation is clearly incorrect in the case of the September 11 attackers, it may still be true for suicide attacks in most other places, such as Lebanon, Israel, Turkey, and Sri Lanka. This question was directly examined in the study of the Palestinian 1993 to 1998 suicides. In that study, the suicides' families were asked about events that could, presumably, provide a reason for a personal grudge. These reasons included the killing of a close family member by Israeli forces, killing of a friend, wounding or beating of the suicide in clashes with Israeli soldiers, and arrest of the suicide. Analysis of the results suggests that a personal grudge has not been a necessary factor and apparently not even a major factor in creating the wish to embark on a suicide mission, although it presumably was a contributing factor in some of the cases. Thus, in only one case of the 34 had a close family member of the suicide been killed by Israeli forces. However, in 11 cases, the interviewees mentioned that a friend of the suicide had been killed before the suicide mission. In seven cases, a close family member (a father or a brother) had been jailed. As to the suicides' personal encounters, in 15 of the cases the suicide had been beaten in clashes with Israeli forces during demonstrations, and 11 of these resulted in some injury. Eighteen of the suicides had been jailed, most of them for short time periods for minor charges, such as participation in violent demonstrations. In assessing these findings as indicative of personal trauma, remember that most of the Palestinian youth were involved in various aspects of the intifada in activities such as stone throwing, demonstrations, distributing leaflets, painting graffiti, and enforcing commerce strikes. In other words, this part of the suicides' personal history does not distinguish them from the average Palestinian youngster in the period under consideration. Indeed, 19 of the suicides were described by their families as "very active" during the intifada and eight were described as "active." In most cases, therefore, a high level of militancy preceded a personal trauma, although such trauma might later add to the already existing hatred and wish for revenge.

Personality Factors and Psychopathology

In none of the cases did interviews with would-be suicides or parents' and siblings' descriptions of the suicides' personality and behavior suggest the existence of clear symptoms of psychopathology. No evidence was found for hospitalization in a mental institution or ambulatory psychological treatment. Furthermore, the descriptions did not reveal a common personality type for all or most of the suicides. (However, relying solely on family descriptions was not a sufficiently sensitive method for characterizing personality types.) Still, significantly, no evidence was found for the existence of risk factors for suicide. Three main risk factors are generally recognized in psychiatry and psychology: the existence of affective disorders (especially depression), substance abuse, and a history of suicide attempts (Barraclough & Hughes, 1987; Jacobs, Brewer, & Klein-Benheim, 1999; Klerman, 1987; Lester & Lester, 1971; Linehan, 1999; Miller & Paulsen, 1999; Moscicki, 1999; World Health Organization, 1993). None of these was present among the Palestinian suicides of the 1993 to 1998 period. It is, however, possible that more sensitive techniques would have revealed more subtle suicidal ideation in at least some of the terrorist suicides.

Furthermore, existing sociological and psychological theories of suicide seem to be inappropriate for explaining suicidal terrorism. A full survey of the compatibility of suicide theories with the phenomenon of terrorist suicide is beyond the scope of this paper; therefore, I address this issue rather succinctly. Of the sociological theories, the closest to explaining this phenomenon seems to be Durkheim's concept of altruistic suicide, more specifically, his subcategory of "optional" altruistic suicide (Durkheim, 1951). Optional altruistic suicide comprises cases in which suicide is considered a merit by society but is not obligatory, such as the Japanese Samurai custom of seppuku (or hara-kiri). However, the suitability of Durkheim's concept to the phenomenon of terrorist suicide is questionable on several grounds. Durkheim used the concept of altruistic suicide to characterize societies, not individuals. He explained the differences in suicide rates of various societies by the attributes of these societies. He inferred the motivation for committing suicide from the characteristics of the society to which the suicides belonged. Thus, he characterized suicides in the military as "altruistic" because of the characteristics that he attributed to the army, such as obedience and a sense of duty. He viewed altruistic suicide as a stable rather than a situational characteristic of the society in question. Altruistic suicide characterizes societies that are highly "integrated," in Durkheim's terms, that is, very cohesive and, therefore, exert much influence on their members. Hence, to apply Durkheim's concept of altruistic suicide to the phenomenon of terrorist suicide is to attribute these suicides to the traits of the societies in which they occurred—a religious group, an ethnic community, a cast, or a social organization such as the army. Terrorist suicide, however, has taken place in very diverse societies. In addition to Lebanese Shiites, Lebanese Sunnis, secular Lebanese, Palestinians, Egyptians, Armenians, Marxist Kurds, and Tamil Hindus, suicide for a political cause has been committed by communist Germans, Catholic Irish, and Protestant Americans (John Wilkes Booth, who assassinated President Lincoln, committed suicide after the murder). It can be argued that the important factor is not the larger social unit—the ethnic group, religious group, or nation—but the microsociety of a terrorist group itself, which provides the social milieu amenable to generating self-sacrificial suicide, in accordance with Durkheim's altruistic variety. The group is highly cohesive, rigorous, and creates rules of conduct and behavior ethics that members are expected to live by. Yet, the great majority of the terrorist groups, regardless of their structure, have not resorted to suicide attacks at all. Furthermore, there is no evidence that terrorist groups that maintain a particularly strict discipline and a tight structure have re-sorted to suicide tactics more than the looser groups. On the contrary, among the Palestinian groups, the Popular Front for the Liberation of Palestine (PFLP) has a much tighter structure and discipline than Hamas. Yet, the PFLP has generated only a few suicide attacks whereas Hamas has carried out many.

Psychological theories of suicide cannot readily explain the phenomenon of terrorist suicide either. Psychoanalytic theories view suicide as a result of an "unconscious identification of the self with another person who is both loved and hated. Thus it becomes possible to treat oneself, or some part of oneself (typically one's disavowed body), as an alien and an enemy" (Maltsberger, 1999, p. 73). While my study did not provide tools for examining the suicides' unconscious processes, no external supportive evidence of this theoretical explanation of suicide was found. A more specific form of this approach was offered by Zilboorg (1996). He stressed the importance of identification with an important person, who died when the suicide was a child. The data does not support this theory. In the Palestinian sample, for instance, only six (of 34) of the suicides lost a parent (at ages that ranged from 2 to 10) before carrying out the attack. It is unlikely, although theoretically possible, that the suicides lost other psychologically important persons in childhood. But these theories would find it difficult to explain the waves of suicide terrorism in the Lebanese, Palestinian, and Sri Lankan cases, as well as the episodes of cluster suicides, such as the September 11, 2001, attacks in the United States, the Irish hunger strikers in 1981, and the cases of Palestinian suicide attacks in duo or trio.

Whereas psychoanalytical theories have basically viewed suicide as aggression (directed internally), other psychological theories emphasize the element of despair. In this view, the wish to commit suicide is almost always caused by intense psychological pain, which is generated by frustrated psychological needs. Suicide is committed by persons who view it as the best way to stop the pain. The prevailing emotion of suicides is the feeling of hopelessness-helplessness (Shneidman, 1985, 1999). Several other researchers (e.g., Beck, Kovacs, & Weissman, 1996; Farber, 1968) also underscored the role of hopelessness in generating the wish to commit suicide. The greater the feeling of hope, the less the likelihood of suicide. Hope is the perceived ability to influence the world and to be satisfied by the world. This concept of hope, however, relates to the individual's expected ability to function within his own social milieu, rather than to a general communal situation, such as being under occupation. Lester and Lester (1971, p. 45) noted that suicidal people tend to see not only the present but also the future as gloomy, expecting to be socially isolated in the future. As to terrorist suicide, however, whereas it can be argued that, at least in some cases, the suicide attacks are motivated by despair at the national or community level (despair that is associated with frustrated *national* needs), there is no evidence that the persons who carried out the suicide attacks suffered from despair at the individual level. It is noteworthy in this respect that, in times of war, when the whole community is under duress, suicide rates tend to go down (Lester & Lester, pp. 109–110).

The profiles of the terrorist suicide gleaned from the interviews did not resemble a typical suicide candidate, as described in the literature. By their family members' accounts, 50% of the 1993 to 1998 Palestinian suicides occasionally said that they wished to carry out an act of martyrdom, and 44% used to talk about paradise. However, the young persons who eventually committed suicide had no record of earlier attempts of self-destruction, were not in conflict with their family and friends, and most of them expressed no feelings of being fed up with life. In the suicides' notes and last messages, the act of self-destruction was presented as a form of struggle rather than as an escape. There was no sense of helplessness-hopelessness. On the contrary, the suicide was an act of projecting power rather than expressing weakness. With all due caution, it seems that most terrorist suicides in the Palestinian sample were not "suicidal" in the usual psychological sense.

The key to understanding terrorist suicide should, therefore, be sought in a realm other than personality disorders and suicidality.

TERRORIST GROUPS AS SUICIDE PRODUCTION LINES

The previous sections suggest that neither demographic nor individual psychological characteristics can explain the phenomenon of terrorist suicide. The suicides were ordinary youngsters, average in all respects. In this sense, suicide terrorism appears to suit Hannah Arendt's (1994) phrase, "the banality of evil."

An important clue to understanding the phenomenon of terrorist sui-cide can be gained from the hunger strike of 10 Irish Republican Army (IRA) and Irish National Liberation Army (INLA) members in Belfast's Maze prison in 1981. Ten Irish nationalists, led by Bobby Sands, starved themselves to death in sequence when their demand to be recognized as political (rather than common criminal) prisoners was rejected by the British government. Although this event does not qualify as an act of suicidal terrorism because the hunger strikers did not kill anyone but themselves, it was an act of self-destruction for a political cause and, as such, can teach us much about the psychological mechanisms involved in suicide terrorism. Self-starvation is an extremely demanding way to die, much more difficult than the instantaneous death caused by a self-inflicted explosion. It took the hunger strikers from 50 to more than 70 days to die. During that time, mothers, wives, and priests begged at least some of the hunger strikers to stop their self-destruction (Beresford, 1987). The force that led them to continue their strike to the very end, ignoring all pressures, must have been very strong. What was this force that sustained their determination? The assumption that all 10 were sui-cidal persons, who happened to be in jail at the same time, is rather im-plausible. It is also unlikely that they were motivated by religious fanaticism and the promise of a place in paradise. The only way to un-derstand this frightening demonstration of human readiness for self-sacrifice is to look at the influence of the group on its individual members. The chain suicide was a product of a group contract that a per-son could not break. The group pressure in that situation was as strong as the group pressure that led hundreds of thousands of soldiers in World War I to charge against enemy machine gun fire and artillery to almost sure death. And, it was even stronger once the first hunger striker died. From that point on, the contract to die could not be broken, because the person who could release the next in line from their commitment was al-ready dead.

A more comprehensive picture of the process of making suicide bombers was gained from data collected on Palestinian suicide terror-ists, including interviews with trainers for such missions and surviving would-be suicides. The findings of these data are supported by circum-stantial evidence from suicide terrorism in other countries. The data suggested that there are three main elements in the preparation of a suicide bomber by an organization, namely, indoctrination, group commitment, and a personal pledge. These elements are described next.

Indoctrination

Throughout the preparation for a suicide mission, the candidate is subjected to indoctrination by authoritative persons in the group. Although the candidate is, presumably, convinced from the start in the justification of the cause for which he or she is willing to die, the indoctrination is intended to further strengthen the motivation and to keep it from dwindling. Indoctrination in the religious Palestinian groups (Hamas and PIJ) included nationalist themes (Palestinian humiliation by Israel, stories of Arab glory in the days of Mohammad and the Caliphate, examples of acts of heroism during the Islamic wars) and religious themes (the act of self-sacrifice is Allah's will and description of the rewards guaranteed for *shahids*—martyrs—in paradise).

Group Commitment

The mutual commitment of candidates for suicide operations to carry out the self-sacrificial attack is a very powerful motivation to stick to the mission despite hesitations and second thoughts. The chain suicide of the Irish hunger strikers in 1981 is an example of this social contract that is extremely difficult to break (Merari, 1990). In Hamas and PIJ, the preparation for suicide attacks is often done in cells, consisting of three to five volunteers. These cells are characterized in the organization as "martyrdom cells" (*haliya istishhadiya*) to differentiate them from ordinary "military cells" (*haliya askariya*). Members of these cells are mutually committed to one another in this kind of an unbreakable social contract. In the LTTE, male and female suicides have been trained in special units called Black Tigers and Birds of Freedom, respectively. Presumably, they are also bonded in a social contract to commit the suicidal mission. In fact, the power of a group commitment and inability to break it was also the basis of the willingness of Japanese pilots in World War II to fly on kamikaze missions. Last letters of kamikazes to their families, written shortly before they took off for their last flight, indicated that while some of them went on their suicidal attack enthusiastically, others regarded it as a duty that they could not evade (Inoguchi &

Nakajima, 1958, pp. 196–208). Presumably, the group commitment element was also influential in the September 11 attacks in the United States.

Personal Commitment

Many Middle Eastern groups adopted a routine of releasing to the media a videotape shortly after a suicide attack. These tapes are also usually presented by the organization to the suicide's family after the operation as a farewell message. Typically, in this tape the suicide is seen, rifle in hand (and, in Islamic groups, a Koran in the other hand), declaring his intention to go on the suicide mission. This act is meant not only for propaganda; it is primarily a ceremony intended to establish an irrevocable personal commitment of the candidate to carry out the suicide attack. This ritual constitutes a point of no return. Having committed himself in front of a television camera (the candidate is also asked at that time to write farewell letters to his family and friends, which are kept by the group alongside the videotape for release after the completion of the suicide mission), the candidate cannot possibly turn back on his promise. In fact, in both Hamas and PIJ, from that point the candidate is formally referred to as "the living martyr" (*al-shahid al-hai*). This title is often used by the candidates themselves in the opening sentence of the video statement, which routinely starts with: "I am [the candidate's name], the living martyr. . . ." At this stage, the candidate is, presumably, in a mental state of a living dead and has already resigned from life.

Public Support

The magnitude of public support for suicide operations seems to affect both the terrorist group's willingness to use this tactic and the number of volunteers for suicide missions. Most, if not all, terrorist groups that have used suicide attacks are not indifferent to the opinions and attitudes of what they view as their constituency—the population whose interests they claim to serve and from which they recruit their members. In choosing tactics and targets, the group tends to act within the boundaries of its constituency's approval. During the last six months of 1995, for example, Hamas refrained from carrying out suicide attacks, because its leadership realized that such actions would not be supported by the Palestinian population at that time and would thus have had an adverse effect on the organization's popularity. In the Palestinian case, public support for terrorist attacks against Israel in general and for suicide attacks in particular has waxed and waned since the Oslo agreement of 1993, ranging from as low as 20% support in May 1996 to more than 70% in May 2002 (Center for Palestine Research and Studies, 2000; Jerusalem Media and Communication Centre, 2002; Palestinian Center for Policy & Survey Research, 2002). The great increase in the frequency of suicide attacks during the second intifada (al-Aqsa intifada) reflects the greater willingness of Palestinian youth to volunteer, or to be recruited, for what is generally regarded in the community as acts of ultimate patriotism and heroism. Songs praising the shahids are the greatest hits, the walls in the streets and alleys of Palestinian towns in the West Bank and the Gaza Strip are covered with graffiti applauding them, and their actions are mimicked in children's games. In this atmosphere, the terrorist groups not only see a public license to continue the suicide attacks but also have a constant flow of youngsters ready to become human bombs. The role of the preparation of the suicide candidate, as described in the previous section, is to make sure that the youngster who, because of social pressure, said yes to an offer to become a shahid, or even the enthusiastic volunteer, would not have second thoughts and change his mind.

The importance of public attitude notwithstanding, it should be emphasized that so far there has not been even a single case of a person who carried out a true terrorist suicide attack (i.e., intentionally killing himself while killing others for a political cause) on his or her own whim. In all cases, it was an organization that decided to use this tactic, chose the target and the time, prepared the explosive charge, and arranged the logistics necessary for getting the human bomb to the target. Evidently, therefore, the terrorist group's decision to use suicide attacks as a tactic and its influence on the candidates are the key elements in this phenomenon.

COPING WITH THE PSYCHOLOGICAL EFFECTS OF SUICIDE TERRORISM

Terrorism in general and suicide attacks in particular constitute a major source of stress. This section deals with the ways adopted to deal with this stress. Because Israel has faced a continuous series of suicide terrorist attacks since 1993, it is an appropriate case in point. Suicide attacks have exacerbated the Israeli-Palestinian conflict and have had a significant adverse political effect on the peace process. They have also had a deleterious impact on the economy. This final section, however, deals only with their individual psychological effect and the ways that Israel has coped with it.

Terrorist events are known to be a source of psychological trauma. In addition to acute stress disorder, which appears immediately following the event, a longer term posttraumatic stress disorder (PTSD) emerges in some of the persons exposed to the traumatic event. In a review of several studies of PTSD among people in various countries who witnessed a terrorist attack, Gidron (2002) found an average PTSD rate of 28%. Symptoms of posttraumatic stress disorder may appear not only among persons present at the site of attack but also among some of those who consider themselves as potential victims, who are exposed to the traumatic event through the mass media or personal accounts of relatives and friends. Studies conducted after the September 11 attacks in New York found PTSD symptoms among people who had not personally witnessed the attack (Galea et al., 2002; Cohen Silver, Holman, McIntosh, Poulin, & Gil-Rivas, 2002). Posttraumatic stress disorder rates were higher among people who lived in close proximity to the site of attack and, therefore, felt a greater direct danger.

Although psychological trauma of civilian victims of terrorism in Israel has been studied since the 1970s, interest in this problem grew in the 1990s at the time when suicide attacks became a frequent occurrence. These attacks intensified in the second intifada, which started on September 29, 2000. The three years of the intifada (as of this writing) have been marked by suicide attacks, which have by far been the most deadly form of terrorism. Although suicide attacks in this period have constituted only about 0.5% of the total number of terrorist attacks, they have accounted for 59% of the civilian fatalities (Israel Defense Forces, 2003). Suicide attacks are more frightening than other forms of terrorism, not only because they cause a larger number of victims but also because these incomprehensible acts of self-sacrifice seem unstoppable. They create a sense of insecurity and lack of control. An explosive charge hidden in an innocent-looking package or a shopping bag can be detected and rendered harmless, but most of the suicides activate their charge on detection. People avoid public places, such as shopping centers, coffee shops, and buses, because these are the targets of suicide attacks.

Surveys conducted in Israel during the recent quarter of a century have consistently found a very high rate of expressed worry of terrorism. Since 1979, in most of the surveys, more than 70% of representative samples of the adult Israeli population have said that they were "very worried" or "worried" that they or members of their families would be hurt in a terrorist attack. The rate of worry was high even in periods when the intensity of terrorism was much lower than during the second intifada (Arian, 2003, p. 19; Merari & Friedland, 1980).

Yet, this high rate of worry is not necessarily associated with stress disorder. A recent survey (Bleich, Gelkopf, & Solomon, 2003) checked the occurrence of PTSD among Israelis. The survey was conducted in April/May 2002, at a time when Israeli civilians were exposed to frequent suicide attacks. Although more than 60% expressed a low sense of safety concerning themselves and their relatives, the authors found that only 9.4% met the symptom criteria for PTSD. This low rate is especially surprising because more than 16% of the sample reported that they had been directly exposed to a terrorist attack, and 37% had a family member or friend who had been exposed. In comparison, in the United States various surveys found that 10% to 20% suffered from several PTSD symptoms a couple of months after September 11 (Cohen Silver et al., 2002; Schlenger et al., 2002). The difference may be explained by methodological variations (e.g., in the duration of time since the exposure to the traumatic event), but also by a habituation process that has taken place in the Israeli population. Another possible explanation is that the Israeli mental health system is more adapted to handle the psychological effects of terrorist attacks.

Coping with the psychological effects of terrorism in general and suicide attacks in particular comprises two general categories: (1) preparatory measures and (2) intervention after the attack. Preparatory measures include training of organizations and units involved in responding to actual or threatened suicide attacks (police, military units of the homeland command, medical corps, public information, etc.). Public knowledge of the existence of an effective response system and trust in its committed and professional performance reduce anxiety and create some sense of control of a situation that is inherently surprising and uncertain. Warnings, based on intelligence information concerning the actual or intended launching of a terrorist attack in a certain area, are followed by a massive effort to dissuade or stop the perpetrator by police and military roadblocks and searches. This effort is often successful and helps to reduce the feeling of uncertainty and gives the public a sense of control over the situation. The credibility of the warnings is highly important for establishing public trust in the authorities. In the absence of trust, public responses might result in a paralysis of economic and social activities. Because suicide bombers target public places, guards are stationed at the entrances to cafes, shopping malls, theaters, and schools. These guards constitute the last line of defense, and some of them have been killed as they prevented the suicide attacker from getting inside the target building, thus saving the lives of many people.

Intervention after the attack necessitates the coordinated action of many organizations. Police, firefighters, medical corps, and victims' identification teams are the first responders on the scene. Concurrently, hospitals in the area of attack are alerted and get ready with medical and mental health teams to take in a large number of casualties. At the same time, the municipalities activate teams whose task is to inform victims' families and provide psychological and social support. Several studies suggest that social support (by the family or community) reduces post-traumatic stress (e.g., Cohen Silver et al., 2002; Solomon et al., 1988).

The activity of social services organizations is especially important in the days and months following the attack. Volunteer organizations are also instrumental at this later stage.

Persons who suffer acute stress reactions, as well as PTSD patients, are entitled to social security compensation for loss of ability to work and for financing of psychological treatment. Following an incident, social security personnel contact patients, who are invited to attend support groups that start a week after the incident. Those who suffer long-range psychological incapacitation get a permanent social security allowance, commensurate with the degree of incapacitation.

In conclusion, the Israeli experience suggests that even a protracted campaign of suicide terrorism does not necessarily cause widespread psychological trauma. A credible warning system and trust in the authorities' effectiveness reduce anxiety. Mental health and social support services may effectively reduce and limit the psychological trauma associated with direct or indirect exposure to terrorist attacks.

REFERENCES

Arendt, H. (1994). *Eichmann in Jerusalem—a report on the banality of evil.* New York: Penguin Classics.

Arian, A. (2003). *Israeli Public Opinion on National Security 2003* (Memorandum No. 67). Tel Aviv: Tel Aviv University, Jaffee Center for Strategic Studies.

Arzt, D. E. (1997). *Refugees into citizens: Palestinians and the end of the Arab-Israeli conflict.* New York: Council on Foreign Relations.

Atran, S. (2003). Genesis of suicide terrorism. *Science, 299,* 1534–1539.

Barraclough, B., & Hughes, J. (1987). *Suicide: Clinical and epidemiological studies.* London: Croom Helm.

Beck, A. T., Kovacs, M., & Weissman, A. (1996). Hopelessness and suicidal behavior. In J. Maltsberger & M. Goldblatt (Eds.), *Essential papers on suicide* (pp. 331–341). New York: New York University Press.

Beresford, D. (1987). *Ten men dead.* London: HarperCollins.

Bleich, A., Gelkopf, M., & Solomon, Z. (2003). Exposure to terrorism, stress-related mental health symptoms, and coping behaviors among a nationally representative sample in Israel. *Journal of the American Medical Association, 290*(5), 612–620.

Center for Palestine Research and Studies. (2000). *Public opinion polls 1–48.* Retrieved May 20, 2000, from http://www.cprs-palestine.org.

Chandran, S. (2001, October 6). Suicide terrorism. *The Hindu Online Edition.* Retrieved July 8, 2003, from http://www.hinduonnet.com/thehindu/2001/10/06/stories/05062524.htm.

Cohen Silver, R., Holman, E. A., McIntosh, D. N., Poulin, M., & Gil-Rivas, V. (2002). Nationwide longitudinal study of psychological responses to September 11. *Journal of the American Medical Association, 288,* 1235–1244.

Durkheim, E. (1951). *Suicide: A study in sociology.* New York: Free Press.

Ergil, D. (2001). Suicide terrorism in Turkey: The Workers' Party of Kurdistan. In The International Policy Institute for Counter Terrorism, *Countering suicide terrorism* (pp. 105–128). Herzliya, Israel: The Interdisciplinary Center.

Farber, M. L. (1968). *Theory of suicide.* New York: Funk & Wagnalls.

Fisk, R. (2001, August 11). What drives a bomber to kill the innocent child? *Independent* (UK). Retrieved January 20, 2002, from http://www.independent.co.uk/story.jsp?story=88134.

Galea, S., Ahern, J., Resnick, H., Kilpatrick, D., Bucuvalas, M., Gold, J., et al. (2002). Psychological sequelae of the September 11 terrorist attacks in New York City. *New England Journal of Medicine, 346*(13), 982–987.

Gidron, Y. (2002). Post-traumatic stress disorder after terrorist attacks: A review. *Journal of Nervous and Mental Diseases, 190,* 118–121.

Gunaratna, R. (2000, October 20). Suicide terrorism: A global threat. *Jane's Intelligence Review.* Retrieved June 1, 2002, from http://www.janes.com /security/international_security/news/usscole/jir001020_1_n.shtml.

Hoffman, B. (1998). *Inside terrorism,* London: Victor Gollancz.

Hurwitz, E. (1999). *Hizballah's military echelon: A social portrait.* Tel Aviv: Tel Aviv University, Dayan Center for Middle Eastern Studies.

Inoguchi, R., & Nakajima, T. (1958). *The divine wind: Japan's Kamikaze force in World War II.* Annapolis, MD: Naval Institute Press.

Israel Defense Forces. (2003). *Casualties since 30.9.00. Updated 20.11.03.* Retrieved November 22, 2003, from http://www.idf.il/daily_statistics /english/1.doc.

Israeli, R. (1997). Islamikaze and their significance. *Terrorism and Political Violence, 9,* 96–121.

Jacobs, D. J., Brewer, M., & Klein-Benheim, M. (1999). Suicide assessment: An overview and recommended protocol. In D. G. Jacobs (Ed.), *The Harvard Medical School guide to suicide assessment and intervention* (pp. 3–39). San Francisco: Jossey-Bass.

Jerusalem Media and Communication Centre (JMCC). (2002). *JMCC public opinion polls 1–48.* Retrieved June 20, 2003, from http://www.jmcc.org.

Joshi, C. L. (2000, June 1). Sri Lanka: Suicide bombers. *Far Eastern Economic Review.* Retrieved June 24, 2002, from http://www.feer.com /_0006_01/p64currents.html.

Klerman, G. L. (1987). Clinical epidemiology of suicide. *Journal of Clinical Psychiatry, 48*(12, Suppl.), 33–38.

Kramer, M. (1991). Sacrifice and fratricide in Shi'ite Lebanon. *Terrorism and Political Violence, 3,* 30–47.

Lester, G., & Lester, D. (1971). *Suicide.* Englewood Cliffs, NJ: Prentice-Hall.

Linehan, M. M. (1999). Standard protocol for assessing and treating suicidal behaviors for patients in treatment. In D. G. Jacobs (Ed.), *The Harvard Medical School guide to suicide assessment and intervention* (pp. 146–187). San Francisco: Jossey-Bass.

Maltsberger, J. T. (1999). The psychodynamic understanding of suicide. In D. G. Jacobs (Ed.), *The Harvard Medical School guide to suicide assessment and intervention* (pp. 72–82). San Francisco: Jossey-Bass.

Merari, A. (1990). The readiness to kill and die: Suicidal terrorism in the Middle East. In W. Reich (Ed.), *Origins of terrorism: Psychologies, ideologies, theologies, states of mind* (pp. 192–207). Cambridge, England: Cambridge University Press.

Merari, A., & Friedland, N. (1980). *Public opinion on terrorism* (Memorandum). Tel Aviv: Tel Aviv University, Center for Strategic Studies.

Miller, M. C., & Paulsen, R. H. (1999). Suicide assessment in the primary care setting. In D. G. Jacobs (Ed.), *The Harvard Medical School guide to suicide assessment and intervention* (pp. 520–539). San Francisco: Jossey-Bass.

Moscicki, E. K. (1999). Epidemiology of suicide. In D. G. Jacobs (Ed.), *The Harvard Medical School guide to suicide assessment and intervention* (pp. 40–51). San Francisco: Jossey-Bass.

Palestinian Central Bureau of Statistics. (1997). *Summary of final results: Population, housing and establishment census—1997.* Retrieved July 28, 2003, from http://www.pcbs.org/english/phc_97/popu.htm.

Palestinian Central Bureau of Statistics. (2002). *Education—Current main indicators.* Retrieved July 30, 2003, from http://www.pcbs.org/inside/selcts.htm.

Palestinian Center for Policy & Survey Research. (2002). *Public opinion polls 1–8.* Retrieved July 1, 2003, from http://www.pcpsr.org.

Post, J. (2001). *Killing in the name of God: Osama bin-Laden and radical Islam.* A presentation at the New York Academy of Medicine, October 30, 2001. Retrieved June 24, 2002, from http://www.theapm.org/cont/Posttext.html.

Schlenger, W. E., Caddell, J. M., Ebert, L., Jordan, B. K., Rourke, K. M., Wilson, D., et al. (2002). Psychological reactions to terrorist attacks: Findings from the national study of American's reactions to September 11. *Journal of the American Medical Association, 288,* 581–588.

Schweitzer, Y. (2001). Suicide terrorism: Developments and main characteristics. In *Countering suicide terrorism* (pp. 75–85). Herzliya, Israel: The Interdisciplinary Center.

Schweitzer, Y., & Shay, S. (2002). *An expected surprise—the September 11th attacks in the USA and their ramifications.* Herzliya, Israel: Mifalot, IDC and ICT Publications.

Shavit, U., & Banna, J. (2001, July 6). The Palestinian dream, the Israeli nightmare [Hebrew]. *Haaretz* (Weekly Suppl.), pp. 18–28.

Shneidman, E. S. (1985). *Definition of suicide.* New York: Wiley.

Shneidman, E. S. (1999). Perturbation and lethality. In D. G. Jacobs (Ed.), *The Harvard Medical School guide to suicide assessment and intervention* (pp. 83–97). San Francisco: Jossey-Bass.

Solomon, Z., Mikulincer, M., & Flum, H. (1988). Negative life events, coping responses, and combat-related psychopathology: A prospective study. *Journal of Abnormal Psychology, 97,* 302–307.

Sprinzak, E. (2000, September/October). Rational fanatics [Electronic version]. *Foreign Policy,* 66–73. Available from http://www.foreignpolicy.com /issue_SeptOct_2001/sprinzak.html.

Taylor, M. (1988). *The terrorist.* London: Brassey's Defence.

World Health Organization. (1993). *Guidelines for the primary prevention of mental, neurological and psychosocial disorders: 4. Suicide.* Geneva, Switzerland: Author. (Publication No. WHO/MNH/MND/93.24)

Zilboorg, G. (1996). Considerations on suicide, with particular reference to that of the young. In J. T. Maltsberger & M. J. Goldblatt (Eds.), *Essential papers on suicide* (pp. 62–82). New York: New York University Press.

Author Index

Subject Index

Abandonment, 212
Abuse, physical and sexual, 239
Acceptance and Commitment
   Therapy (ACT), 287
Acquiescence response set, 72
Acting-out, 249, 282
Activation of benign cycles, 177
Active listening, 145, 341
Active passivity, 281
Addictions, in voice therapy, 261
Affective disorder, 210
Affect regulation, 214
Ageism, 308
Akathisia, 412
Al-Aqsa intifada, 438
Alcoholics Anonymous (AA), 283,
   313
Al-Qaeda, 433–434
Altruistic suicide, 440
Ambivalence, 126, 129, 167
American Association of
   Suicidology (AAS), 173, 339
   guidelines for discharge, 413
Anger, 131
Annihilation, threat of, 241
Antidepressants, 411
Anti-self system, 235, 242, 245,
   246–249, 260
Antisocial personality disorder, 111
Apparent competence, 281
Applied Suicide Intervention Skills
   Training (ASIST), 394

Armenia, 440
Assassins, 432, 433
Assertiveness training, 154, 221,
   285
Assessment, 171
   on campus, 390
Attempted suicide, 1, 29, 66–71,
   207, 380, 384
   repeaters, 193, 280
Attributional style, 31, 35, 213

Baader-Meinhof Gang, 437
Base rates, 30, 64, 94, 207
BDI-II, 40, 41
Beck Anxiety Inventory (BAI), 43,
   50
Beck Depression Inventory (BDI),
   39, 50
Beck Hopelessness Scale (BHS), 10,
   40, 44
Beck's scales, x, 29–61, 134
Behavioral contracting, 153, 185
Behavior therapy, 156, 183, 282
Beirut attack in 1981, 433
Bereavement, 330
Berne, Eric, 184
Bibliotherapy, 221
Big Ten Student Suicide Study,
   380
Birds of Freedom, 436, 444
Black Tigers, 444
Blaming, 306